The OXFORD World Atlas

© Oxford University Press 1994
© Maps copyright Oxford University Press

Oxford University Press, Great Clarendon Street, Oxford, OX2 6DP

All rights reserved. No part of this publication may be
reproduced, stored in a retrieval system, or transmitted,
in any form or by any means, without the prior
permission in writing of Oxford University Press.
Within the U.K., exceptions are allowed in respect of any
fair dealing for the purpose of research or private study,
or criticism or review, as permitted under the Copyright,
Designs and Patents Act, 1988, or in the case of
reprographic reproduction in accordance with the terms
of licences issued by the Copyright Licensing Agency.
Enquiries concerning reproduction outside those
terms and in other countries should be sent to the
Rights Department, Oxford University Press,
at the address above.

Oxford New York
Athens Auckland Bangkok Bogotá Buenos Aires
Calcutta Cape Town Chennai Dar es Salaam
Delhi Florence Hong Kong Istanbul Karachi
Kuala Lumpur Madrid Melbourne Mexico City
Mumbai Nairobi Paris São Paulo Singapore
Taipei Tokyo Toronto Warsaw

and associated companies in
Berlin Ibadan

Oxford is a trade mark of Oxford University Press

ISBN 0 19 831784 0 hdbk
ISBN 0 19 831797 2   pbk

First published 1994
Reprinted 1995 and July 1996 with corrections,
and 1997, 1999

Printed in Hong Kong

Oxford University Press

2 Contents

Contents 3

Country	Land Area thousand sq km	Capital city	Total Population millions	Density of Population per sq km	Birth Rate per thousand	Death Rate per thousand	People living in cities percent	GNP per capita US $
Afghanistan	652	Kābul	16.9	26	51	23	18	450
Albania	27	Tiranë	3.3	113	23	6	36	800
Algeria	2382	Algers (Algiers)	26.0	11	35	8	50	2060
Andorra	0.5	Andorra-la-Vella	0.05	104	13	4	...	...
Angola	1247	Luanda	8.9	8	47	19	26	620
Anguilla	0.16	The Valley	0.007	77	25	10	...	...
Antigua & Barbuda	0.4	St. John's	0.1	190	15	5	58	4600
Argentina	2767	Buenos Aires	33.1	12	21	9	86	2370
Armenia	30	Yerevan	3.5	...	24	7	68	...
Australia	7687	Canberra	17.8	2	15	8	85	17080
Austria	84	Wien (Vienna)	7.9	89	12	12	55	19240
Azerbaijan	87	Baku	7.1	...	26	6	53	...
Bahamas, The	14	Nassau	0.3	18	20	5	75	11510
Bahrain	0.6	Al'Manāmah (Manama)	0.5	829	27	3	81	6610
Bangladesh	144	Dhaka	111.4	803	41	15	14	200
Barbados	0.4	Bridgetown	0.3	606	16	9	32	6540
Belarus	207	Minsk	10.3	...	14	11	67	...
Belgium	31	Bruxelles (Brussels)	10.0	326	12	12	95	15440
Belize	23	Belmopan	0.2	8	37	6	50	1970
Benin	113	Porto Novo	5.0	42	49	19	39	360
Bermuda	0.05	Hamilton	0.058	1160	16	7	100	25000
Bhutan	47	Thimphu	0.7	32	38	16	13	190
Bolivia	1099	La Paz	7.8	7	42	13	51	620
Bosnia-Herzegovina	51	Sarajevo	4.2	...	14	6	36	...
Botswana	582	Gaborone	1.4	2	46	11	24	2040
Brazil	8512	Brasília	150.8	18	27	8	74	2680
Brunei Darussalam	6	Bandar Seri Begawan	0.3	42	29	3	59	14120
Bulgaria	111	Sofiya	8.9	81	13	12	68	2210
Burkina	274	Ougadougou	9.6	33	47	18	18	330
Burundi	28	Bujumbura	5.8	196	47	17	5	210
Cambodia	181	Phnom Penh	9.1	46	39	16	13	75
Cameroon	475	Yaoundé	12.7	24	47	14	42	940
Canada	9976	Ottawa	27.4	3	14	8	78	20450
Cape Verde Islands	4	Praia	0.4	94	38	10	33	890
Cayman Islands	0.3	George Town	0.25	...	15	4	100	...
Central African Republic	623	Bangui	3.2	5	45	17	43	390
Chad	1284	Ndjamena	5.2	4	44	19	30	190
Chile	757	Santiago	13.6	17	23	6	85	1940
China	9597	Beijing (Peking)	1165.8	118	21	7	26	370
Colombia	1139	Bogotá	34.3	28	27	6	68	1240
Comoros	2	Moroni	0.5	239	47	13	26	480
Congo	342	Brazzaville	2.4	6	46	14	41	1010
Cook Islands	0.3	Rarotonga	0.018	90	24	5	35	...
Costa Rica	51	San José	3.2	59	27	4	45	1910
Côte d'Ivoire	322	Yamoussoukro	13.0	39	50	14	43	730
Croatia	56	Zagreb	4.6	...	12	11	51	...
Cuba	111	La Habana (Havana)	10.8	93	18	7	73	1500
Cyprus	9	Nicosia	0.7	76	19	7	62	8040
Czech Republic	79	Praha (Prague)	15.7	...	14	12	347	3140
Denmark	43	København (Copenhagen)	5.2	119	11	11	85	22090
Djibouti	22	Djibouti	0.4	18	47	18	79	1000
Dominica	0.7	Roseau	0.1	109	26	5	...	1940
Dominican Republic	49	Santo Domingo	7.5	147	30	7	58	820
Ecuador	284	Quito	10.2	38	32	7	55	960
Egypt	1001	El Qâ'hira (Cairo)	55.7	54	33	10	45	600
El Salvador	21	San Salvador	5.6	250	36	8	48	1100
Equatorial Guinea	28	Malabo	0.4	16	43	17	28	330
Eritrea	117	Asmera	3	...	...	...	...	...
Estonia	45	Tallinn	1.6	...	16	12	71	...
Ethiopia	1105	Ādis Ābeba (Addis Ababa)	54.3	15	...	...	...	120
Fiji	18	Suva	0.8	41	27	6	39	1770
Finland	338	Helsinki	5.0	15	12	10	62	26070
France	547	Paris	56.9	103	14	10	73	19480
French Polynesia	4	Papeete	0.2	56	28	5	62	6000
Gabon	268	Libreville	1.1	4	41	16	43	3220
Gambia, The	11	Banjul	0.9	76	47	21	22	260
Georgia	70	Tbilisi	5.5	...	17	9	56	...
Germany	357	Berlin	80.6	218	11	12	90	20750
Ghana	239	Accra	16.0	63	44	13	32	390
Greece	132	Athínai (Athens)	10.3	76	12	10	58	6000
Grenada	0.4	St George's	0.1	247	37	7	...	2120
Guam	0.5	Agaña	0.1	218	27	4	...	...
Guatemala	109	Guatemala	9.7	84	40	8	39	900
Guinea	246	Conakry	7.8	28	51	21	22	480
Guinea Bissau	36	Bissau	1.0	27	43	22	27	180
Guyana	215	Georgetown	0.8	5	24	5	35	370
Haiti	28	Port-au-Prince	6.4	234	36	13	28	370
Honduras	112	Tegucigalpa	5.5	46	39	8	44	590
Hong Kong	1	Victoria	5.7	5589	13	6	93	11540
Hungary	93	Budapest	10.3	113	12	13	63	2780
Iceland	103	Reykjavik	0.3	2	19	7	90	21150
India	3288	New Delhi	882.6	260	32	11	26	350
Indonesia	1905	Jakarta	184.5	9	28	9	31	560
Iran	1648	Tehrān	59.7	34	34	7	54	2450
Iraq	438	Baghdād	18.2	44	42	7	73	2000
Irish Republic	70	Dublin	3.5	53	18	9	56	9550
Israel	21	Jerusalem	5.2	221	22	7	91	10970
Italy	301	Roma (Rome)	58.0	190	10	10	72	16850
Jamaica	11	Kingston	2.5	229	23	6	51	1510
Japan	378	Tōkyō	124.4	327	11	7	77	25430
Jordan	98	Amman	3.6	44	39	6	70	1240
Kazakhstan	2717	Alma-Ata	16.9	...	22	8	58	...
Kenya	580	Nairobi	26.2	43	47	11	22	370
Kirgyzstan	199	Bishkek	4.5	...	29	7	38	...
Kiribati	0.7	Tarawa	0.06	92	...	...	36	760
Korea, North	121	Pyongyang	22.2	190	24	5	64	700
Korea, South	99	Soul (Seoul)	44.3	443	16	6	74	5400
Kuwait	18	Al Kuwayt	1.4	117	27	2	96	16380
Laos	237	Viangchan (Vientiane)	4.4	17	45	16	16	200
Latvia	65	Riga	2.7	...	15	12	71	...
Lebanon	10	Beyrouth (Beirut)	3.4	285	31	8	84	2000
Lesotho	30	Maseru	1.9	58	41	12	19	470
Liberia	98	Monrovia	2.8	23	47	15	44	500
Libya	1760	Tarābulus (Tripoli)	4.5	3	44	9	76	6000
Liechtenstein	0.2	Vaduz	0.03	175	14	6	28	16600

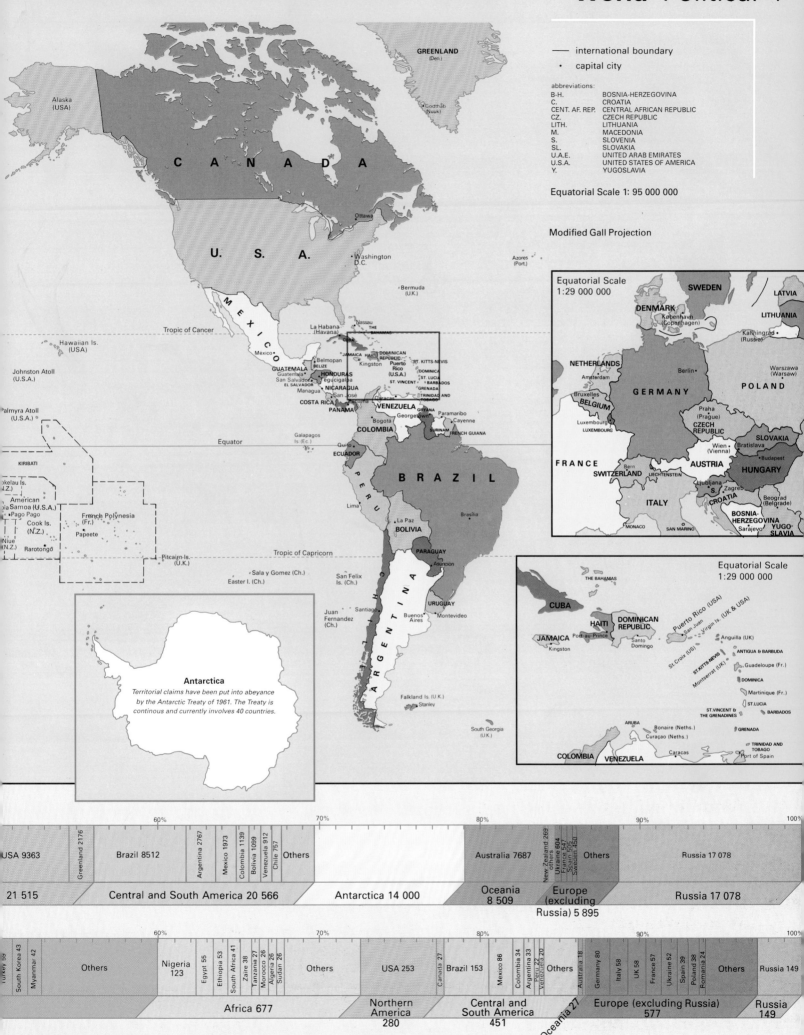

international boundary
capital city
abbreviations:
B-H. BOSNIA-HERZEGOVINA
C. CROATIA
CENT. AF. REP. CENTRAL AFRICAN REPUBLIC
CZ. CZECH REPUBLIC
LITH. LITHUANIA
M. MACEDONIA
S. SLOVENIA
SL. SLOVAKIA
U.A.E. UNITED ARAB EMIRATES
U.S.A. UNITED STATES OF AMERICA
Y. YUGOSLAVIA
Equatorial Scale 1: 95 000 000
Modified Gall Projection
GREENLAND (Den.)
Godthåb (Nuuk)
Alaska (USA)
C A N A D A
Ottawa
U. S. A.
Washington D.C.
Azores (Port.)
Bermuda (U.K.)
M E X I C O
México
Tropic of Cancer
Hawaiian Is. (USA)
Johnston Atoll (U.S.A.)
Palmyra Atoll (U.S.A.)
La Habana (Havana)
CUBA
Nassau
THE BAHAMAS
JAMAICA
Kingston
HAITI
DOMINICAN REPUBLIC
Puerto Rico (U.S.A.)
ST. KITTS-NEVIS
DOMINICA
ST. LUCIA
BARBADOS
ST. VINCENT
GRENADA
TRINIDAD AND TOBAGO
Belmopan
BELIZE
GUATEMALA
Guatemala
San Salvador
EL SALVADOR
HONDURAS
Tegucigalpa
NICARAGUA
Managua
San José
COSTA RICA
Panamá
PANAMA
Caracas
VENEZUELA
GUYANA
Georgetown
Paramaribo
SURINAM
Cayenne
FRENCH GUIANA
Bogotá
COLOMBIA
Equator
Galapagos Is. (Ec.)
Quito
ECUADOR
KIRIBATI
Tokelau Is. (N.Z.)
American Samoa (U.S.A.)
Pago Pago
Cook Is. (N.Z.)
Niue (N.Z.)
Rarotonga
French Polynesia (Fr.)
Papeete
Pitcairn Is. (U.K.)
P E R U
Lima
B R A Z I L
Brasília
La Paz
BOLIVIA
PARAGUAY
Asunción
Tropic of Capricorn
Sala y Gomez (Ch.)
Easter I. (Ch.)
San Felix Is. (Ch.)
Juan Fernandez (Ch.)
Santiago
C H I L E
A R G E N T I N A
URUGUAY
Buenos Aires
Montevideo
Falkland Is. (U.K.)
Stanley
South Georgia (U.K.)
Antarctica
Territorial claims have been put into abeyance by the Antarctic Treaty of 1961. The Treaty is continous and currently involves 40 countries.
Equatorial Scale 1:29 000 000
SWEDEN
LATVIA
DENMARK
København (Copenhagen)
LITHUANIA
Kaliningrad (Russia)
NETHERLANDS
Amsterdam
Berlin
Warszawa (Warsaw)
GERMANY
POLAND
Bruxelles
BELGIUM
Luxembourg
LUXEMBOURG
Praha (Prague)
CZECH REPUBLIC
SLOVAKIA
Bratislava
Wien (Vienna)
Budapest
FRANCE
Bern
SWITZERLAND
LIECHTENSTEIN
AUSTRIA
HUNGARY
Ljubljana
S.
Zagreb
CROATIA
ITALY
Beograd (Belgrade)
BOSNIA-HERZEGOVINA
Sarajevo
YUGOSLAVIA
MONACO
SAN MARINO
Equatorial Scale 1:29 000 000
THE BAHAMAS
CUBA
HAITI
DOMINICAN REPUBLIC
Port-au-Prince
Santo Domingo
JAMAICA
Kingston
Puerto Rico (USA)
San Juan
Virgin Is. (UK & USA)
Anguilla (UK)
ANTIGUA & BARBUDA
St.Croix (US)
ST.KITTS-NEVIS
Montserrat (UK)
Guadeloupe (Fr.)
DOMINICA
Martinique (Fr.)
ST.LUCIA
ST.VINCENT & THE GRENADINES
BARBADOS
ARUBA
Bonaire (Neths.)
Curaçao (Neths.)
GRENADA
TRINIDAD AND TOBAGO
Port of Spain
Caracas
COLOMBIA
VENEZUELA
60%
70%
80%
90%
100%
USA 9363
Greenland 2176
Brazil 8512
Argentina 2767
Mexico 1973
Colombia 1139
Bolivia 1099
Venezuela 912
Chile 757
Others
Australia 7687
New Zealand 269
others
Ukraine 604
France 547
Spain 505
Sweden 450
Others
Russia 17 078
21 515
Central and South America 20 566
Antarctica 14 000
Oceania 8 509
Europe (excluding Russia) 5 895
Russia 17 078
Turkey 59
South Korea 43
Myanmar 42
Others
Nigeria 123
Egypt 55
Ethiopia 53
South Africa 41
Zaire 38
Tanzania 27
Morocco 26
Algeria 26
Sudan 26
Others
USA 253
Canada 27
Brazil 153
Mexico 86
Colombia 34
Argentina 33
Peru 22
Venezuela 20
Others
Australia 18
Germany 80
Italy 58
UK 58
France 57
Ukraine 52
Spain 39
Poland 38
Romania 24
Others
Russia 149
Africa 677
Northern America 280
Central and South America 451
Oceania 27
Europe (excluding Russia) 577
Russia 149

Plate tectonics

The present positions of the major tectonic plates are shown with the white areas representing the smaller plates.

Plate boundaries

- ▲▲ subduction zones
- ═══ ridge zones
- ⇉ transform zones
- ➤ direction of sea-floor spreading
- — major fracture zones

Gall Projection

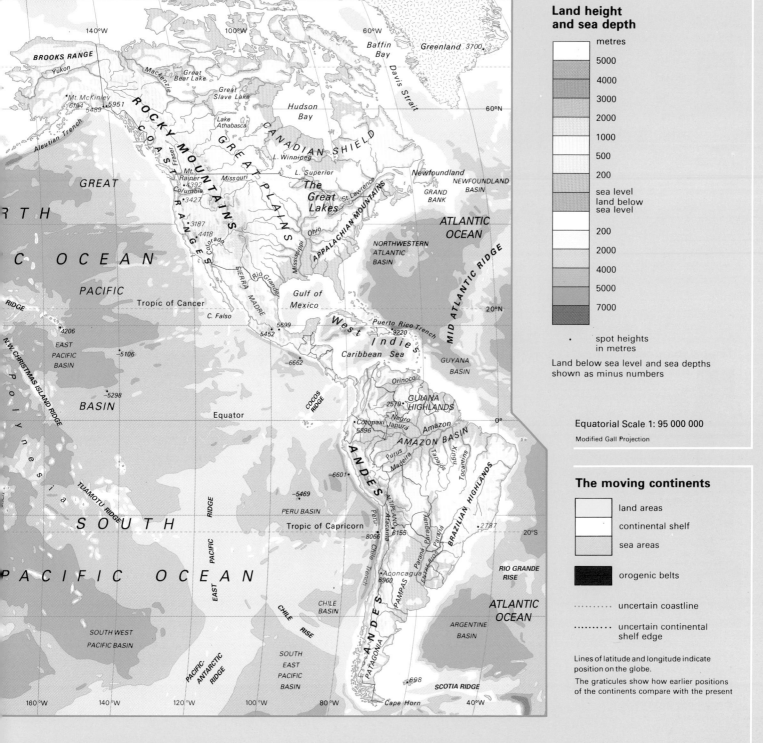

Land height and sea depth

metres

5000
4000
3000
2000
1000
500
200

sea level
land below sea level

200
2000
4000
5000
7000

• spot heights in metres

Land below sea level and sea depths shown as minus numbers

Equatorial Scale 1: 95 000 000

Modified Gall Projection

The moving continents

land areas
continental shelf
sea areas

orogenic belts

.... uncertain coastline

.... uncertain continental shelf edge

Lines of latitude and longitude indicate position on the globe.

The graticules show how earlier positions of the continents compare with the present

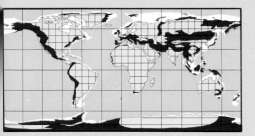

Present day

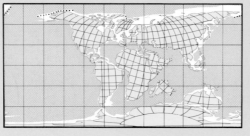

100 million years ago

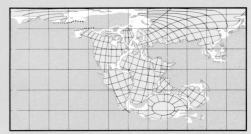

200 million years ago

© Oxford University Press

Rainfall
and other forms of precipitation

	mm
	over 400
	250–400
	150–250
	50–150
	25–50
	under 25

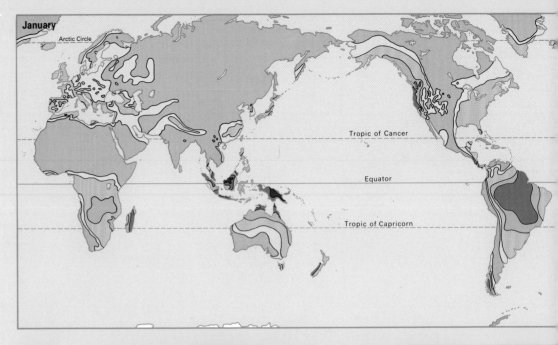

January

Arctic Circle

Tropic of Cancer

Equator

Tropic of Capricorn

Temperature, ocean currents

	actual temperature °C
	32
	24
	16
	8
	0
	−8
	−16
	−24

Ocean currents

cold

warm

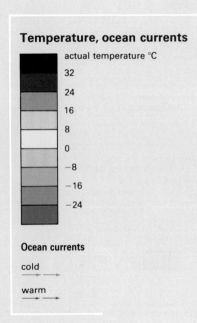

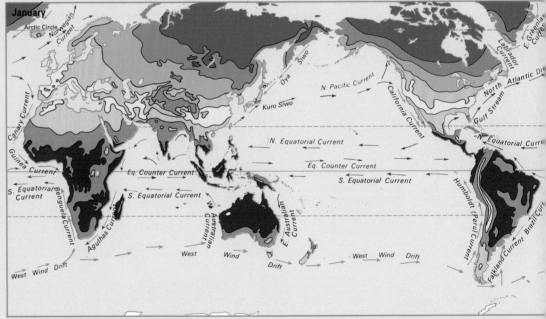

January

Arctic Circle

Norwegian Current
Canary Current
Guinea Current
S. Equatorial Current
Benguela Current
Agulhas Current
West Wind Drift
Oya Siwo
Kuro Siwo
N. Pacific Current
California Current
N. Equatorial Current
Eq. Counter Current
S. Equatorial Current
W. Australian Current
E. Australian Current
West Wind Drift
West Wind Drift
Labrador Current
E. Greenland Current
North Atlantic Drift
Gulf Stream
N. Equatorial Current
Humboldt (Peru) Current
Falkland Current
Brazil Current

Pressure and winds

Pressure reduced to sea level

1035 millibars
1030
1025
1020
1015
1010
1005
1000
995

H high pressure cell

L low pressure cell

Prevailing winds
Arrows fly with the wind:
the heavier the arrow, the
more regular ('constant')
the direction of the wind

January

Arctic Circle

Westerlies
N. E. Monsoon
N. W. Monsoon
N. E. Trades
S. E. Trades
Westerlies
Westerlies
Roaring Fort

Equatorial scale 1: 240 000 000

Modified Gall Projection

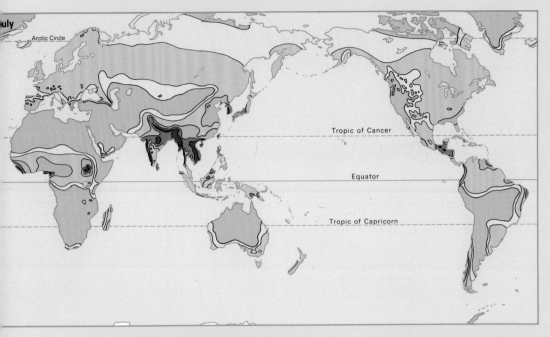

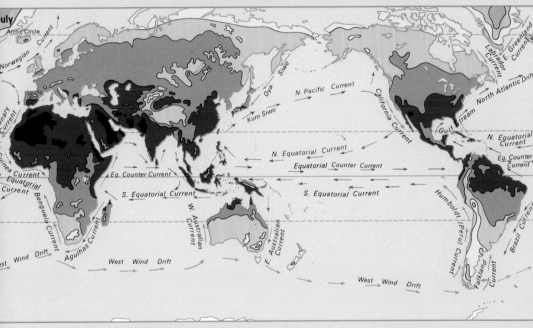

Tropical revolving storms

temperature 27°C and over at mean sea level

Northern hemisphere
Maximum frequency August - September

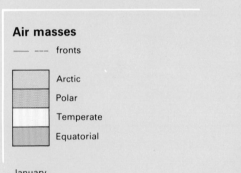

Southern hemisphere
Maximum frequency January - March

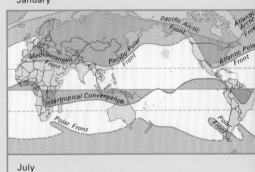

Air masses

- - - fronts

Arctic

Polar

Temperate

Equatorial

January

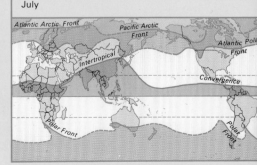

July

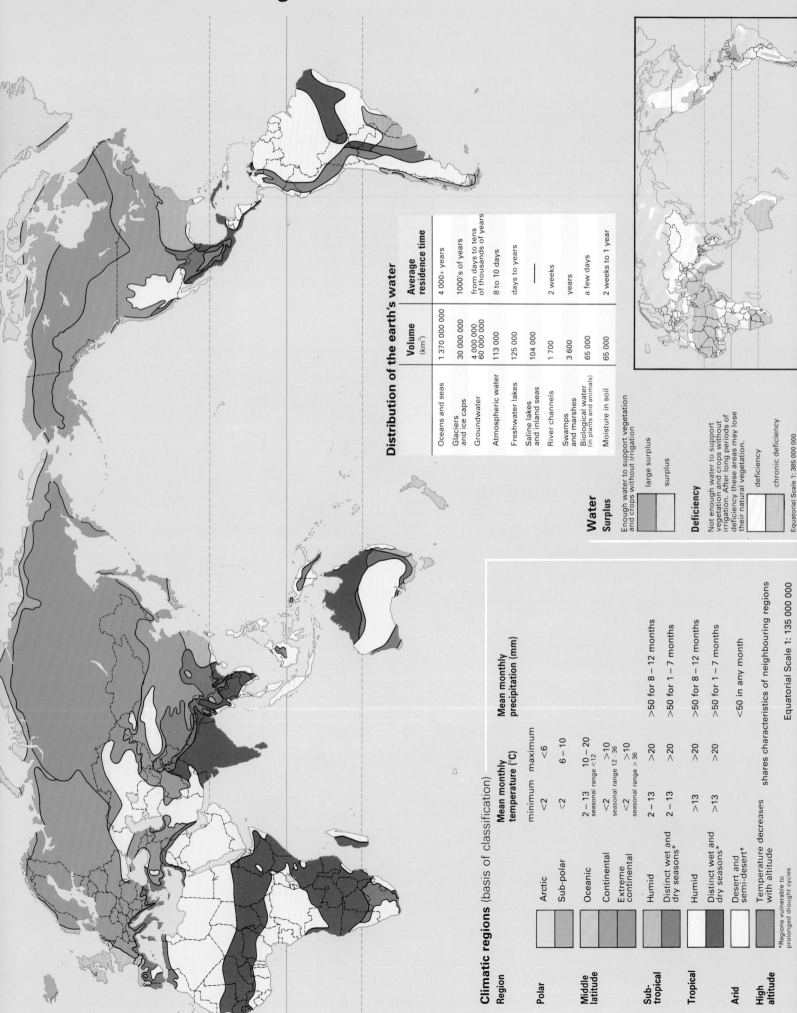

Distribution of the earth's water

	Volume (km³)	Average residence time
Oceans and seas	1 370 000 000	4 000+ years
Glaciers and ice caps	30 000 000	1000's of years
Groundwater	4 000 000 / 60 000 000	from days to tens of thousands of years
Atmospheric water	113 000	8 to 10 days
Freshwater lakes	125 000	days to years
Saline lakes and inland seas	104 000	—
River channels	1 700	2 weeks
Swamps and marshes	3 600	years
Biological water (in plants and animals)	65 000	a few days
Moisture in soil	65 000	2 weeks to 1 year

Water

Surplus

Enough water to support vegetation and crops without irrigation

large surplus

surplus

Deficiency

Not enough water to support vegetation and crops without irrigation. After long periods of deficiency these areas may lose their natural vegetation.

deficiency

chronic deficiency

Equatorial Scale 1: 385 000 000

Climatic regions (basis of classification)

Region		Mean monthly temperature (°C)		Mean monthly precipitation (mm)
		minimum	maximum	
Polar	Arctic	<2	<6	
	Sub-polar	<2	6 – 10	
Middle latitude	Oceanic	2 – 13	10 – 20	
	Continental	<2 seasonal range 12 - 36	>10	
	Extreme continental	<2 seasonal range > 36	>10	
Sub-tropical	Humid	2 – 13	>20	>50 for 8 – 12 months
	Distinct wet and dry seasons*	2 – 13	>20	>50 for 1 – 7 months
Tropical	Humid	>13	>20	>50 for 8 – 12 months
	Distinct wet and dry seasons*	>13	>20	>50 for 1 – 7 months
Arid	Desert and semi-desert*			<50 in any month
High altitude	Temperature decreases with altitude			shares characteristics of neighbouring regions

*Regions vulnerable to prolonged drought cycles

Equatorial Scale 1: 135 000 000

© Oxford University Press

Equatorial Scale 1: 135 000 000

Equatorial Scale 1: 385 000 000

Earthquakes and volcanoes

Areas susceptible to earthquakes

fold mountains and
East African rift valley

continental shelf

oceanic ridges and valleys

deep ocean trenches

Volcanoes

▲ active volcanoes

* strong earthquakes this century
(7.0 to 8.5 on the Richter scale)

* catastrophic earthquakes this century
(major loss of life – more than 1000 deaths)

Storms and floods

→ paths of revolving tropical storms

areas affected by tropical storms

coast vulnerable to tsunamis
(seismic sea waves)

· major floods
(more than 1000 deaths, 1960-91)

major river flood plains, some
partially controlled, which are
susceptible to flooding

areas affected by tornadoes

– · – the Tropics

Modified Gall Projection   © Oxford University Press

14 **World** Population

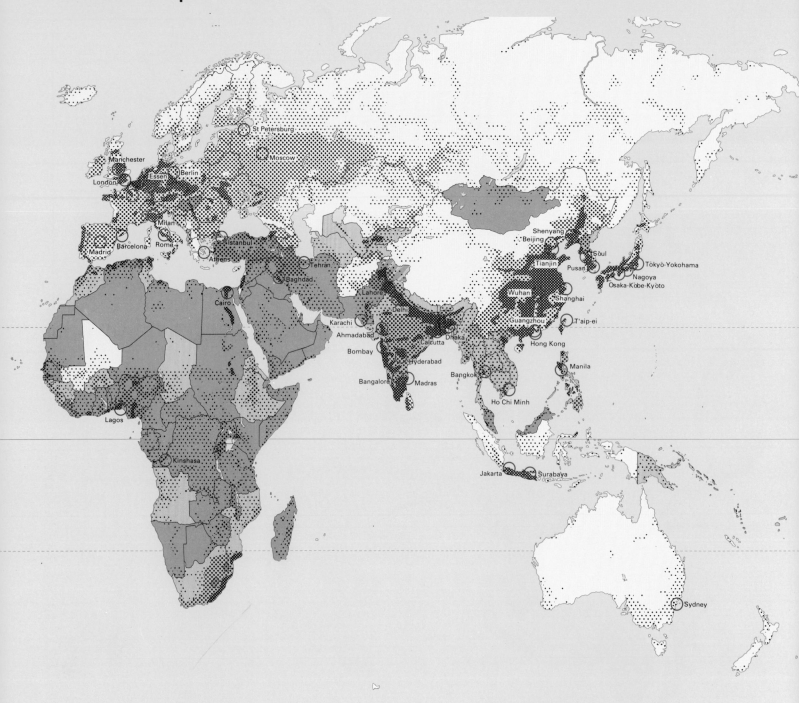

World population growth

Past growth (1AD to 1990)

Green Revolution: development of new varieties of cereals such as
rice, wheat and maize increasing food production in many countries

Medical and Sanitary Revolutions: elimination of many diseases
and a reduction of incidence of many others

Industrial and Agricultural Revolutions in Europe and North America:
technological advances in food production, distribution and exchange
for industrial goods

Black Death: bubonic plague spread from Central Asia devastating
the populations of China and Europe

Recent growth (1900 to 1990), projected to the year 2020

developing regions

developed regions

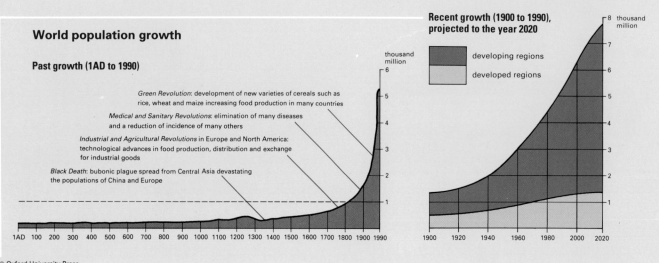

© Oxford University Press

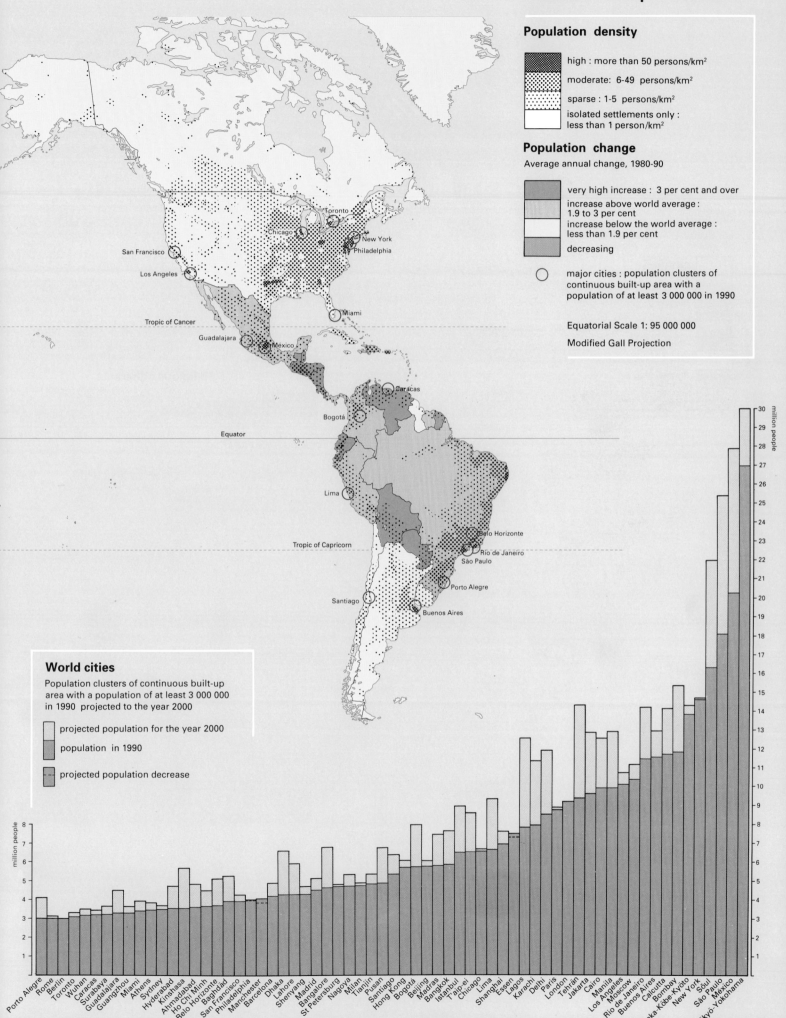

Population density

high : more than 50 persons/km²

moderate: 6-49 persons/km²

sparse : 1-5 persons/km²

isolated settlements only : less than 1 person/km²

Population change

Average annual change, 1980-90

very high increase : 3 per cent and over

increase above world average : 1.9 to 3 per cent

increase below the world average : less than 1.9 per cent

decreasing

○ major cities : population clusters of continuous built-up area with a population of at least 3 000 000 in 1990

Equatorial Scale 1: 95 000 000

Modified Gall Projection

World cities

Population clusters of continuous built-up area with a population of at least 3 000 000 in 1990 projected to the year 2000

projected population for the year 2000

population in 1990

projected population decrease

Tropic of Cancer

Equator

Tropic of Capricorn

Toronto
Chicago
New York
San Francisco
Philadelphia
Los Angeles
Miami
Guadalajara
México
Caracas
Bogotá
Lima
Belo Horizonte
Rio de Janeiro
São Paulo
Porto Alegre
Santiago
Buenos Aires

million people

Porto Alegre · Rome · Berlin · Toronto · Wuhan · Caracas · Surabaya · Guadalajara · Guangzhou · Miami · Athens · Sydney · Hyderabad · Kinshasa · Ahmadabad · Ho Chi Minh · Belo Horizonte · Baghdad · San Francisco · Philadelphia · Manchester · Barcelona · Dhaka · Lahore · Shenyang · Madrid · Bangalore · St Petersburg · Nagoya · Milan · Tianjin · Pusan · Santiago · Hong Kong · Bogotá · Beijing · Madras · Bangkok · Istanbul · T'aip-ei · Chicago · Lima · Shanghai · Essen · Lagos · Karachi · Delhi · Paris · London · Tehrān · Jakarta · Cairo · Manila · Los Angeles · Moscow · Rio de Janeiro · Buenos Aires · Calcutta · Bombay · Ōsaka-Kōbe-Kyōto · New York · Sŏul · São Paulo · México · Tōkyō-Yokohama

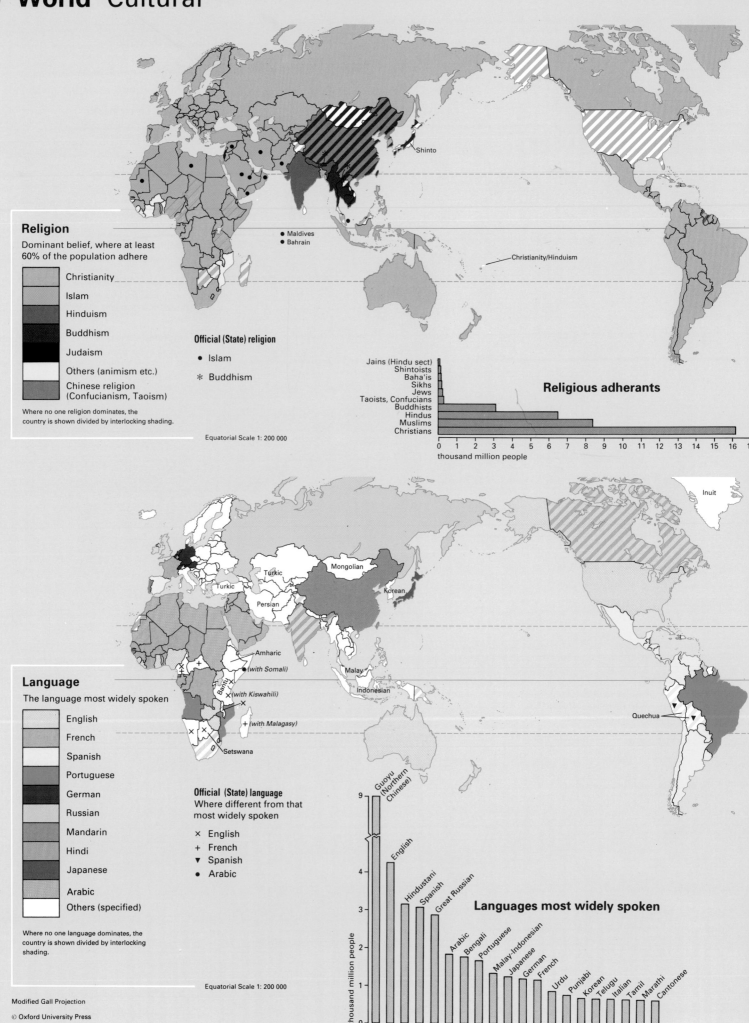

Religion

Dominant belief, where at least
60% of the population adhere

- Christianity
- Islam
- Hinduism
- Buddhism
- Judaism
- Others (animism etc.)
- Chinese religion
  (Confucianism, Taoism)

Where no one religion dominates, the
country is shown divided by interlocking shading.

Shinto

● Maldives
● Bahrain

Christianity/Hinduism

Official (State) religion

● Islam

✳ Buddhism

Equatorial Scale 1: 200 000

Religious adherants

Jains (Hindu sect)
Shintoists
Baha'is
Sikhs
Jews
Taoists, Confucians
Buddhists
Hindus
Muslims
Christians

0 1 2 3 4 5 6 7 8 9 10 11 12 13 14 15 16 17
thousand million people

Language

The language most widely spoken

- English
- French
- Spanish
- Portuguese
- German
- Russian
- Mandarin
- Hindi
- Japanese
- Arabic
- Others (specified)

Where no one language dominates, the
country is shown divided by interlocking
shading.

Inuit

Turkic
Turkic
Persian
Mongolian
Korean
Malay
Indonesian

Amharic
● (with Somali)
Bantu
✕ (with Kiswahili)
✕

＋ (with Malagasy)
✕ ✕
Setswana

Quechua ▼ ▼

Official (State) language
Where different from that
most widely spoken

✕ English
＋ French
▼ Spanish
● Arabic

Equatorial Scale 1: 200 000

Languages most widely spoken

Guoyu (Northern Chinese)
English
Hindustani
Spanish
Great Russian
Arabic
Bengali
Portuguese
Malay-Indonesian
Japanese
German
French
Urdu
Punjabi
Korean
Telugu
Italian
Tamil
Marathi
Cantonese

9
4
3
2
1
0
thousand million people

Modified Gall Projection

© Oxford University Press

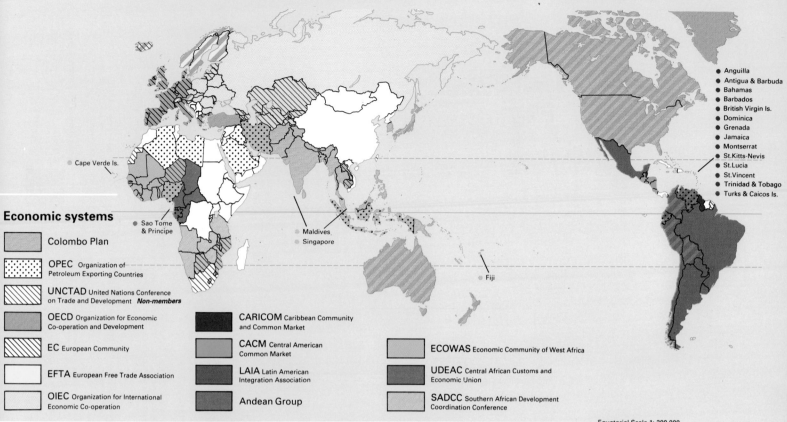

Economic systems

	Colombo Plan
	OPEC Organization of Petroleum Exporting Countries
	UNCTAD United Nations Conference on Trade and Development *Non-members*
	OECD Organization for Economic Co-operation and Development
	EC European Community
	EFTA European Free Trade Association
	OIEC Organization for International Economic Co-operation

	CARICOM Caribbean Community and Common Market
	CACM Central American Common Market
	LAIA Latin American Integration Association
	Andean Group

	ECOWAS Economic Community of West Africa
	UDEAC Central African Customs and Economic Union
	SADCC Southern African Development Coordination Conference

- Anguilla
- Antigua & Barbuda
- Bahamas
- Barbados
- British Virgin Is.
- Dominica
- Grenada
- Jamaica
- Montserrat
- St.Kitts-Nevis
- St.Lucia
- St.Vincent
- Trinidad & Tobago
- Turks & Caicos Is.

Cape Verde Is.

Sao Tome & Principe

Maldives
Singapore

Fiji

Equatorial Scale 1: 200 000

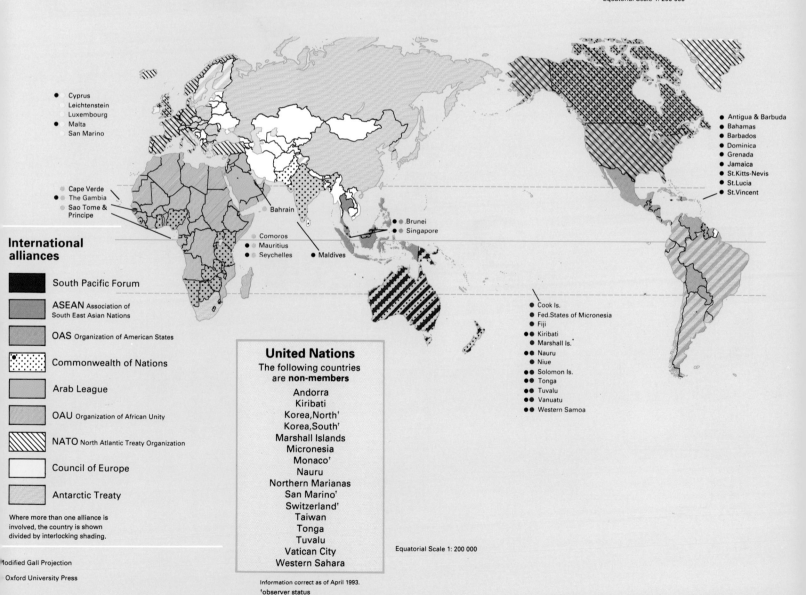

- Cyprus
- Leichtenstein
- Luxembourg
- Malta
- San Marino

- Cape Verde
- The Gambia
- Sao Tome & Principe

Bahrain

Comoros
Mauritius
Seychelles
Maldives

Brunei
Singapore

- Antigua & Barbuda
- Bahamas
- Barbados
- Dominica
- Grenada
- Jamaica
- St.Kitts-Nevis
- St.Lucia
- St.Vincent

- Cook Is.
- Fed.States of Micronesia
- Fiji
- Kiribati
- Marshall Is.'
- Nauru
- Niue
- Solomon Is.
- Tonga
- Tuvalu
- Vanuatu
- Western Samoa

International alliances

	South Pacific Forum
	ASEAN Association of South East Asian Nations
	OAS Organization of American States
	Commonwealth of Nations
	Arab League
	OAU Organization of African Unity
	NATO North Atlantic Treaty Organization
	Council of Europe
	Antarctic Treaty

Where more than one alliance is involved, the country is shown divided by interlocking shading.

Modified Gall Projection

Oxford University Press

United Nations
The following countries are non-members

Andorra
Kiribati
Korea,North'
Korea,South'
Marshall Islands
Micronesia
Monaco'
Nauru
Northern Marianas
San Marino'
Switzerland'
Taiwan
Tonga
Tuvalu
Vatican City
Western Sahara

Equatorial Scale 1: 200 000

Information correct as of April 1993.

'observer status

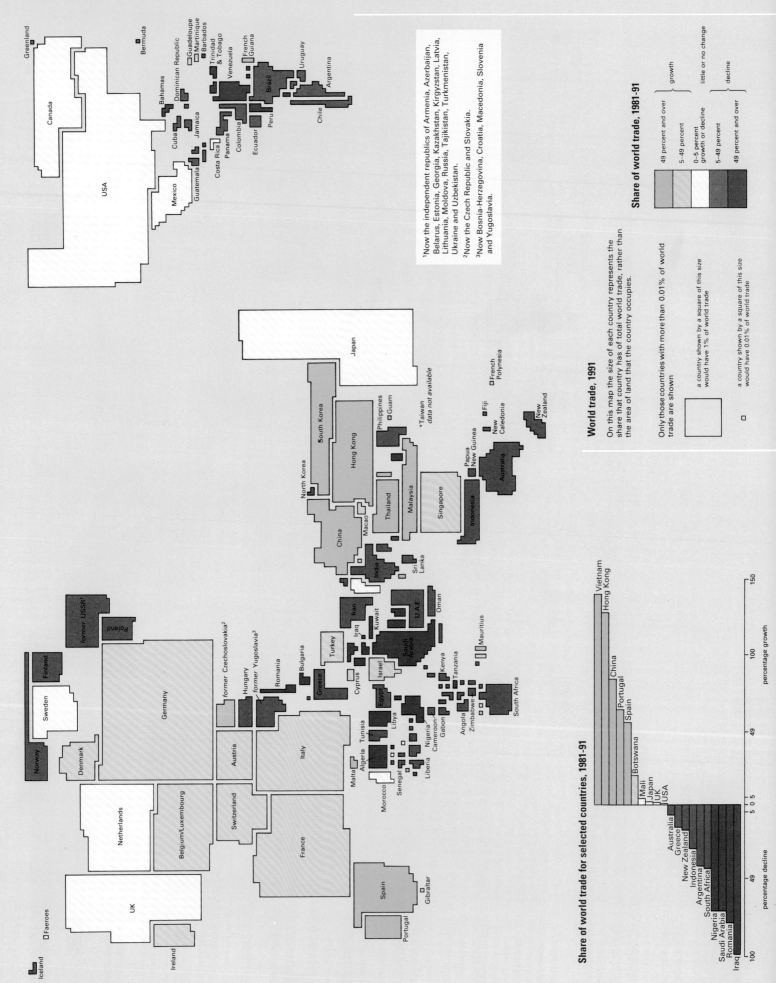

[1] Now the independent republics of Armenia, Azerbaijan, Belarus, Estonia, Georgia, Kazakhstan, Kirgyzstan, Latvia, Lithuania, Moldova, Russia, Tajikistan, Turkmenistan, Ukraine and Uzbekistan.

[2] Now the Czech Republic and Slovakia.

[3] Now Bosnia-Herzegovina, Croatia, Macedonia, Slovenia and Yugoslavia.

Share of world trade, 1981-91

- 49 percent and over — growth
- 5-49 percent
- 0-5 percent growth or decline — little or no change
- 5-49 percent
- 49 percent and over — decline

World trade, 1991

On this map the size of each country represents the share that country has of total world trade, rather than the area of land that the country occupies.

Only those countries with more than 0.01% of world trade are shown

a country shown by a square of this size would have 1% of world trade

a country shown by a square of this size would have 0.01% of world trade

Share of world trade for selected countries, 1981-91

© Oxford University Press

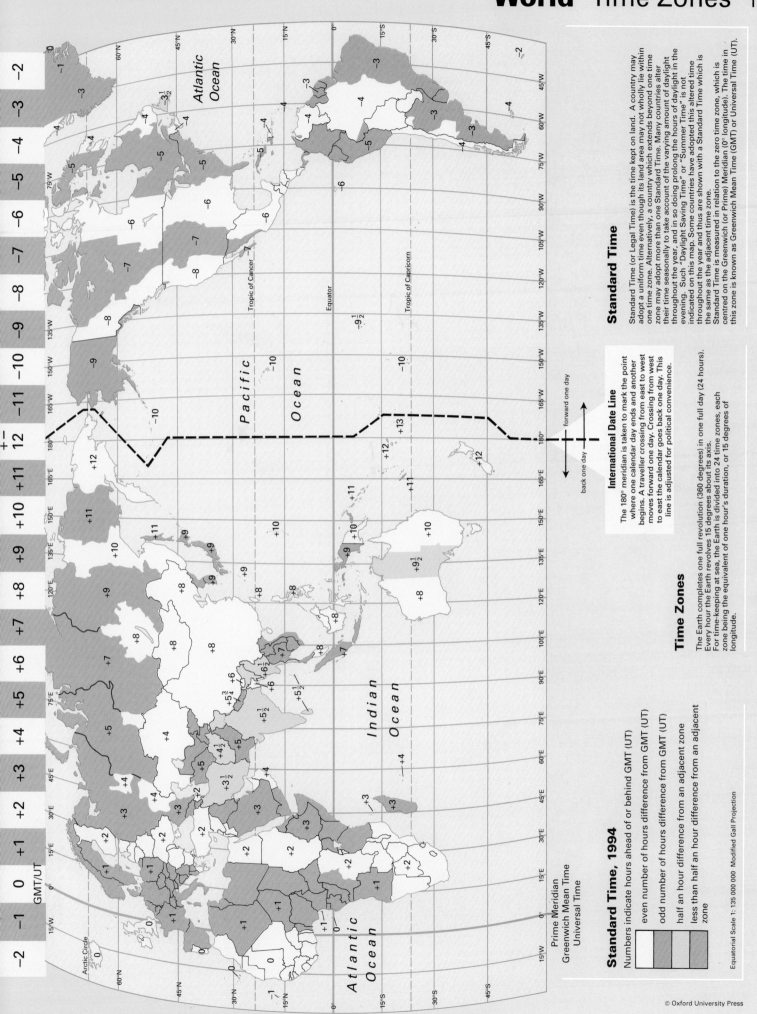

Standard Time, 1994

Numbers indicate hours ahead of or behind GMT (UT)

- even number of hours difference from GMT (UT)
- odd number of hours difference from GMT (UT)
- half an hour difference from an adjacent zone
- less than half an hour difference from an adjacent zone

Prime Meridian
Greenwich Mean Time
Universal Time

Equatorial Scale 1: 135 000 000 Modified Gall Projection

Time Zones

The Earth completes one full revolution (360 degrees) in one full day (24 hours). Every hour the Earth revolves 15 degrees about its axis. For time-keeping at sea, the Earth is divided into 24 time zones, each zone being the equivalent of one hour's duration, or 15 degrees of longitude.

International Date Line

The 180° meridian is taken to mark the point where one calendar day ends and another begins. A traveller crossing from east to west moves forward one day. Crossing from west to east the calendar goes back one day. This line is adjusted for political convenience.

forward one day
back one day

Standard Time

Standard Time (or Legal Time) is the time kept on land. A country may adopt a uniform time even though its land area may not wholly lie within one time zone. Alternatively, a country which extends beyond one time zone may adopt more than one Standard Time. Many countries alter their time seasonally to take account of the varying amount of daylight in the evening. Such "Daylight Saving Time" or "Summer Time" is not indicated on this map. Some countries have adopted this altered time throughout the year and thus are shown with a Standard Time which is the same as the adjacent time zone. Standard Time is measured in relation to the zero time zone, which is centred on the Greenwich (or Prime) Meridian (0° longitude). The time in this zone is known as Greenwich Mean Time (GMT) or Universal Time (UT).

© Oxford University Press

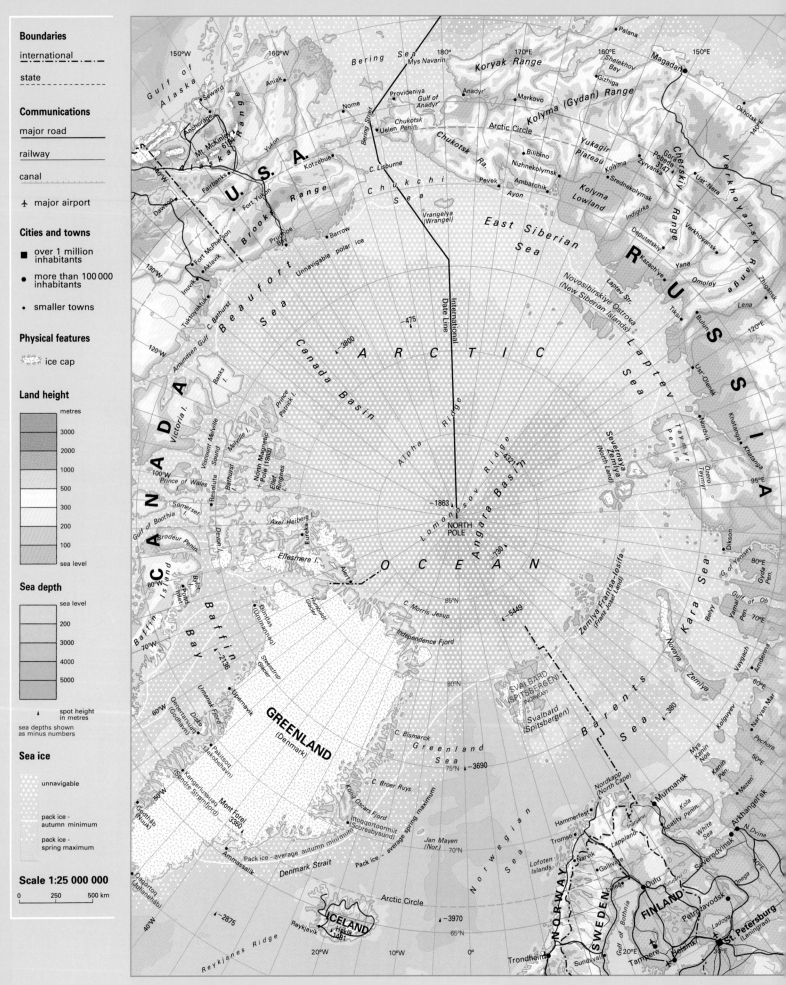

Boundaries

international

state

Communications

major road

railway

canal

✈ major airport

Cities and towns

■ over 1 million inhabitants

● more than 100 000 inhabitants

• smaller towns

Physical features

ice cap

Land height

metres
3000
2000
1000
500
300
200
100
sea level

Sea depth

sea level
200
3000
4000
5000

▲ spot height in metres
sea depths shown as minus numbers

Sea ice

unnavigable

pack ice - autumn minimum

pack ice - spring maximum

Scale 1:25 000 000

0   250   500 km

Zenithal Equidistant Projection

© Oxford University Press

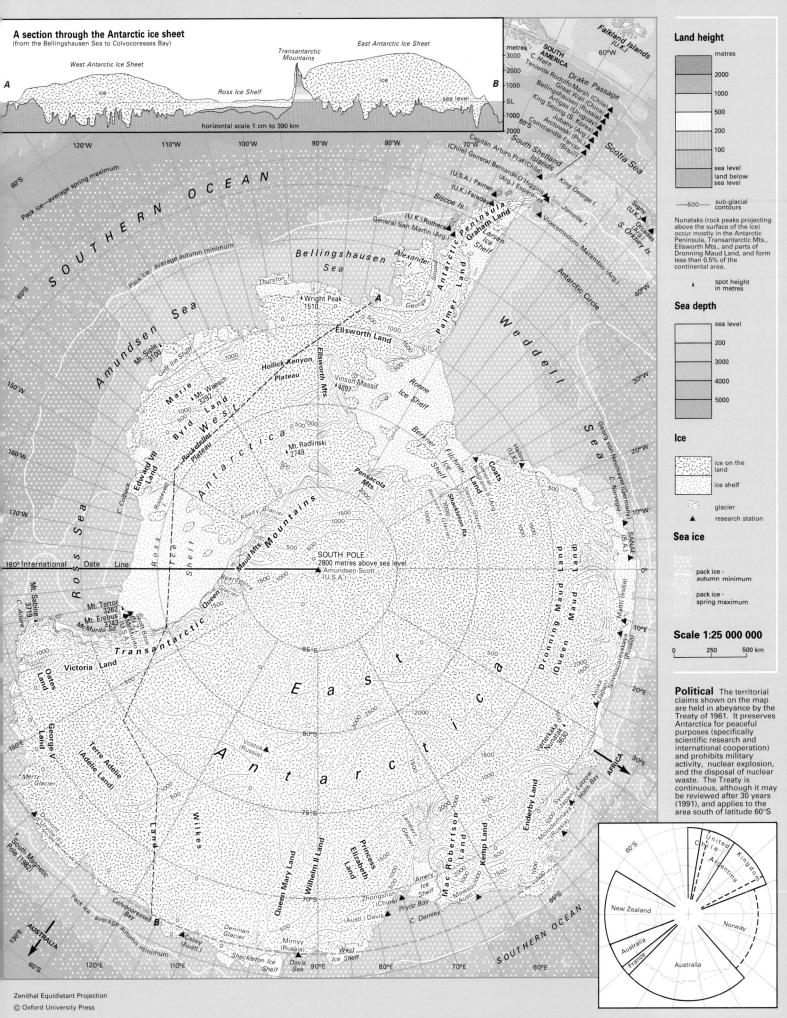

A section through the Antarctic ice sheet
(from the Bellingshausen Sea to Colvocoresses Bay)

West Antarctic Ice Sheet

East Antarctic Ice Sheet

Transantarctic Mountains

A

B

ice

Ross Ice Shelf

sea level

horizontal scale 1 cm to 390 km

Land height

metres
2000
1000
500
200
100
sea level
land below sea level

—500— sub-glacial contours

Nunataks (rock peaks projecting above the surface of the ice) occur mostly in the Antarctic Peninsula, Transantarctic Mts., Ellsworth Mts., and parts of Dronning Maud Land, and form less than 0.5% of the continental area.

▲ spot height in metres

Sea depth

sea level
200
3000
4000
5000

Ice

ice on the land

ice shelf

glacier

▲ research station

Sea ice

pack ice - autumn minimum

pack ice - spring maximum

Scale 1:25 000 000

0   250   500 km

Political The territorial claims shown on the map are held in abeyance by the Treaty of 1961. It preserves Antarctica for peaceful purposes (specifically scientific research and international cooperation) and prohibits military activity, nuclear explosion, and the disposal of nuclear waste. The Treaty is continuous, although it may be reviewed after 30 years (1991), and applies to the area south of latitude 60°S.

Zenithal Equidistant Projection

© Oxford University Press

Pacific Rim

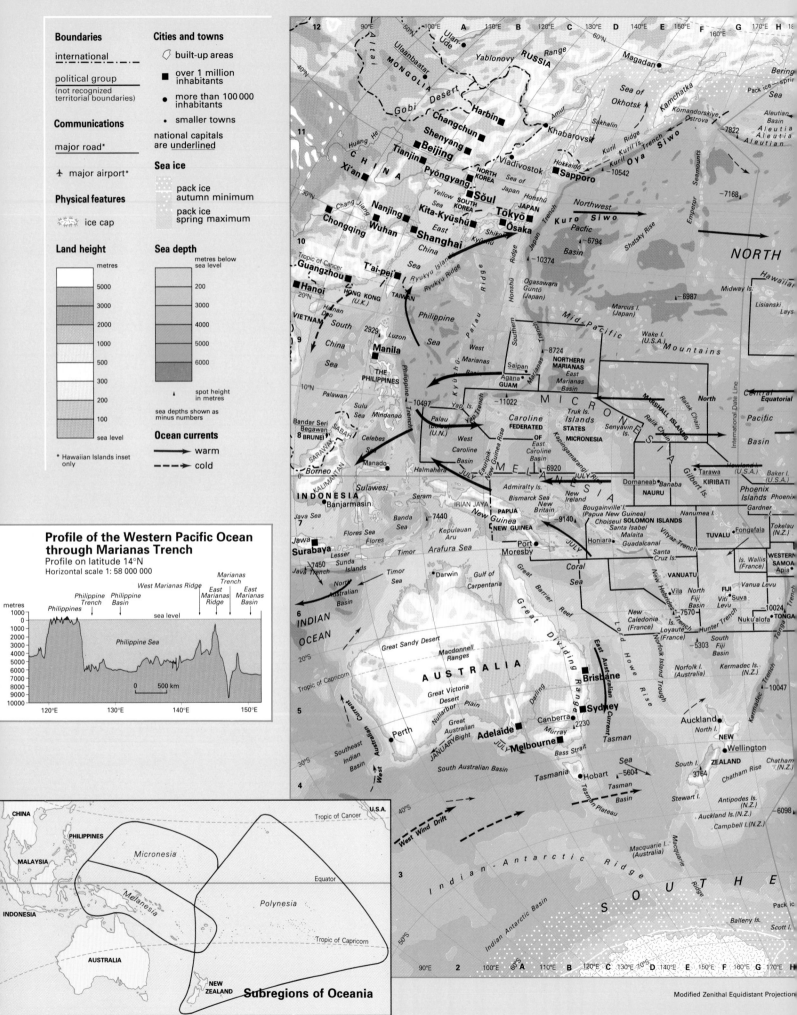

Boundaries
international
political group
(not recognized territorial boundaries)
Communications
major road*
major airport*
Physical features
ice cap
Land height
metres
5000
3000
2000
1000
500
300
200
100
sea level
* Hawaiian Islands inset only
Cities and towns
built-up areas
over 1 million inhabitants
more than 100 000 inhabitants
smaller towns
national capitals are underlined
Sea ice
pack ice autumn minimum
pack ice spring maximum
Sea depth
metres below sea level
200
3000
4000
5000
6000
spot height in metres
sea depths shown as minus numbers
Ocean currents
warm
cold
Profile of the Western Pacific Ocean through Marianas Trench
Profile on latitude 14°N
Horizontal scale 1: 58 000 000
metres
Philippines
Philippine Trench
Philippine Basin
West Marianas Ridge
East Marianas Ridge
Marianas Trench
East Marianas Basin
sea level
Philippine Sea
0 500 km
120°E
130°E
140°E
150°E
Subregions of Oceania
CHINA
PHILIPPINES
MALAYSIA
INDONESIA
AUSTRALIA
NEW ZEALAND
U.S.A.
Micronesia
Melanesia
Polynesia
Tropic of Cancer
Equator
Tropic of Capricorn
MONGOLIA
RUSSIA
CHINA
Gobi Desert
Altai
Yablonovy Range
Ulan-Ude
Ulaanbaatar
Harbin
Changchun
Shenyang
Beijing
Tianjin
Xi'an
Huang He
Chang Jiang
Chongqing
Wuhan
Nanjing
Shanghai
Guangzhou
Hanoi
HONG KONG (U.K.)
Hainan Dao
VIETNAM
TAIWAN
T'ai-pei
NORTH KOREA
SOUTH KOREA
Pyŏngyang
Sŏul
Kita-Kyūshū
Yellow Sea
East China Sea
Sea of Japan
Vladivostok
Khabarovsk
Amur
Sakhalin
Hokkaidō
Sapporo
Honshū
JAPAN
Tōkyō
Ōsaka
Shikoku
Kyūshū
Magadan
Sea of Okhotsk
Kamchatka
Komandorskiye Ostrova
Bering Sea
Aleutian Basin
Aleutian Trench
Kuril Is.
Kuril Ridge
Kuril Trench
Oya Siwo
Kuro Siwo
Northwest Pacific Basin
Shatsky Rise
Emperor Seamounts
Japan Trench
Ryukyu Islands
Ryukyu Ridge
Ogasawara Guntō (Japan)
Philippine Sea
Palau Ridge
Marcus I. (Japan)
Mid-Pacific Mountains
Wake I. (U.S.A.)
Midway Is.
Hawaiian
Lisianski
NORTH
South China Sea
Luzon
Manila
THE PHILIPPINES
Palawan
Sulu Sea
Mindanao
Philippine Trench
Bandar Seri Begawan
BRUNEI
SABAH
SARAWAK
Borneo
KALIMANTAN
Celebes Sea
Manado
Halmahera
Sulawesi
INDONESIA
Banjarmasin
Java Sea
Jawa
Surabaya
Java Trench
Lesser Sunda Islands
Flores Sea
Banda Sea
Seram
Timor
Timor Sea
Arafura Sea
Kepulauan Aru
Saipan
NORTHERN MARIANAS
Agana
GUAM
Marianas Trench
East Marianas Basin
West Marianas
Yap Is.
Yap Trench
Palau (Belau) (U.N.)
West Caroline Basin
Caroline Islands
FEDERATED STATES OF MICRONESIA
East Caroline Basin
MICRONESIA
MELANESIA
Kapingamarangi Rise
Eauripik New Guinea Rise
Truk Is.
Senyavin Is.
MARSHALL ISLANDS
Ratak Chain
Ralik Chain
IRIAN JAYA
New Guinea
PAPUA NEW GUINEA
Port Moresby
Admiralty Is.
Bismarck Sea
New Ireland
New Britain
Bougainville I. (Papua New Guinea)
Choiseul
SOLOMON ISLANDS
Santa Isabel
Malaita
Honiara
Guadalcanal
Santa Cruz Is.
Vityaz Trench
Domaneab
NAURU
Banaba
Tarawa
KIRIBATI
Gilbert Is.
Howland I. (U.S.A.)
Baker I. (U.S.A.)
Phoenix Islands
Gardner
Nanumea I.
TUVALU
Fongafala
Tokelau (N.Z.)
Is. Wallis (France)
WESTERN SAMOA
Apia
VANUATU
Vila
New Hebrides Trench
North Fiji Basin
FIJI
Viti Levu
Vanua Levu
Suva
Nuku'alofa
TONGA
Tonga Trench
New Caledonia (France)
Loyauté Is. (France)
Hunter Trench
South Fiji Basin
Kermadec Is. (N.Z.)
Kermadec Trench
Norfolk I. (Australia)
Norfolk Island Trough
Lord Howe Rise
Coral Sea
Great Barrier Reef
Great Dividing Range
Gulf of Carpentaria
Darwin
North Australian Basin
INDIAN OCEAN
Great Sandy Desert
Macdonnell Ranges
AUSTRALIA
Great Victoria Desert
Nullarbor Plain
Great Australian Bight
Tropic of Capricorn
Perth
Adelaide
Darling
Murray
Canberra
Melbourne
Sydney
Brisbane
Bass Strait
Tasmania
Hobart
East Australian Current
West Australian Current
Southeast Indian Basin
South Australian Basin
Tasman Sea
Tasman Basin
Tasman Plateau
Auckland
North I.
NEW ZEALAND
Wellington
South I.
Stewart I.
Chatham Rise
Chatham Is. (N.Z.)
Antipodes Is. (N.Z.)
Auckland Is. (N.Z.)
Campbell I. (N.Z.)
Macquarie I. (Australia)
Macquarie Ridge
West Wind Drift
Indian-Antarctic Ridge
Indian Antarctic Basin
SOUTH
Balleny Is.
Scott I.
Pack ice
Central Pacific Basin
North Equatorial
International Date Line
JULY
JANUARY
-10542
-7822
-7168
-6794
-10374
-6987
-8724
-11022
-10497
-6920
-9140
-7440
-7450
-7570
-5303
-10024
-10047
-5604
-6098
2929
2230
3764
Modified Zenithal Equidistant Projection

PACIFIC OCEAN

NORTH ATLANTIC OCEAN

CANADA

UNITED STATES

MEXICO

Gulf of Mexico

SOUTH PACIFIC OCEAN

Equatorial Counter Current

Equator

Scale 1 : 63 000 000

0   500   1000   1500 km

© Oxford University Press

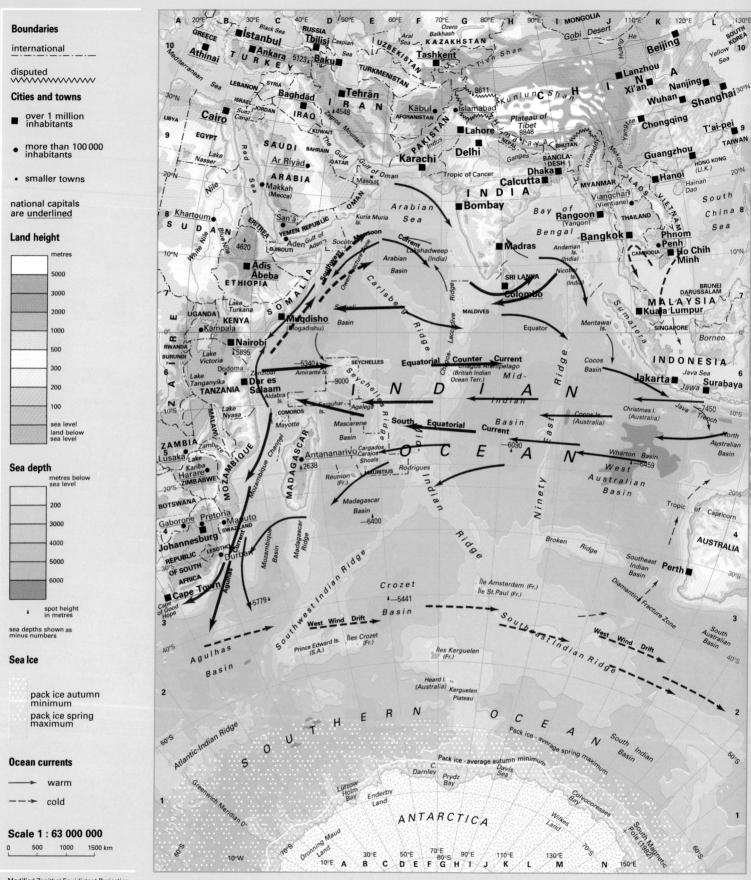

Boundaries

international

disputed

Cities and towns

■ over 1 million inhabitants

● more than 100 000 inhabitants

• smaller towns

national capitals are underlined

Land height

metres
5000
3000
2000
1000
500
300
200
100
sea level
land below sea level

Sea depth

metres below sea level
200
3000
4000
5000
6000

▲ spot height in metres

sea depths shown as minus numbers

Sea ice

pack ice autumn minimum

pack ice spring maximum

Ocean currents

→ warm

--→ cold

Scale 1 : 63 000 000

0   500   1000   1500 km

Modified Zenithal Equidistant Projection

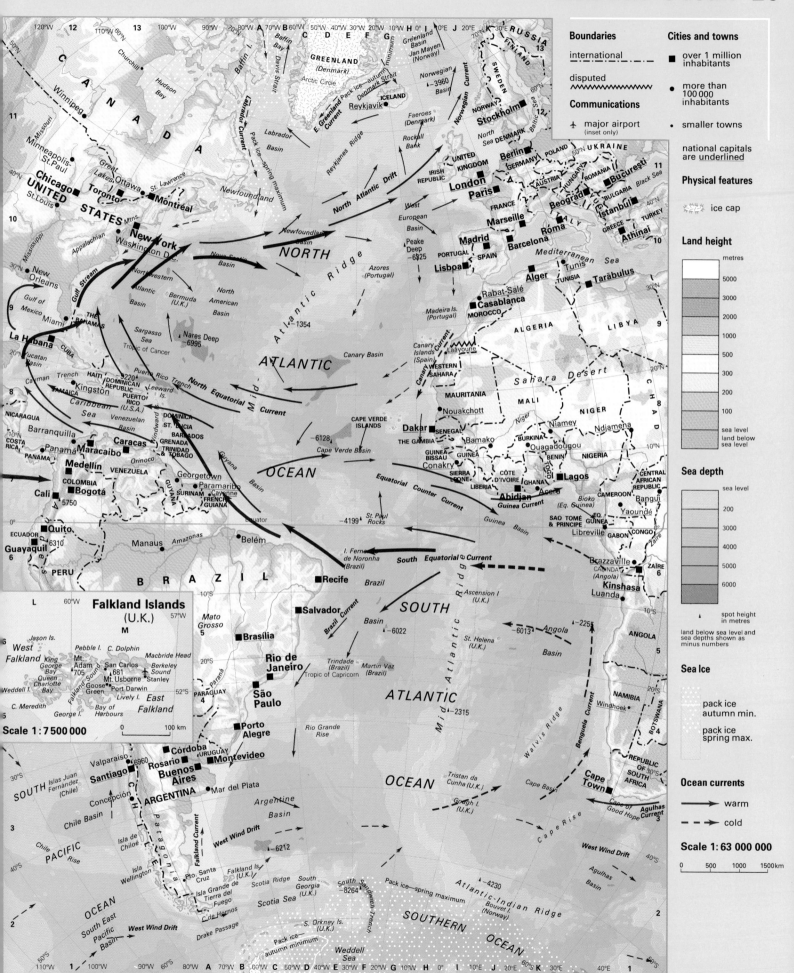

Boundaries

international ————

disputed ∿∿∿∿∿

Communications

✈ major airport (inset only)

Cities and towns

■ over 1 million inhabitants

● more than 100 000 inhabitants

• smaller towns

national capitals are <u>underlined</u>

Physical features

✲ ice cap

Land height

metres
5000
3000
2000
1000
500
300
200
100
sea level
land below sea level

Sea depth

sea level
200
3000
4000
5000
6000

▲ spot height in metres

land below sea level and sea depths shown as minus numbers

Sea Ice

pack ice autumn min.

pack ice spring max.

Ocean currents

→ warm

⇢ cold

Scale 1: 63 000 000

0   500   1000   1500km

Falkland Islands (U.K.)

L   60°W   57°W
M

West Falkland
Jason Is.
Pebble I.   C. Dolphin
King George Bay   Mt. Adam 705   San Carlos   Macbride Head
Queen Charlotte Bay   Mt. Usborne 681   Berkeley Sound
Weddell I.   Goose Green   Port Darwin   Stanley
C. Meredith   George I.   Lively I.   *East Falkland*
Bay of Harbours

Scale 1: 7 500 000

0   100 km

Land height

metres
5000
3000
2000
1000
500
300
200
100
sea level
land below sea level

spot height in metres

Sea depth

sea level
200
3000
4000
5000
6000

⌣ maximum extent of glaciation

ice cap

sand desert

Land below sea level and sea depths shown as minus numbers

–·–·– international boundary

Scale 1 : 44 000 000

0   500   1000 km

Zenithal Equal Area Project

Political

— international boundary

• capital city

Abbreviations:
A	ARMENIA Yerevan
AZ	AZERBAIJAN Baku
B	BAHRAIN Manama
G	GEORGIA Tbilisi
I	ISRAEL Jerusalem
J	JORDAN Amman
K	KUWAIT Al Kuwayt
KIR	KIRGYZSTAN Bishkek (Frunze)
L	LITHUANIA Vilnius
LA	LATVIA Riga
LEB	LEBANON Beyrouth (Beirut)
M	MOLDOVA Kishinev
Q	QATAR Ad Dawhah (Doha)
S	SYRIA Dimashq (Damascus)
T	TAJIKISTAN Dushanbe
UAE	UNITED ARAB EMIRATES Abu Zabi (Abu Dhabi)

Scale 1: 60 000 000

0   500   1000 km

China: Population, 1982

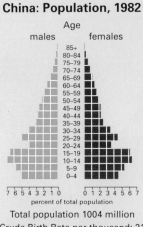

Age
males — females

percent of total population

Total population 1004 million
Crude Birth Rate per thousand: 21
Crude Death Rate per thousand: 7

Japan: Population, 1986

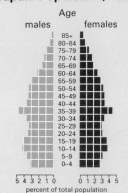

Age
males — females

percent of total population

Total population 122 million
Crude Birth Rate per thousand: 12
Crude Death Rate per thousand: 6

Philippines: Population, 1988

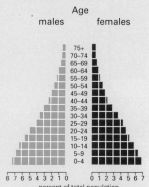

Age
males — females

percent of total population

Total population 59 million
Crude Birth Rate per thousand: 33
Crude Death Rate per thousand: 8

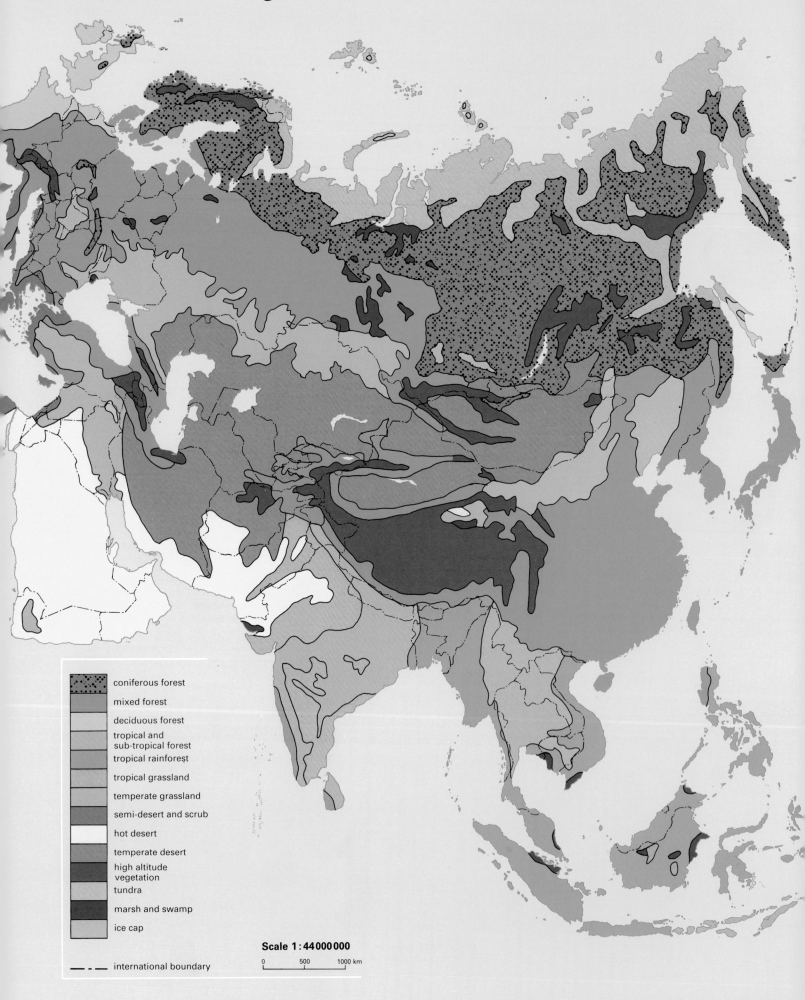

coniferous forest

mixed forest

deciduous forest

tropical and
sub-tropical forest

tropical rainforest

tropical grassland

temperate grassland

semi-desert and scrub

hot desert

temperate desert

high altitude
vegetation

tundra

marsh and swamp

ice cap

Scale 1 : 44 000 000

0   500   1000 km

– · – international boundary

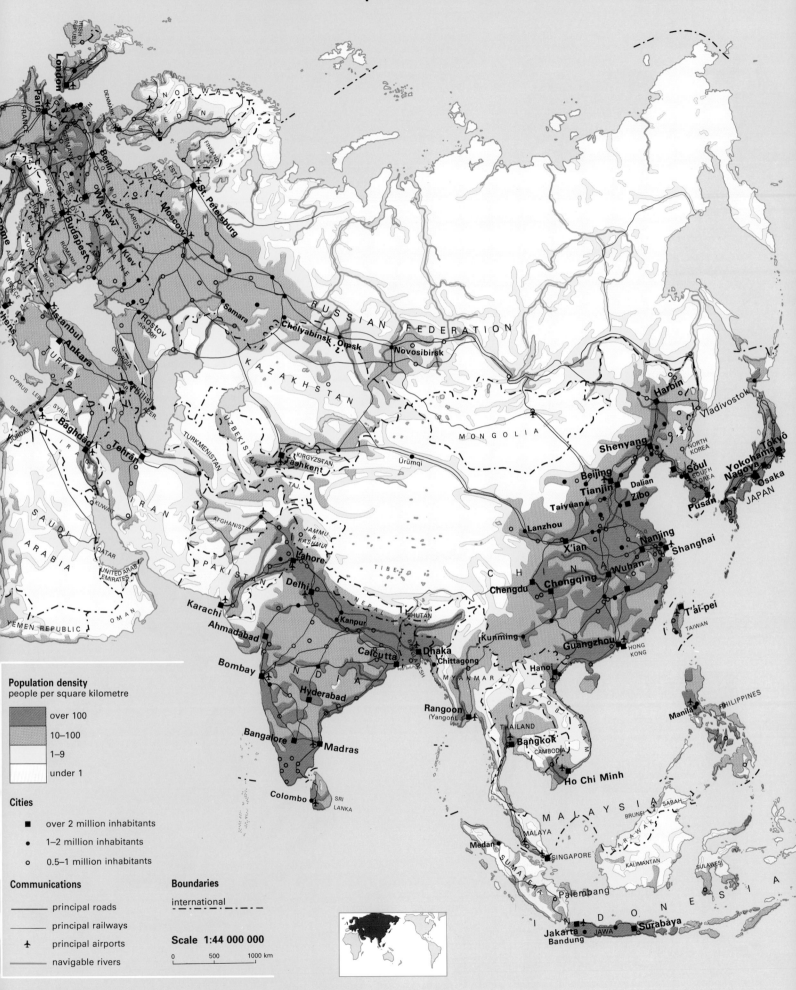

Population density
people per square kilometre

- over 100
- 10–100
- 1–9
- under 1

Cities

- ■ over 2 million inhabitants
- • 1–2 million inhabitants
- ○ 0.5–1 million inhabitants

Communications

- ——— principal roads
- ——— principal railways
- ✈ principal airports
- ——— navigable rivers

Boundaries

international

Scale 1:44 000 000

0   500   1000 km

Zenithal Equal Area Projection
© Oxford University Press

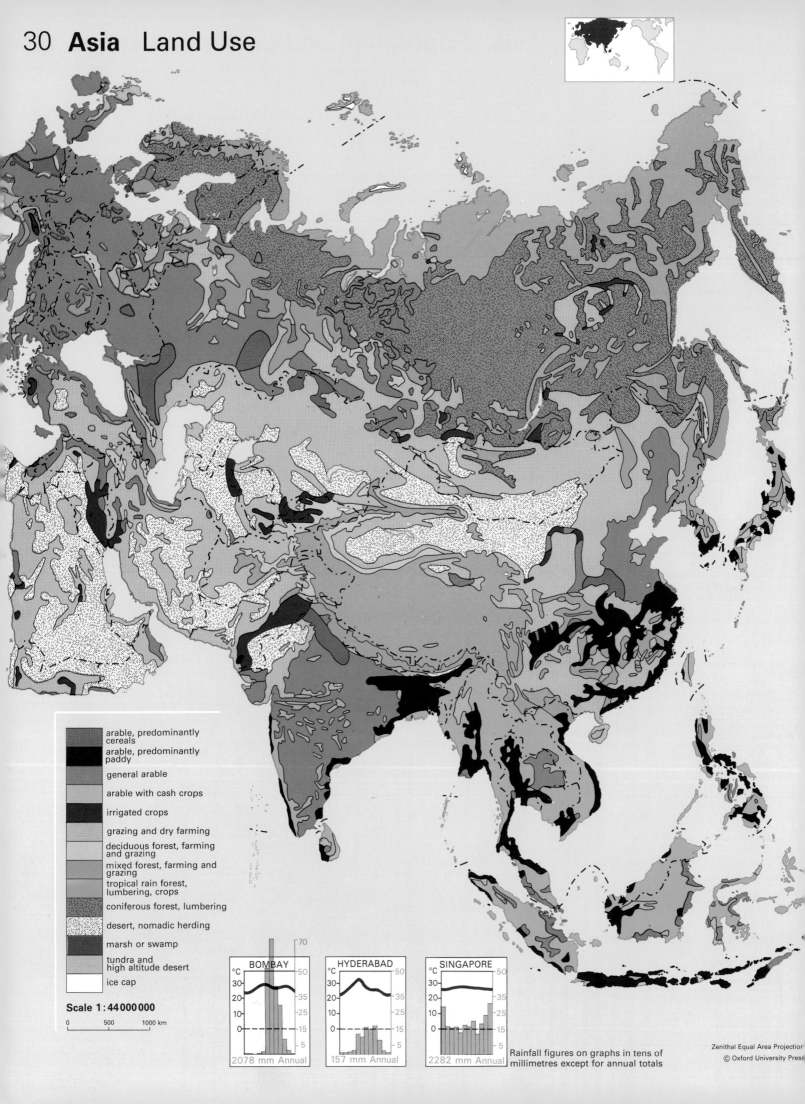

Legend:

- arable, predominantly cereals
- arable, predominantly paddy
- general arable
- arable with cash crops
- irrigated crops
- grazing and dry farming
- deciduous forest, farming and grazing
- mixed forest, farming and grazing
- tropical rain forest, lumbering, crops
- coniferous forest, lumbering
- desert, nomadic herding
- marsh or swamp
- tundra and high altitude desert
- ice cap

Scale 1:44 000 000

0   500   1000 km

BOMBAY
°C
30
20
10
0
70
50
35
25
15
5
2078 mm Annual

HYDERABAD
°C
30
20
10
0
50
35
25
15
5
157 mm Annual

SINGAPORE
°C
30
20
10
0
50
35
25
15
5
2282 mm Annual

Rainfall figures on graphs in tens of millimetres except for annual totals

Zenithal Equal Area Projection

© Oxford University Press

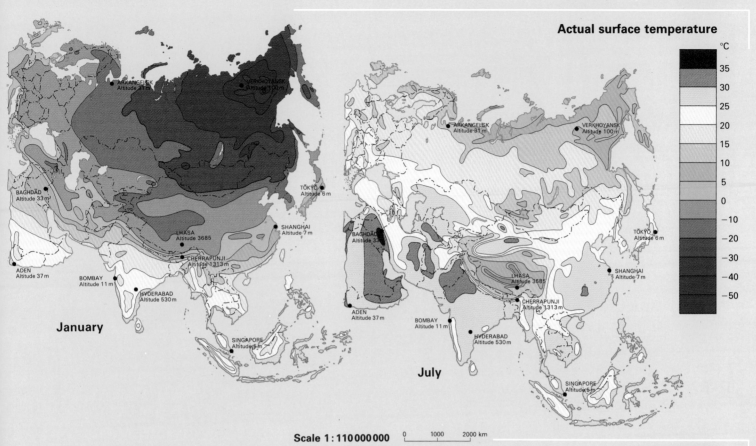

Actual surface temperature

°C
35
30
25
20
15
10
5
0
−10
−20
−30
−40
−50

January

July

Scale 1:110 000 000

0   1000   2000 km

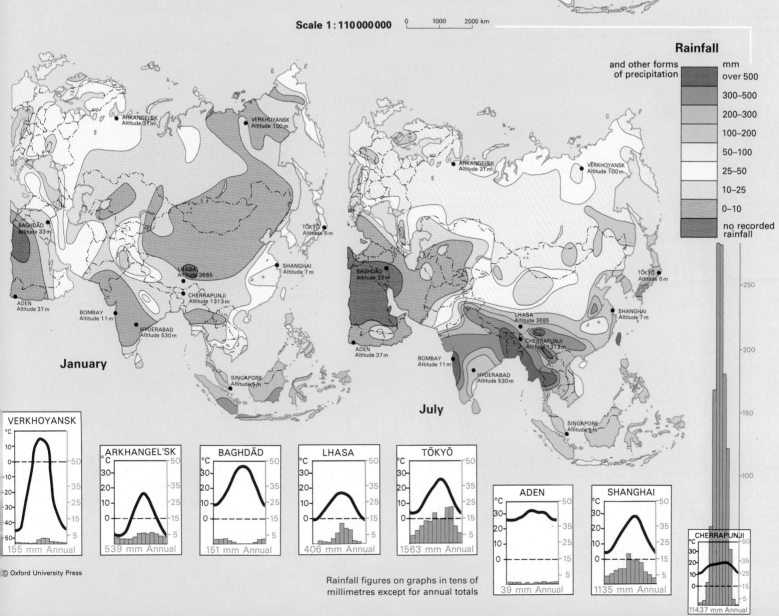

Rainfall

and other forms
of precipitation

mm
over 500
300–500
200–300
100–200
50–100
25–50
10–25
0–10
no recorded
rainfall

January

July

VERKHOYANSK
°C
10
0
−10
−20
−30
−40
−50
155 mm Annual

ARKHANGEL'SK
°C
30
20
10
0
−10
50
35
25
15
5
539 mm Annual

BAGHDĀD
°C
30
20
10
0
50
35
25
15
5
151 mm Annual

LHASA
°C
30
20
10
0
50
35
25
15
5
406 mm Annual

TŌKYŌ
°C
30
20
10
0
50
35
25
15
5
1563 mm Annual

ADEN
°C
30
20
10
0
50
35
25
15
5
39 mm Annual

SHANGHAI
°C
30
20
10
0
50
35
25
15
5
1135 mm Annual

250

200

150

100

CHERRAPUNJI
°C
30
20
10
0
50
35
25
15
5
11437 mm Annual

Rainfall figures on graphs in tens of
millimetres except for annual totals

© Oxford University Press

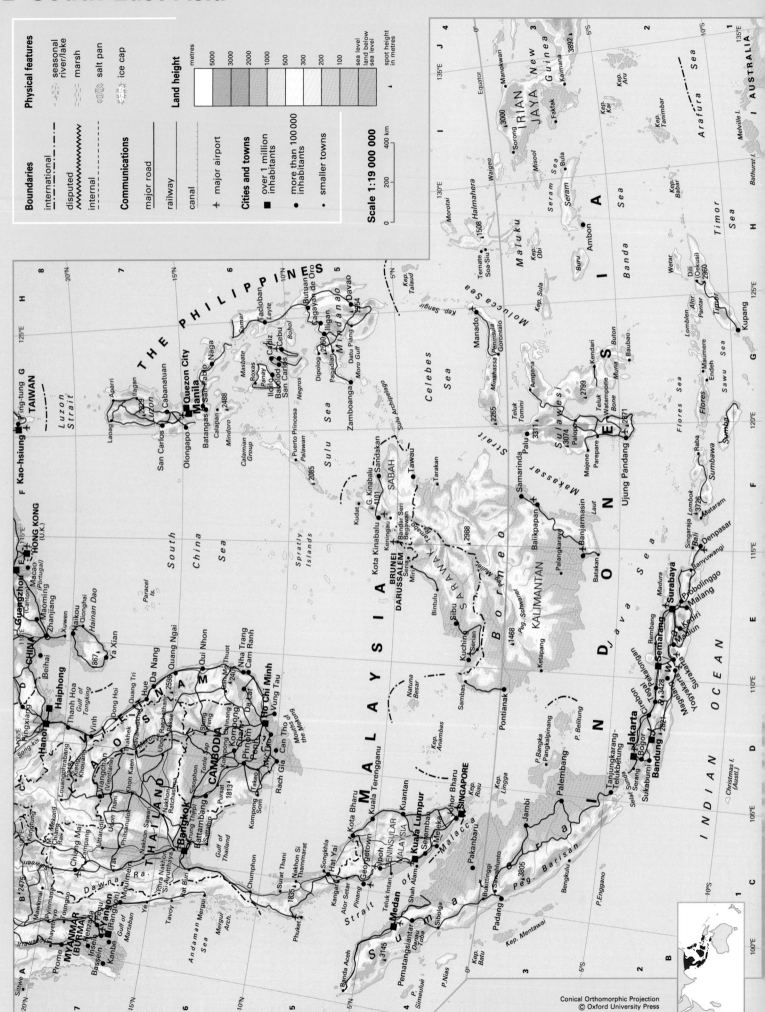

Physical features
- ---·-- seasonal river/lake
- ----- marsh
- salt pan
- ice cap

Boundaries
- ---·--- international
- ⋀⋀⋀⋀ disputed
- ----- internal

Communications
- ——— major road
- ——— railway
- ——— canal

Cities and towns
- ■ over 1 million inhabitants
- ● more than 100 000 inhabitants
- · smaller towns

✈ major airport

Land height

| metres | 5000 | 3000 | 2000 | 1000 | 500 | 300 | 200 | 100 | sea level / land below sea level |

· spot height in metres

Scale 1:19 000 000

0   200   400 km

Conical Orthomorphic Projection
© Oxford University Press

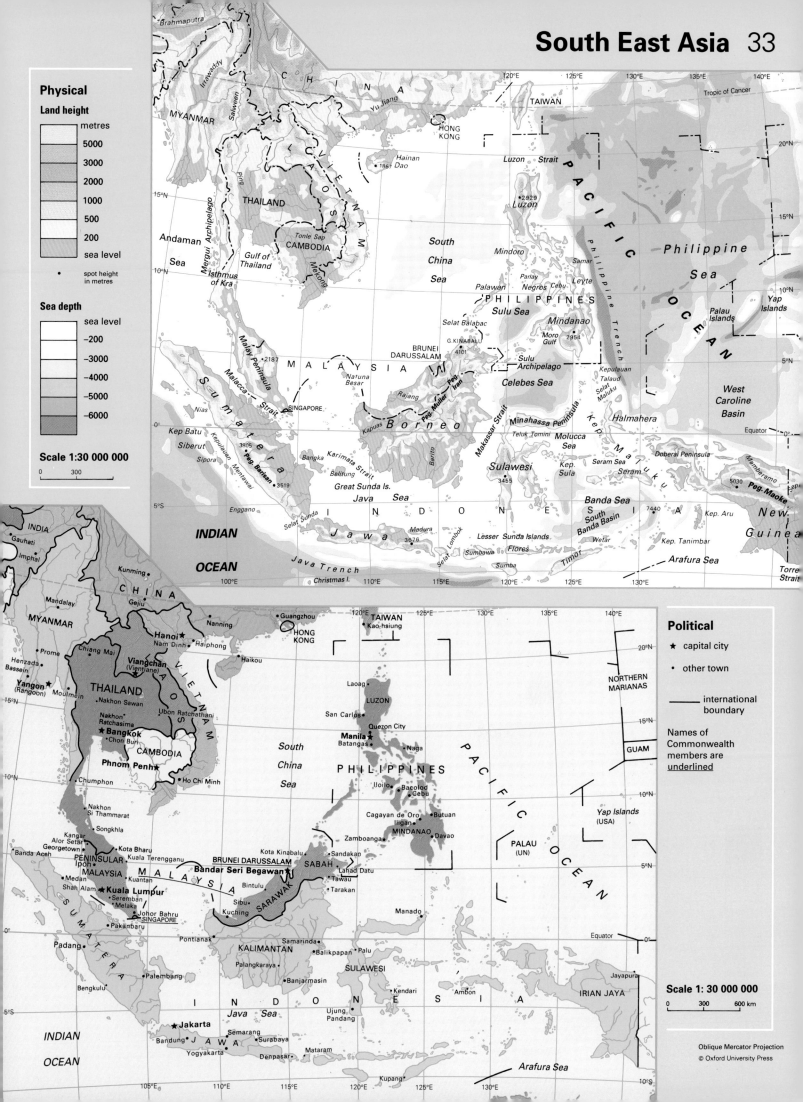

Physical

Land height

metres
- 5000
- 3000
- 2000
- 1000
- 500
- 200
- sea level
- • spot height in metres

Sea depth

sea level
- -200
- -3000
- -4000
- -5000
- -6000

Scale 1:30 000 000

0 — 300

Political

- ★ capital city
- • other town
- — international boundary

Names of Commonwealth members are <u>underlined</u>

Scale 1: 30 000 000

0 — 300 — 600 km

Oblique Mercator Projection
© Oxford University Press

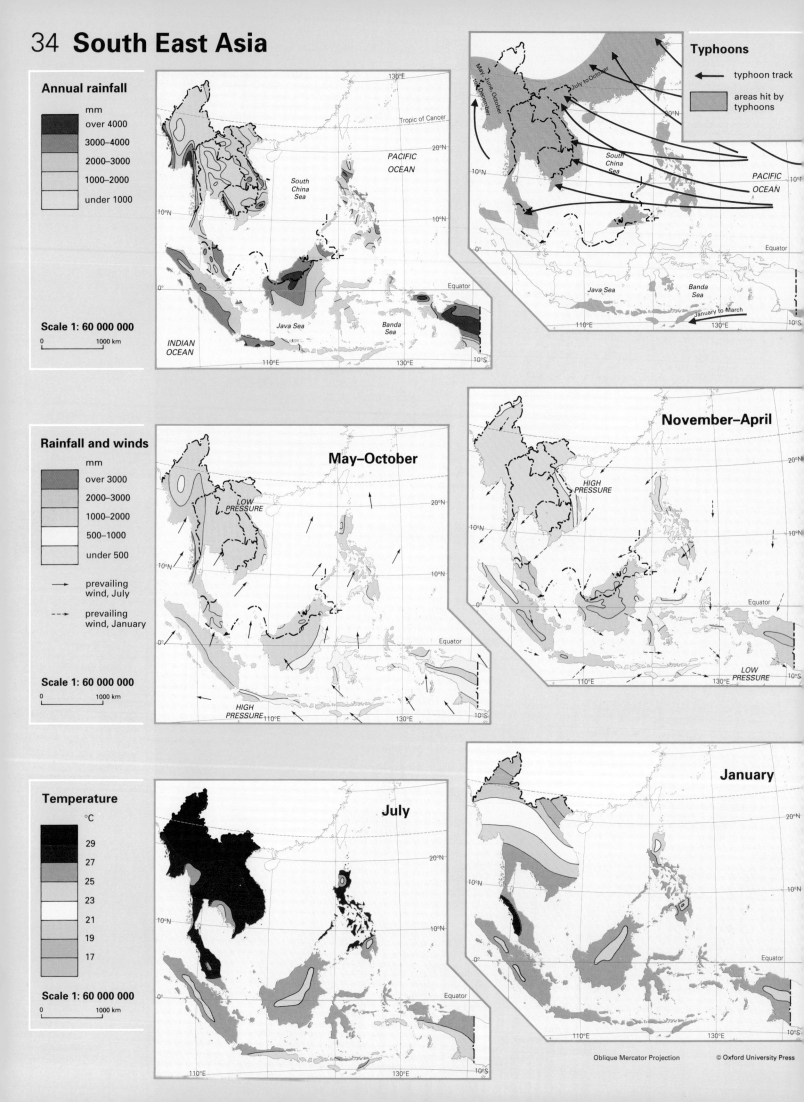

Annual rainfall

mm
- over 4000
- 3000–4000
- 2000–3000
- 1000–2000
- under 1000

Scale 1: 60 000 000

0   1000 km

Tropic of Cancer

130°E

20°N

PACIFIC OCEAN

South China Sea

10°N

10°N

0°

Equator

Java Sea

Banda Sea

110°E

130°E

INDIAN OCEAN

10°S

Typhoons

→ typhoon track

areas hit by typhoons

May, June, October to December

July to October

South China Sea

PACIFIC OCEAN

10°N

Java Sea

Banda Sea

Equator

January to March

110°E

130°E

10°S

Rainfall and winds

mm
- over 3000
- 2000–3000
- 1000–2000
- 500–1000
- under 500

→ prevailing wind, July

--→ prevailing wind, January

Scale 1: 60 000 000

0   1000 km

May–October

LOW PRESSURE

20°N

10°N

10°N

0°

Equator

110°E

130°E

HIGH PRESSURE

10°S

November–April

HIGH PRESSURE

20°N

10°N

0°

Equator

LOW PRESSURE

110°E

130°E

10°S

Temperature

°C
- 29
- 27
- 25
- 23
- 21
- 19
- 17

Scale 1: 60 000 000

0   1000 km

July

20°N

10°N

10°N

Equator

110°E

130°E

10°S

January

20°N

10°N

10°N

Equator

110°E

130°E

10°S

Oblique Mercator Projection   © Oxford University Press

Land use

- cultivated land
- cultivated land, rice dominant
- scrub, non-agricultural land
- forest and jungle
- swamp forest and swamp

- shifting cultivation
- plantations

Scale 1: 30 000 000

0   300   600 km

Andaman Sea

Gulf of Thailand

South China Sea

Sulu Sea

Celebes Sea

PACIFIC OCEAN

Java Sea

Banda Sea

Arafura Sea

INDIAN OCEAN

Equator

INDIA

Population

Population density
people per square kilometre

- more than 700
- 100–700
- 10–100
- 1–9
- less than 1

Cities and towns

- ■ over 2 million
- ● 1–2 million
- ○ 0.5–1 million

Scale 1: 30 000 000

0   300   600 km

MYANMAR

○ Mandalay

Hanoi ■
Haiphong ●

Yangon (Rangoon) ■

C H I N A

THAILAND

L A O S

V I E T N A M

Bangkok ●

CAMBODIA
Phnom Penh ○

■ **Ho Chi Minh**

Andaman Sea

Gulf of Thailand

HONG KONG

TAIWAN

South China Sea

Manila ■ ● Quezon City

PHILIPPINES

○Cebu

○Davao

Sulu Sea

BRUNEI DARUSSALAM

Celebes Sea

PACIFIC OCEAN

NORTHERN MARIANAS

GUAM

○ YAP ISLANDS

PALAU

Medan ●

Kuala Lumpur ●

M A L A Y S I A

■ **Singapore**

I N D O N E S I A

○ Palembang

Java Sea

Jakarta ■ ● Bandung Semarang ● ■ **Surabaya**
○ Malang

Ujung Pandang ○

Banda Sea

INDIAN OCEAN

Arafura Sea

Equator

Scale 1: 12 500 000

0   200   400 km

Transverse Mercator Projection

© Oxford University Press

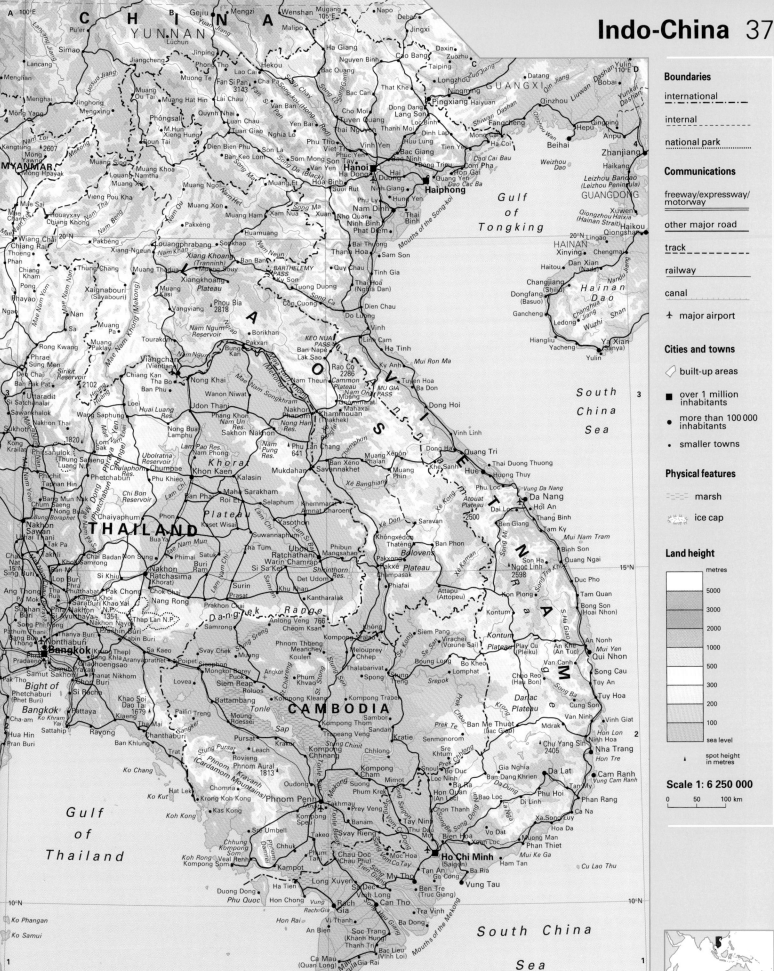

Boundaries

international

internal

national park

Communications

freeway/expressway/
motorway

other major road

track

railway

canal

✈ major airport

Cities and towns

◇ built-up areas

■ over 1 million
inhabitants

● more than 100 000
inhabitants

• smaller towns

Physical features

marsh

ice cap

Land height

metres
5000
3000
2000
1000
500
300
200
100
sea level

▲ spot height
in metres

Scale 1: 6 250 000

0   50   100 km

CHINA

YUNNAN

MYANMAR

THAILAND

LAOS

VIETNAM

CAMBODIA

GUANGXI

GUANGDONG

HAINAN

Gulf
of
Tongking

South
China
Sea

Gulf
of
Thailand

Bight of
Phetchaburi
(Phet Buri)

Bangkok
Bay

South China
Sea

Hanoi

Haiphong

Bangkok

Phnom Penh

Ho Chi Minh
(Saigon)

Da Nang

Hue

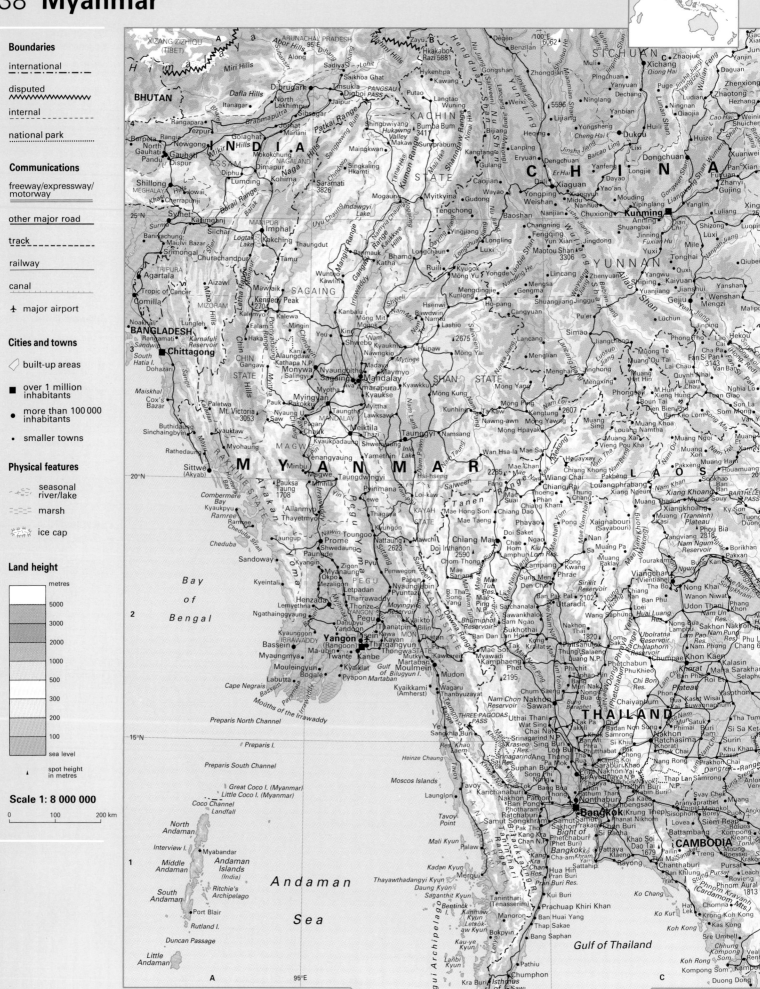

Boundaries

international
disputed
internal
national park

Communications

freeway/expressway/
motorway

other major road

track

railway

canal

✈ major airport

Cities and towns

◇ built-up areas

■ over 1 million
inhabitants

● more than 100 000
inhabitants

• smaller towns

Physical features

seasonal
river/lake

marsh

ice cap

Land height

metres
5000
3000
2000
1000
500
300
200
100
sea level

▲ spot height
in metres

Scale 1: 8 000 000

0   100   200 km

Conic Projection

© Oxford University Press

Boundaries

international

internal

national park

Communications

freeway/expressway/motorway

other major road

track

railway

canal

✈ major airport

Cities and towns

built-up areas

■ over 1 million inhabitants

● more than 100 000 inhabitants

• smaller towns

Physical features

marsh

Land height

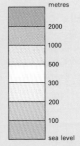

metres

2000

1000

500

300

200

100

sea level

▲ spot height in metres

Scale 1: 6 250 000

0   50   100 km

Conic Projection
© Oxford University Press

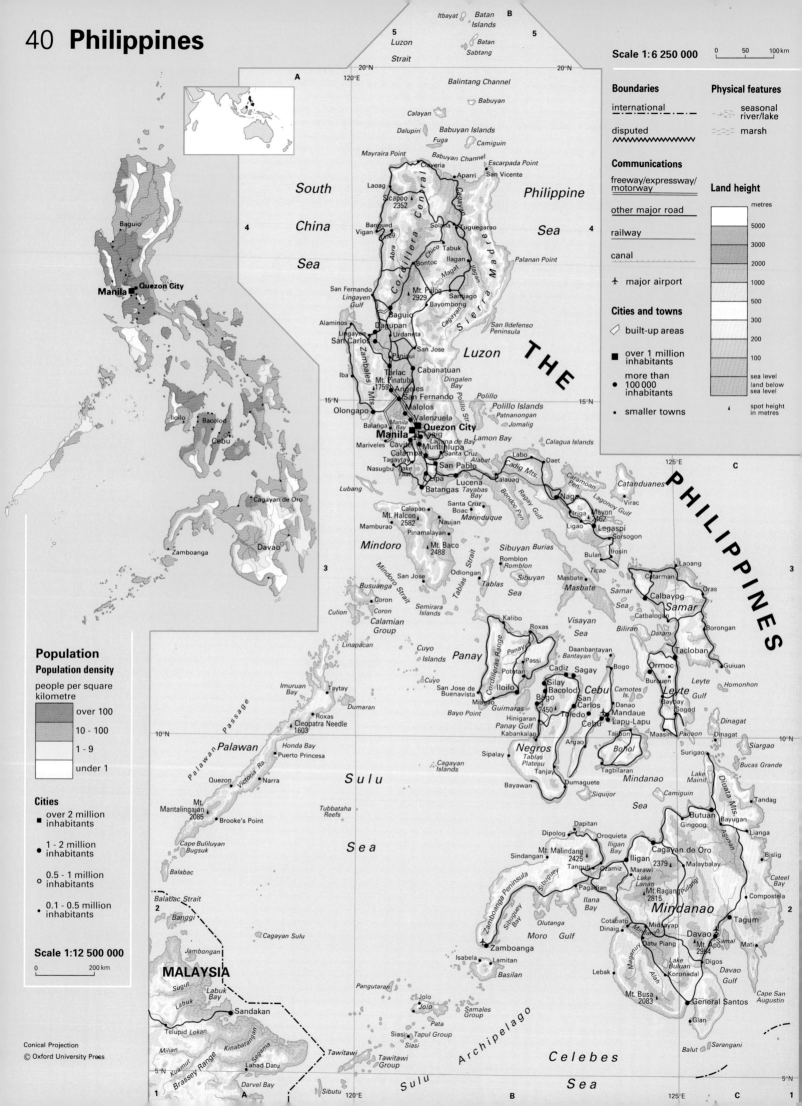

40 Philippines

Conical Projection
© Oxford University Press

Scale 1: 200 000

0 2 4 km

Cassini Projection
© Oxford University Press

Land height

metres	
140	
100	
60	
40	
20	
sea level	

▲ spot height in metres

Boundaries

international

anchorage

Communications

freeway/expressway/motorway

other major road

railway

canal

✈ major airport

Cities and towns

built-up areas

• smaller towns

Labels on map

MALAYSIA
JOHOR BAHRU
INDONESIA

Straits of Singapore (Selat Singapura)
Selat Johor
S·e·l·a·t J·o·h·o·r
Nenas Channel

Pulau Tekong
Pulau Tekong Reservoir
P. Tekong Kechil
P. Unum
Sea Embankment
P. Chek Jawa
Tg. Chek Jawa
Pulau Ubin
Serangoon Ketam Channel
P. Ketam
Serangoon Harbour

Changi International Airport
S. Changi Point
Changi
Loyang
Yan Kit
Simei
Tampines
Bedok
S. Bedok
Pasir Ris
Hun Yeang
Bedok Reservoir
Ulu Bedok
Katong
Geylang Serai
Geylang

Punggol
Tg. Punggol
Jalan Kayu
Kg. Pinang
Hougang
Paya Lebar
Serangoon
Chia Keng
Bradell Heights
Seletar
Sungai Seletar Reservoir
Seletar Reservoir

Woodlands
Sembawang
S. Sembawang
Chong Pang
Yishun
Chye Kay
Nee Soon
Mandai Road
Lower Peirce Reservoir
Upper Peirce Reservoir
MacRitchie Reservoir
Public Utilities Board Catchment Area and Nature Reserve

Yio Chu Kang
Ang Mo Kio
Bishan
Toa Payoh
Thomson
Kallang R.
Central Expressway
Bukit Timah Expressway
Bt. Timah ▲162
Bukit Timah
Pan-Island Expressway

Sungei Seletar
S. Simpang
S. Khatib Bongsu

Kranji Reservoir
Kranji
S. Kranji
P. Buloh
S. Buloh Besar
Murai Reservoir
Poyan Reservoir
Tengeh Reservoir
Sarimbun Reservoir
Lim Chu Kang
S. Kangkar
Thong Hoe
Ama Keng
Lim Chu Kang Road
Choa Chu Kang
S. Tengah
S. Peng Siang
Nanyang Technological Institute
S. Pang Sua
Bt. Mandai 129
Bt. Gombak ▲133
Bukit Mandai
Yew Tee
S. Mandai
Bukit Batok
Bukit Panjang
Bukit Timah
Hong Kah
Bulim
Lam San
Jurong
Jurong Lake
Jurong Industrial Area
Jurong Road
Gul Basin
Tuas Basin

Clementi
Singapore Polytechnic
Ngee Ann Polytechnic
Ulu Pandan
Dunearn Road
Bukit Timah Road
Holland Village
Holland Road
Institute of Education
Singapore Botanical Gardens
Race Course
Queenstown
Alexandra
Telok Blangah ▲106
Pasir Panjang
National University of Singapore
Ayer Rajah Expressway
West Coast Road
Pandan Reservoir
S. Pandan
Buona Vista
Terumbu Retan Laut

Singapore
Railway Station
Tanjong Pagar
Keppel Harbour
Tg. Berlayar
Pulau Brani
Sentosa
P. Blakang Mati
Tg. Rimau

Marina East
Marina South
Kallang R.
Rochor R.
Stadium
Wilampoa
Serangoon R.
Kampong Bugis

East Coast Parkway
Pan-Island Expressway

Anchorages
Anchorage for awaiting Singapore Pilot
Eastern Explosives Anchorage
Eastern Special Purposes Anchorage
Laid-up Vessels Anchorage
Small Craft Anchorage
Eastern Petroleum A Anchorage
Eastern Petroleum B Anchorage
Explosives Anchorage
Man-of-War Anchorage
Eastern Quarantine A Anchorage
Eastern Working Anchorage
Eastern Quarantine and Immigration Anchorage
Western Quarantine and Immigration Anchorage
Western Working Anchorage
Western Petroleum Anchorage
Reserved Anchorage
Dangerous Goods Anchorage
Coastal Anchorage
Selat Pauh Anchorage
Sultan Shoal Quarantine and Immigration Anchorage
West Jurong Petroleum Anchorage
North Tuas Basin Anchorage
Jurong Petroleum Anchorage

Islands
P. Kusu
P. Tembakul (P. Tembakul, Peak I.)
P. Seringat (P. Renget)
P. Sakijang Pelepah (Lazarus Island)
P. Sakijang Bendera (St John's Island)
Buran Darat
Tg. China
P. Sebarok
P. Tekukor (P. Penyabong)
P. Jong
P. Semakau
P. Sakeng
P. Bukum
P. Bukum Kechil
P. Hantu
P. Ular
P. Busing
P. Salu
P. Pesek
P. Pesek Kechil
P. Sakra
P. Meskol
P. Seraya
P. Ayer Chawan
P. Ayer Merbau
P. Merlimau
P. Mesemut Laut
P. Mesemut Kechil
P. Samulun
P. Damar Laut
P. Buaya
P. Pawai
P. Senang
P. Sudong
P. Senang
P. Biola
P. Satumu ▲ 103°45′E

Straits of Singapore (Selat Singapura)
Selat Pandan
Selat Jurong
Tg. Skopek
Tg. Chenting

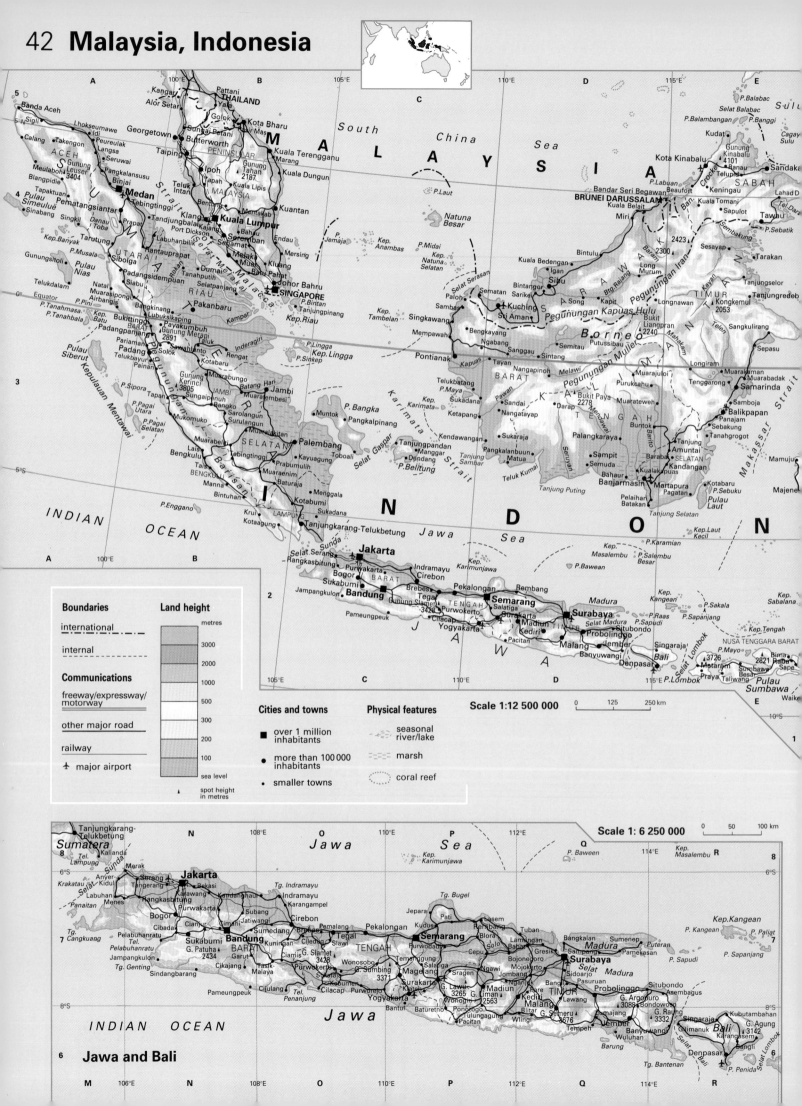

Jawa and Bali

Boundaries
international
internal

Communications
freeway/expressway/motorway
other major road
railway
✈ major airport

Land height
metres
3000
2000
1000
500
300
200
100
sea level
▲ spot height in metres

Cities and towns
■ over 1 million inhabitants
● more than 100 000 inhabitants
• smaller towns

Physical features
seasonal river/lake
marsh
coral reef

Scale 1:12 500 000
0   125   250 km

Scale 1: 6 250 000
0   50   100 km

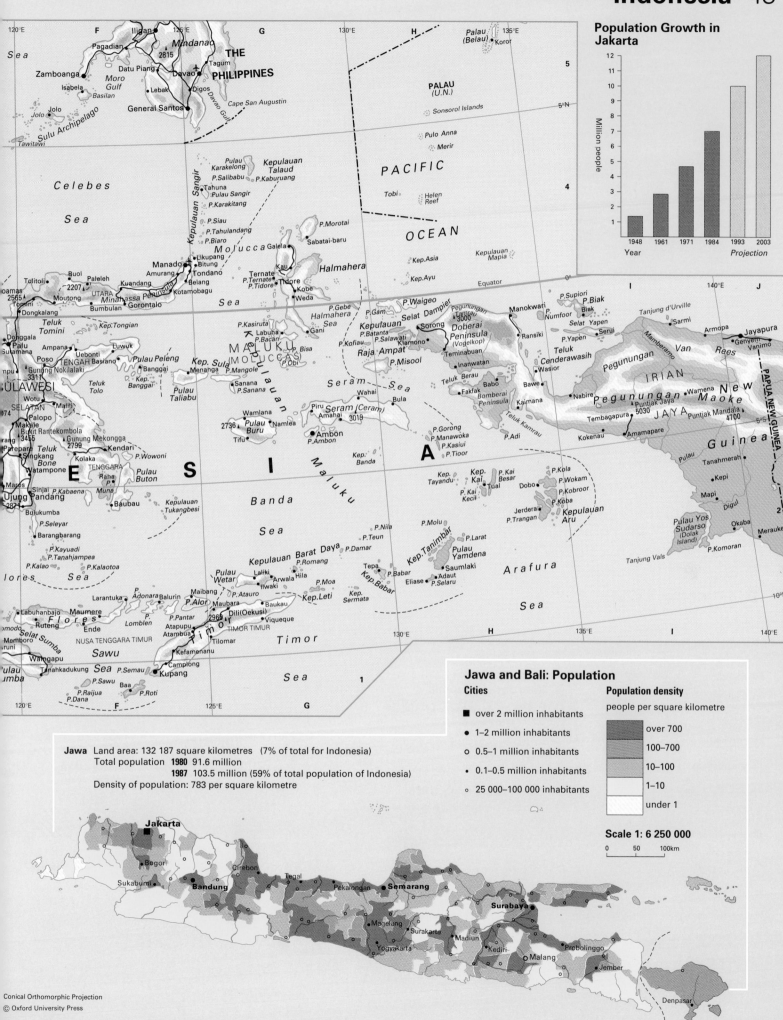

Indonesia 43

Population Growth in Jakarta

Million people

12
11
10
9
8
7
6
5
4
3
2
1

| 1948 | 1961 | 1971 | 1984 | 1993 | 2003 |
| Year | | | | | Projection |

THE PHILIPPINES

Mindanao
Iligan
Pagadian
2815
Datu Piang
Zamboanga   Moro   Davao
Isabela   Gulf   Tagum
Basilan   Digos
Jolo   General Santos
Jolo   Cape San Augustin
Sulu Archipelago
Tawitawi

Palau (Belau)
Koror
PALAU (U.N.)
Sonsorol Islands
Pulo Anna
Merir

PACIFIC OCEAN

Tobi   Helen Reef

Kepulauan Sangir
Pulau Karakelong
P.Salibabu
Kepulauan Talaud
P.Kaburuang
Tahuna
Pulau Sangir
P.Karakitang
P.Siau
P.Tahulandang
P.Biaro

P.Morotai
Sabatai-baru

Kep.Asia
Kepulauan Mapia

Equator   0°

Celebes Sea

Molucca Sea
Galela
Likupang
Manado
Amurang   Bitung
Tondano
Belang   Ternate   Kobe
Kotamobagu   P.Ternate   Tidore   Weda
P.Tidore
Halmahera
Kau

Buol
Tolitoli   2207   Paleleh
Kuandang
Moutong   UTARA   Minahassa Peninsula
2565   Tomini   Bumbulan   Gorontalo
Toamas
Dongkalang   Teluk Tomini
Donggala   Kep.Tongian
Palu   Ampana   Uebonti   Luwuk
Sulamana   TENGAH   Basiano   Pulau Peleng
Gunung Nokilalaki   Banggai
3311   Poso   Kep.Sula
Kep.Banggai
SULAWESI   Teluk Tolo   Pulau Taliabu
Wotu   Maliti
SELATAN   Palopo
874   Makale   Bukit Rantekombola
rang   3455   Gunung Mekongga
Parepare   Teluk   2799   Kendari
Singkang   Bone   P.Wowoni
Watampone   Kolaka
E   TENGGARA   Pulau Buton
S   Raha   Pulau
Sinjai   P.Kabaena   Muna
Maros   287
Ujung Pandang   Baubau
Bulukumba
P.Seleyar   Kepulauan Tukangbesi
Barangbarang

Halmahera Sea
P.Gebe
P.Gam   P.Waigeo
P.Kasiruta   P.Batanta   Selat Dampier
P.Bacan   Kep.Kofiau   P.Salawati
P.Bisa   Kepulauan   Sorong
P.Obi   Raja Ampat   Doberai Peninsula (Vogelkop)
Gani   P.Misool   Teminabuan
Inanwatan

MALUKU
MOLUCCAS
Kep.Sula
P.Mangole
Menanga
P.Sanana
Sanana

Seram Sea
Wahai
Piru   Seram (Ceram)
Wamlana   Amahai   3019   Bula
2736   Pulau Buru
Namlea
Tifu   Ambon
P.Ambon
Kep.Banda

Manokwari
Tamrau   Numfoor   P.Supiori   P.Biak
3000   P.Yapen   Biak
Ransiki   Serui
Teluk   Selat Yapen
Pegunungan   Teluk Cenderawasih
Sorong   Nabire
Bawe
Teluk Berau   Wasior
Babo
Fakfak   Bomberai Peninsula
Teluk Kamrau
Kaimana
P.Adi   Kokenau   Tembagapura
Amamapare

Mamberamo
Tanjung d'Urville
Sarmi
Armopa
Van   Genyem   Jayapura
Rees   Vanimo
IRIAN
Pegunungan   Maoke   New
Puntjak Jaya   Wamena
5030   JAYA   Puntjak Mandala
4700   Guinea
Pulau   Tanahmerah
Sudarso   Kepi
Mapi
Digul
Okaba   Merauke
P.Komoran

PAPUA NEW GUINEA

Banda Sea
Kep.Tayandu
P.Kai Kecil
Tual   P.Kai Besar
Dobo
Jerdera
P.Nila   P.Kola
P.Wokam
P.Kobroor
P.Koba
Kepulauan Aru
P.Trangan

Kepulauan Barat Daya
P.Romang   P.Molu
P.Teun   P.Damar
Laliki   Tepa   P.Larat
Pulau Wetar   Arwala Hila   P.Babar   Pulau Yamdena
Ilwaki   Kep.Tanimbar
P.Moa   Saumlaki
Kep.Leti   Eliase   Adaut
Kep.Sermata   P.Selaru

Arafura Sea
Tanjung Vals

Flores Sea
P.Kayuadi
P.Tanahjampea
P.Kalao   P.Kalaotoa

Flores Sea
Labuhanbajo   Maumere
Ruteng   Larantuka   P.Adonara   Balurin
Ende   P.Alor   Maubara
Lomblen   P.Pantar   Maibang   Baukau
P.Ataura   Dili (Oekusi)   Viqueque
2960
Atambua   TIMOR TIMUR
Kefamenanu   Tilomar
komodo   NUSA TENGGARA TIMUR
runi   Memboro
Waingapu   Sawu Sea
ulau   Tanahkadukung   Kupang
umba   P.Semau
P.Sawu   Baa
P.Raijua   P.Roti
P.Dana

Timor Sea

Jawa and Bali: Population

Cities

■ over 2 million inhabitants

● 1–2 million inhabitants

○ 0.5–1 million inhabitants

● 0.1–0.5 million inhabitants

○ 25 000–100 000 inhabitants

Population density

people per square kilometre

over 700
100–700
10–100
1–10
under 1

Scale 1: 6 250 000

0   50   100km

Jawa   Land area: 132 187 square kilometres (7% of total for Indonesia)
Total population   **1980** 91.6 million
              1987 103.5 million (59% of total population of Indonesia)
Density of population: 783 per square kilometre

Jakarta
Bogor
Sukabumi   Cirebon
Bandung   Tegal
Pekalongan   Semarang
Magelang   Surakarta   Surabaya
Yogyakarta   Madiun
Kediri   Probolinggo
Malang   Jember
Denpasar

Conical Orthomorphic Projection
© Oxford University Press

Legend

Boundaries
international
internal
national park

Communications
major road
✈ major airport

Cities and towns
● more than 100 000 inhabitants
• smaller towns

Physical features
seasonal river/lake
marsh

Scale 1: 8 000 000
Conical Equidistant Projection

0 — 100 km

Land height
metres
5000
3000
2000
1000
500
300
200
100
sea level
▲ spot height in metres

Irian Jaya Economic
areas considered for transmigration settlement (see map on page 65)
oil concession boundaries
+ alluvial extraction of minerals
● mineral mines
* major mining prospect
logging concession area

Timor Gap Treaty, 1988
1971 1972 Australian-Indonesian seabed boundary agreements
the "Timor Gap"

Zone of cooperation, sub-areas:
area subject to Indonesian laws covering petroleum exploration and exploitation
central area, subject to Australian/Indonesian development regime, regulated by a ministerial council and a joint authority
area subject to Australian laws covering petroleum exploration and exploitation

Scale 1: 14 000 000
0 — 200 — 400 km

© Oxford University Press

Papua New Guinea

Scale 1: 11 500 000

0   200 km

Political Boundaries

international

province

district

Headquarters

● provincial

· district

Daru provincial/district

Population, 1995

estimate by province

Thousand people

more than 400

325-400

250-325

175-250

100-175

25-100

District	Headquarters		
1 GEMBOGL	Gembogl	15 PORGERA	Porgera
2 KUNDIAWA	Kundiawa	16 KANDEP	Kandep
3 SINA SINA	Kamtai	17 WAPENAMANDA	Wapenamanda
4 CHUAVE	Chuave	18 TAMBUL	Tambul
5 GUMINE	Gumine	19 HAGEN CENTRAL	Mt.Hagen
6 KEROWAGI	Kerowagi	20 MENDI	Mendi
7 WAHGI	Minj	21 IALIBU	Ialibu
8 JIMI	Tabibuga	22 PANGIA	Pangia
9 HAGEN NORTH	Muglamp	23 KARIMUI	Karimui
10 LUFA	Lufa	24 OKAPA	Okapa
11 HENGANOFI	Henganofi	25 GOROKA	Goroka
12 KOMPIAM	Kompiam	26 KAINANTU	Kainantu
13 WABAG	Wabag	27 MARAWAKA	Marawaka
14 LAGAIP	Laiagam	28 KIRA	Kira

Net internal migration, 1980
percent by province

+4%
0
-4
-8
-12
-16
-20
-24
-28

Western Highlands
N. Solomons
Enga
Sandaun
Milne Bay
Southern Highlands
Western
Madang
Eastern Highlands
New Ireland
West New Britain
Chimbu
East Sepik
Oro
Central
East New Britain
Manus
Morobe
Gulf
NCD

46 Japan

Scale 1: 2 000 000

0   25   50 km

Zenithal Equidistant Projection

Scale 1 : 6 250 000

0   50   100 km

© Oxford University Press

Legend

Boundaries
international
internal
national park

Communications
freeway/expressway/motorway
other major road
railway
canal
✈ major airport

Cities and towns
built-up areas
■ over 1 million inhabitants
● more than 100 000 inhabitants
• smaller towns

Land height

metres
3000
2000
1000
500
300
200
100
sea level

▲ spot height in metres

Seas and regions
Sea of Okhotsk
Sea of Japan
PACIFIC OCEAN
Hokkaidō
Honshū
Shikoku
Kyūshū
Kuril Islands
Kunashir (RUSSIA)
Shikotan (occupied)

Selected place names
Tōkyō, Kawasaki, Yokohama, Chiba, Kyōto, Ōsaka, Kōbe, Nagoya, Sapporo, Fukuoka, Kita Kyūshū, Hiroshima, Sendai, Niigata, Kanazawa, Nagasaki, Kumamoto, Kagoshima, Matsuyama, Kōchi, Okayama, Takamatsu, Tottori, Matsue, Yamaguchi, Shimonoseki, Wakkanai, Asahikawa, Kushiro, Hakodate, Aomori, Akita, Morioka, Yamagata, Fukushima, Kōriyama, Nagano, Matsumoto, Gifu, Tsu, Otsu, Nara, Wakayama, Shizuoka, Hamamatsu

Tōkyō-wan, Ōsaka-wan, Ise-wan, Wakasa-wan, Sagami-wan, Tsugaru-kaikyō, Nemuro-kaikyō, Higashi-suidō, Tsushima-suidō, Kii-suidō, Bungo-suidō, Harima-nada, Iyo-nada, Suō-nada, Sagami-nada, Tosa-wan

Biwa-ko, Ou-sannyaku, Chūgoku-sanchi, Kii-sanchi, Shima-hantō, Bōsō-hantō, Miura-hantō, Chita-hantō, Atsumi-hantō

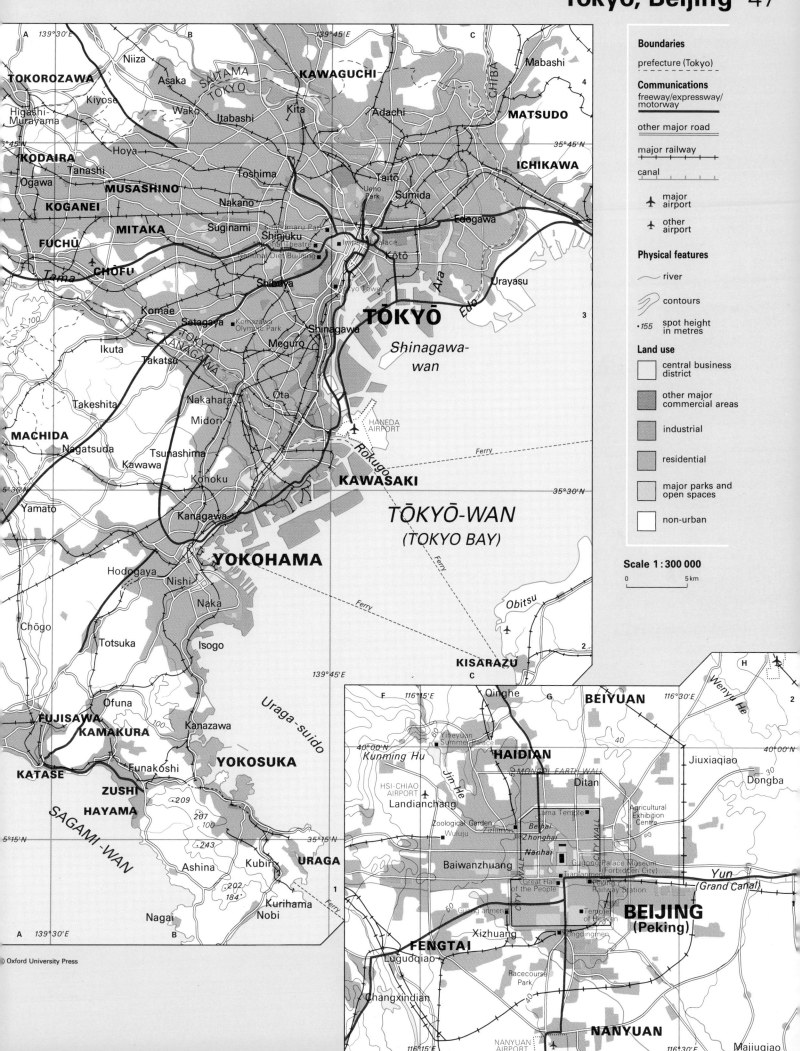

Boundaries

prefecture (Tokyo)

Communications
freeway/expressway/
motorway

other major road

major railway

canal

major airport

other airport

Physical features

river

contours

·155 spot height
in metres

Land use

central business
district

other major
commercial areas

industrial

residential

major parks and
open spaces

non-urban

Scale 1 : 300 000

0   5 km

TOKOROZAWA

Niiza

Higashi-Murayama

Kiyose

Asaka

Wako

KAWAGUCHI

Mabashi

SAITAMA
TOKYO

Kita

Adachi

MATSUDO

Itabashi

KODAIRA

Hoya

Toshima

Taitō

Ueno
Park

Sumida

ICHIKAWA

KOGANEI

Ogawa

Tanashi

MUSASHINO

Nakano

Edogawa

CHIBA

MITAKA

Suginami

Shinjuku

Kitanomaru Park
National Theatre
Imperial Palace

Kōtō

FUCHŪ

Komae

National Diet Building

Kōtō

Edo

Urayasu

CHŌFU

Tama

Shibuya

Tokyo Tower

TŌKYŌ

Ara

Satagaya

Komazawa
Olympic Park

Meguro

Ōta

Shinagawa

Shinagawa-
wan

MACHIDA

Ikuta

Takeshita

Nakahara

Midori

HANEDA
AIRPORT

Nagatsuda

Tsunashima

Kawawa

Kohoku

Rōkugo

Ferry

KAWASAKI

Yamato

Kanagawa

TŌKYŌ-WAN
(TOKYO BAY)

YOKOHAMA

Hodogaya

Nishi

Naka

Ferry

Chōgo

Totsuka

Isogo

Obitsu

Ferry

KISARAZU

FUJISAWA

Ofuna

Kanazawa

Uraga-suido

KAMAKURA

KATASE

ZUSHI

HAYAMA

Funakoshi

YOKOSUKA

SAGAMI-WAN

·209

·207

100

·243

·202

·184

Ashina

Kubiri

URAGA

Nagai

Kurihama
Nobi

Ferry

© Oxford University Press

Beijing inset

Qinghe

BEIYUAN

Wenyu He

Yiheyuan
Summer Palace

HAIDIAN

Jin He

Kunming Hu

MONGOL EARTH WALL

Ditan

Jiuxiaqiao

HSI-CHIAO
AIRPORT

Dongba

Landianchang

Zoological Garden
Wuluju

Zizhumen

Lama Temple

Agricultural
Exhibition
Centre

Belhai
Zhonghai

Nanhai

CITY WALL

Baiwanzhuang

Gugong Palace Museum
(Forbidden City)
Tiananmen

Yun
(Grand Canal)

Great Hall
of the People

Peking
Railway Station

Guang'anmen

BEIJING
(Peking)

Temple of
Heaven

Xizhuang

Yongdingmen

FENGTAI

Luguoqiao

Racecourse
Park

Changxindian

NANYUAN
AIRPORT

NANYUAN

Majiuqiao

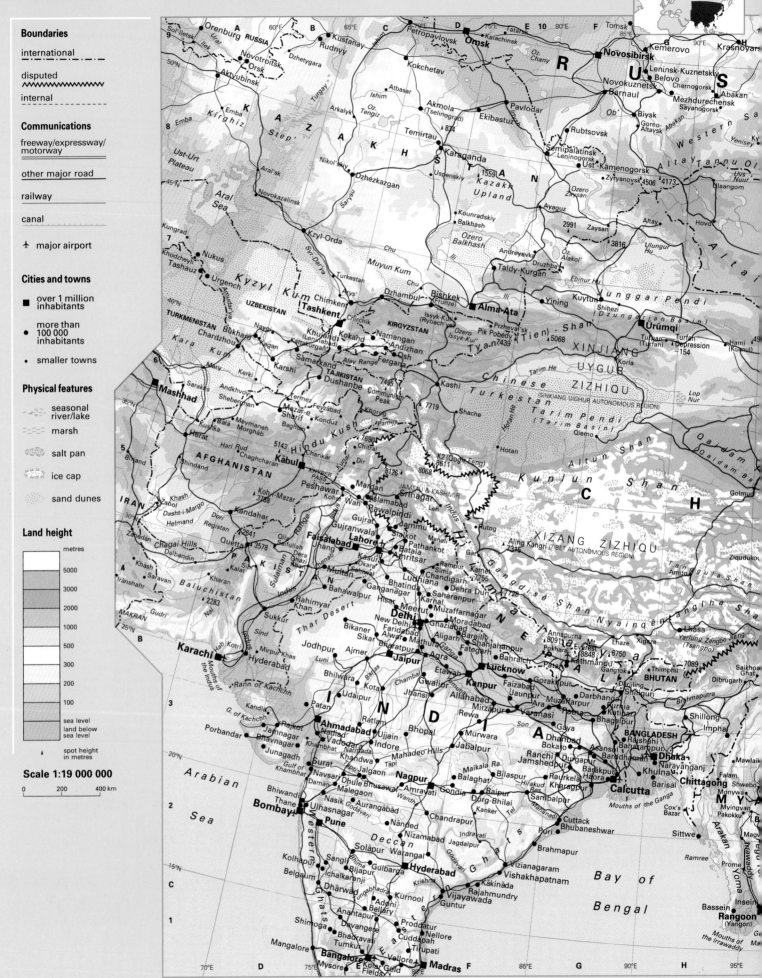

Boundaries

international

disputed

internal

Communications

freeway/expressway/ motorway

other major road

railway

canal

✈ major airport

Cities and towns

■ over 1 million inhabitants

● more than 100 000 inhabitants

• smaller towns

Physical features

seasonal river/lake

marsh

salt pan

ice cap

sand dunes

Land height

metres

5000

3000

2000

1000

500

300

200

100

sea level

land below sea level

▲ spot height in metres

Scale 1:19 000 000

0   200   400 km

© Oxford University Press

50 Korea

Boundaries

international

internal

Communications

freeway/expressway/motorway

other major road

railway

✈ major airport

Cities and towns

▱ built-up areas

■ over 1 million inhabitants

● more than 100 000 inhabitants

• smaller towns

Physical features

marsh

Land height

metres
3000
2000
1000
500
300
200
100
sea level

▲ spot height in metres

Scale 1: 4 000 000

0   50   100 km

Conic Projection

© Oxford University Press

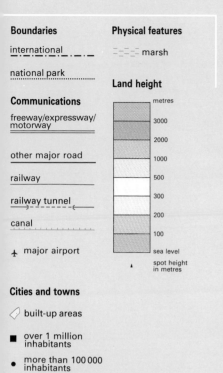

Boundaries

international

national park

Communications

freeway/expressway/
motorway

other major road

railway

railway tunnel

canal

✈ major airport

Physical features

--- marsh

Land height

metres
3000
2000
1000
500
300
200
100
sea level
▲ spot height in metres

Cities and towns

⬦ built-up areas

■ over 1 million inhabitants

● more than 100 000 inhabitants

• smaller towns

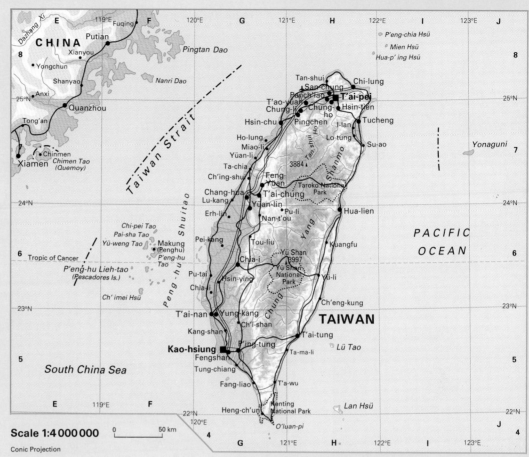

CHINA

Dazhang Xi · Fuqing
Putian
Xianyou · Yongchun
Shanyao
Anxi · Quanzhou
Tong'an
Xiamen
Chinmen
Chimen Tao (Quemoy)

Pingtan Dao

Nanri Dao

Tan-shui · San-chung
Panch'iao · Chung-ho · T'ai-pei
T'ao-yuan · Chung-ho · Hsin-tien
Hsin-chu · Pingchen · I-lan
Ho-lung · Lo-tung · Su-ao
Miao-li
Yüan-li
Ta-chia
Ch'ing-shui · Feng-Yüan
Chang-hua · T'ai-chung
Lu-kang · Yüan-lin
Erh-lin · Pu-li
Nan-t'ou

Chi-lung

Hsin-ten
Tucheng

3884 ▲

Taroko National Park

Hua-lien

Kuangfu

Taiwan Strait

Yang

Shuitao

P'eng-hu

Peng-hu Shuitao

Chi-pei Tao
Pai-sha Tao
Yü-weng Tao
Makung (Penghu)
P'eng-hu Tao

Tropic of Cancer

P'eng-hu Lieh-tao (Pescadores Is.)

Ch'imei Hsü

Pei-kang
Tou-liu
Yü Shan 3997 Yü Shan National Park
Yü-li
Chia-i
Hsin-ying
Pu-tai
Chia-li
T'ai-nan · Yung-kang
Ch'i-shan
Kang-shan
Kao-hsiung
Fengshan
Tung-chiang
Fang-liao
Heng-ch'un
Kenting National Park
O'luan-pi

P'eng-chia Hsü
Mien Hsü
Hua-p'ing Hsü

Yonaguni

PACIFIC OCEAN

TAIWAN

Ch'eng-kung
T'ai-tung
Ta-ma-li
Lü Tao
T'a-wu
Lan Hsü

South China Sea

Scale 1:4 000 000

0   50 km

Conic Projection

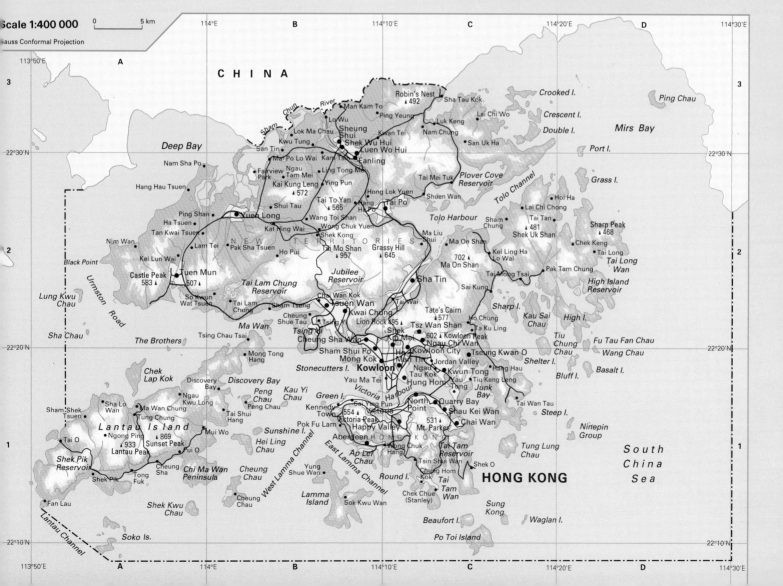

Scale 1:400 000

0   5 km

Gauss Conformal Projection

CHINA

Sham Chun River

Man Kam To
Lo Wu
Lok Ma Chau
Kwu Tung
San Tin
Mai Po Lo Wai
Fairview Park
Ngau Tam Mei
Kai Kung Leng ▲ 572
Shui Tau
Ping Shan
Ha Tsuen
Tan Kwai Tsuen
Nim Wan
Kei Lun Wai
Lam Tei
Pak Sha Tsuen
Castle Peak 583 ▲
Yuen Mun ▲ 507
So Kwun Wat Tsuen
Tai Lam Chung

Sheung Shui
Shek Wu Hui
Luen Wo Hui
Fanling
Kam Tsin
Ling Tong Mei
Ying Pun
Tai To Yan ▲ 565
Wang Toi Shan
Wong Chuk Yuen
Shek Kong
Ho Pui

Robin's Nest ▲ 492
Ping Yeung
Kwan Tei
Nam Chung
Hong Lok Yuen
Tai Mei Tuk
Ha Po
Tai Po

Sha Tau Kok
Lai Chi Wo
Luk Keng
San Uk Ha
Shuen Wan

Crooked I.
Crescent I.
Double I.
Port I.

Mirs Bay

Ping Chau

Plover Cove Reservoir

Sham Chung
Lai Chi Chong
Tai Tan ▲ 481
Shek Uk Shan
Hoi Ha
Grass I.

Tolo Channel

Tolo Harbour

Ma Liu Shui
Ma On Shan ▲ 702
Kei Ling Ha Lo Wai
Tai Mong Tsai
Pak Tam Chung

Sharp Peak ▲ 468
Chek Keng
Tai Long
Tai Long Wan
High Island Reservoir

NEW TERRITORIES

Tai Mo Shan ▲ 957
Grassy Hill ▲ 645
Jubilee Reservoir

Tai Lam Chung Reservoir

Chai Wan Kok
Tsuen Wan
Kwai Chung
Tsing Yi
Cheung Shue Tau
Ma Wan
Tsing Chau Tsai

Sha Tin
Tai Wai
Lion Rock ▲ 495
Tsz Wan Shan
Tate's Cairn ▲ 577
Shek ▲ 602 Kowloon Peak
Kowloon City
Ho Chung
Sai Kung
Ma On Shan

Ku Ling
Kau Sai Chau
High I.
Sharp I.
Tiu Chung Chau
Fu Tau Fan Chau
Wang Chau
Shelter I.
Bluff I.

Deep Bay

Nam Sha Po
Hang Hau Tsuen

Yuen Long
Kat Hing Wai

HONG KONG

Chek Lap Kok
Sha Lo Wan
Ngau Kwu Long
Ma Wan Chung
Tung Chung
Sham Shek Tsuen
Tai O
Ngong Ping ▲ 869
Lantau Peak ▲ 933
Sunset Peak
Pui O
Shek Pik Reservoir
Shek Pik
Tong Fuk
Fan Lau

Lantau Island

Chi Ma Wan Peninsula

Mui Wo
Cheung Sha

Discovery Bay
Peng Chau
Kau Yi Chau
Green I.
Sunshine I.
Hei Ling Chau
Tai Shui Hang

Mong Tong Hang
Stonecutters I.
Kowloon
Sham Shui Po
Mong Kok
Yau Ma Tei
Kwun Tong
Ngau Tau Kok
Lam Tin
Tseung Kwan O
Hang Hau
Tai Kok
Kwai Chung
Kowloon Tong

Kennedy Town
Sai Ying Pun
Victoria ▲ 554
Victoria Peak
Pok Fu Lam
Happy Valley
Aberdeen
Ap Lei Chau
Wong Chuk Hang
Mt Parker ▲ 531
North Point
Quarry Bay
Shau Kei Wan
Chai Wan
Tai Tam Reservoir

Victoria Harbour

Hung Hom
Junk Bay
Jordan Valley

Tai Wan Tau
Steep I.

Ninepin Group

Tung Lung Chau

South China Sea

Tin Hau
Shek O
Tai Tam
Tai Tam Wan
Tsin Shui Wan
Chung Hom Kok
Stanley (Chek Chue)

Pok Liu Chau
Sok Kwu Wan
Lamma Island
Yung Shue Wan

West Lamma Channel
East Lamma Channel

Cheung Chau
Peng Chau

Discovery Bay

Sunshine I.

Soko Is.
Lantau Channel

Beaufort I.
Sung Kong
Waglan I.
Po Toi Island

Urmston Road
Lung Kwu Chau
Sha Chau
Black Point
The Brothers

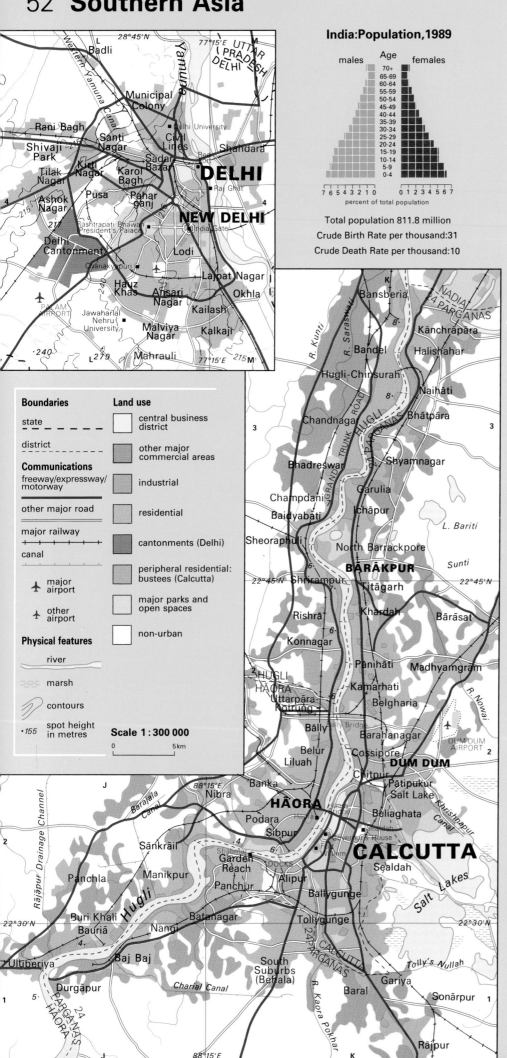

India: Population, 1989

males | Age | females
70+
65-69
60-64
55-59
50-54
45-49
40-44
35-39
30-34
25-29
20-24
15-19
10-14
5-9
0-4

7 6 5 4 3 2 1 0   0 1 2 3 4 5 6 7
percent of total population

Total population 811.8 million
Crude Birth Rate per thousand:31
Crude Death Rate per thousand:10

Boundaries
state
district

Communications
freeway/expressway/motorway
other major road
major railway
canal

✈ major airport
✈ other airport

Physical features
river
marsh
contours
·155 spot height in metres

Land use
central business district
other major commercial areas
industrial
residential
cantonments (Delhi)
peripheral residential: bustees (Calcutta)
major parks and open spaces
non-urban

Scale 1 : 300 000
0   5km

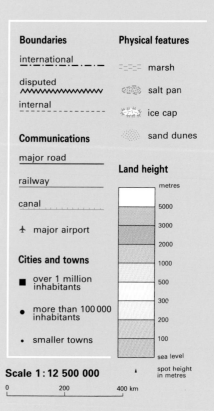

Boundaries
international
disputed
internal

Communications
major road
railway
canal
✈ major airport

Cities and towns
■ over 1 million inhabitants
● more than 100 000 inhabitants
· smaller towns

Physical features
marsh
salt pan
ice cap
sand dunes

Land height
metres
5000
3000
2000
1000
500
300
200
100
sea level
▲ spot height in metres

Scale 1 : 12 500 000
0   200   400 km

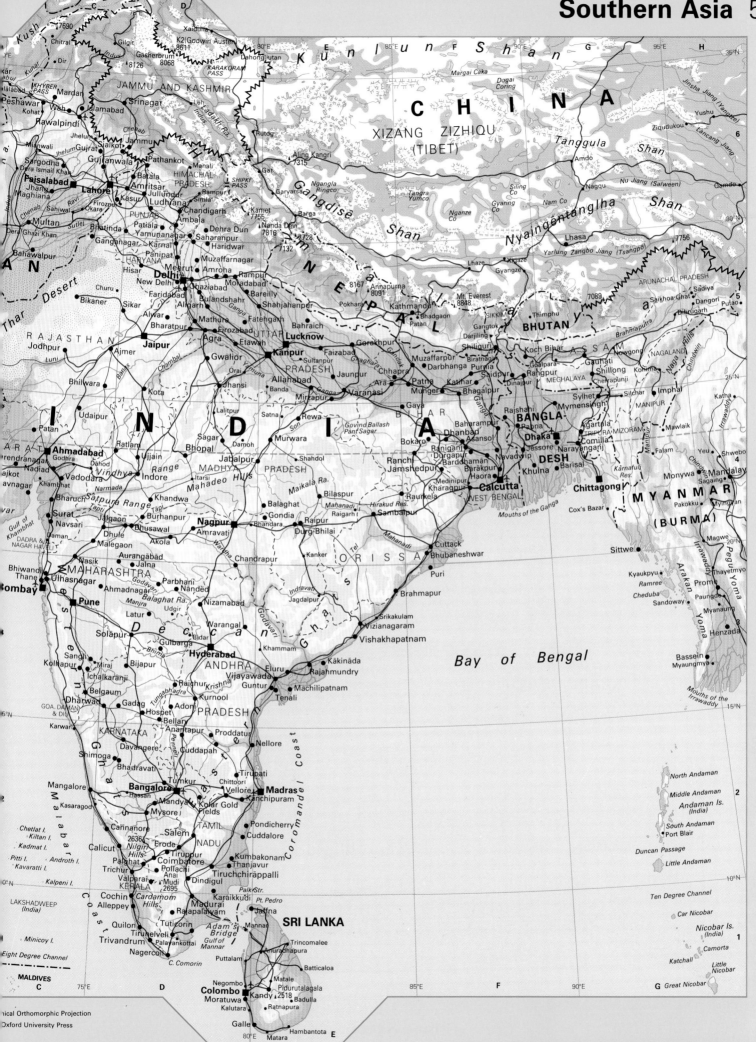
CHINA
XIZANG ZIZHIQU
(TIBET)
Kunlun Shan
Tanggula Shan
Nyainqentanglha Shan
Gangdisê Shan
Himalaya
Karakoram Pass
JAMMU AND KASHMIR
HIMACHAL PRADESH
PUNJAB
HARYANA
RAJASTHAN
Thar Desert
UTTAR PRADESH
BIHAR
MADHYA PRADESH
MAHARASHTRA
ORISSA
ANDHRA PRADESH
KARNATAKA
TAMIL NADU
KERALA
WEST BENGAL
ASSAM
MEGHALAYA
NAGALAND
MANIPUR
TRIPURA
MIZORAM
ARUNACHAL PRADESH
SIKKIM
INDIA
NEPAL
BHUTAN
BANGLADESH
MYANMAR
(BURMA)
SRI LANKA
MALDIVES
LAKSHADWEEP
(India)
Andaman Is.
(India)
Nicobar Is.
(India)
Bay of Bengal
Gulf of Khambhat
Gulf of Mannar
Palk Str.
Adam's Bridge
Mouths of the Ganga
Mouths of the Irrawaddy
Ten Degree Channel
Duncan Passage
Eight Degree Channel
Coromandel Coast
Malabar Coast
Deccan
Western Ghats
Eastern Ghats
Vindhya Range
Satpura Range
Mahadeo Hills
Maikala Ra.
Balaghat Ra.
Nilgiri Hills
Cardamom Hills
Arakan Yoma
Pegu Yoma
Naga Hills
Ganga
Yamuna
Brahmaputra
Indus
Narmada
Tapti
Godavari
Krishna
Mahanadi
Irrawaddy
Chindwin
Delhi
New Delhi
Calcutta
Bombay
Madras
Bangalore
Hyderabad
Ahmadabad
Kanpur
Lucknow
Nagpur
Pune
Jaipur
Kathmandu
Thimphu
Dhaka
Chittagong
Lahore
Faisalabad
Islamabad
Rawalpindi
Lhasa
Mandalay
Colombo
Jaffna
Kandy
Mt. Everest
8848
K2 (Godwin Austen)
8611
Annapurna
8091
Nanda Devi
7816
Port Blair
Sittwe
Cox's Bazar
C. Comorin
Conical Orthomorphic Projection
Oxford University Press

Israel & Lebanon

Scale 1:4 000 000

0   50   100 km

Conical Orthomorphic Projection

Boundaries

international

disputed

internal

Communications

freeway/expressway/
motorway

other major road

railway

canal

✈ major airport

Cities and towns

■ over 1 million
inhabitants

● more than 100 000
inhabitants

• smaller towns

+ historic sites

Physical features

seasonal
river/lake

marsh

salt pan

ice cap

sand dunes

Land height

	metres
	5000
	3000
	2000
	1000
	500
	300
	200
	100
	sea level
	land below sea level

▲ spot height in metres

Scale 1:12 500 000

0   125   250 km

© Oxford University Press

Boundaries

international

disputed

internal

Communications

freeway/expressway/motorway

other major road

railway

canal

✈ major airport

Cities and towns

■ over 1 million inhabitants

● more than 100 000 inhabitants

• smaller towns

Scale 1 : 25 000 000

0   250   500 km

Physical features

seasonal river/lake

marsh

salt pan

ice cap

sand dunes

Land height

metres
5000
3000
2000
1000
500
300
200
100
sea level
land below sea level

▲ spot height in metres

Sea Ice

unnavigable polar ice

pack ice autumn minimum

pack ice spring maximum

Boundaries

city limit/oblast

Land use

central business district

other major commercial areas

industrial

residential

major parks and open spaces

non-urban

Refer to page 52 for complete legend

Scale 1 : 300 000

0   5 km

Conical Orthomorphic Projection

Moscow inset

KHIMKI
Khimki–Khovrino
Mitino
TUSHINO
Strogino
KUNTSEVO
Matveyevskoye
Gagarin
Semenovskoye
Ochakovo
Solntsevo
ORLOVO AIRPORT
Medvedkovo
BABUSHKIN
Beskudnikovo
Economic Exhibition Grounds
Kuybyshev Forest
Ostankino
Cherkizovsky
SOKOLNIKI Park
Timiryazev Park
NORTH PORT
Khimki Reservoir
CENTRAL AIRPORT
Khorochevo
Mnevniki
FILI AIRFIELD
WEST PORT
Kremlin
Moscow University
MOSKVA (Moscow)
Gorkiy Park
Cheremushki
Chertanovo
LYUBLINO
Kuz'minki
SOUTH PORT
Izmaylovskiy Park
REUTOV
PEROVO
Yauza
Lenino
Krasny Stroitel
Butovo
Moskva
MOSCOW CITY
MOSCOW OBLAST

37°30'E   37°45'E   55°45'N

Boundaries
international
disputed

Communications
freeway/expressway/
motorway

other major road

railway

canal

✈ major airport

Cities and towns
■ over 1 million
inhabitants

● more than 100 000
inhabitants

• smaller towns

Physical features
seasonal
river/lake

marsh

salt pan

ice cap

sand dunes

salt lake

Sea Ice
pack ice
spring max.

Land height

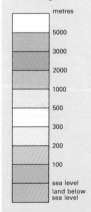

metres
5000
3000
2000
1000
500
300
200
100
sea level
land below
sea level

▲ spot height
in metres

Scale 1: 12 500 000

0   100   200   300 km

Conical Orthomorphic Projection

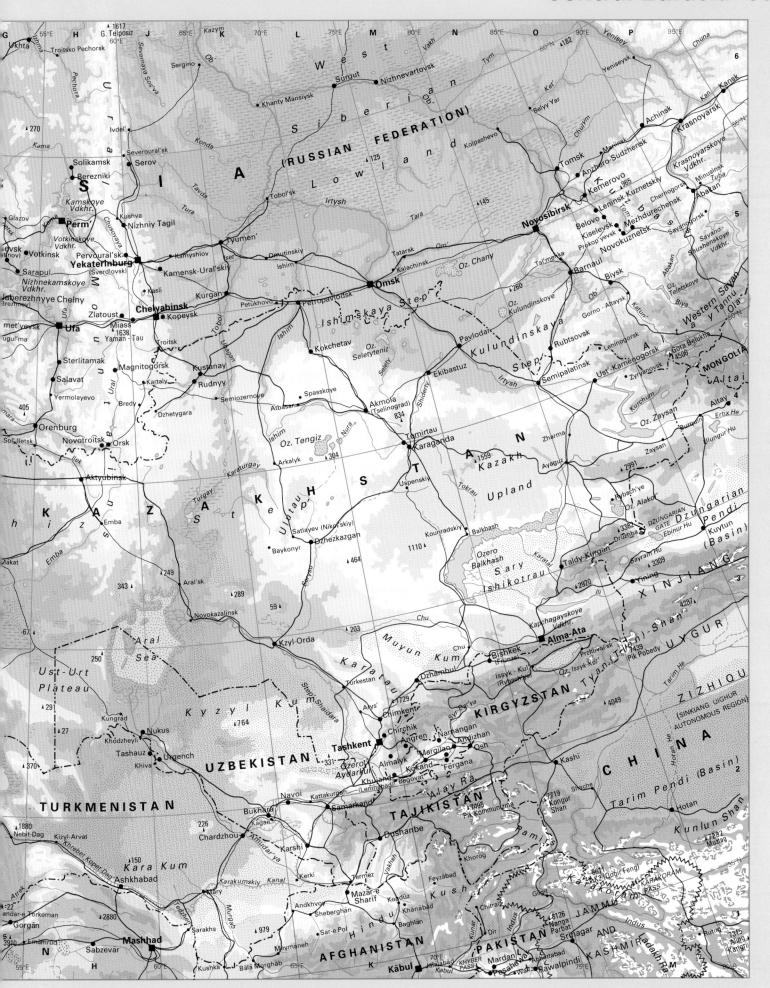

Arctic Circle
C. Kanin
Kola Peninsula
White Sea
Lake Onega
Lake Ladoga
Rybinsk Reservoir
North Cape
Inarijärvi
Lappland
Salpausselkä
Gulf of Finland
Lake Peipus
G. of Riga
West Dvina
Pripet Marshes
Dnepr
Bug
Dnestr
Black Sea
Bosphorus
Sea of Marmara
Dardanelles
Aegean Sea
Euboea
Cyclades
Crete
Peloponnese
Ionian Is.
Ionian Sea
OLYMPUS 2917
5121
Balkan Mts
Rodopi Planina
Pindhos Mountains
Danube
Carpathian Mountains
Tisza
Hungarian Basin
Tatra Mts
Drava
Sava
Dinaric Alps
Neman
Vistula
North European Plain
Oder
Baltic Sea
Gulf of Bothnia
Åland
Gotland
Öland
Bornholm
Pomeranian Bay
Scandinavia
Lofoten Is.
Dovrefjell
Jostedalsbreen
Hardangervidda
Skerryguard
Mälaren
Vänern
Vättern
Skåne
Kattegat
Sjælland
Fyn
Jylland
Skagerrak
Elbe
Weser
Harz Mts
Erzgebirge
Bohemian Massif
1603
Danube
Inn
Tauern
Alps
Bodensee
Schwäbische Alb
MONT BLANC 4807
Po
Ligurian Sea
Appennini
Adriatic Sea
VESUVIUS 1277
Golfo di Taranto
MT ETNA 3323
Sicily
Malta
Tyrrhenian Sea
Corsica
Sardinia
Mediterranean Sea
Balearic Is.
Golfe du Lyon
Rhône
Saône
Alpes Maritimes
Jura
Vosges
Rhine
Ardennes
Maas
Waal
IJsselmeer
Frisian Is.
−36
Scheldt Est.
Marne
Seine
Paris Basin
Loire
Massif Central
Garonne
Pyrenees
3401
Ebro
Bay of Biscay
Cantabrian Mts
Duero
Central Cordillera
Tagus
Guadiana
Guadalquivir
Betican Cordillera
Algarve
Str. of Gibraltar
C. Finnisterre
Str. of Dover
English Channel
Cotentin
Channel Is.
Brittany Pen.
The Wash
Thames
Pennines
Cambrian Mts
Southern Uplands
Grampians
Moray Firth
C. Wrath
The Minch
Skye
Outer Hebrides
Orkney Is.
Shetland Is.
North Sea
Faeroe Islands
−3970
Malin Hd
St George's Channel
Central Plain
Shannon
Scilly Is.
Iceland
Vatnajökull
HEKLA 1491
Greenland Sea
ATLANTIC OCEAN
65°N 60°N 55°N 50°N 45°N 40°N 35°N
25°W 20°W 15°W 10°W 5°W 0° 5°E 10°E 15°E 20°E 25°E 30°E 40°E

© Oxford University Press

Conical Orthomorphic Projection

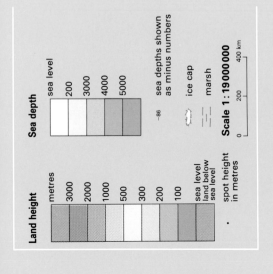

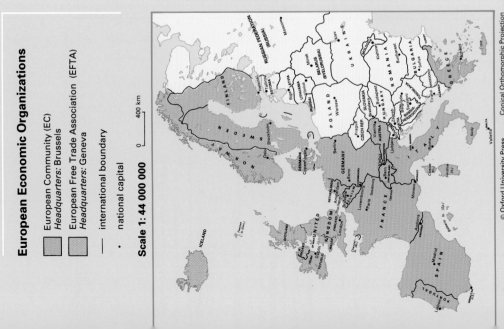

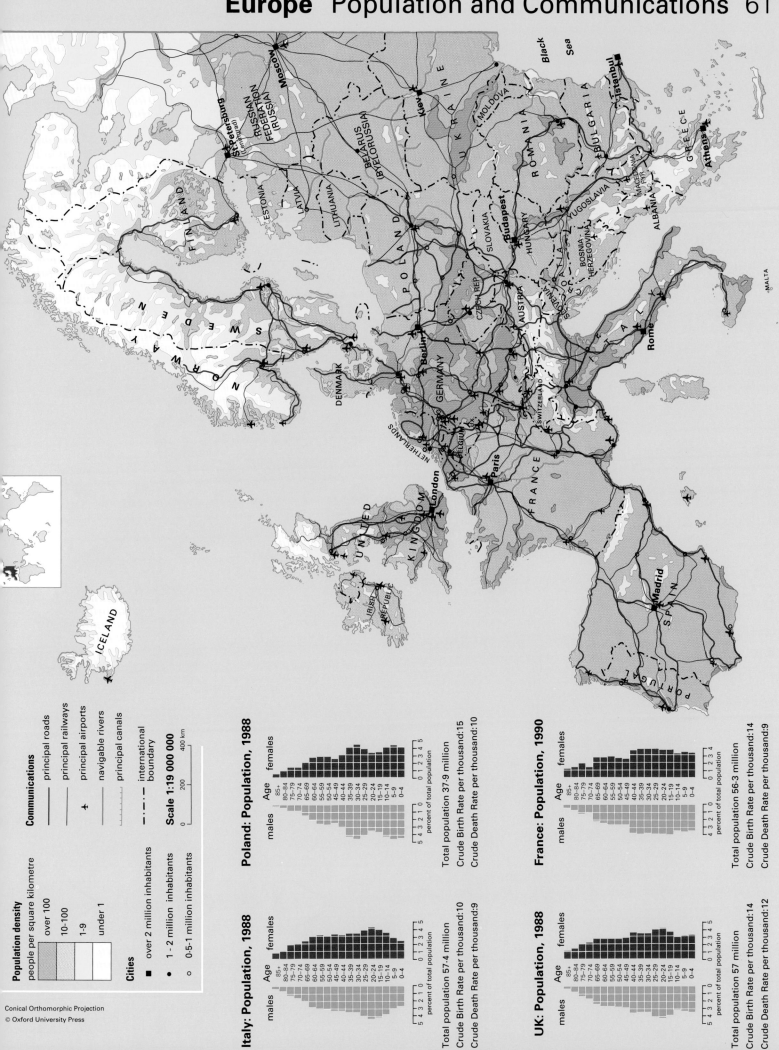

Population density
people per square kilometre
- over 100
- 10–100
- 1–9
- under 1

Cities
- ■ over 2 million inhabitants
- ● 1 – 2 million inhabitants
- ○ 0·5–1 million inhabitants

Communications
- —— principal roads
- —— principal railways
- + principal airports
- —— navigable rivers
- ···· principal canals
- –·–·– international boundary

Scale 1:19 000 000
0   200   400 km

Conical Orthomorphic Projection
© Oxford University Press

Italy: Population, 1988

males   Age   females

85+
80–84
75–79
70–74
65–69
60–64
55–59
50–54
45–49
40–44
35–39
30–34
25–29
20–24
15–19
10–14
5–9
0–4

5 4 3 2 1 0   0 1 2 3 4 5
percent of total population

Total population 57·4 million
Crude Birth Rate per thousand:10
Crude Death Rate per thousand:9

UK: Population, 1988

males   Age   females

85+
80–84
75–79
70–74
65–69
60–64
55–59
50–54
45–49
40–44
35–39
30–34
25–29
20–24
15–19
10–14
5–9
0–4

5 4 3 2 1 0   0 1 2 3 4 5
percent of total population

Total population 57 million
Crude Birth Rate per thousand:14
Crude Death Rate per thousand:12

Poland: Population, 1988

males   Age   females

85+
80–84
75–79
70–74
65–69
60–64
55–59
50–54
45–49
40–44
35–39
30–34
25–29
20–24
15–19
10–14
5–9
0–4

5 4 3 2 1 0   0 1 2 3 4 5
percent of total population

Total population 37·9 million
Crude Birth Rate per thousand:15
Crude Death Rate per thousand:10

France: Population, 1990

males   Age   females

85+
80–84
75–79
70–74
65–69
60–64
55–59
50–54
45–49
40–44
35–39
30–34
25–29
20–24
15–19
10–14
5–9
0–4

4 3 2 1 0   0 1 2 3 4
percent of total population

Total population 56·3 million
Crude Birth Rate per thousand:14
Crude Death Rate per thousand:9

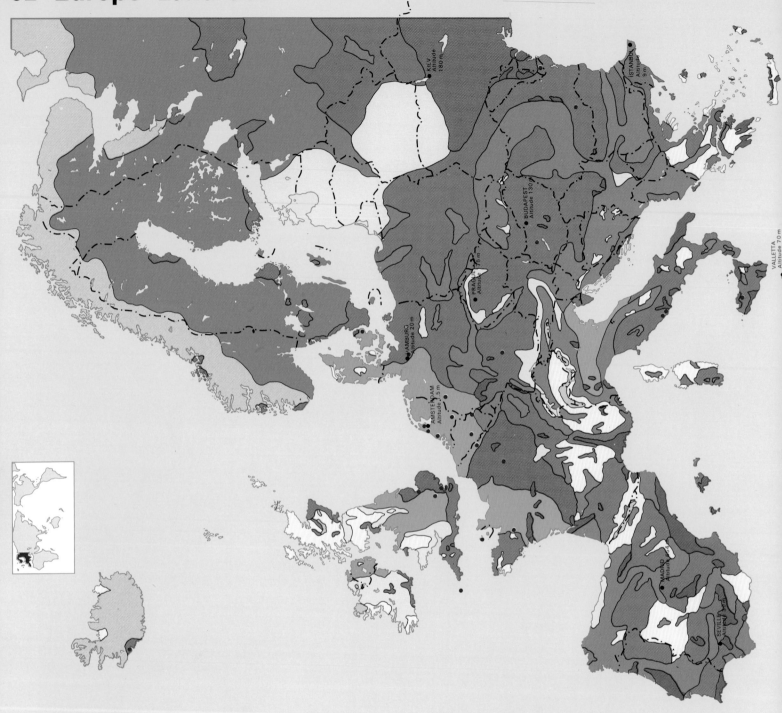

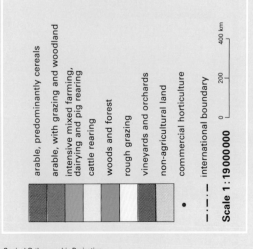

arable, predominantly cereals

arable, with grazing and woodland

intensive mixed farming, dairying and pig rearing

cattle rearing

woods and forest

rough grazing

vineyards and orchards

non-agricultural land

commercial horticulture

international boundary

●

Scale 1:19 000 000

0   200   400 km

Conical Orthomorphic Projection

© Oxford University Press

Rainfall figures on graphs in tens of
millimetres except for annual totals

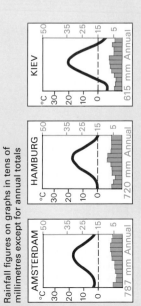

KIEV

°C
50
30 · 35
20 · 25
10 · 15
0 · 5
615 mm Annual

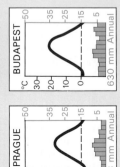

HAMBURG

°C
50
30 · 35
20 · 25
10 · 15
0 · 5
720 mm Annual

BUDAPEST

°C
50
30 · 35
20 · 25
10 · 15
0 · 5
630 mm Annual

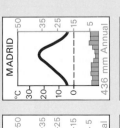

MADRID

°C
50
30 · 35
20 · 25
10 · 15
0 · 5
436 mm Annual

ISTANBUL

°C
50
30 · 35
20 · 25
10 · 15
0 · 5
669 mm Annual

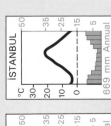

AMSTERDAM

°C
50
30 · 35
20 · 25
10 · 15
0 · 5
787 mm Annual

PRAGUE

°C
50
30 · 35
20 · 25
10 · 15
0 · 5
508 mm Annual

SEVILLE

°C
50
30 · 35
20 · 25
10 · 15
0 · 5
559 mm Annual

VALLETTA

°C
50
30 · 35
20 · 25
10 · 15
0 · 5
516 mm Annual

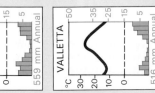

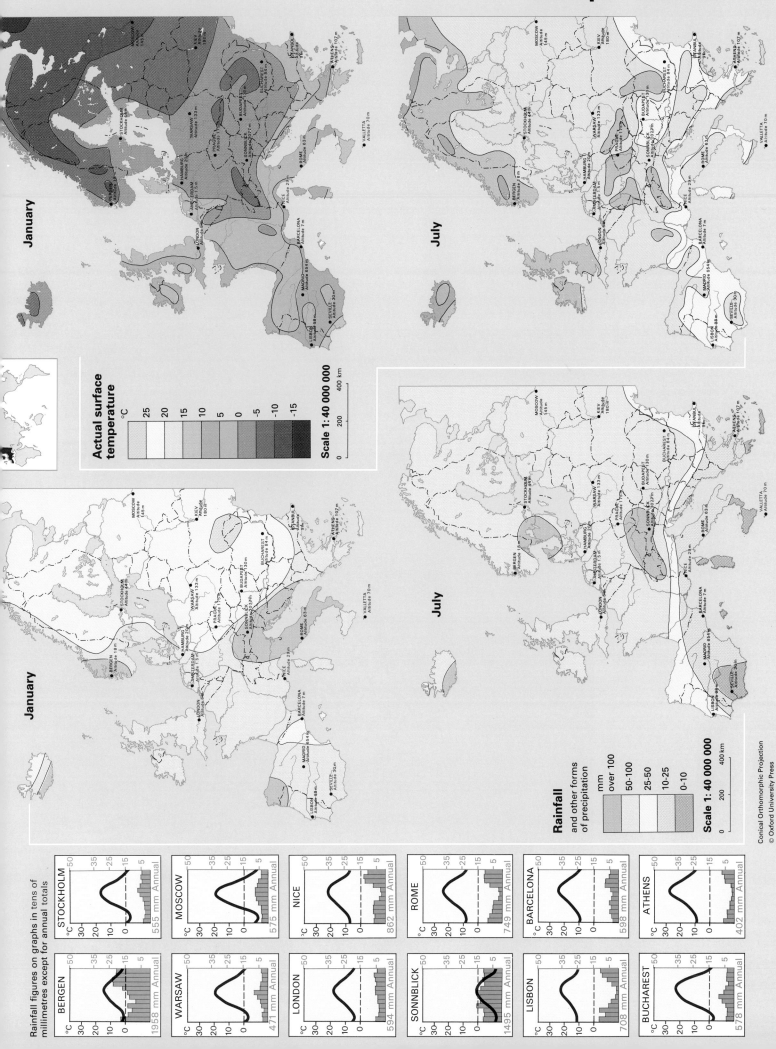

January

July

January

July

Actual surface temperature

°C
25
20
15
10
5
0
-5
-10
-15

Scale 1: 40 000 000

0 200 400 km

Rainfall
and other forms of precipitation

mm
over 100
50-100
25-50
10-25
0-10

Scale 1: 40 000 000

0 200 400 km

Conical Orthomorphic Projection
© Oxford University Press

Rainfall figures on graphs in tens of millimetres except for annual totals

STOCKHOLM — 555 mm Annual
MOSCOW — 575 mm Annual
NICE — 862 mm Annual
ROME — 749 mm Annual
BARCELONA — 598 mm Annual
ATHENS — 402 mm Annual
BERGEN — 1958 mm Annual
WARSAW — 471 mm Annual
LONDON — 594 mm Annual
SONNBLICK — 1495 mm Annual
LISBON — 708 mm Annual
BUCHAREST — 578 mm Annual

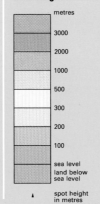

Boundaries

international — · — · —

disputed ∧∧∧∧∧∧∧∧∧

internal — — — — —

Communications

freeway/expressway/
motorway ════════

other major road ════════

railway ────────

canal ────────

✈ major airport

Cities and towns

■ over 1 million
inhabitants

● more than 100 000
inhabitants

• smaller towns

Physical features

seasonal
river/lake

marsh

salt pan

ice cap

sand dunes

Sea Ice

pack ice
spring max.

Land height

metres
3000
2000
1000
500
300
200
100
sea level
land below sea level
▲ spot height in metres

Scale 1 : 12 500 000

0   125   250 km

Conical Orthomorphic Projection

© Oxford University Press

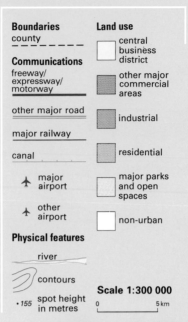

Boundaries
county

Communications
freeway/
expressway/
motorway

other major road

major railway

canal

✈ major airport

✈ other airport

Physical features

river

contours

·155 spot height in metres

Land use

central business district

other major commercial areas

industrial

residential

major parks and open spaces

non-urban

This image of London, United Kingdom was produced by a Landsat satellite orbiting the earth at an altitude of approximately 900 km.

Scale 1:600 000

Scale 1:300 000

0   5km

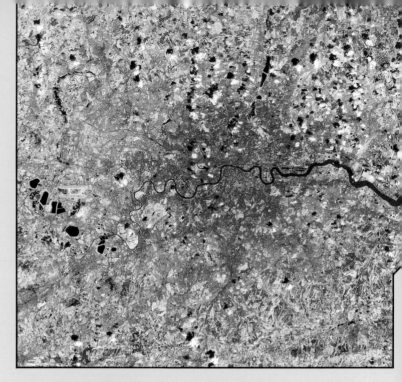

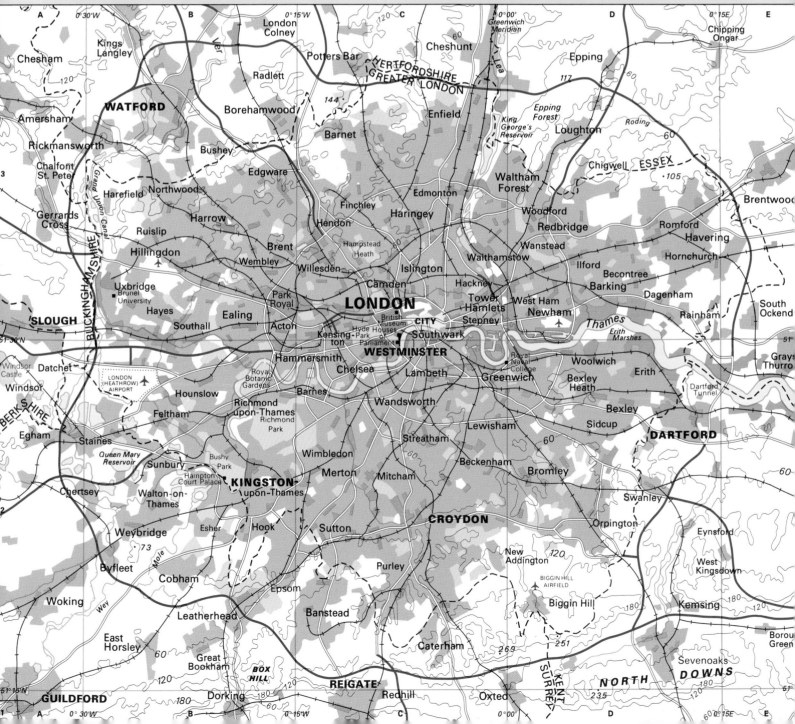

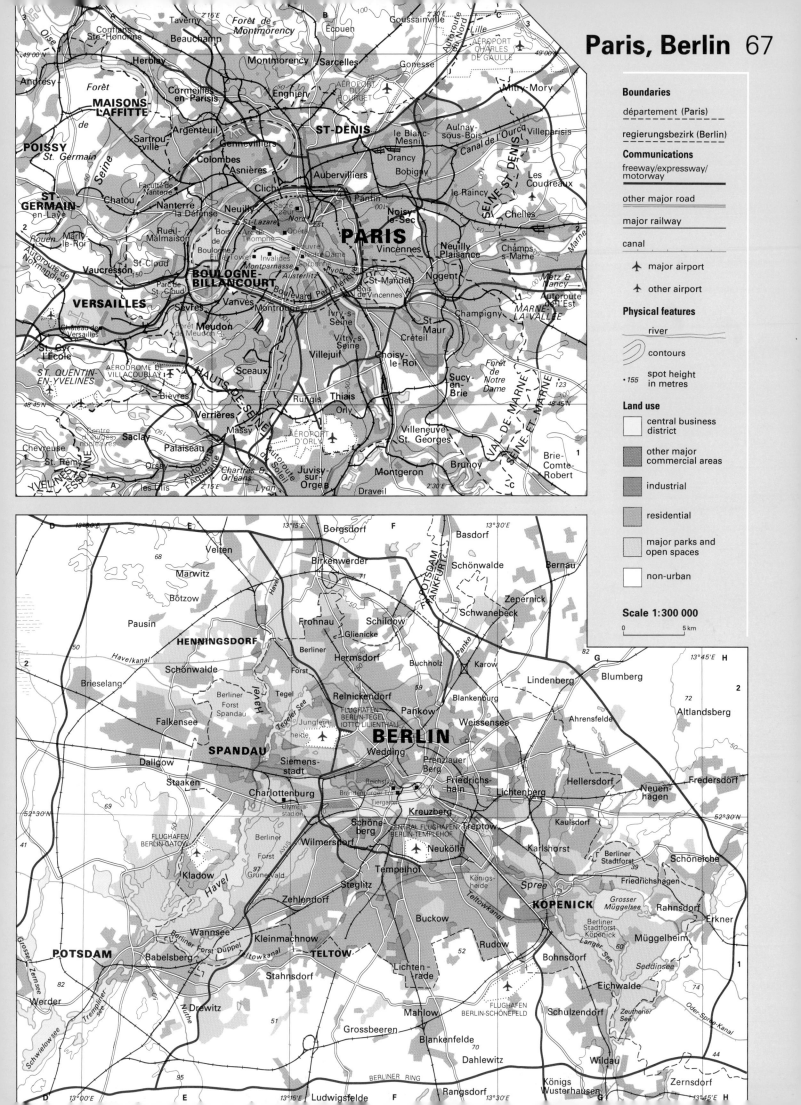
Boundaries
département (Paris)
regierungsbezirk (Berlin)
Communications
freeway/expressway/motorway
other major road
major railway
canal
major airport
other airport
Physical features
river
contours
155 spot height in metres
Land use
central business district
other major commercial areas
industrial
residential
major parks and open spaces
non-urban
Scale 1:300 000
0
5 km
PARIS
ST-DENIS
MAISONS-LAFFITTE
POISSY
ST-GERMAIN-en-Laye
VERSAILLES
BOULOGNE-BILLANCOURT
Taverny
Forêt de Montmorency
Écouen
Goussainville
Conflans Ste-Honorine
Beauchamp
Herblay
Montmorency
Sarcelles
Gonesse
AÉROPORT CHARLES DE GAULLE
Andrésy
Cormeilles-en-Parisis
Enghien
AÉROPORT DU BOURGET
Mitry-Mory
Argenteuil
Sartrouville
Gennevilliers
le Blanc-Mesnil
Aulnay-sous-Bois
Villeparisis
Canal de l'Ourcq
St. Germain
Seine
Colombes
Asnières
Drancy
Bobigny
Aubervilliers
Les Coudreaux
Clichy
Chatou
Nanterre
la Défense
Neuilly
Sacré Coeur
Pantin
Noisy-le-Sec
le Raincy
SEINE-ST.-DENIS
Chelles
Rueil-Malmaison
Marly-le-Roi
Bois de Boulogne
Arc de Triomphe
St-Lazare
Opéra
Nord
Est
Louvre
Notre Dame
Eiffel Tower
Invalides
Montparnasse
Sorbonne
Lyon
Austerlitz
Vincennes
Neuilly Plaisance
Champs-s-Marne
Marne
Autoroute de Normandie
Vaucresson
St-Cloud
Parc de St. Cloud
Boulevard Périphérique
St-Mandé
Bois de Vincennes
Nogent
Metz & Nancy
Autoroute de l'Est
Sèvres
Vanves
Montrouge
Ivry-s-Seine
Champigny
MARNE-LA-VALLÉE
Château de Versailles
Forêt de Meudon
Meudon
Vitry-s-Seine
St. Maur
Créteil
St. Cyr-l'École
Villejuif
Choisy-le-Roi
Forêt de Notre Dame
AÉRODROME DE VILLACOUBLAY
ST. QUENTIN-EN-YVELINES
HAUTS-DE-SEINE
Sceaux
Sucy-en-Brie
Bièvres
Rungis
Thiais
Orly
Verrières
VAL-DE-MARNE
SEINE-ET-MARNE
Centre d'études nucléaires
Saclay
Massy
AÉROPORT D'ORLY
Villeneuve-St. Georges
Chevreuse
Palaiseau
St. Rémy
Orsay
Autoroute l'Aquitaine
Chartres & Orléans
Autoroute du Soleil
Juvisy-sur-Orge
Montgeron
Brunoy
Brie-Comte-Robert
YVELINES
ESSONNE
les Ulis
Lyon
Draveil
BERLIN
SPANDAU
HENNINGSDORF
POTSDAM
KÖPENICK
TELTOW
Borgsdorf
Basdorf
Velten
Birkenwerder
Schönwalde
Bernau
Marwitz
Bötzow
Havel
POTSDAM FRANKFURT
Zepernick
Schwanebeck
Pausin
Frohnau
Schildow
Glienicke
Havelkanal
Berliner
Hermsdorf
Buchholz
Panke
Karow
Lindenberg
Blumberg
Schönwalde
Forst
Brieselang
Berliner Forst Spandau
Tegel
Reinickendorf
Blankenburg
Altlandsberg
Tegeler See
FLUGHAFEN BERLIN-TEGEL (OTTO LILIENTHAL)
Pankow
Weissensee
Ahrensfelde
Falkensee
Jungfernheide
Wedding
Dallgow
Siemensstadt
Prenzlauer Berg
Friedrichshain
Hellersdorf
Staaken
Charlottenburg
Reichstag
Dom
Lichtenberg
Neuenhagen
Fredersdorf
Brandenburger Tor
Tiergarten
Olympia-stadion
Kreuzberg
Schöneberg
ZENTRAL FLUGHAFEN BERLIN-TEMPELHOF
Treptow
Kaulsdorf
FLUGHAFEN BERLIN-GATOW
Berliner Forst Grunewald
AVUS
Wilmersdorf
Neukölln
Karlshorst
Berliner Stadtforst
Schöneiche
Tempelhof
Kladow
Königsheide
Spree
Friedrichshagen
Steglitz
Teltowkanal
Zehlendorf
Grosser Müggelsee
Rahnsdorf
Buckow
Erkner
Wannsee
Kleinmachnow
Berliner Stadtforst Köpenick
Müggelheim
Berliner Forst Düppel
Rudow
Langer See
Babelsberg
Bohnsdorf
Seddinsee
Grosser Zernsee
Stahnsdorf
Lichtenrade
Eichwalde
FLUGHAFEN BERLIN-SCHÖNEFELD
Werder
Drewitz
Templiner See
Nuthe
Mahlow
Schulzendorf
Zeuthener See
Oder-Spree-Kanal
Schwielowsee
Grossbeeren
Blankenfelde
Dahlewitz
Wildau
BERLINER RING
Rangsdorf
Königs Wusterhausen
Zernsdorf
Ludwigsfelde

Boundaries

international
internal

Communications

freeway/expressway/motorway
other major road
railway

✈ major airport

Cities and towns

◇ major built-up areas
■ over 1 million inhabitants
● more than 100 000 inhabitants
• smaller towns

Land height

metres
1000
500
200
100
sea level
land below sea level
▲ spot height in metres

Scale 1:4 500 000

0   50   100 km

Transverse Mercator Projection
© Oxford University Press

SCOTLAND
UNITED KINGDOM
NORTHERN IRELAND
IRISH REPUBLIC
ENGLAND
WALES
FRANCE

Shetland Islands
Unst
Yell
Fetlar
Mainland
Lerwick
Foula
Sumburgh Head
Fair Isle
Orkney Islands
Westray
Sanday
Stronsay
Mainland
Kirkwall
Hoy
Duncansby Head
Pentland Firth
Thurso
Wick
Cape Wrath
Butt of Lewis
Rona
Lewis
Stornoway
Harris
St. Kilda
North Uist
Benbecula
South Uist
Barra
Skye
Kyle of Lochalsh
Mallaig
Rhum
Eigg
Coll
Tiree
Iona
Mull
Oban
Colonsay
Jura
Islay
Sound of Jura
Firth of Lorn
The Minch
Little Minch
Inner Hebrides
Outer Hebrides
North West Highlands
Ullapool
Loch Shin
Dornoch Firth
Ben Wyvis 1046
Dingwall
Inverness
Moray Firth
Elgin
Loch Ness
Monadhliath Mtns.
Spey
Fraserburgh
Peterhead
1009
1183
Cairngorms
1310
Ben Macdhui
Aberdeen
Grampian Mountains
Fort William
Ben Nevis 1344
Loch Linnhe
Dee
Don
Esk
Tay
Perth
Dundee
St. Andrews
Arbroath
Sidlaw Hills
Loch Tay
Stirling
Alloa
Kirkcaldy
Firth of Forth
Dunfermline
Firth of Forth
Loch Lomond
Greenock
Clydebank
Glasgow
Paisley
East Kilbride
Motherwell
Cumbernauld
Edinburgh
St. Abb's Head
Falkirk
Lammermuir Hills
Kilmarnock
Ayr
Galashiels
Berwick-upon-Tweed
Holy Island
Southern Uplands
Hawick
840
Cheviot Hills
Tweed
Coquet
Bute
Arran
Campbeltown
Rathlin I.
Mull of Kintyre
Firth of Clyde
North Channel
Stranraer
Dumfries
Kirkcudbright
Mull of Galloway
Solway Firth
Newcastle upon Tyne
Blyth
Gateshead
Sunderland
Carlisle
Penrith
Durham
Hartlepool
893
Workington
Whitehaven
St. Bees Head
Eden
Cumbrian Mtns.
978 Scafell Pike
Stockton-on-Tees
Darlington
Middlesbrough
North York Moors
Scarborough
Barrow-in-Furness
Kendal
Lancaster
Ribble
Harrogate
York
Yorkshire Wolds
Flamborough Head
Blackpool
Preston
Southport
Blackburn
Bolton
Bradford
Leeds
Whaley
Kingston upon Hull
Spurn Head
Humber
Liverpool
Birkenhead
St. Helens
Manchester
Stockport
Sheffield
Doncaster
Scunthorpe
Grimsby
Colwyn
Bangor Bay
Chester
Crewe
Stoke-on-Trent
Chesterfield
Lincoln
Lincoln Wolds
Skegness
Wrexham
Derby
Nottingham
The Wash
Boston
1085 Snowdon
Cambrian Mtns.
Shrewsbury
Telford
Stafford
Leicester
Peterborough
The Fens
King's Lynn
Wensum
Great Yarmouth
Norwich
Lowestoft
892
Wolverhampton
Walsall
Dudley
Birmingham
Coventry
Solihull
Rugby
Northampton
Bedford
Cambridge
Ipswich
Felixstowe
Harwich
Aberystwyth
Cardigan Bay
WALES
Hereford
Worcester
Banbury
Milton Keynes
Colchester
Teifi
Carmarthen
Black Mtns.
Cheltenham
Gloucester
Oxford
Chiltern Hills
Luton
Watford
St. Albans
Chelmsford
Basildon
St. David's Head
Fishguard
Milford Haven
Brecon Beacons
Merthyr Tydfil
Cwmbran
Swindon
Thames
Slough
London
Southend-on-Sea
Llanelli
Neath
Rhondda
Newport
Gloucester
Cotswold Hills
Reading
Gillingham
Margate
Swansea
Cardiff
Barry
Bristol
Bath
Mendip Hills
Salisbury Plain
Basingstoke
Guildford
Maidstone
Canterbury
Bristol Channel
Lundy
Mendip Hills
Bridgwater
Salisbury
Winchester
Crawley
North Downs
Dover
Barnstaple
Exmoor Hills
Taunton
Avon
Southampton
South Downs
The Weald
Folkestone
Hastings
Hartland Point
Quantock Hills
Exe
Portsmouth
Brighton
Eastbourne
Beachy Head
Strait of Dover
Bodmin Moor
Dartmoor
619
Lyme Bay
Weymouth
Bournemouth
Poole
Isle of Wight
Worthing
Penzance
Truro
Plymouth
Torbay
Exeter
Land's End
Isles of Scilly
Lizard Point
Start Point
English Channel
Celtic Sea
Boulogne-sur-Mer
le Touquet–Paris–Plage
le Tréport
Dieppe
C. de la Hague
Alderney
Guernsey
St. Peter Port
Sark
Channel Islands
Jersey
St. Helier
Cherbourg
Baie de la Seine
le Havre
Caen
Rouen
Seine

Irish Sea
Isle of Man
621 Snaefell
Douglas
Anglesey
Holy I.
Holyhead
Caernarfon
Bangor
Malin Head
Bloody Foreland
Lough Foyle
Lough Swilly
Donegal Mtns.
Aran I.
Londonderry
Coleraine
Ballymena
Antrim Mtns.
Larne
Donegal Bay
Donegal
Sligo
Enniskillen
Lower Lough Erne
Omagh
NORTHERN IRELAND
Lough Neagh
Newtownabbey
Bangor
Belfast
Lisburn
Lurgan
Portadown
Armagh
Newry
Mourne Mtns.
852
Slieve Donard
Dundalk
Drogheda
Errris Head
Achill I.
Castlebar
Westport
Lough Conn
Lough Mask
Slyne Head
Lough Corrib
Galway
Galway Bay
Aran Is.
Clare
Lough Ree
Suck
Longford
Kells
Boyne
Mullingar
Athlone
Tullamore
Dublin
Dún Laoghaire
Bray
IRISH REPUBLIC
Naas
Wicklow Mtns.
926
Portlaoise
Barrow
Nore
Shannon
Slaney
Wexford
Rosslare
Carnsore Point
Limerick
Kilkenny
Clonmel
Suir
Waterford
1041
Carrauntoohill
Tralee
Killarney
Galty Mtns.
Blackwater
Lee
Cork
Youghal
Caha Mtns.
Dingle Bay
Loop Head
Bantry Bay
Mizen Head
Cape Clear
Old Head of Kinsale
St. George's Channel
Loch Lomond

Legend

Boundaries

international

internal

Communications

freeway/expressway/motorway

other major road

railway

canal

✈ major airport

Cities and towns

■ over 1 million inhabitants

● more than 100 000 inhabitants

• smaller towns

Land height

metres

2000

1000

500

300

200

100

sea level

land below sea level

▲ spot height in metres

Physical features

marsh

ice cap

Scale 1:8 500 000

100   200 km

Modified Conical Orthomorphic Projection

© Oxford University Press

Iceland inset

ICELAND

Grimsey

Siglufjördur

Ísafjördur   925

Húsavik

Akureyri   Vopnafjördur

Neskaupstadur

65°N

Breidha Fjördur

Stykkishólmur

Langjökull   Hofsjökull

Faxaflói   Akranes   Pjórsá   2000   Vatnajökull

Reykjavik   Hekla   Höfn

Keflavik   1491   Myrdals-

Hafnarfjördur   jökull

Vestmannaeyjar

Arctic Circle

Main map labels

ARCTIC OCEAN

Nordkapp (North Cape)

Barents Sea

Hammerfest   Sørøya   Lopphavet   Varangerhalvøya   Vardø

Vanna   Lakselv   637   Varangerfjorden

Ringvassøy   Alta   1139   Teno/oki   Pechenga   Murmansk

Tromsø   1067   Jiesjavrre   623   637   Tuloma

Senja   Karasjok   Inarijärvi   Lotta   Pudunskoye More

Langøya   1144   Rasto   Maanselka   Monchegorsk   1208

Hinnøya   1681   Enontekiö   807   Porttipahdan tekojarvi   636   Ozero Imandra   Apatity

Lofoten Is.   Narvik   Torne-   555   Lokan tekojarvi   Kholayarvi   Kandalakshskiy Zaliv (White Sea)

Vestfjorden   1901   träsk   Sodankylä   Kemijoki   Ozero Pyazero

Nordfold   2111   Kiruna   Ounasjoki   Yü-kitka   Kuusamo   Ozero Topozero

Bodø   2013   Stora Lulevattern   Gällivare   431   Muojoki   Ozero

Saltdal   1908   2021   Jokkmokk   Rovaniemi   Kemijärvi   Kiantajärvi   Kuhmo   Ozero Nyuk

1599   1754   1694   Kalix älv   Övertorneå   Tornio   Pudasjärvi   Kalevala

Mo-i-Rana   Hornavan   Lule älv   Boden   Tornio   Oulu   Ozero Sredneye Kuyto

Dønna   Røssvatnet   Arjeplog   Pite älv   Luleå   Hailuoto   Oulu järvi   355   Ozero Leksozero

Vega   1764   Uddjaur   Skellefte älv   Piteå   Raahe   Kajaani   Pielinen   409

Mosjøen   1588   Storuman   Vindelälven   Skellefteå   Pulkkila   Iisalmi

Brønnøysund   1703   Vilhelmina   Umeå   Kokkola   Pyhäjärvi   Kuopio   Joensuu

Kolvereid   Lycksele   Ångermanälven   Jakobstad   Keitele   Suvasvesi

Vikna   Namdalen   Hoting   Vännäs   Vaasa   Lappajärvi   Varkhaus   Pytäselkä

Folda   1337   Örnsköldsvik   Lapua   Jyväskylä   Haukivesi   Pyhäjärvi

Namsos   Dragan   Storsjön   Sollefteå   Kaskö   Kurikka   Puulavesi   Puruvesi

Frøya   Innherad   Tunnsjøen   Östersund   Härnösand   Parkano   Näsijärvi   Mikkeli   Saimaa   Imatra

Hitra   Fosna   Kallsjön   Storsjön   Sundsvall   Pori   Tampere   Päijänne   Ladozhskoye Ozero

Smøla   Brekstad   1441   1796   Åsarna   Indalsälven   Rauma   Hämeenlinna   Lahti   Kouvola   Vyborg

Kristiansund   Trondheim   Berkåk   Storsjön   Deljen   Pyhäjärvi   Forssa   Salpausselkä

Ålesund   Andalsnes   Trollheimen   1277   Östervall   Ljusnan   Åland   Porssa   Hyvinkää   Kotka

Måløy   Nordfjord   2083   2286   Tynset   Linsell   Ytterhogdal   Ljus   Turku   Salo   Vantaa   Kronstadt

Florø   2469   Jostedalsbreen   Dombås   Femund   1755   Idre   Voxnan   Mariehamn   Espoo   Helsinki (Helsingfors)

Jotunheimen   Gudbrandsdalen   887   Österdalälven   Bollnäs   Hangö   Tallinn   St. Petersburg (Leningrad)   Gatchina

Sognefjorden   Lillehammer   Mora   Söderhamn   Kohtla-Järve   Narva   Luga

Bergen   Laerdalsøyri   Valdres   Amungen   Siljan   Gävle   Hiiumaa   Haapsalu   Tápa   Luga

Voss   1962   Hamar   Falun   Hedesunda-fjärdarna   Saaremaa   Pärnu   Tartu   Pskov

Hardangerfjorden   Hardanger-vidda   Mjøsa   Borlänge   Ludvika   Avesta   ESTONIA   Ozero Chudskoye   318

Haugesund   1660   Odda   Telemark   Kløfta   Oslo   Uppsala   Kuressaare   Võrtsjärv   Võru

Stavanger   Boknafjorden   Drammen   Arvika   Västerås   Mälaren   Hangö   Ozero Pskovskoye

Setesdal   Moss   Karlstad   Eskilstuna   Stockholm   Fårön   Valga   LATVIA

Flekkefjord   Tønsberg   Sarpsborg   Karlskoga   Örebro   Södertälje   Mazirbe   Gulf of Riga   Valmiera   Rēzekne

Skien   Frederikstad   Vänern   Katrineholm   Nyköping   Ventspils   Riga   Alūksne

Arendal   Porsgrunn   Skövde   Norrköping   Visby   Gotland   Kuldīga   Tukums   Daugavpils   Opochka

Kristiansand   Uddevalla   Trollhättan   Linköping   Västervik   Saldus   Jelgava

Mandal   Sommen   Öland   Liepāja   Šiauliai   Panevēžys   Polotsk

Göteborg   Borås   Jönköping   Borgholm   Venta   Plunge   LITHUANIA

Skagerrak   Mölndal   Nässjö   Värnamo   Kalmar   Klaipėda   Plunge   Vilnius   BELARUS (BYELORUSSIA)

North Sea   Hjørring   Frederikshavn   Bolmen   Vetlanda   Kristianstad   Karlskrona   Lida

Ålborg   Växjö   Almhult   Kurshskiy Zaliv   Kaunas   Marijampole   Molodechno

Viborg   Randers   Halmstad   Agnen   Hanöbukten   Gdynia   Gdansk   KALININGRAD (RUSSIA)   Grodno   Minsk

DENMARK   Herning   Århus   Helsingborg   Landskrona   Lund   Kaliningrad   Elbląg   Vilna

Ringkøbing Fjord   Vejle   København (Copenhagen)   Malmö   Sassnitz   Koszalin   Olsztyn   Ełk   Sniardwy

Esbjerg   Kolding   Roskilde   Sjaelland   Bornholm (Denmark)   Szczecin   Ploty

Odense   Naestved   Gdansk   Tczew

Nord-friesische Inseln   Sønderborg   Lolland   Nyköbing   Pomeranian Bay   Świnoujście

Heligoland Bight   Schleswig   Flensburg   Rügen   POLAND

GERMANY   Rendsburg   Kiel   Mecklenburg Bay   Stralsund

Groningen   Cuxhaven   Neumünster   Lübeck   Wismar   Rostock   Schwerin

NETHERLANDS   Bremerhaven   Hamburg   Bremen

Gulf of Bothnia

Baltic Sea

Gulf of Finland

Kattegat

Limfjorden

Arctic Circle

NORWAY   SWEDEN   FINLAND   RUSSIA (RUSSIAN FEDERATION)   LAPLAND

70°N   65°N   60°N   55°N

Benelux: Political

Boundaries
international
région
province

Cities
■ national capital
· provincial capital

Scale 1 : 4 000 000
0   50   100 km

NETHERLANDS
GRONINGEN
Leeuwarden · Groningen
FRIESLAND
· Assen
DRENTHE
NOORD-HOLLAND
Haarlem · Amsterdam
ZWOLLE
OVERIJSSEL
's-Gravenhage (Den Haag, The Hague)
ZUID-HOLLAND
UTRECHT · Utrecht
GELDERLAND
· Arnhem
's-Hertogenbosch
NOORD-BRABANT
Middelburg
ZEELAND
Brugge (Bruges)
WEST-VLANDEREN
OOST-VLANDEREN
Gent (Gand)
ANTWERPEN
Antwerpen (Anvers)
LIMBURG
· Hasselt
Maastricht
BRABANT
Bruxelles (Brussel, Brussels)

BELGIUM
HAINAUT · Mons
NAMUR · Namur
· Liège
LIÈGE
WALLONIE
LUXEMBOURG
Arlon · Luxembourg
LUXEMBOURG

Boundaries
international
internal

Communications
freeway/expressway/motorway
other major road
railway
canal
✈ major airport

Physical features
- - - marsh

Cities and towns
built-up areas
■ over 1 million inhabitants
● more than 100 000 inhabitants
· smaller towns

Land height
metres
500
300
200
100
sea level
land below sea level
▲ spot height in metres

Scale 1 : 2 000 000
0   25   50 km

North Sea

NETHERLANDS
FRIESLAND
GRONINGEN
DRENTHE
OVERIJSSEL
NOORD-HOLLAND
ZUID-HOLLAND
Amsterdam
Rotterdam
's-Gravenhage (Den Haag, The Hague)
GELDERLAND
ZEELAND
NOORD BRABANT
Eindhoven
Breda
Tilburg
LIMBURG

ANTWERPEN
Antwerpen (Anvers)
OOST-VLANDEREN
WEST-VLANDEREN
Gent (Gand)
Brugge (Bruges)
BELGIUM
Bruxelles (Brussel, Brussels)
BRABANT
HAINAUT
NAMUR
LIÈGE
LUXEMBOURG

U.K.
Strait of Dover (Pas de Calais)
PAS-DE-CALAIS
FRANCE
ARDENNES
AISNE

GERMANY
FEDERAL REPUBLIC
NORDRHEIN WESTFALEN
RHEINLAND PFALZ

Conical Orthomorphic Projection   © Oxford University Press

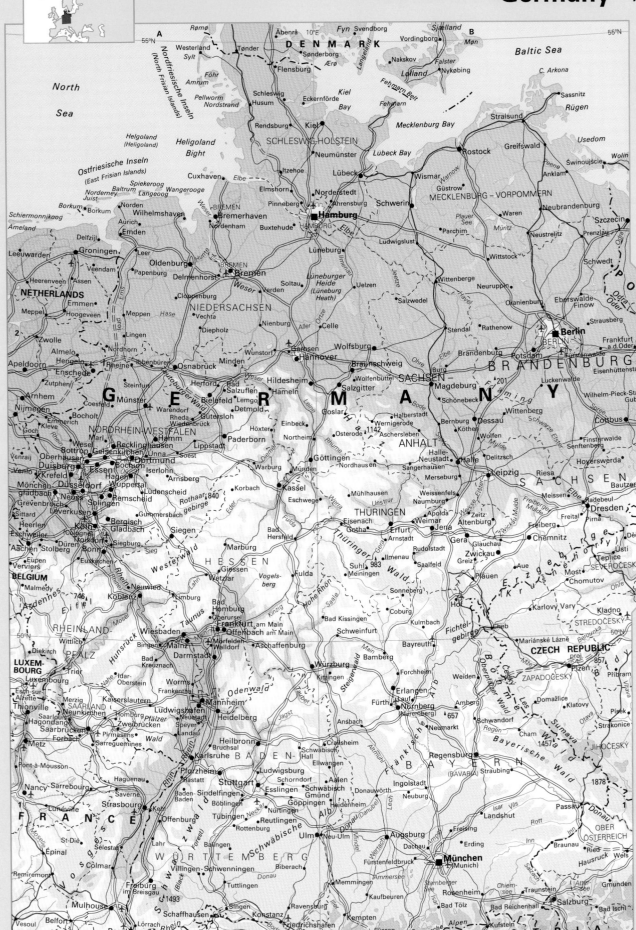

Boundaries
international
internal

Communications
freeway/expressway/motorway
other major road
railway
canal
✈ major airport

Cities and towns
built-up areas
over 1 million inhabitants
more than 100 000 inhabitants
smaller towns

Physical features
marsh
ice cap

Land height
metres
3000
2000
1000
500
300
200
100
sea level
land below sea level

▲ spot height in metres

Scale 1:3 500 000
25   50 km

Conical Orthomorphic Projection
© Oxford University Press

Bay of Biscay

FRANCE
Pyrénées
Pirineos
ANDORRA
Andorra la Vella

Cabo Finisterre
C. Ortegal
El Ferrol del Caudillo
La Coruña (Corunna)
Ortigueira
Villalba
Luarca
Avilés
C. de Peñas
Gijón
Santander
San Sebastián
Biarritz
Bayonne
Arcachon
Marmande
Figeac
Cahors
Agen
Montauban
Mimizan
Mont-de-Marsan
Dax
Tarbes
Pau
Lourdes
St-Gaudens
Toulouse
Castres
Béziers
Narbonne
Carcassonne
Pamiers
Foix
Perpignan
Gerona
San Feliú de Guixols
C. de Creus
Figueras
Santiago de Compostela
Lugo
Oviedo
Mieres
Torrelavega
Reinosa
Baracaldo
Bilbao
Vitoria
Irún
Tolosa
Pamplona
Jaca
Huesca
Barbastro
Lérida (Lleida)
Manresa
Sabadell
Tarrasa
Hospitalet
Barcelona
Badalona
Mataró
Pontevedra
Ponferrada
León
Benavente
Burgos
Branda de Ebro
Logroño
Calahorra
Tudela
Zaragoza
Reus
Tarragona
Tortosa
Vigo
Tuy
Orense
Verin
Bragança
Palencia
Valladolid
Zamora
Soria
Calatayud
Daroca
Alcañiz
Vinaroz
Benicarló
Viana do Castelo
Braga
Guimarães
Vila Real
Lamego
Tordesillas
Medina del Campo
Segovia
Sigüenza
Teruel
Castellón de la Plana
Matosinhos
Porto (Oporto)
Vila Nova de Gaia
Aveiro
Visau
Salamanca
Ávila
Guadalajara
Alcalá de Henares
Cuenca
Sagunto
Valencia
Figueira da Foz
Coimbra
Guarda
Covilhã
Ciudad Rodrigo
Madrid
Leganés
Móstoles
Getafe
Aranjuez
Alcira
Leiria
Caldas da Rainha
Castelo Branco
Plasencia
Talavera de la Reina
Toledo
Villarrobledo
Tomar
Santarém
Portalegre
Cáceres
Trujillo
Alcázar de San Juan
Albacete
Almansa
Alcoy
Sintra
Cascais
Lisboa (Lisbon)
Almada
Barreiro
Setúbal
Elvas
Mérida
Badajoz
Don Benito
Ciudad Real
Manzanares
Valdepeñas
Hellín
Elda
Elche
Alicante
Orihuela
C. Espichel
Évora
Zafra
Jerez de los Caballeros
Almadén
Puertollano
Murcia
Sines
Beja
Aljustrel
Peñarroya-Pueblonuevo
Andújar
Linares
Cartagena
C. de Palos
Portimão
Silves
Almodóvar
Nerva
Córdoba
Jaén
Baza
Lorca
Aguilas
C. de São Vicente
Lagos
Faro
Olhão
Tavira
Ayamonte
Huelva
Sevilla (Seville)
Utrera
Écija
Lucena
Guadix
Granada
Almería
C. de Gata
Sanlúcar de Barrameda
Jerez de la Frontera
Puerto de Sta. María
Cádiz
San Fernando
Ronda
Marbella
Antequera
Loja
Málaga
Motril
Adra
Algeciras
La Línea de la Concepción
GIBRALTAR (U.K.)
Ceuta (Sp.)
Melilla (Sp.)
Nador
Tanger (Tangiers)
Asilah
Larache
Ksar-el-Kebir
Tétouan
Al Hoceima
Ouezzane
Kénitra

ATLANTIC OCEAN
Mediterranean Sea
Gulf of Valencia
Costa Blanca
C. de la Nao
Ibiza
Formentera
Balearic Islands (Spain)
Palma de Mallorca
Sóller
Inca
Manacor
Mallorca
Cabrera
Menorca
Ciudadela
Mahón
Alcudia

ALGERIA
Alger (Algiers)
Blida
Boufarik
Médéa
Tizi Ouzou
Dellys
Cherchell
Miliana
Ech Cheliff
El Bayadh
Massif de l'Ouarsenis
Oran
Arzew
Mostaganem
Mohammadia
Mascara
Aïn Témouchent
Beni Saf
Sidi Bel Abbès
Tlemcen
Saïda
Tiaret
Ksar El Boukhari
Bou Saâda
Djelfa
Bougzoul

MOROCCO
Rif Mts.
Oujda
C. des Trois Fourches

SPAIN
PORTUGAL
Cordillera Cantabrica (Cantabrian Mts.)
Montañas de León
Sierra Morena
La Mancha
Sa. de Gredos
Sa. de Guadarrama
Serranía de Cuenca
Sierra Nevada
Mulhacén 3482
Costa del Sol
Costa Brava
Costa Dorada

Douro / Duero
Ebro
Tajo / Tejo (Tagus)
Guadiana
Guadalquivir
Júcar
Segura

Scale 1 : 6 250 000
0   50   100 km

Boundaries
international

Communications
freeway/expressway/motorway
other major road
railway
canal
✈ major airport

Cities and towns
▱ built-up areas
■ over 1 million inhabitants
● more than 100 000 inhabitants
• smaller towns

Physical features
seasonal river/lake
marsh
▲ spot height in metres

Land height
metres
3000
2000
1000
500
300
200
100
sea level

Balearic Islands (Spain)

Mediterranean Sea
Mallorca (Majorca)
Sóller
Sa. de Alfabia
I. Dragonera
Andraitx
Calvia
C. de Cala Figuera
Palma de Mallorca
Lluchmayor
Sineu
Inca
Pollensa
Alcudia
La Puebla
C. de Formentor
C. d'Artrutx
Arta
Manacor
Felanitx
Campos del Puerto
Santañy
C. de Salinas
Conejera
Cabrera
Menorca (Minorca)
Ciudadela
C. Caballeria
Fornells
Alayor
Mahón
C. Freu

Ibiza
San Antonio Abad
San José
San Juan Bautista
Sta. Eulalia del Rio
Ibiza
C. de Barberia
San Francisco Javier
Formentera

Scale 1 : 3 000 000
0   25   50 km

Conical Orthomorphic Projection
© Oxford University Press

UNITED KINGDOM
English Channel (La Manche)
Channel Islands
Bay of Biscay
FRANCE
BELGIUM
LUXEMBOURG
FEDERAL REPUBLIC OF GERMANY
SWITZERLAND
AUSTRIA
LIECHTENSTEIN
ITALY
SPAIN
ANDORRA
MONACO
Mediterranean Sea
Ligurian Sea
Golfe du Lion
Corse (Corsica) (France)
Sardegna (Sardinia) (Italy)
Paris
Lyon
Marseille
Bruxelles (Brussel)
Milano (Milan)
Torino (Turin)
Bordeaux
Toulouse
Nantes
Lille
Strasbourg
Nice
Grenoble
Massif Central
Pyrénées
Alpes
Jura
Vosges
Ardennes
Boundaries
international
Communications
freeway/expressway/motorway
other major road
railway
canal
major airport
Cities and towns
built-up areas
over 1 million inhabitants
more than 100 000 inhabitants
smaller towns
Physical features
marsh
ice cap
Land height
metres
3000
2000
1000
500
300
200
100
sea level
land below sea level
spot height in metres
Scale 1: 5 000 000
0
50
100 km
Conical Orthomorphic Projection
© Oxford University Press

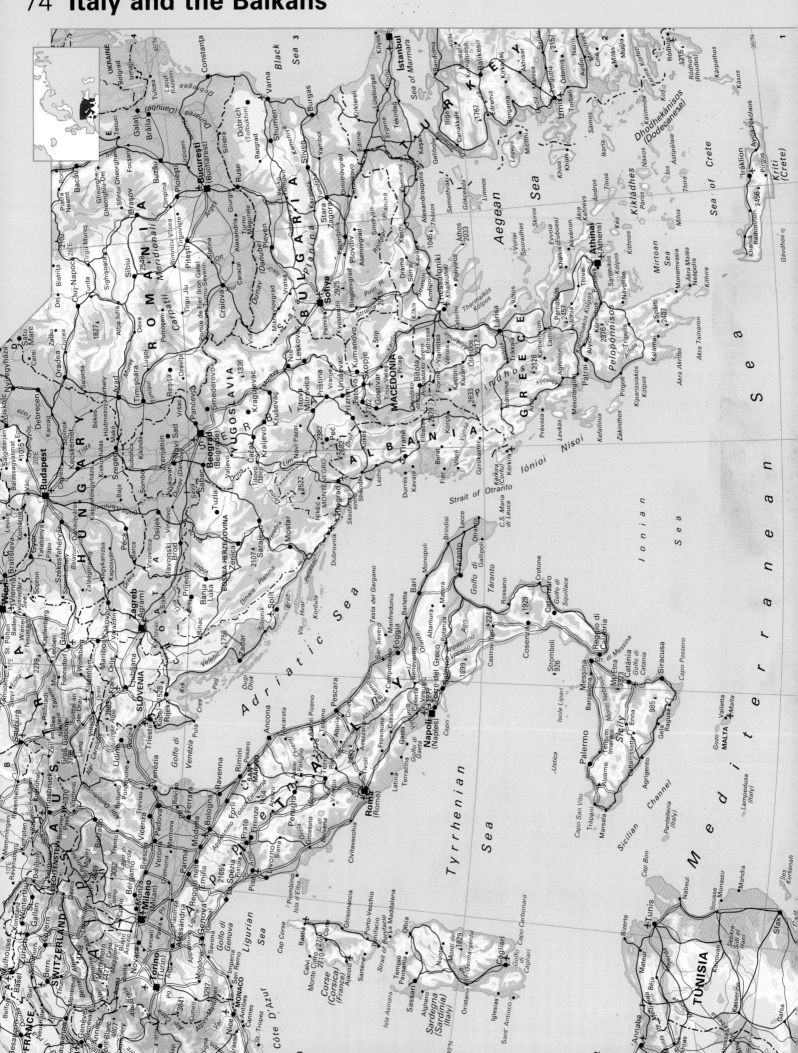

FRANCE
SWITZERLAND
LIECHTENSTEIN
AUSTRIA
HUNGARY
ROMANIA
UKRAINE
SLOVENIA
CROATIA
BOSNIA-HERZEGOVINA
YUGOSLAVIA
SERBIA
MONTENEGRO
MACEDONIA
ALBANIA
BULGARIA
GREECE
TURKEY
ITALY
SAN MARINO
MONACO
TUNISIA
MALTA
Black Sea
Sea of Marmara
Aegean Sea
Sea of Crete
Mirtoan Sea
Ionian Sea
Mediterranean Sea
Adriatic Sea
Tyrrhenian Sea
Ligurian Sea
Sicilian Channel
Strait of Otranto
Golfo di Táranto
Golfo di Venézia
Golfo di Genova
Strait of Bonifacio
Côte D'Azur
Wien (Vienna)
Budapest
Bucureşti (Bucharest)
Sofiya
Beograd (Belgrade)
Zagreb (Agram)
Ljubljana
Sarajevo
Skopje
Tiranë
Athinai (Athens)
İstanbul
Roma (Rome)
Napoli (Naples)
Milano (Milan)
Torino (Turin)
Genova (Genoa)
Venézia
Bologna
Firenze
Palermo
Messina
Bari
Brindisi
Thessaloníki
Varna
Burgas
Constanța
Cluj-Napoca
Timişoara
Debrecen
Szeged
Split
Zadar
Rijeka
Trieste
Dubrovnik
Tunis
Sfax
Corse (Corsica) (France)
Sardegna (Sardinia) (Italy)
Sicily
Kríti (Crete)
Pelopónnisos
Dhodhekánisos (Dodecanese)
Kikládhes
Lampedusa (Italy)
Pantelleria (Italy)
Dunărea (Danube)
Dunav (Danube)
Carpații Meridionali
Stara Planina
Pindhos
Appennino
Alps

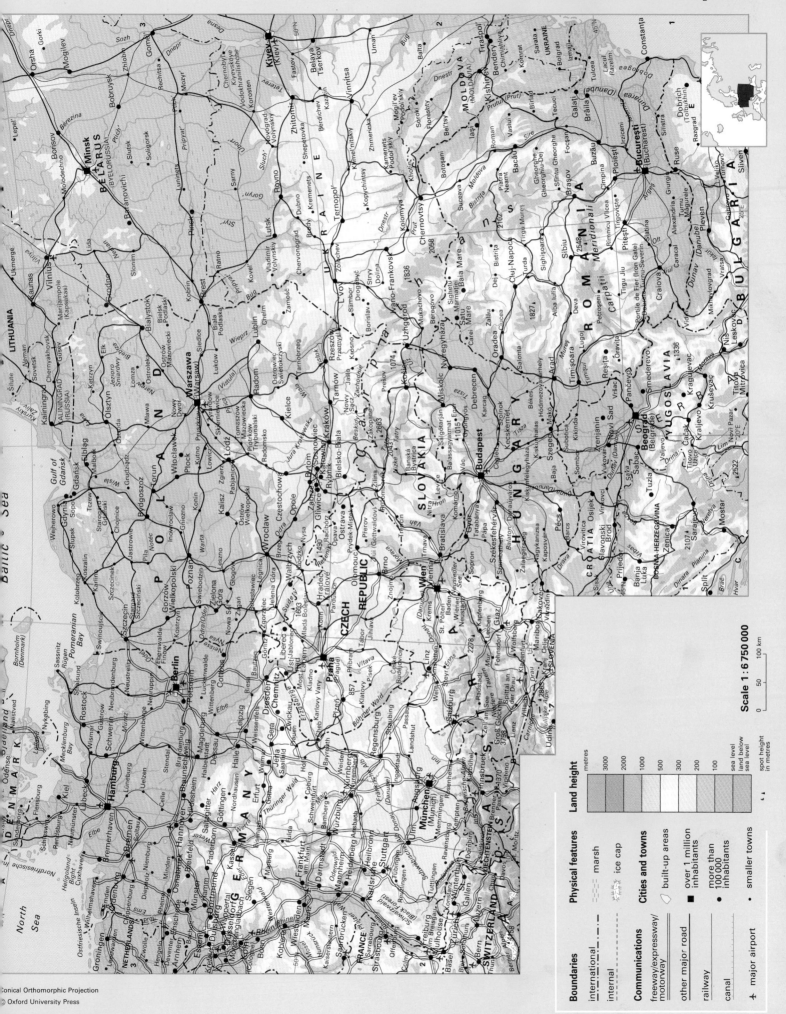

Scale 1 : 6 750 000

0   50   100 km

Boundaries
international
internal

Communications
freeway/expressway/ motorway
other major road
railway
canal

Physical features
marsh
ice cap

Cities and towns
built-up areas
over 1 million inhabitants
more than 100 000 inhabitants
smaller towns
major airport

Land height
	metres
	3000
	2000
	1000
	500
	300
	200
	100
	sea level
	land below sea level

spot height in metres

Conical Orthomorphic Projection
© Oxford University Press

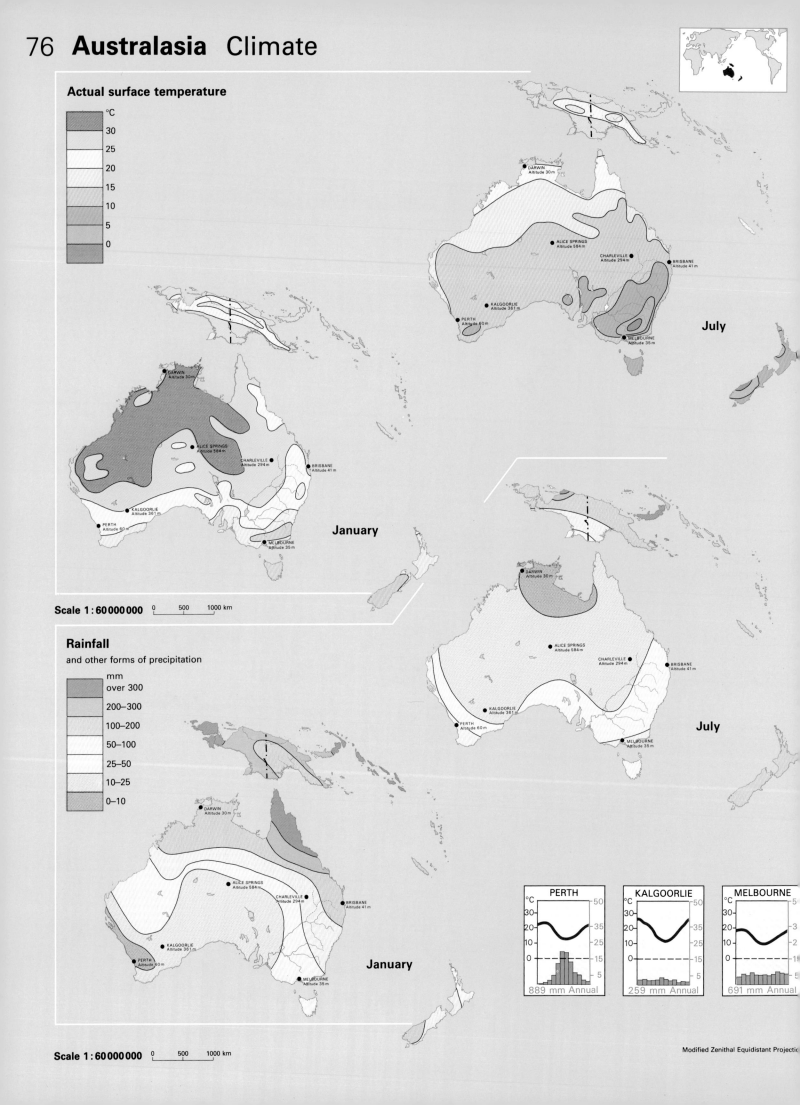

Actual surface temperature

	°C
	30
	25
	20
	15
	10
	5
	0

July

January

Scale 1:60 000 000   0   500   1000 km

Rainfall
and other forms of precipitation

	mm
	over 300
	200–300
	100–200
	50–100
	25–50
	10–25
	0–10

July

January

Scale 1:60 000 000   0   500   1000 km

DARWIN Altitude 30 m
ALICE SPRINGS Altitude 584 m
CHARLEVILLE Altitude 294 m
BRISBANE Altitude 41 m
KALGOORLIE Altitude 361 m
PERTH Altitude 60 m
MELBOURNE Altitude 35 m

PERTH
889 mm Annual

KALGOORLIE
259 mm Annual

MELBOURNE
691 mm Annual

Modified Zenithal Equidistant Projection

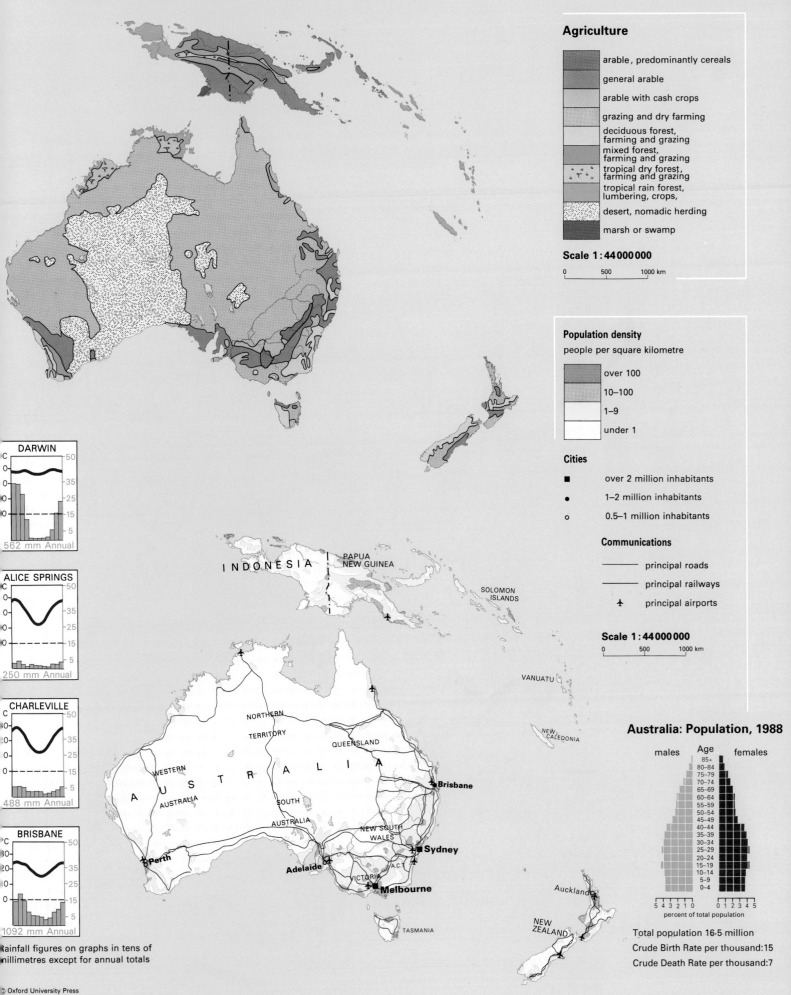

Agriculture

- arable, predominantly cereals
- general arable
- arable with cash crops
- grazing and dry farming
- deciduous forest, farming and grazing
- mixed forest, farming and grazing
- tropical dry forest, farming and grazing
- tropical rain forest, lumbering, crops,
- desert, nomadic herding
- marsh or swamp

Scale 1 : 44 000 000

0   500   1000 km

Population density

people per square kilometre

- over 100
- 10–100
- 1–9
- under 1

Cities

- ■ over 2 million inhabitants
- ● 1–2 million inhabitants
- ○ 0.5–1 million inhabitants

Communications

- —— principal roads
- —— principal railways
- ✈ principal airports

Scale 1 : 44 000 000

0   500   1000 km

DARWIN
562 mm Annual

ALICE SPRINGS
250 mm Annual

CHARLEVILLE
488 mm Annual

BRISBANE
1092 mm Annual

Rainfall figures on graphs in tens of millimetres except for annual totals

INDONESIA

PAPUA NEW GUINEA

SOLOMON ISLANDS

VANUATU

NEW CALEDONIA

WESTERN AUSTRALIA

NORTHERN TERRITORY

QUEENSLAND

SOUTH AUSTRALIA

NEW SOUTH WALES

A U S T R A L I A

● Perth

Adelaide

VICTORIA

A.C.T.

■ Sydney

■ Brisbane

■ Melbourne

TASMANIA

Auckland

NEW ZEALAND

Australia: Population, 1988

males	Age	females
	85+	
	80–84	
	75–79	
	70–74	
	65–69	
	60–64	
	55–59	
	50–54	
	45–49	
	40–44	
	35–39	
	30–34	
	25–29	
	20–24	
	15–19	
	10–14	
	5–9	
	0–4	

5 4 3 2 1 0   0 1 2 3 4 5
percent of total population

Total population 16·5 million
Crude Birth Rate per thousand: 15
Crude Death Rate per thousand: 7

© Oxford University Press

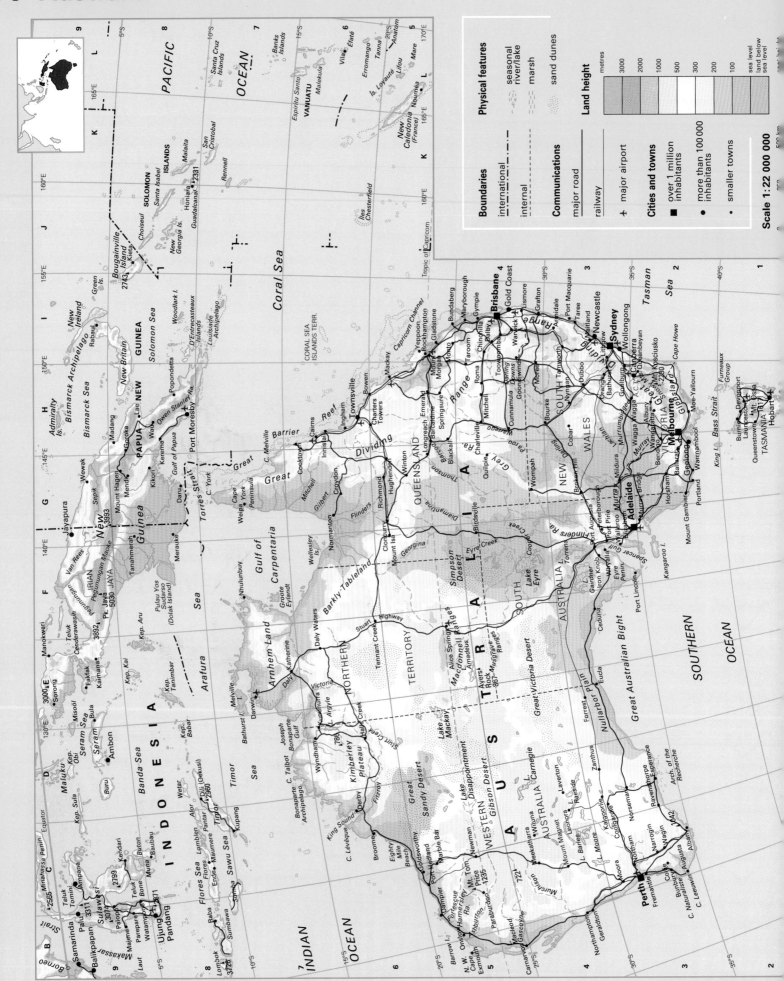

Zenithal Equidistant Projecti
© Oxford University Pre

Land height

metres	
3000	
2000	
1000	
500	
300	
200	
100	
sea level	

▴ spot height in metres

Communications

— major road
▬ railway
✈ major airport

Cities and towns

● more than 100 000 inhabitants
· smaller towns

Scale 1:7 500 000

0 50 100 150 km

Conical Orthomorphic Projection
© Oxford University Press

North Island

Three Kings Is.
North Cape
C. Maria van Diemen
Ninety Mile Beach
Kaitaia 751
Kaikohe
Bay of Islands
Russell
Kerikeri
Whangarei
Dargaville
Kaipara Harbour
Wellsford
Great Barrier I.
Coromandel Peninsula
Hauraki Gulf
Takapuna
Manukau
Auckland
Manukau Harbour
Thames
Bay of Plenty
Te Aroha
Morrinsville
Tauranga
Paeroa
Waihi
Katikati
Huntly
Ngaruawahia
Cambridge
Hamilton
Waikato
Te Awamutu
Te Kuiti
Rotorua
Raukumara
East Cape
Gisborne
Poverty Bay
Whakatane
Mahia Peninsula
Illkurangi 1754
Mt Ruapehu 2751
L. Taupo
Taupo
Mt Ngauruhoe 2291
Waitara
New Plymouth
Mt Egmont 2518
C. Egmont
Hawera
Patea
Wanganui
Waikaremoana
Wairoa
Hawke Bay
Napier
Hastings
Waipawa
Dannevirke
Woodville
Feilding
Palmerston North
Levin
Masterton
Otaki
Porirua
Upper Hutt
Lower Hutt 663
Wellington
Cook Strait
C. Palliser

Tasman Sea

South Island

Farewell Spit
Golden Bay
Tasman Bay
Collingwood
Motueka
Nelson
Richmond
Mt Owen 1875
Westport
Buller
Mt Travers 2338
Tapuaenuku 2885
Picton
Blenheim
Kaikoura
Rangiora
Kaiapoi
Lyttelton
Christchurch
Akaroa
Banks Peninsula
Pegasus Bay
Canterbury Bight
Ashburton
Temuka
Timaru
Waimate
Oamaru
LEWIS PASS
ARTHUR'S PASS 1867
C. Foulwind
Runanga
Greymouth
Hokitika
Southern Alps
Mt Cook 3764
Mt Aspiring 3036
HAAST PASS
LINDIS PASS
Lake Tekapo
Lake Benmore
Lake Waitaki
Lake Hawea
Lake Wanaka
Wanaka
Cromwell
Alexandra
Roxburgh
Mossburn
Milton
Balclutha
Port Chalmers
Dunedin
Clutha
Queenstown
Lake Wakatipu
Lake Te Anau
Milford Sound 2095
Fiordland
Gore
Mataura
Riverton
Winton
Invercargill
Bluff
Foveaux Strait
Stewart I. 980 750
Southwest Cape
Jackson Head
Mt Travers
Canterbury Plains

SOUTH PACIFIC OCEAN

Scale 1:300 000

freeway/expressway/motorway
other major road
major railway
✈ major airport
✈ other airport

Physical features
river
marsh
contours
·155 spot height in metres

Land use
central business district
other major commercial areas
industrial
residential
major parks and open spaces
non-urban

0 5 km

Sydney

Barranjoey Head
Palm Beach
Pitt Water
Newport
Mona Vale
Narrabeen
Dee Why
Brookvale
Terrey Hills
Frenchs Forest
MANLY
Balgowlah
North Head
Mosman
Crows Nest
Middle Harbour
Port Jackson
South Head
SYDNEY
Sydney Harbour Bridge
Opera House
Bondi Beach
Woollahra
Centennial Park
Randwick
University of New South Wales
Maroubra
La Perouse
Cape Banks
Cape Solander
Kurnell
Botany Bay
Bate Bay
Cronulla
Port Hacking Point
Bundeena
Royal National Park
Ku-ring-gai Chase National Park
Cowan Creek
SYDNEY–NEWCASTLE FREEWAY
Berowra
Asquith
Galston
Dural
Kenthurst
Castle Hill
Baulkham Hills
HORNSBY
Turramurra
Pennant Hills
St Ives
Gordon
Lindfield
Chatswood
Macquarie University
PACIFIC HIGHWAY
Epping
Eastwood
Ryde
Gladesville
Drummoyne
Balmain
Leichhardt
University of Sydney
Mascot
KINGSFORD SMITH INTERNATIONAL AIRPORT
Marrickville
Rockdale
Kingsgrove
Hurstville
Parramatta River
PARRAMATTA
Merrylands
Ashfield
Strathfield
Lidcombe
Canterbury
Revesby
East Hills
BANKSTOWN
BANKSTOWN AIRPORT
HUME HIGHWAY
Fairfield
LIVERPOOL
Chipping Norton
Georges River
Menai
SUTHERLAND
Caringbah
Port Hacking
PRINCES HIGHWAY
Heathcote
GREAT WESTERN HIGHWAY
Woronora River
Waterfall
Woronora Reservoir

15°00'E 151°15'E 33°45'S 34°00'S

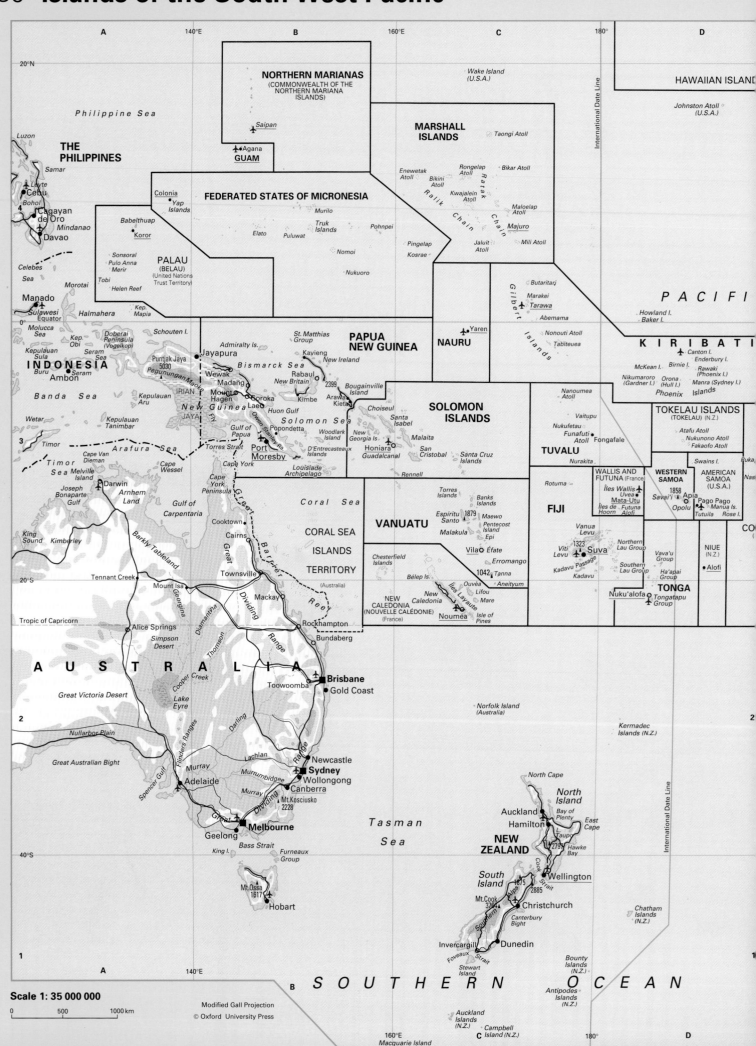

0   500   1000 km

Modified Gall Projection
© Oxford University Press

Norfolk Island
Scale 1: 100 000

6
J 167°55'E K 167°57'E L 167°59'E M 6

Point Vincent
Point Howe
Point Duncombe Bay
29°00'S
Anson Pt.
Captain Cook Monument
Bird Rock
PACIFIC OCEAN
Anson Bay Reserve
Mount Bates ▲321
Anson Bay
NORFOLK ISLAND
Selwyn Recreational Reserve
Mount Pitt ▲320
NATIONAL PARK
Cascade Bay
Jacobs Rock
Broken Bridge Ck.
Cascade
Cascade Ck.
Cascade Reserve
Cascade
Steels Point
Puppys Point
Botanic Garden
5
29°02'S
Burnt Pine
Cascade Creek
Stockyard Creek
Middlegate
Bucks Point Reserve
Two Chimneys Reserve
Headstone Reserve
Ball Bay Reserve
Point Blackbourne
Headstone Point
Ball Bay
Collins Head
Rocky Point Reserve
Watermill Dam
Town Ck.
Rocky Point
Sumbora Reserve
Kingston Common Reserve
Kingston
4
Point Ross Reserve
Government House
Point Hunter Reserve
Cemetery Bay
Point Ross
Sydney Bay
Point Hunter
29°04'S

J 167°55'E K 167°57'E L M
Transverse Mercator Projection

0 1 2 km

3

Phillip Island
2
K 167°57'E L 2
Nepean Island
Cow Bay
Red Stone
Dar Moo-oo Bay
29°07'S
West End Pt.
East End Point
Phillip Island
Dar Tomato Bay
Spin Bay
Juvenile Point
1
Garnet Pt.
PACIFIC OCEAN
K 167°57'E L

Boundaries
- international
- state, territory
- island group (not a recognised territorial boundary)
- national park *

Communications
- main road
- railway
- ✈ main airport

Cities and towns
- ◇ built-up areas *
- ■ over 1 million inhabitants
- ● more than 100 000 inhabitants
- ○ 10 000 - 100 000 inhabitants
- • smaller towns

Physical features
- seasonal river/lake
- marsh
- coral reef
- quarry *

Land height (main map)
	metres
	2000
	1000
	500
	200
	sea level
	land below sea level

Land height (insets)
	metres
	300
	200
	100
	sea level

▲ spot height in metres

*insets only

Christmas Island (Australia)

R
105°35'E 105°40'E
Rocky Point
North East Point
10°25'S
Q
Settlement
Silver City
Poon Saan
Smith Point
Phosphate Hill
Drumsite
North West Point
Irvine Hill
INDIAN OCEAN
2
Waterfall
Low Pt.
Steep Pt.
Murray Hill 361
Stewart Hill
Wright Pt.
10°30'S
Egeria Pt.
Middle Point
Smithson Bight
Wharton Hill 284
Ross Hill
INDIAN OCEAN
John D. Point
1
West Quarry
East Quarry
INDIAN OCEAN
Stubbings Point
Medwin Pt.
Q 105°40'E R
P 105°35'E

Scale 1: 200 000
0 1 2 3 4 5 km

Transverse Mercator Projection

Population, Gross National Product, and Infant Mortality

Population
On this map the size of each country represents the number of people living there, rather than the area of land that the country occupies.

- □ One small square represents 10 000 people, *except* countries of less than 10 000 people are shown by a spot (●)
- ■ One small square represents 200 000 people in Indonesia and Malaysia

Gross National Product (GNP)
$ US per capita, 1989

	10 000 - 20 000
	5000 - 10 000
	1000 - 5000
	750 - 1000
	500 - 750
	no data

Infant Mortality, 1990
Deaths per 1000 live births

	over 70
	50 - 70
	30 - 50
	20 - 30
	10 - 20
	less than 10
	no data

Malaysia
Indonesia
Singapore
Northern Marianas
Guam
Palau
Papua New Guinea
Marshall Is.
Micronesia
Nauru
Kiribati
Wallis and Futuna
Western Samoa
Tokelau Islands
American Samoa
Tuvalu
Solomon Is.
New Caledonia
Niue
Cook Is.
French Polynesia
Fiji
Vanuatu
Tonga
Coral Sea Islands Territory

Australia

New Zealand

(Left inset map)
160°W
Kauai
Oahu
Molokai
Lanai
Maui
E
20°N
Hawaii

Kingman Reef
Palmyra Atoll
Teraina (Washington I.)
Tabuaeran (Fanning I.)
Kiritimati (Christmas I.)
Jarvis I.
Line Islands
0°
Malden I.
Starbuck I.
Vostok I.
Caroline I.
Flint I.
OCEAN
Penrhyn
ahanga
anihiki
warrow
LANDS
nd)
nerston
ll
Aitutaki
Hervey
Atiu Mitiaro
✈ Rarotonga
Mangaia
Maria
Rurutu
Rimatara
Tubuai
Raivavae
Tubuai or Austral Islands
Nuku Hiva
Hiva Hoa
Marquesas Islands
3
F
Rangiroa
Fangatau
FRENCH POLYNESIA
(France)
Tuamotu Archipelago
Marutea
Fangatau
Mooréa
Tahiti
○ Papeete
Society Archipelago
Hao
Pukarua
20°S
Actaeon Islands
Muraroa Atoll
Gambier Islands
Pitcairn I. (U.K.)
160°W
E
140°W
F

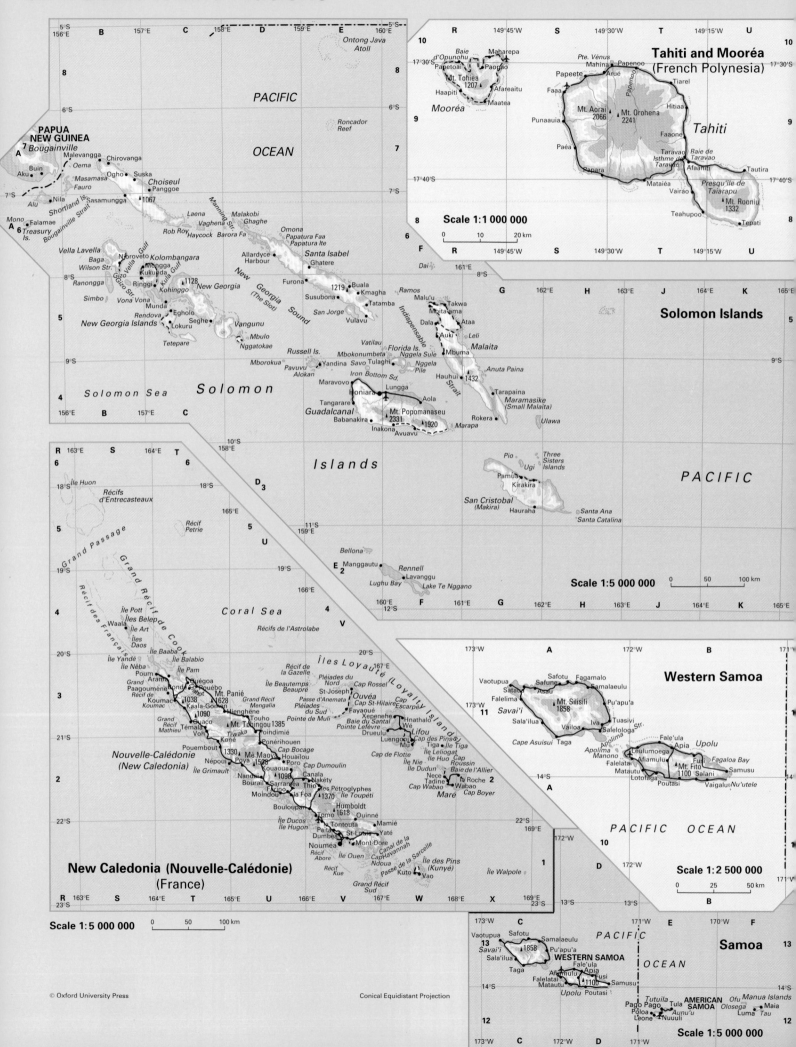

Tahiti and Mooréa (French Polynesia)

Scale 1:1 000 000

0   10   20 km

Solomon Islands

PACIFIC OCEAN

Scale 1:5 000 000

0   50   100 km

Western Samoa

Scale 1:2 500 000

0   25   50 km

New Caledonia (Nouvelle-Calédonie) (France)

Scale 1:5 000 000

0   50   100 km

Samoa

Scale 1:5 000 000

© Oxford University Press

Conical Equidistant Projection

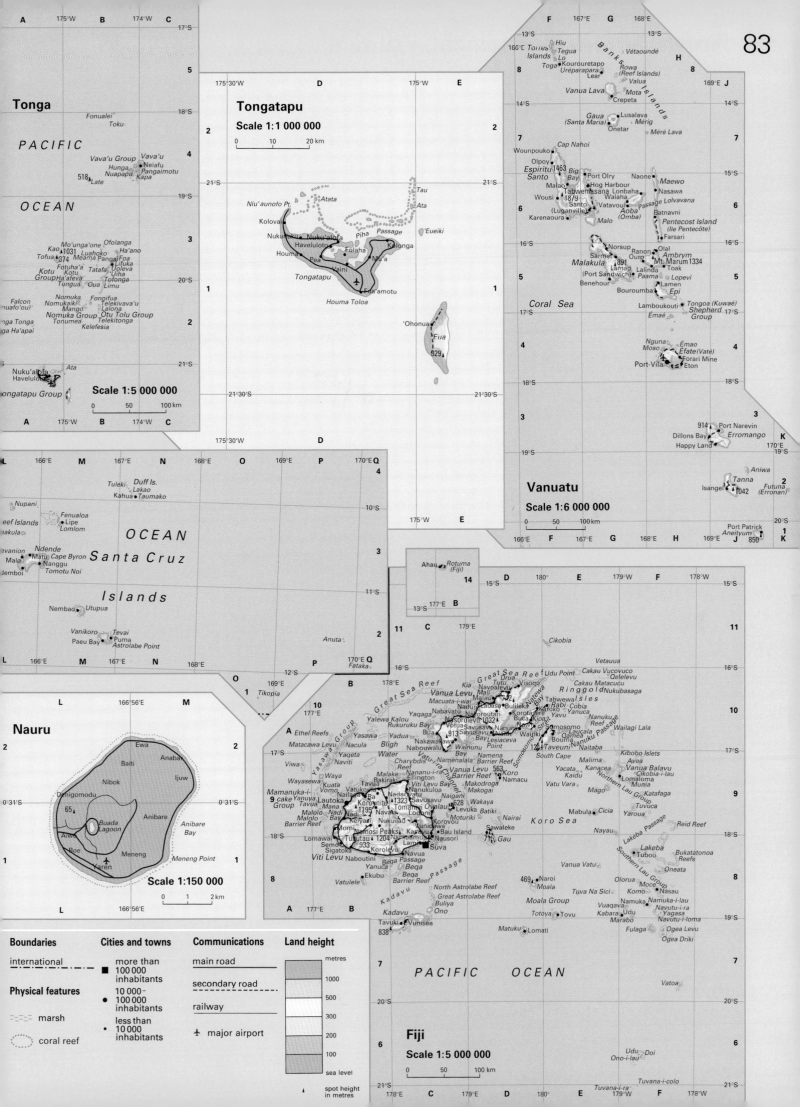
Tonga
PACIFIC
OCEAN
Fonualei
Toku
Vava'u Group
Vava'u
Hunga
Neiafu
Nuapapu
Pangaimotu
Kapa
518
Late
Kao
1031
Tofua
374
Mo'unga'one
Ofolanga
Luahoko
Ha'ano
Meama
Pangai
Foa
Lifuka
Kotu
Uoleva
Fotuha'a
Tatafa
'Uiha
Group
Ha'afeva
Tofonga
Tungua
Oua
Limu
Nomuka
Fonoifua
Nomukaiki
Telekivava'u
Mango
Lalona
Nomuka Group
Otu Tolu Group
Tonumea
Telekitonga
Kelefesia
Falcon
Ata
Nuku'alofa
Havelulofo
Tongatapu Group
Scale 1:5 000 000
0 50 100 km
Tongatapu
Scale 1:1 000 000
0 10 20 km
Atata
Niu'aunofo Pt.
Tau
Ata
Kolovai
'Eueiki
Nukunuku
Nuku'alofa
Piha Passage
Haveluloto
Kolonga
Folaha
Houma
Pea
Mu'a
Vaini
Tongatapu
Fua'amotu
Houma Toloa
'Ohonua
Fua
329
Vanuatu
Scale 1:6 000 000
0 50 100 km
Torres Islands
Hiu
Tegua
Lo
Toga
Kouroureotapo
Uréparapara
Lear
Banks Islands
Vétaoundé
Rowa (Reef Islands)
Valua
Vanua Lava
Mota
Crepeta
Gaua (Santa Maria)
Lusalava
Mérig
Onetar
Méré Lava
Cap Nahoi
Wounpouko
Olpoy
Espiritu Santo
1463
Big Bay
Port Olry
Naone
Maewo
Malao
Hog Harbour
Tabwemasana
Lonbaha
Nasawa
Wousi
1879
Walaha
Passage
Lolvavana
Santo (Luganville)
Vatavoui
Aoba (Omba)
Karenaoura
Malo
Batnavni
Pentecost Island (Ile Pentecôte)
Farsari
Norsup
Olal
Sarmet
Ranon
Ambrym
Malakula
891
Ouro
Mt. Marum 1334
Lamap
Lalinda
Toak
(Port Sandwich)
Paama
Lopevi
Benehour
Lamen
Bouroumba
Epi
Coral Sea
Lamboukouti
Tongoa (Kuwaé)
Shepherd Group
Émaé
Nguna
Émao
Moso
Éfate (Vaté)
Forari Mine
Port-Vila
Eton
914
Port Narevin
Dillons Bay
Erromango
Happy Land
Aniwa
Tanna
Isangel
1042
Futuna (Erronan)
Port Patrick
Aneityum
850
Duff Is.
Tuleki
Lakao
Kahua
Taumako
Nupani
Fenualoa
Lipe
Lomlom
OCEAN
Ndende
Matu
Cape Byron
Nanggu
Tomotu Noi
Santa Cruz Islands
Nembao
Utupua
Vanikoro
Tevai
Paeu Bay
Puma
Astrolabe Point
Anuta
Fataka
Tikopia
Nauru
Scale 1:150 000
0 1 2 km
Ewa
Anabar
Baiti
Ijuw
Nibok
Denigomodu
65
Anibare
Buada Lagoon
Anibare Bay
Aiwo
Boe
Meneng
Meneng Point
Yaren
Ahau
Rotuma (Fiji)
Fiji
Scale 1:5 000 000
0 50 100 km
Cikobia
Vetauua
Udu Point
Cakau Vucovuco
Qelelevu
Cakau Matacucu
Nukubasaga
Great Sea Reef
Ringgold Isles
Vanua Levu
Labasa
Tabwewa
Rabi
Cobia
Yanuca
Savusavu
Natewa Bay
Taveuni
Somosomo
Laucala
Qamea
Nanuku Passage
Wailagi Lala
Naitaba
South Cape
Kibobo Islets
Vanua Balavu
Cikobia-i-lau
Lomaloma
Munia
Northern Lau Group
Katafaga
Tuvuca
Yaroua
Cicia
Mabula
Reid Reef
Lakeba Passage
Lakeba
Tubou
Bukatatonoa Reefs
Oneata
Southern Lau Group
Moce
Nasau
Komo
Namuka
Namuka-i-lau
Kabara
Navutu-i-ra
Yagasa
Navutu-i-loma
Fulaga
Ogea Levu
Ogea Driki
Vatoa
Ono-i-lau
Doi
Tuvana-i-colo
Tuvana-i-ra
Koro Sea
Koro
Namacu
Vatu Vara
Naigani
Wakaya
Makogai
Batiki
Nairai
Gau
Levuka
Moturiki
Bau Island
Nausori
Suva
Viti Levu
Lautoka
Nadi
Ba
Tavua
Rakiraki
Vatukoula
1323
Tomanivi
Nanukuloa
Ellington
Vatu-i-ra Channel
Namosi Peaks
1204
Sigatoka
Korolevu
Navua
Beqa Passage
Beqa
Beqa Barrier Reef
Kadavu Passage
North Astrolabe Reef
Great Astrolabe Reef
Buliya
Ono
Kadavu
Vunisea
Tavuki
838
Yasawa Group
Yasawa
Nacula
Naviti
Waya
Viwa
Wayasewa
Mamanuka-i-cake Group
Malolo
Malolo Barrier Reef
Yanuya
Tavua
Mana
Vatulele
Ekubu
Lomawai
Yanuca
Moala Group
Moala
469
Naroi
Totoya
Tovu
Matuku
Lomati
Vanua Vatu
Tuva Na Sici
Olorua
Vuaqava
Marabo
Udu
PACIFIC OCEAN
Boundaries
international
Physical features
marsh
coral reef
Cities and towns
more than 100 000 inhabitants
10 000 – 100 000 inhabitants
less than 10 000 inhabitants
Communications
main road
secondary road
railway
major airport
Land height
metres
1000
500
300
200
100
sea level
spot height in metres

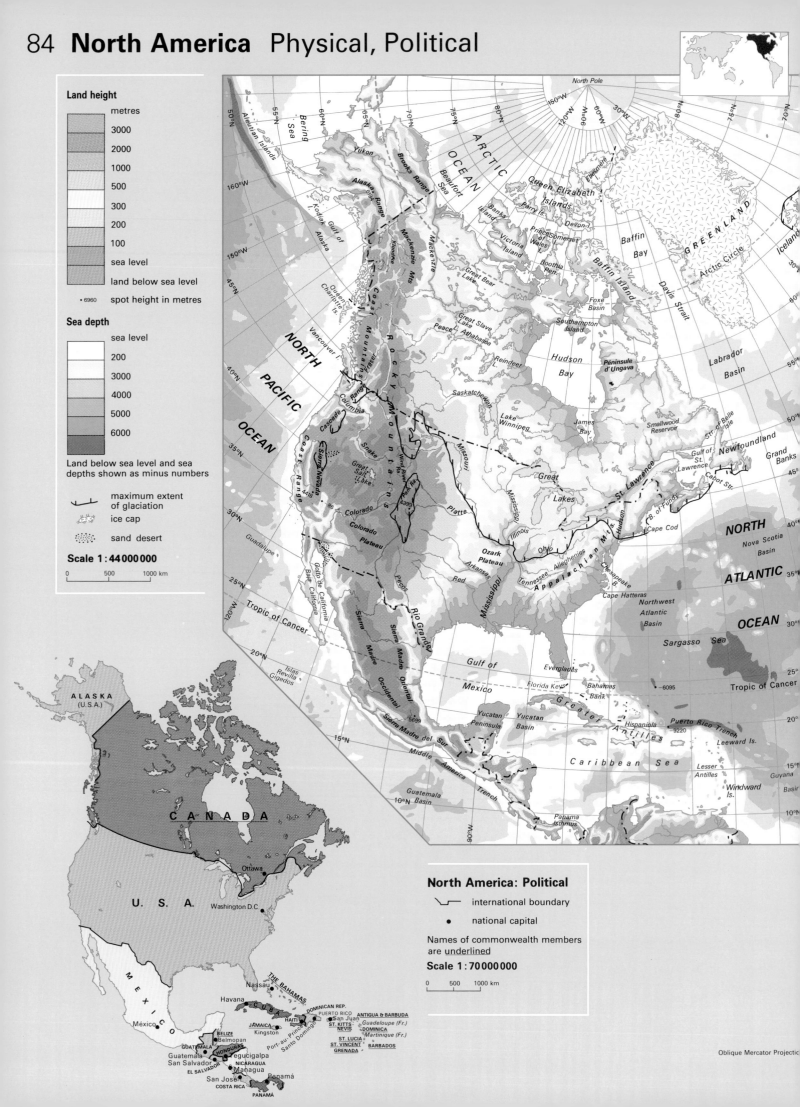

Land height

metres

3000
2000
1000
500
300
200
100
sea level
land below sea level

• 6960   spot height in metres

Sea depth

sea level
200
3000
4000
5000
6000

Land below sea level and sea
depths shown as minus numbers

maximum extent
of glaciation

ice cap

sand desert

Scale 1 : 44 000 000

0   500   1000 km

North America: Political

international boundary

• national capital

Names of commonwealth members
are underlined

Scale 1 : 70 000 000

0   500   1000 km

Oblique Mercator Projection

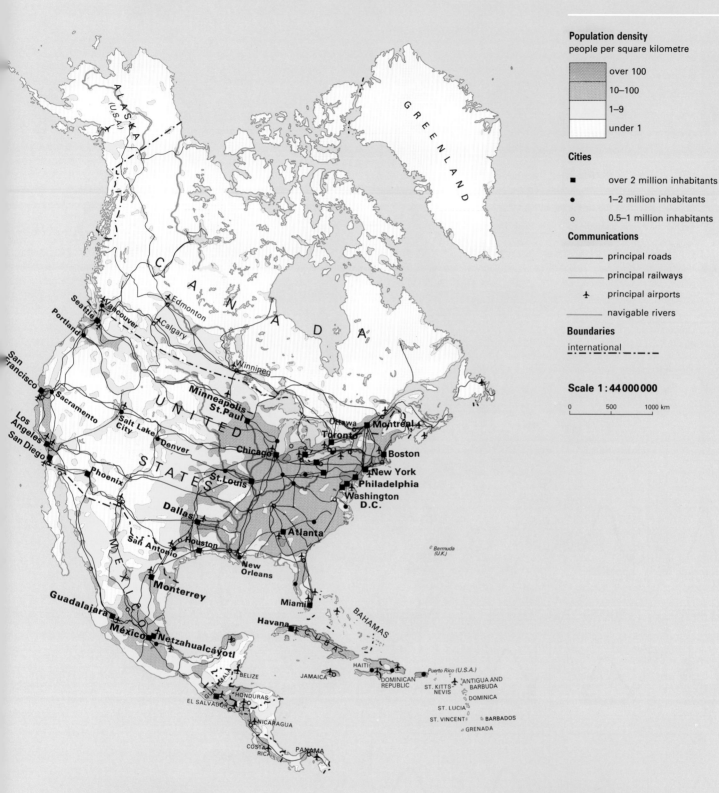

Population density
people per square kilometre

- over 100
- 10–100
- 1–9
- under 1

Cities

- ■ over 2 million inhabitants
- ● 1–2 million inhabitants
- ○ 0.5–1 million inhabitants

Communications

- ——— principal roads
- ——— principal railways
- ✈ principal airports
- ——— navigable rivers

Boundaries

international

Scale 1 : 44 000 000

0   500   1000 km

Canada:Population,1990

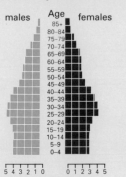

males   Age   females

85+
80–84
75–79
70–74
65–69
60–64
55–59
50–54
45–49
40–44
35–39
30–34
25–29
20–24
15–19
10–14
5–9
0–4

5 4 3 2 1 0   0 1 2 3 4 5
percent of total population

Total population:26.6 million
Crude Birth Rate per thousand:15
Crude Death Rate per thousand:7

Mexico:Population,1985

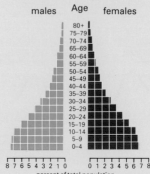

males   Age   females

80+
75–79
70–74
65–69
60–64
55–59
50–54
45–49
40–44
35–39
30–34
25–29
20–24
15–19
10–14
5–9
0–4

8 7 6 5 4 3 2 1 0   0 1 2 3 4 5 6 7 8
percent of total population

Total population:78.5 million
Crude Birth Rate per thousand:29
Crude Death Rate per thousand:6

© Oxford University Press

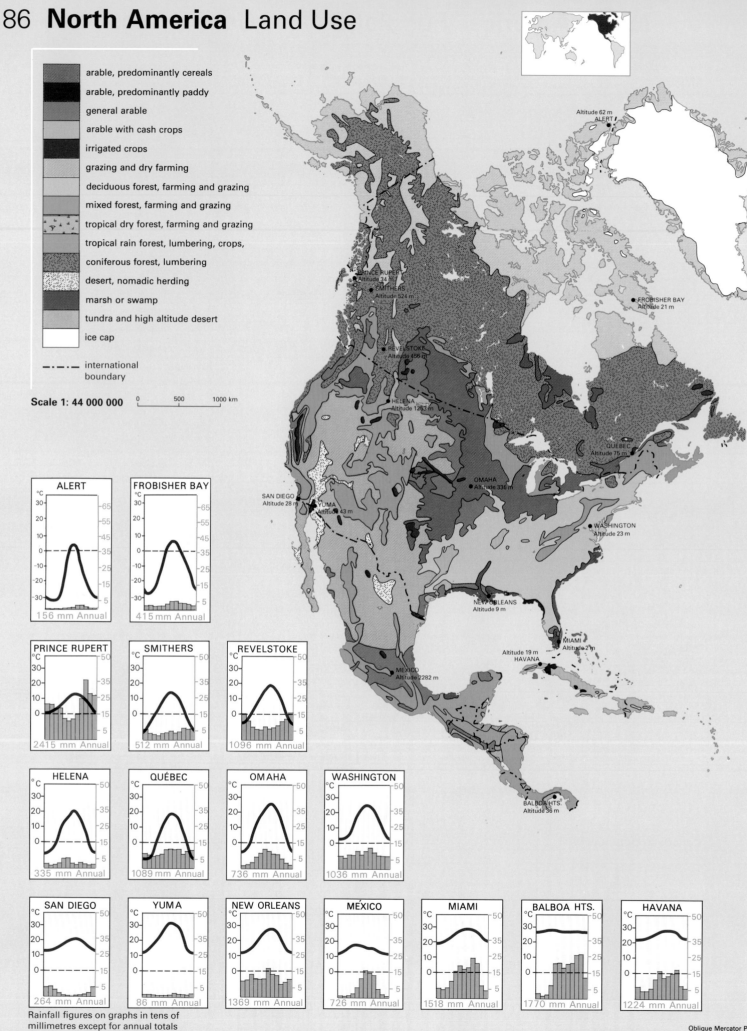

Legend:
- arable, predominantly cereals
- arable, predominantly paddy
- general arable
- arable with cash crops
- irrigated crops
- grazing and dry farming
- deciduous forest, farming and grazing
- mixed forest, farming and grazing
- tropical dry forest, farming and grazing
- tropical rain forest, lumbering, crops,
- coniferous forest, lumbering
- desert, nomadic herding
- marsh or swamp
- tundra and high altitude desert
- ice cap

–·–·– international boundary

Scale 1: 44 000 000

0   500   1000 km

ALERT — 156 mm Annual

FROBISHER BAY — 415 mm Annual

PRINCE RUPERT — 2415 mm Annual

SMITHERS — 512 mm Annual

REVELSTOKE — 1096 mm Annual

HELENA — 335 mm Annual

QUÉBEC — 1089 mm Annual

OMAHA — 736 mm Annual

WASHINGTON — 1036 mm Annual

SAN DIEGO — 264 mm Annual

YUMA — 86 mm Annual

NEW ORLEANS — 1369 mm Annual

MÉXICO — 726 mm Annual

MIAMI — 1518 mm Annual

BALBOA HTS. — 1770 mm Annual

HAVANA — 1224 mm Annual

Rainfall figures on graphs in tens of millimetres except for annual totals

Map labels:
- Altitude 62 m / ALERT
- FROBISHER BAY / Altitude 21 m
- PRINCE RUPERT / Altitude 34 m
- SMITHERS / Altitude 524 m
- REVELSTOKE / Altitude 456 m
- HELENA / Altitude 1253 m
- QUÉBEC / Altitude 75 m
- OMAHA / Altitude 336 m
- SAN DIEGO / Altitude 28 m
- YUMA / Altitude 43 m
- WASHINGTON / Altitude 23 m
- NEW ORLEANS / Altitude 9 m
- MIAMI / Altitude 2 m
- Altitude 19 m / HAVANA
- MÉXICO / Altitude 2282 m
- BALBOA HTS. / Altitude 36 m

Oblique Mercator Projection

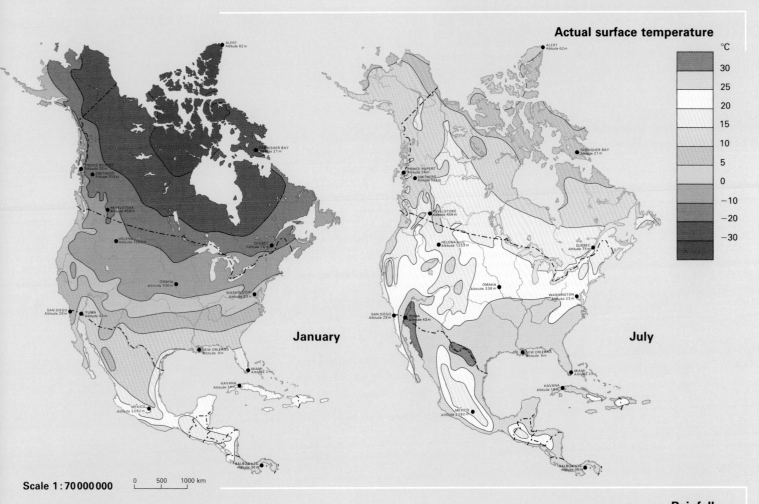

Actual surface temperature

°C
30
25
20
15
10
5
0
−10
−20
−30

January

July

Scale 1 : 70 000 000

0   500   1000 km

© Oxford University Press

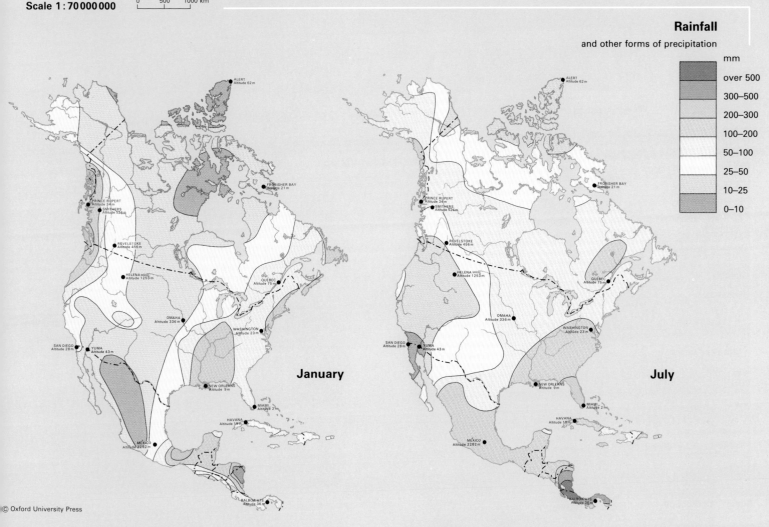

Rainfall

and other forms of precipitation

mm
over 500
300–500
200–300
100–200
50–100
25–50
10–25
0–10

January

July

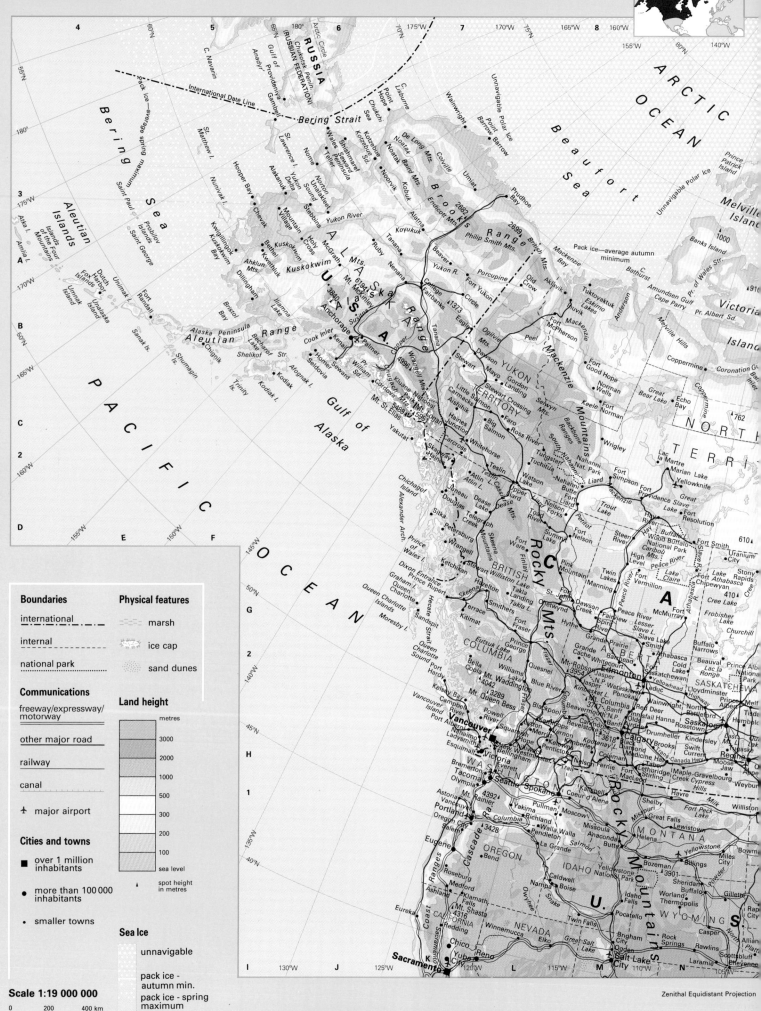

ARCTIC OCEAN
Beaufort Sea
PACIFIC OCEAN
Bering Sea
Aleutian Islands
Gulf of Alaska

RUSSIA (RUSSIAN FEDERATION)
U.S.A. ALASKA
YUKON TERRITORY
BRITISH COLUMBIA
ALBERTA
SASKATCHEWAN
NORTHWEST TERRITORIES
ROCKY Mts.
WASHINGTON
OREGON
IDAHO
MONTANA
WYOMING
NEVADA
CALIFORNIA
U.S.A.

Boundaries
international
internal
national park

Communications
freeway/expressway/motorway
other major road
railway
canal
✈ major airport

Cities and towns
■ over 1 million inhabitants
● more than 100 000 inhabitants
• smaller towns

Physical features
marsh
ice cap
sand dunes

Land height
metres
3000
2000
1000
500
300
200
100
sea level
▲ spot height in metres

Sea Ice
unnavigable
pack ice - autumn min.
pack ice - spring maximum

Scale 1:19 000 000
0   200   400 km

Zenithal Equidistant Projection

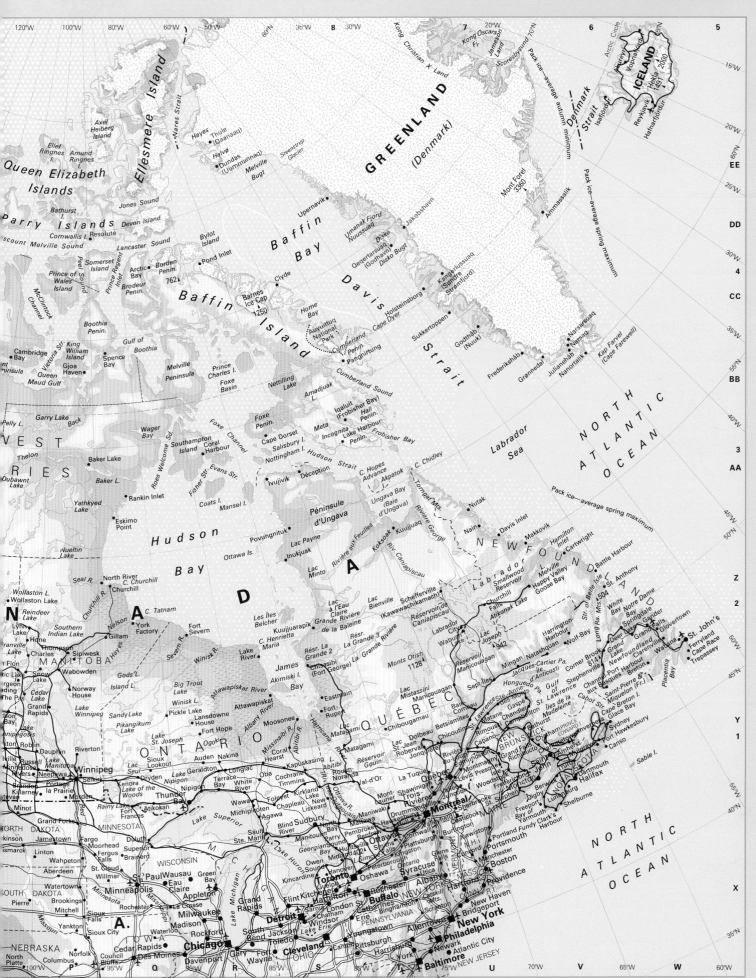

© Oxford University Press

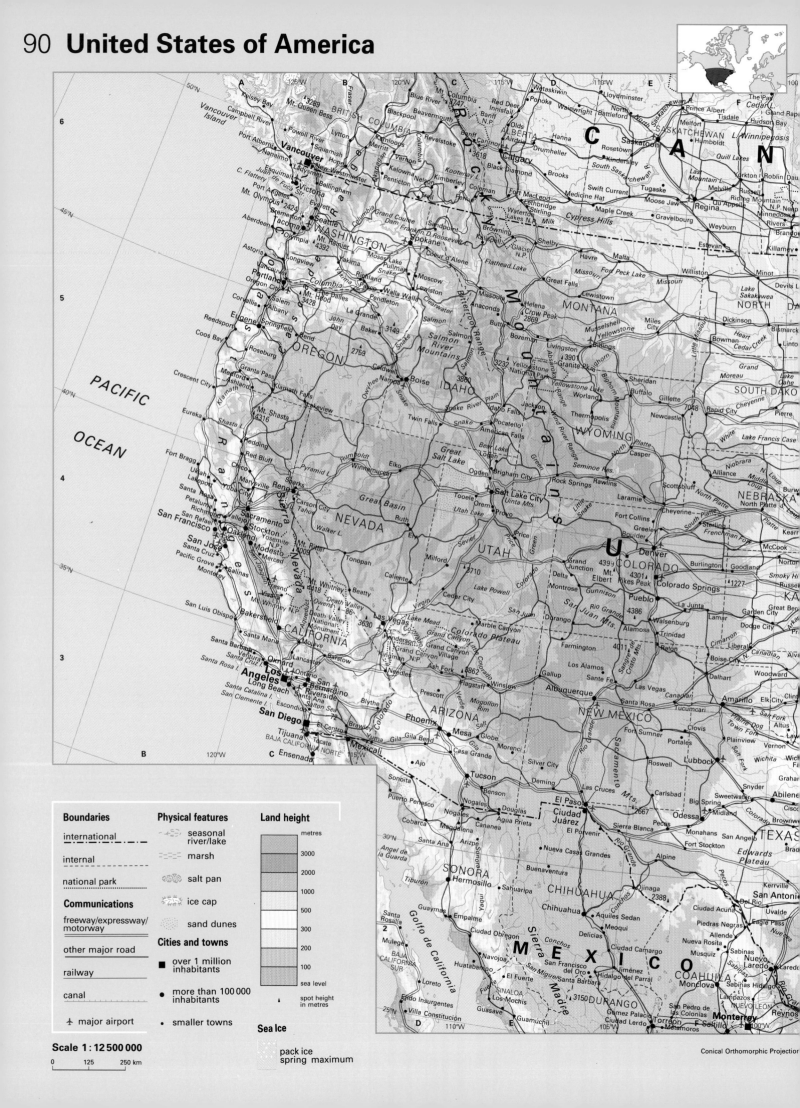

Boundaries

international

internal

national park

Communications

freeway/expressway/motorway

other major road

railway

canal

✈ major airport

Physical features

seasonal river/lake

marsh

salt pan

ice cap

sand dunes

Cities and towns

■ over 1 million inhabitants

● more than 100 000 inhabitants

• smaller towns

Land height

metres
3000
2000
1000
500
300
200
100
sea level

▲ spot height in metres

Sea Ice

pack ice
spring maximum

Scale 1 : 12 500 000

0   125   250 km

Conical Orthomorphic Projection

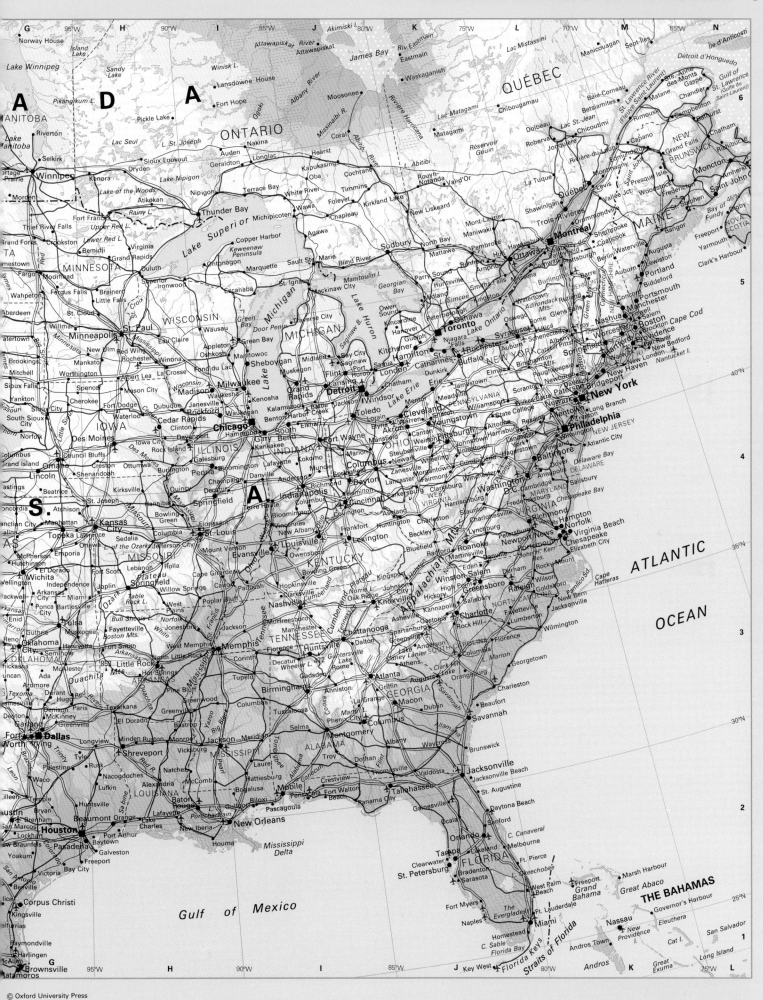

© Oxford University Press

Boundaries

international

internal

national park

Communications

freeway/expressway/
motorway

other major road

railway

canal

✈ major airport

Cities and towns

◇ built-up areas

■ over 1 million
inhabitants

● more than 100 000
inhabitants

• smaller towns

Physical features

seasonal
river/lake

marsh

Land height

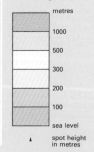

metres
1000
500
300
200
100
sea level

▲ spot height
in metres

Scale 1 : 6 250 000

0   25   50 km

Conical Orthomorphic Projection

© Oxford University Press

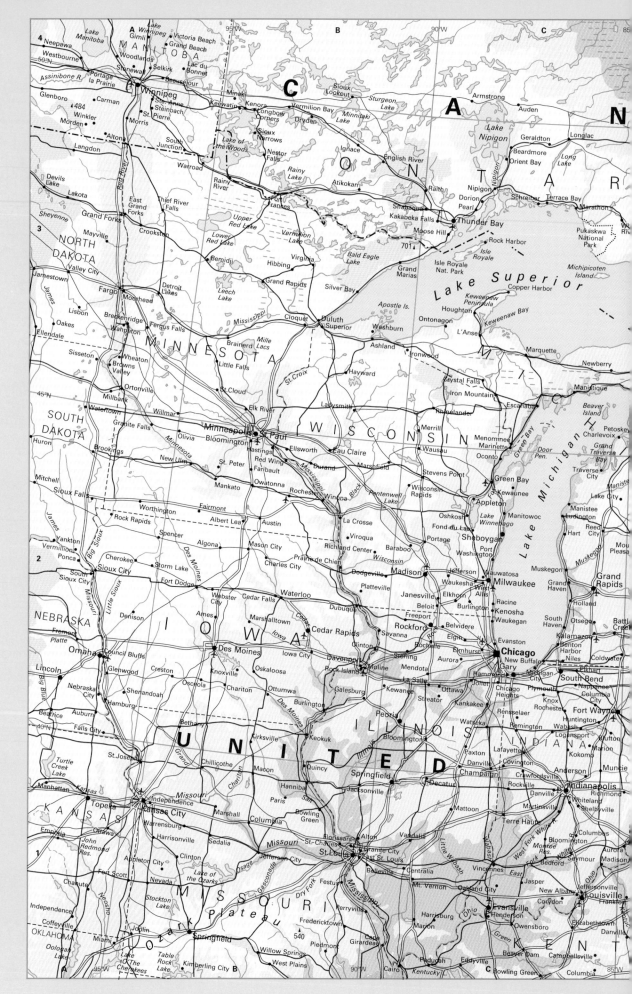

C A N A D A
Q U É B E C
O N T A R I O
U N I T E D S T A T E S
NEW YORK
PENNSYLVANIA
OHIO
WEST VIRGINIA
VIRGINIA
MAINE
NEW HAMPSHIRE
VERMONT
NEW BRUNSWICK
NEW JERSEY
DELAWARE
MARYLAND
ATLANTIC OCEAN
James Bay
Lake Huron
Georgian Bay
Lake Erie
Lake Ontario
Lake Champlain
Lake Abitibi
Réservoir Gouin
Réservoir Cabonga
Réservoir Baskatong
Lac Mistassini
Lac Manouane
Lac Matagami
Kesagami Lake
Lac St.-Jean
Saguenay R.
St. Lawrence (St. Laurent)
Ottawa
Moose River
Abitibi River
Albany River
Missinaibi River
Mattagami River
Groundhog
Harricanaw R.
Nottaway R.
Rivière aux Outardes
Manicouagan
Péribonca R.
Saginaw Bay
Long Island Sd.
Long Island
Cape Cod
Cape Ann
Massachusetts Bay
Nantucket Sd.
Nantucket I.
Martha's Vineyard
Delaware Bay
Chesapeake Bay
Adirondack Mountains
Green Mts.
White Mts.
Catskill Mts.
Allegheny Mts.
Appalachian Mountains
Blue Ridge
Shenandoah Mts.
Moosonee
Fort Rupert
Baie-du-Poste
Chibougamau
Otter Rapids
Coral
Hearst
Mattice
Kapuskasing
Cochrane
Iroquois Falls
Timmins
Foleyet
Kirkland Lake
Noranda
Rouyn
Val-d'Or
Malartic
Chapleau
Englehart
New Liskeard
Angliers
Témiscaming
North Bay
Sudbury
Coniston
Mattawa
Deep River
Pembroke
Maniwaki
Mont-Laurier
L'Annonciation
La Tuque
Dolbeau
Mistassini
St.-Félicien
Roberval
Alma
Jonquière
Chicoutimi
Tadoussac
Baie Comeau
Chute-aux-Outardes
Betsiamites
Forestville
Baie Trinité
Matane
Sayabec
Mont-Joli
Rimouski
Trois-Pistoles
Rivière-du-Loup
Québec
Lévis
Trois Rivières
Montréal
Sherbrooke
Ottawa
Kingston
Toronto
Mississauga
Hamilton
Kitchener
London
Windsor
Sarnia
St. Catharines
Niagara Falls
Buffalo
Rochester
Syracuse
Utica
Albany
Schenectady
Binghamton
Erie
Cleveland
Toledo
Detroit
Lansing
Flint
Saginaw
Akron
Youngstown
Canton
Pittsburgh
Columbus
Dayton
Springfield
Cincinnati
Harrisburg
Allentown
Scranton
Reading
Philadelphia
New York
Newark
Brooklyn
Bronx
Manhattan
Queens
Trenton
Baltimore
Washington D.C.
Annapolis
Richmond
Norfolk
Portsmouth
Newport News
Hampton
Roanoke
Lynchburg
Charleston
Huntington
Wheeling
Morgantown
Hagerstown
Wilmington
Atlantic City
Cape May
Ocean City
Dover
Hartford
New Haven
Bridgeport
Providence
Worcester
Boston
Springfield
Manchester
Nashua
Concord
Portsmouth
Portland
Augusta
Bangor
Lewiston
Burlington
Montpelier
Plattsburgh
New Bedford
Fall River
Provincetown
80°W
75°W
70°W
50°N
45°N
40°N
1190
1628
1605
1916
1281
774
1481

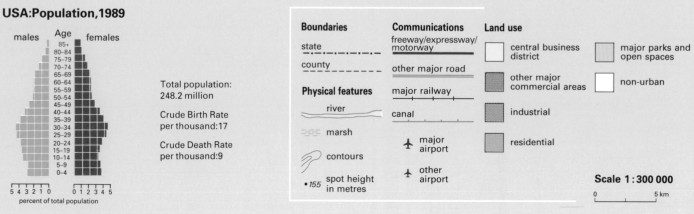

USA:Population, 1989

males   Age   females

Age
85+
80–84
75–79
70–74
65–69
60–64
55–59
50–54
45–49
40–44
35–39
30–34
25–29
20–24
15–19
10–14
5–9
0–4

5 4 3 2 1 0   0 1 2 3 4 5
percent of total population

Total population:
248.2 million

Crude Birth Rate
per thousand: 17

Crude Death Rate
per thousand: 9

Boundaries
state
county

Physical features
river
marsh
contours
•155 spot height
in metres

Communications
freeway/expressway/
motorway
other major road
major railway
canal
✈ major
airport
✈ other
airport

Land use
central business
district
other major
commercial areas
industrial
residential
major parks and
open spaces
non-urban

Scale 1 : 300 000
0   5 km

San Fernando Airport
Van Norman Lake
San Fernando
GOLDEN STATE FREEWAY
Sunland
Tujunga
MOUNT LUKENS 1853
La Crescenta
La Canada
Altadena

SAN GABRIEL MOUNTAINS
Big Tujunga Reservoir
ANGELES NATIONAL FOREST
Mount Wilson Observatory 1740
Cogswell Reservoir
San Gabriel Reservoir
1569

STA. MONICA MOUNTAINS
Van Nuys
Sepulveda Dam Recreational Area
North Hollywood
Los Angeles River
HOLLYWOOD BURBANK AIRPORT
BURBANK
Brand Park
Devils Gate Reservoir
Rose Bowl
PASADENA
Eaton Wash Reservoir
Arcadia
Azusa
Big Santa Anita Reservoir
Sawpit Canyon Reservoir
Morris Reservoir

GLENDALE
Griffith Park
Hollywood Reservoir
Hollywood Bowl
Stone Canyon Reservoir 397
Franklin Canyon Reservoir
Beverly Hills
Hollywood
Silver Lake Reservoir
HOLLYWOOD FREEWAY
Elysian Park
ALHAMBRA
San Gabriel
Rosemead
EL MONTE AIRPORT
El Monte
Temple City
Santa Fe Flood Control Basin
Baldwin Park
Glendora
Covina
West Covina

LOS ANGELES
SANTA MONICA
West Los Angeles
SANTA MONICA FREEWAY
Civic Center
East Los Angeles
Monterey Park
Montebello
Whittier Narrows Dam Reservoir Area
La Puente
SAN BERNADINO FREEWAY
POMONA FREEWAY

SANTA MONICA AIRPORT
Culver City
Marina del Rey
INGLEWOOD
LOS ANGELES AIRPORT
Hawthorne
Manhattan Beach
Lawndale
Gardena
Redondo Beach
SOUTH GATE
DOWNEY
Pico Rivera
Rio Hondo
San Gabriel River
SAN GABRIEL RIVER FREEWAY
Whittier
431
LOS ANGELES COUNTY
ORANGE COUNTY
La Habra
NORWALK
Fullerton Reservoir
Brea Reservoir
FULLERTON AIRPORT
FULLERTON

COMPTON
COMPTON AIRPORT
Bellflower
LONG BEACH FREEWAY
LAKEWOOD
Los Angeles River
HARBOR FREEWAY
TORRANCE
Carson
TORRANCE AIRPORT
LONG BEACH AIRPORT
SANTA ANA FREEWAY
Buena Park
RIVERSIDE FREEWAY
Knotts Berry Farm
ANAHEIM
Disneyland
GARDEN GROVE
Orange
Santa Ana River

PALOS VERDES HILLS
San Pedro 396
300
150
Marineland of the Pacific
LONG BEACH
San Pedro Bay
Coyote Creek
Westminster
SAN DIEGO FREEWAY
SANTA ANA
Sunset Beach
Fountain Valley
Huntington Beach

Pacific Ocean
San Pedro Channel

118°15'W
118°00'W
900
1830
1525
1220
34°15'N
600
900
1220
600
300
34°00'N
150
33°45'N

© Oxford University Press

Boundaries
international
internal
national park

Communications
freeway/expressway/motorway
other major road
track
railway
canal

✈ major airport

Cities and towns
◊ built-up areas
■ over 1 million inhabitants
● more than 100 000 inhabitants
• smaller towns

Physical features
seasonal river/lake
marsh
sand dunes

Land height

metres
3000
2000
1000
500
300
200
100
sea level
land below sea level

▲ spot height in metres

Scale 1:16 000 000
0   200   400km
main map only

Scale 1:1 250 000
0   25 km

Trinidad

Barbados

Scale 1:1 000 000
0

PACIFIC OCEAN

Gulf of

Caribbean Sea

ATLANTIC OCEAN

Gulf of Paria

Columbus Channel

ATLANTIC OCEAN

Panama Canal
Scale 1:1 500 000

The canal, opened in 1914, is 82 km long, including approaches (actual canal 64 km). Minimum depth 12 m, minimum width 152 m (Gaillard Cut). Time of passage 8 hours. In 1990 11 941 vessels used the canal carrying 157 072 978 tonnes of cargo. In 1979 Panama assumed control of the former Canal Zone, with the USA retaining majority representation on the Panama Commission until 1989. US military forces will remain in Panama until the year 2000 and the USA will be entitled to defend the Canal's neutrality thereafter.

Jamaica

Zenithal Equidistant Projection
© Oxford University Press

Scale 1:3 000 000

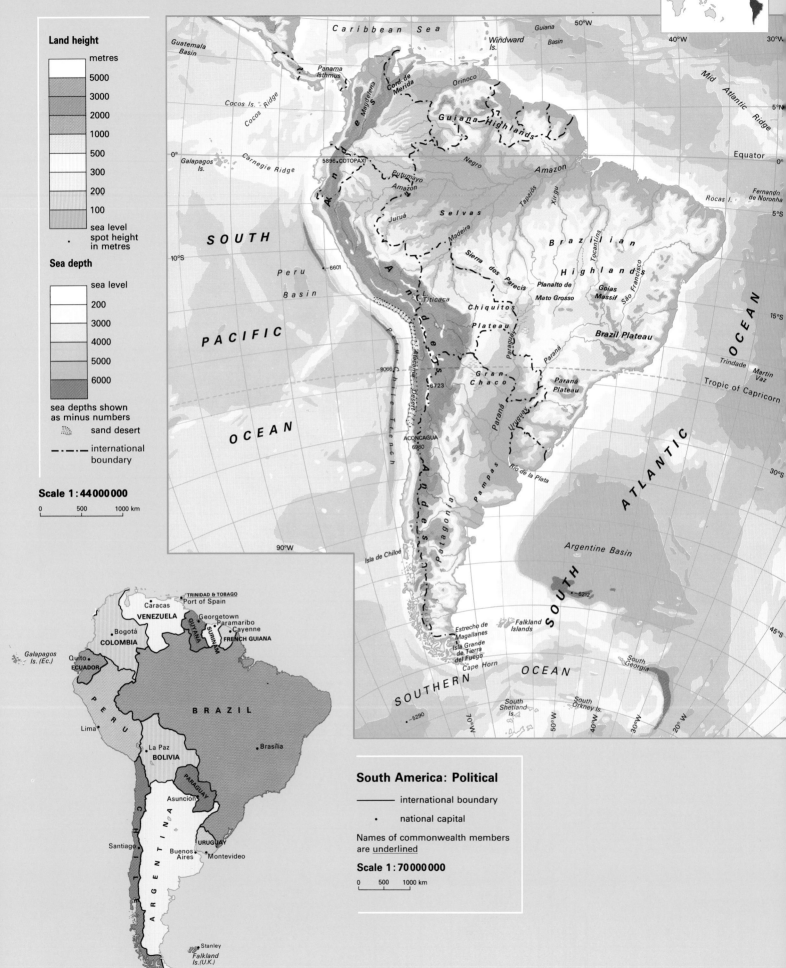

Land height

metres
5000
3000
2000
1000
500
300
200
100
sea level

• spot height in metres

Sea depth

sea level
200
3000
4000
5000
6000

sea depths shown as minus numbers

sand desert

international boundary

Scale 1 : 44 000 000

0   500   1000 km

Caribbean Sea

Guatemala Basin

Panama Isthmus

Cocos Is. Ridge

Cocos Is.

Galapagos Is.

Carnegie Ridge

Windward Is.

Guiana Basin

Mid Atlantic Ridge

Orinoco

Cord. de Merida

Guiana Highlands

Magdalena

Anders

Putumayo

Amazon

5896 COTOPAXI

Amazon

Negro

Juruá

Selvas

Madeira

Tapajós

Xingu

Rocas I.

Fernando de Noronha

SOUTH

Peru Basin

6601

Sierra dos Parecis

B r a z i l i a n

H i g h l a n d s

Tocantins

São Francisco

Titicaca

Planalto de Mato Grosso

Goias Massif

PACIFIC

Chiquitos Plateau

Brazil Plateau

8066

Atacama Desert

6723

G r a n   C h a c o

Paraguay

Paraná

Paraná Plateau

Trindade

Martin Vaz

Tropic of Capricorn

OCEAN

ACONCAGUA 6960

Uruguay

Paraná

Río de la Plata

ATLANTIC

Pampas

Patagonia

Argentine Basin

SOUTH

OCEAN

Isla de Chiloé

6212

Estrecho de Magallanes

Isla Grande de Tierra del Fuego

Cape Horn

Falkland Islands

South Georgia

SOUTHERN   OCEAN

5290

South Shetland Is.

South Orkney Is.

Oblique Mercator Projection

TRINIDAD & TOBAGO
Port of Spain

Caracas

VENEZUELA

Georgetown

Paramaribo

Cayenne

Bogotá

COLOMBIA

GUYANA

SURINAM

FRENCH GUIANA

Galapagos Is. (Ec.)

Quito

ECUADOR

Lima

PERU

B R A Z I L

La Paz

BOLIVIA

Brasília

PARAGUAY

Asunción

CHILE

ARGENTINA

Santiago

Buenos Aires

URUGUAY

Montevideo

Stanley

Falkland Is. (U.K.)

South America: Political

—— international boundary

• national capital

Names of commonwealth members are underlined

Scale 1 : 70 000 000

0   500   1000 km

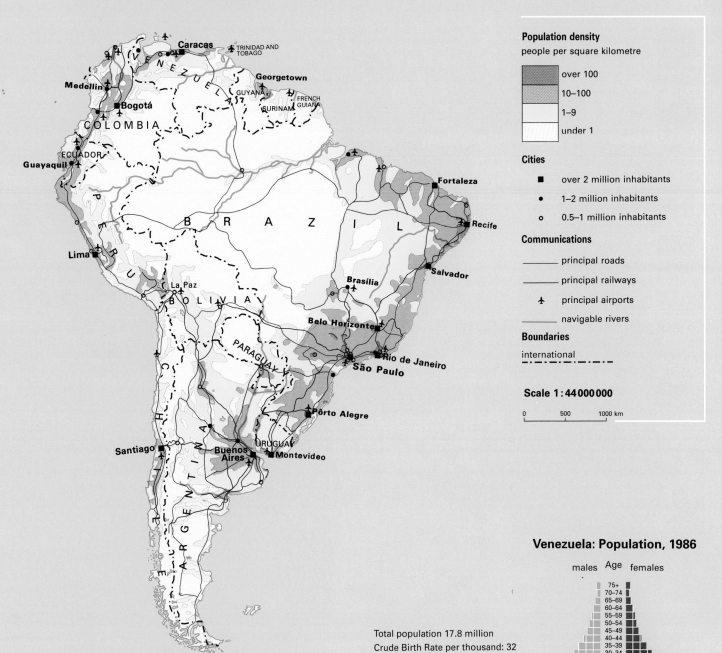

Population density
people per square kilometre

	over 100
	10–100
	1–9
	under 1

Cities

■ over 2 million inhabitants

● 1–2 million inhabitants

○ 0.5–1 million inhabitants

Communications

―――― principal roads

―――― principal railways

✈ principal airports

―――― navigable rivers

Boundaries

–·–·–·–·– international

Scale 1 : 44 000 000

0   500   1000 km

Venezuela: Population, 1986

males   Age   females

Total population 17.8 million
Crude Birth Rate per thousand: 32
Crude Death Rate per thousand: 5

percent of total population

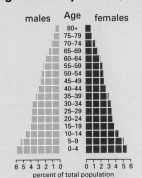

Argentina: Population, 1985

males   Age   females

percent of total population

Total population 30.6 million
Crude Birth Rate per thousand: 24
Crude Death Rate per thousand: 9

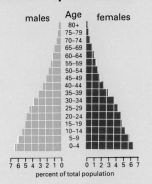

Brazil: Population, 1988

males   Age   females

percent of total population

Total population 144.4 million
Crude Birth Rate per thousand: 27
Crude Death Rate per thousand: 8

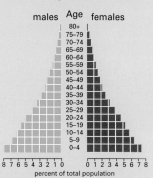

Peru: Population, 1985

males   Age   females

percent of total population

Total population 19.7 million
Crude Birth Rate per thousand: 33
Crude Death Rate per thousand: 10

Oblique Mercator Projection

© Oxford University Press

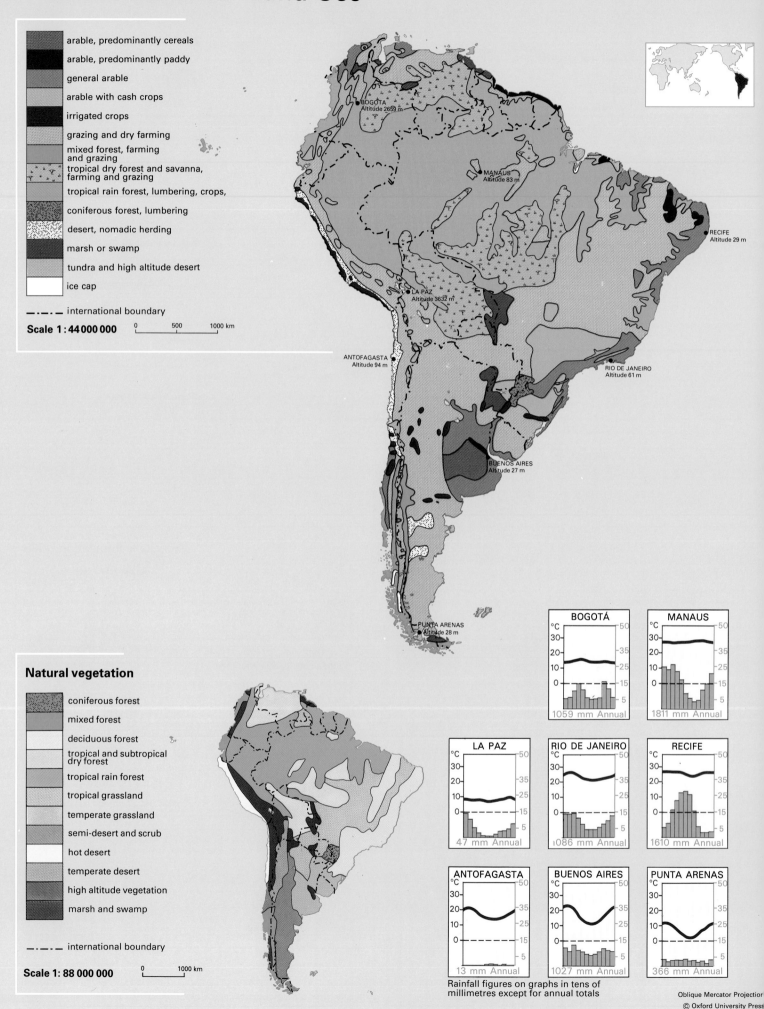

arable, predominantly cereals
arable, predominantly paddy
general arable
arable with cash crops
irrigated crops
grazing and dry farming
mixed forest, farming and grazing
tropical dry forest and savanna, farming and grazing
tropical rain forest, lumbering, crops,
coniferous forest, lumbering
desert, nomadic herding
marsh or swamp
tundra and high altitude desert
ice cap

— · — · — international boundary

Scale 1 : 44 000 000

0   500   1000 km

BOGOTÁ
Altitude 2659 m

MANAUS
Altitude 83 m

RECIFE
Altitude 29 m

LA PAZ
Altitude 3632 m

ANTOFAGASTA
Altitude 94 m

RIO DE JANEIRO
Altitude 61 m

BUENOS AIRES
Altitude 27 m

PUNTA ARENAS
Altitude 28 m

Natural vegetation

coniferous forest
mixed forest
deciduous forest
tropical and subtropical dry forest
tropical rain forest
tropical grassland
temperate grassland
semi-desert and scrub
hot desert
temperate desert
high altitude vegetation
marsh and swamp

— · — · — international boundary

Scale 1 : 88 000 000

0   1000 km

BOGOTÁ
°C   50
30   35
20   25
10   5
0   15
1059 mm Annual

MANAUS
°C   50
30   35
20   25
10   5
0   15
1811 mm Annual

LA PAZ
°C   50
30   35
20   25
10   5
0   15
47 mm Annual

RIO DE JANEIRO
°C   50
30   35
20   25
10   5
0   15
1086 mm Annual

RECIFE
°C   50
30   35
20   25
10   5
0   15
1610 mm Annual

ANTOFAGASTA
°C   50
30   35
20   25
10   5
0   15
13 mm Annual

BUENOS AIRES
°C   50
30   35
20   25
10   5
0   15
1027 mm Annual

PUNTA ARENAS
°C   50
30   35
20   25
10   5
0   15
366 mm Annual

Rainfall figures on graphs in tens of millimetres except for annual totals

Oblique Mercator Projection

© Oxford University Press

South America Climate 101

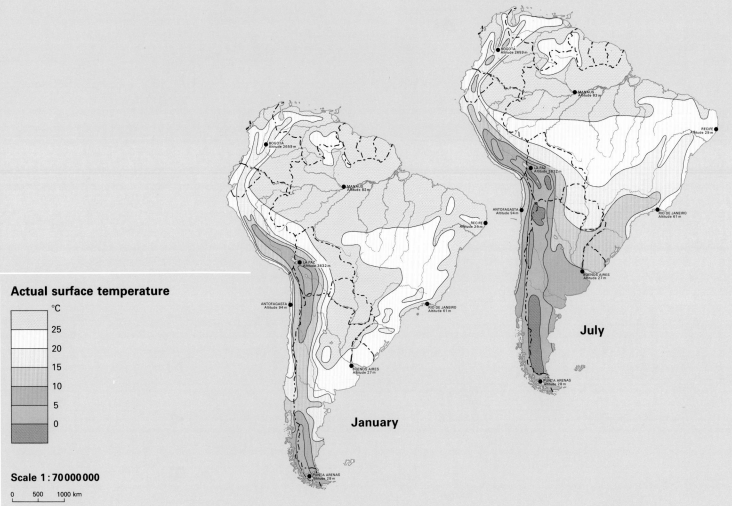

Actual surface temperature

°C
- 25
- 20
- 15
- 10
- 5
- 0

Scale 1 : 70 000 000

0   500   1000 km

January

July

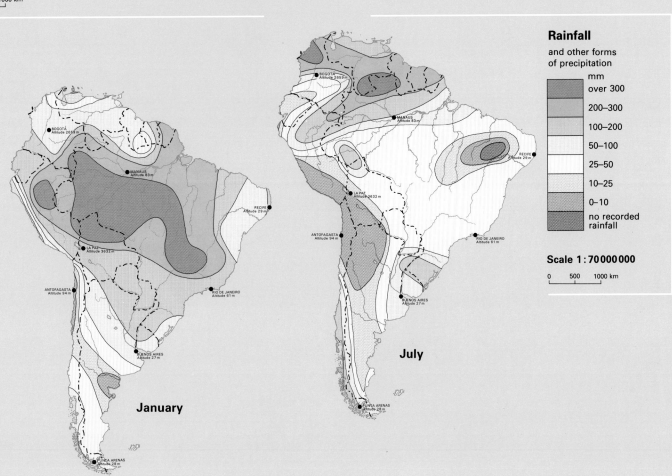

Rainfall
and other forms
of precipitation

mm
- over 300
- 200–300
- 100–200
- 50–100
- 25–50
- 10–25
- 0–10
- no recorded rainfall

Scale 1 : 70 000 000

0   500   1000 km

January

July

© Oxford University Press

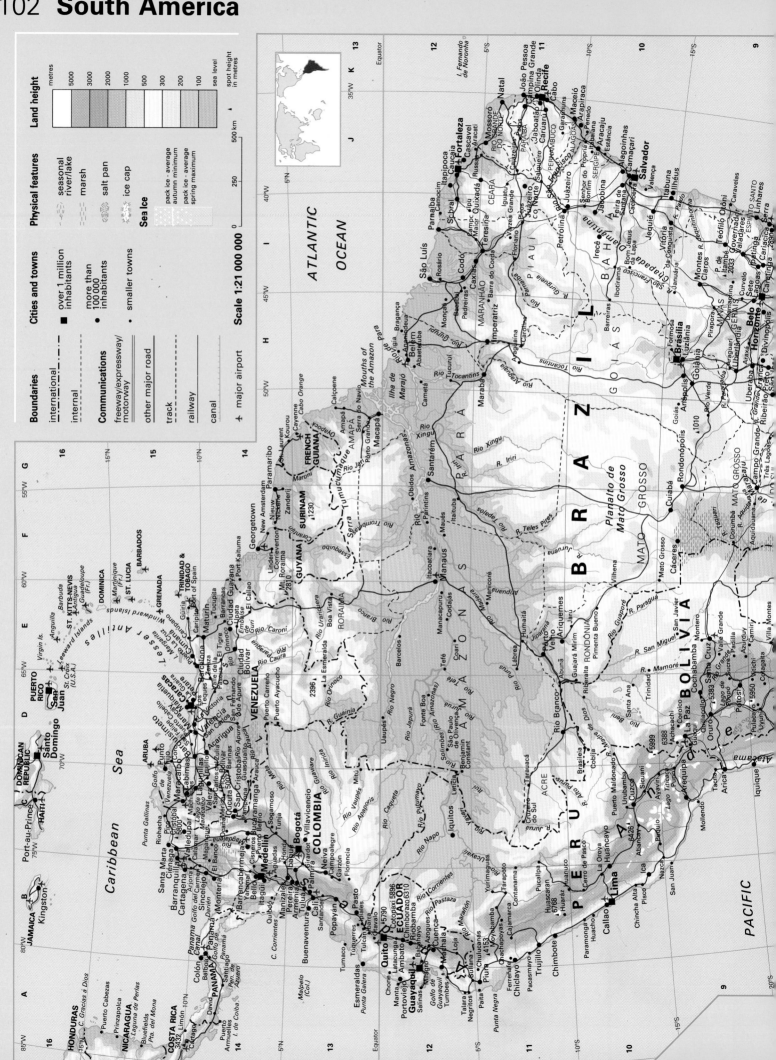
Boundaries
international
internal
Communications
freeway/expressway/motorway
other major road
track
railway
canal
major airport
Cities and towns
over 1 million inhabitants
more than 100 000 inhabitants
smaller towns
Scale 1:21 000 000
0
250
500 km
Physical features
seasonal river/lake
marsh
salt pan
ice cap
Sea Ice
pack ice - average autumn minimum
pack ice - average spring maximum
Land height
metres
5000
3000
2000
1000
500
300
200
100
sea level
spot height in metres
Caribbean Sea
ATLANTIC OCEAN
PACIFIC
Lesser Antilles
Leeward Islands
Windward Islands
JAMAICA
Kingston
HAITI
Port-au-Prince
DOMINICAN REPUBLIC
Santo Domingo
PUERTO RICO
San Juan
ST. KITTS-NEVIS
DOMINICA
ST. LUCIA
BARBADOS
GRENADA
TRINIDAD & TOBAGO
Port of Spain
ARUBA
HONDURAS
NICARAGUA
COSTA RICA
PANAMA
VENEZUELA
Caracas
Maracaibo
COLOMBIA
Bogotá
Medellín
Cali
ECUADOR
Quito
Guayaquil
PERU
Lima
BOLIVIA
La Paz
GUYANA
Georgetown
SURINAM
Paramaribo
FRENCH GUIANA
Cayenne
BRAZIL
AMAZONAS
PARÁ
Manaus
Belém
São Luís
Fortaleza
Natal
Recife
Salvador
Brasília
Goiânia
Belo Horizonte
Planalto de Mato Grosso
MATO GROSSO
Mouths of the Amazon
Ilha de Marajó
Rio Amazonas
Equator

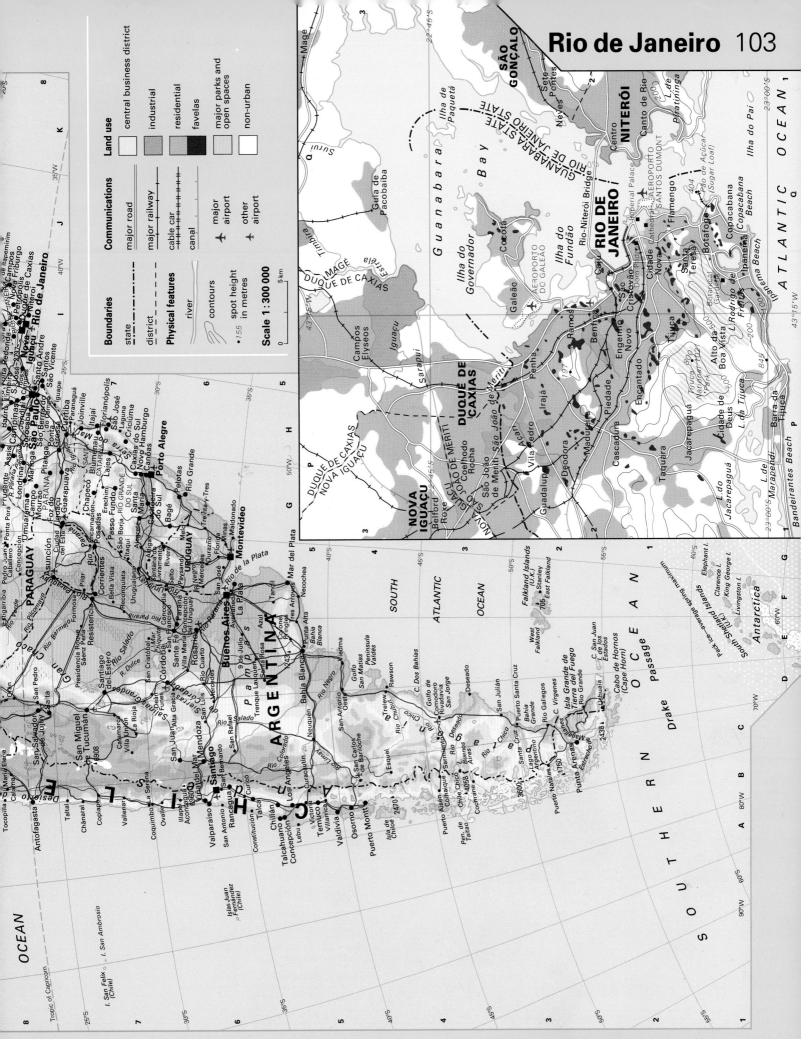

Boundaries
state
district

Physical features
river
canal

contours
• 55 spot height in metres

Communications
major road
major railway
cable car

✈ major airport
✈ other airport

Land use
central business district
industrial
residential
favelas
major parks and open spaces
non-urban

Scale 1 : 300 000

0   5 km

Transverse Mercator Projection
© Oxford University Press

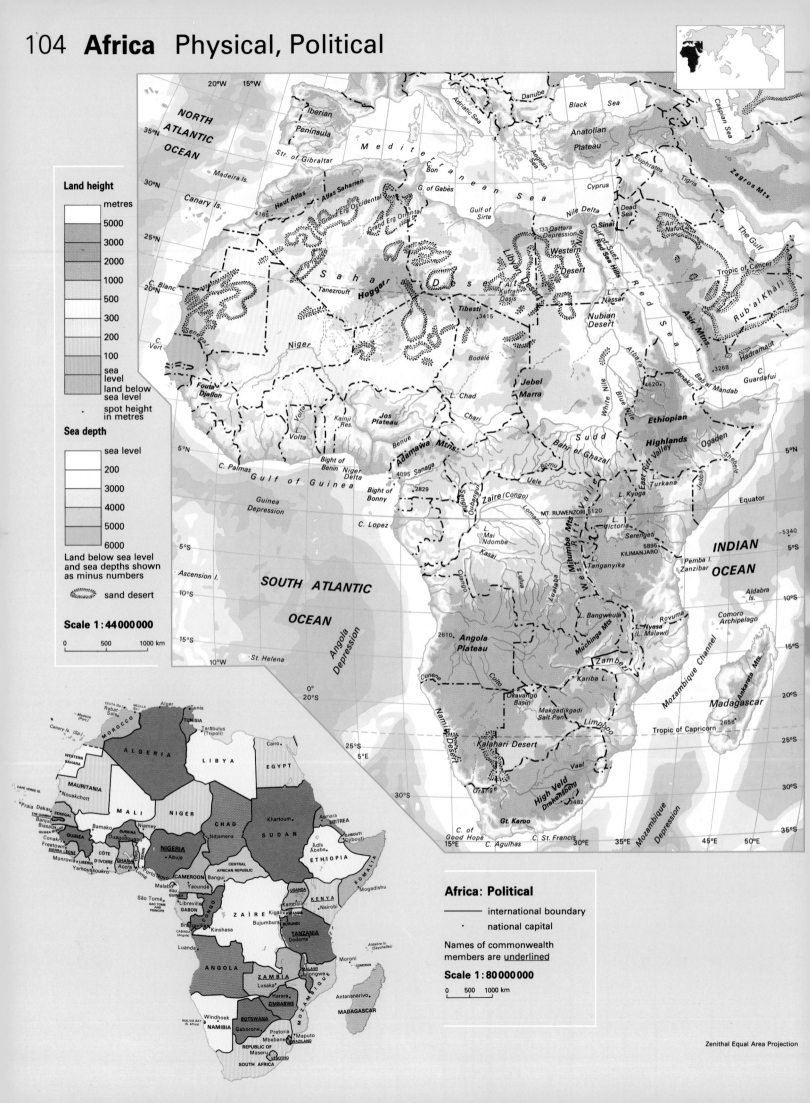

Land height

metres
5000
3000
2000
1000
500
300
200
100
sea level
land below sea level

. spot height in metres

Sea depth

sea level	
200	
3000	
4000	
5000	
6000	

Land below sea level and sea depths shown as minus numbers

 sand desert

Scale 1 : 44 000 000

0   500   1000 km

NORTH ATLANTIC OCEAN

SOUTH ATLANTIC OCEAN

INDIAN OCEAN

Mediterranean Sea

Red Sea

Sahara Desert

Libyan Desert

Western Desert

Nubian Desert

Ethiopian Highlands

Kalahari Desert

Namib Desert

Madagascar

Equator

Tropic of Cancer

Tropic of Capricorn

Africa: Political

—— international boundary

· national capital

Names of commonwealth members are underlined

Scale 1 : 80 000 000

0   500   1000 km

MOROCCO
WESTERN SAHARA
ALGERIA
TUNISIA
LIBYA
EGYPT
MAURITANIA
MALI
NIGER
CHAD
SUDAN
ERITREA
DJIBOUTI
ETHIOPIA
SOMALIA
SENEGAL
THE GAMBIA
GUINEA-BISSAU
GUINEA
SIERRA LEONE
LIBERIA
CÔTE D'IVOIRE
BURKINA
GHANA
TOGO
BENIN
NIGERIA
CAMEROON
CENTRAL AFRICAN REPUBLIC
EQU. GUINEA
GABON
CONGO
ZAÏRE
UGANDA
KENYA
RWANDA
BURUNDI
TANZANIA
ANGOLA
ZAMBIA
MALAWI
MOZAMBIQUE
ZIMBABWE
BOTSWANA
NAMIBIA
SOUTH AFRICA
SWAZILAND
LESOTHO
COMOROS
MADAGASCAR
CAPE VERDE IS.

Zenithal Equal Area Projection

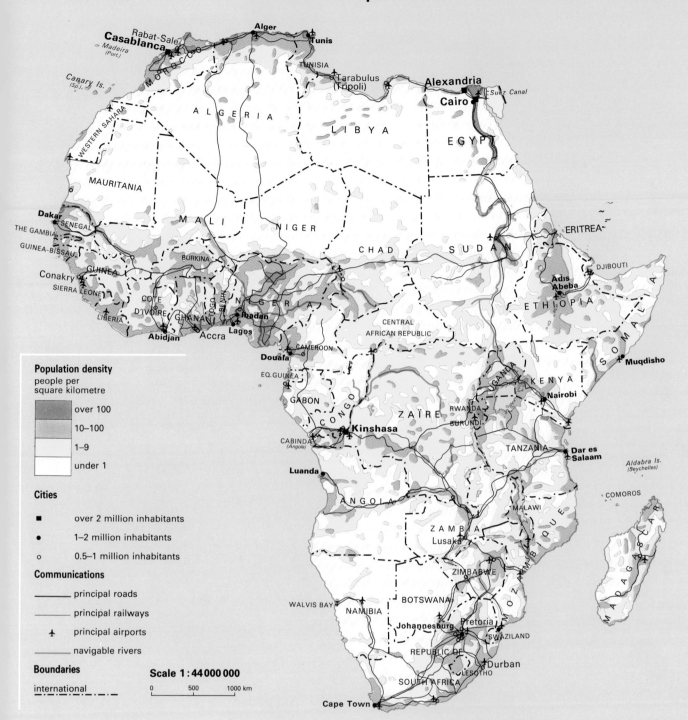

Population density

people per square kilometre

- over 100
- 10–100
- 1–9
- under 1

Cities

- ■ over 2 million inhabitants
- ● 1–2 million inhabitants
- ○ 0.5–1 million inhabitants

Communications

- —— principal roads
- —— principal railways
- ✈ principal airports
- —— navigable rivers

Boundaries

- international

Scale 1 : 44 000 000

0   500   1000 km

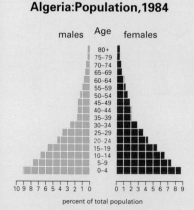

Algeria:Population,1984

males   Age   females

80+
75–79
70–74
65–69
60–64
55–59
50–54
45–49
40–44
35–39
30–34
25–29
20–24
15–19
10–14
5–9
0–4

10 9 8 7 6 5 4 3 2 1 0   0 1 2 3 4 5 6 7 8 9

percent of total population

Total Population:20.8 million

Crude Birth Rate per thousand:37

Crude Death Rate per thousand:10

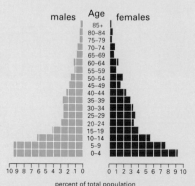

Ethiopia:Population,1989

males   Age   females

85+
80–84
75–79
70–74
65–69
60–64
55–59
50–54
45–49
40–44
35–39
30–34
25–29
20–24
15–19
10–14
5–9
0–4

10 9 8 7 6 5 4 3 2 1 0   0 1 2 3 4 5 6 7 8 9 10

percent of total population

Total population:49.5 million

Crude Birth Rate per thousand:49

Crude Death Rate per thousand:20

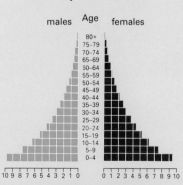

Zaïre:Population,1985

males   Age   females

80+
75–79
70–74
65–69
60–64
55–59
50–54
45–49
40–44
35–39
30–34
25–29
20–24
15–19
10–14
5–9
0–4

10 9 8 7 6 5 4 3 2 1 0   0 1 2 3 4 5 6 7 8 9 10

percent of total population

Total population:31 million

Crude Birth Rate per thousand:46

Crude Death Rate per thousand:14

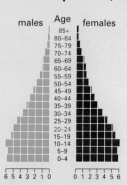

South Africa:Population,1985

males   Age   females

85+
80–84
75–79
70–74
65–69
60–64
55–59
50–54
45–49
40–44
35–39
30–34
25–29
20–24
15–19
10–14
5–9
0–4

6 5 4 3 2 1 0   0 1 2 3 4 5 6

percent of total population

Total population:23.4 million

Crude Birth Rate per thousand:35

Crude Death Rate per thousand:8

© Oxford University Press

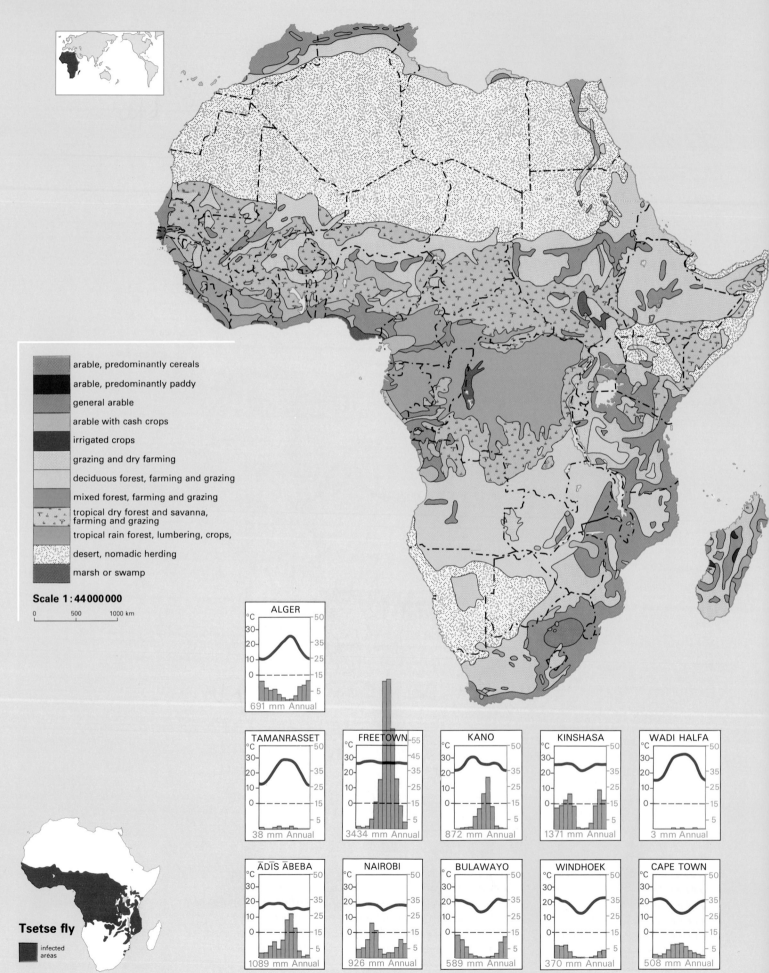

arable, predominantly cereals

arable, predominantly paddy

general arable

arable with cash crops

irrigated crops

grazing and dry farming

deciduous forest, farming and grazing

mixed forest, farming and grazing

tropical dry forest and savanna, farming and grazing

tropical rain forest, lumbering, crops,

desert, nomadic herding

marsh or swamp

Scale 1:44 000 000

0   500   1000 km

Tsetse fly

infected areas

ALGER
°C   50
30
20   35
10   25
0   15
          5
691 mm Annual

TAMANRASSET
°C   50
30
20   35
10   25
0   15
          5
38 mm Annual

FREETOWN
°C   55
30   45
20   35
10   25
0   15
          5
3434 mm Annual

KANO
°C   50
30
20   35
10   25
0   15
          5
872 mm Annual

KINSHASA
°C   50
30
20   35
10   25
0   15
          5
1371 mm Annual

WADI HALFA
°C   50
30
20   35
10   25
0   15
          5
3 mm Annual

ĀDĪS ĀBEBA
°C   50
30
20   35
10   25
0   15
          5
1089 mm Annual

NAIROBI
°C   50
30
20   35
10   25
0   15
          5
926 mm Annual

BULAWAYO
°C   50
30
20   35
10   25
0   15
          5
589 mm Annual

WINDHOEK
°C   50
30
20   35
10   25
0   15
          5
370 mm Annual

CAPE TOWN
°C   50
30
20   35
10   25
0   15
          5
508 mm Annual

Rainfall figures on graphs in tens of millimetres except for annual totals

Zenithal Equal Area Projection

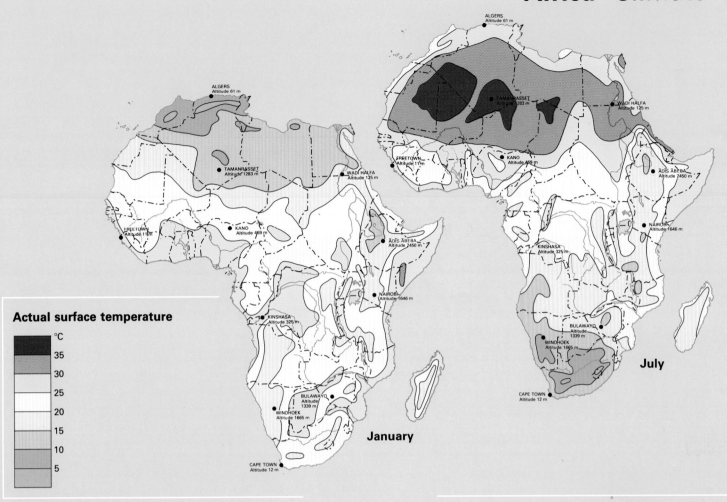

Actual surface temperature

	°C
	35
	30
	25
	20
	15
	10
	5

January

July

Scale 1 : 80 000 000

0   500   1000 km

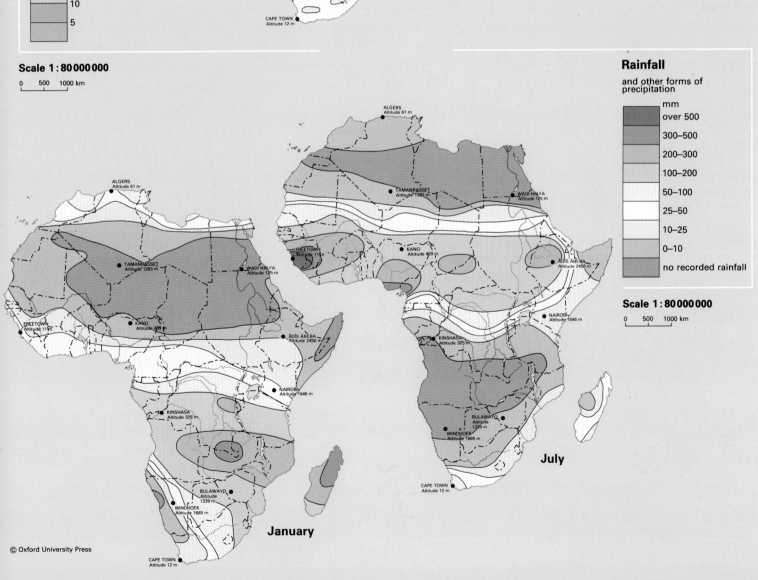

Rainfall

and other forms of
precipitation

	mm
	over 500
	300–500
	200–300
	100–200
	50–100
	25–50
	10–25
	0–10
	no recorded rainfall

Scale 1 : 80 000 000

0   500   1000 km

January

July

© Oxford University Press

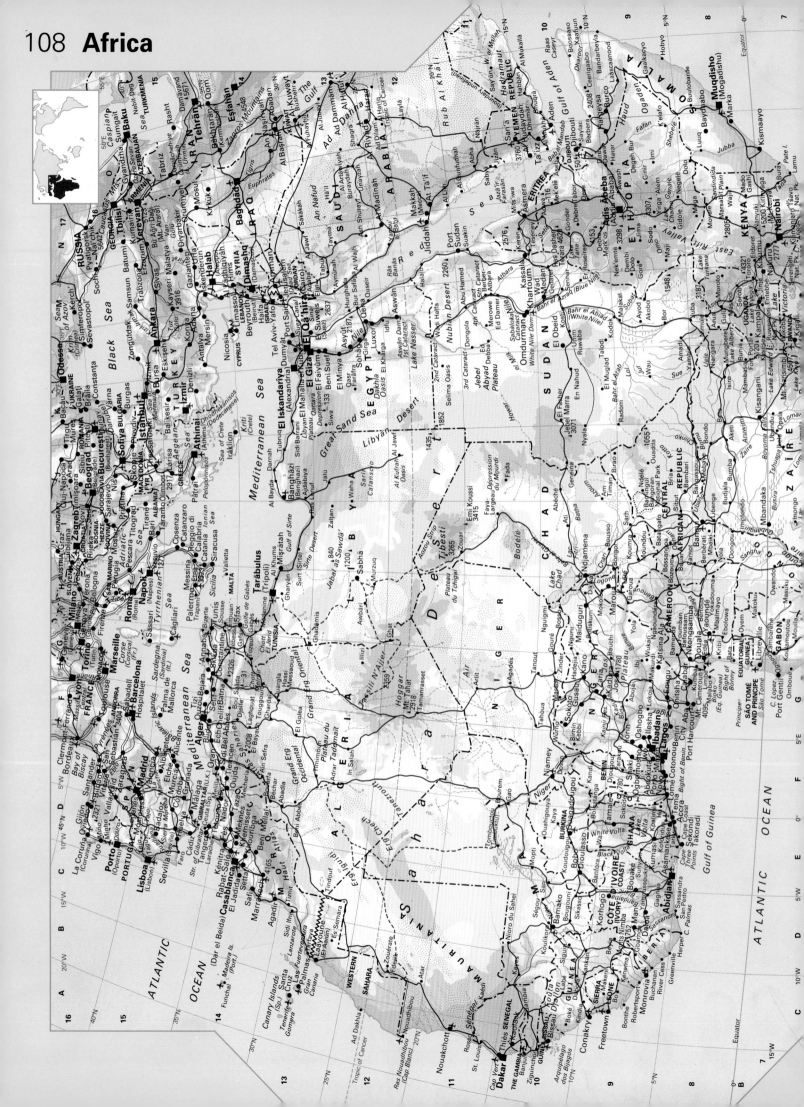
ATLANTIC OCEAN
Mediterranean Sea
Black Sea
Red Sea
Gulf of Aden
Gulf of Guinea
Sahara Desert
Libyan Desert
Nubian Desert
ALGERIA
LIBYA
EGYPT
SUDAN
CHAD
NIGER
MALI
MAURITANIA
NIGERIA
ETHIOPIA
SOMALIA
KENYA
SAUDI ARABIA
IRAQ
IRAN
TURKEY
ZAÏRE

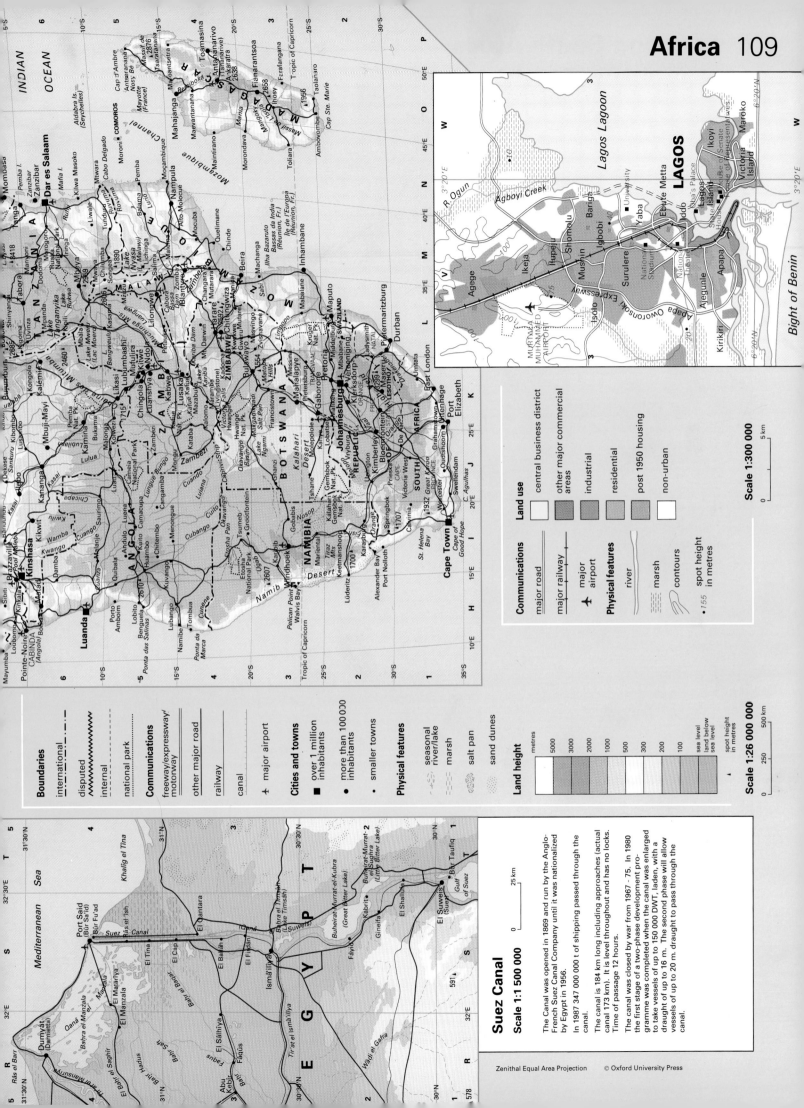

Suez Canal

Scale 1:1 500 000

The Canal was opened in 1869 and run by the Anglo-French Suez Canal Company until it was nationalized by Egypt in 1956.

In 1987 347 000 000 t of shipping passed through the canal.

The canal is 184 km long including approaches (actual canal 173 km). It is level throughout and has no locks. Time of passage 12 hours.

The canal was closed by war from 1967 - 75. In 1980 the first stage of a two-phase development programme was completed when the canal was enlarged to take vessels of up to 150 000 DWT, laden, with a draught of up to 16 m. The second phase will allow vessels of up to 20 m. draught to pass through the canal.

Zenithal Equal Area Projection   © Oxford University Press

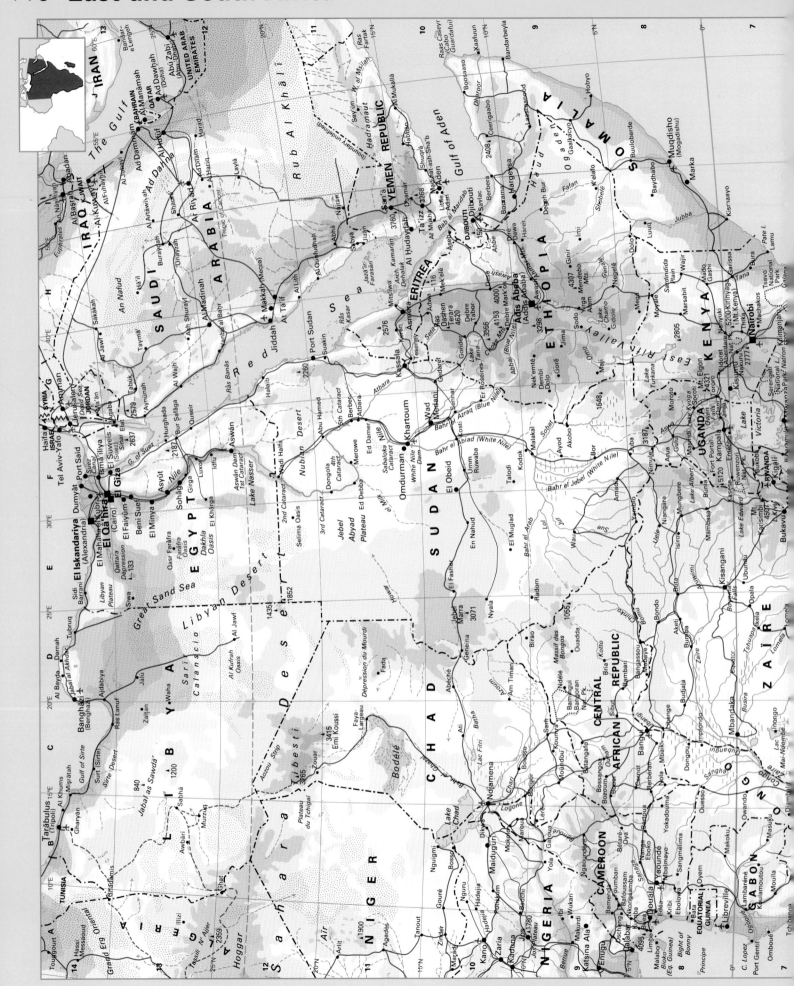

Zenithal Equal Area Projection

© Oxford University Press

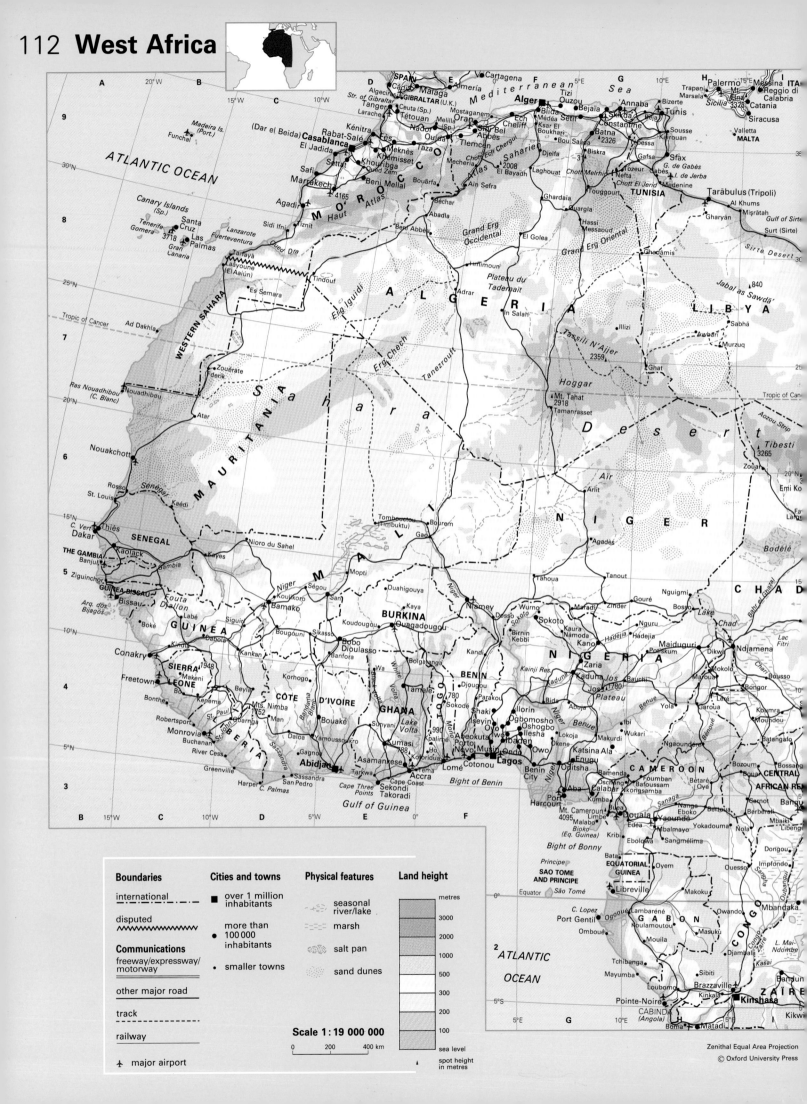

Boundaries
international
disputed

Cities and towns
■ over 1 million inhabitants
● more than 100 000 inhabitants
• smaller towns

Physical features
seasonal river/lake
marsh
salt pan
sand dunes

Land height

metres
3000
2000
1000
500
300
200
100
sea level

Communications
freeway/expressway/motorway
other major road
track
railway
✈ major airport

▲ spot height in metres

Scale 1 : 19 000 000

0   200   400 km

Zenithal Equal Area Projection
© Oxford University Press

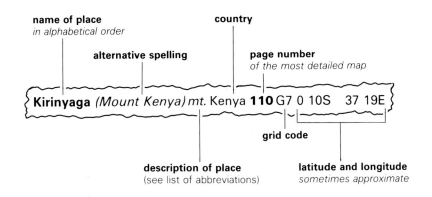

name of place
in alphabetical order

country

alternative spelling

page number
of the most detailed map

Kirinyaga *(Mount Kenya) mt.* Kenya **110** G7 0 10S 37 19E

grid code

description of place
(see list of abbreviations)

latitude and longitude
sometimes approximate

How to use the gazetteer

To find a place on an atlas map
use either the grid code or
latitude and longitude.

Grid code

Latitude and Longitude

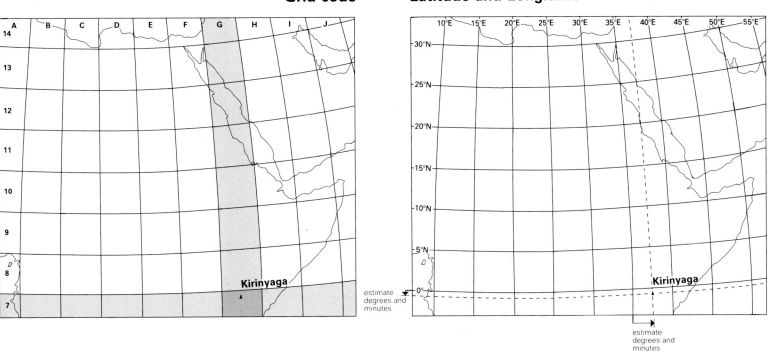

Kirinyaga is in grid square G7

Kirinyaga is at latitude 0 10S longitude 37 19E

Kirinyaga *(Mount Kenya) mt.* Kenya **110** G7 0 10S 37 19E

Kirinyaga *(Mount Kenya) mt.* Kenya **110** G7 0 10S 37 19E

A

Aa r. France 70 B2 50 50N 2 10E
Aachen Germany 71 A2 50 46N 6 06E
Aalen Germany 71 B1 48 50N 10 07E
Aalsmeer Netherlands 70 D4 52 16N 4 45E
Aalst Belgium 70 D2 50 57N 4 03E
Aalten Belgium 70 C3 51 56N 6 35E
Aare r. Switzerland 73 C2 47 00N 7 05E
Aarschot Belgium 70 D2 50 59N 4 50E
Aba Nigeria 112 G4 5 06N 7 21E
Ābādān Iran 55 G5 30 20N 48 15E
Abadla Algeria 112 E9 31 01N 2 45W
Abaetetuba Brazil 102 H12 1 45S 48 54W
Abakan Russia 57 L6 53 43N 91 25E
Abakan r. Russia 57 K6 52 00N 90 00E
Abancay Peru 102 C10 13 37S 72 52W
Abashiri Japan 46 D3 44 02N 114 17E
Abau Papua New Guinea 45 N1 10 13S 148 44E
Abbe, Lake Ethiopia 110 H10 11 00N 44 00E
Abbeville France 73 B3 50 06N 1 51E
Ābd al Kūrī i. Socotra 55 H1 11 55N 52 20E
Abéché Chad 110 D10 13 49N 20 49E
Abemama i. Pacific Ocean 80 C4 0 20N 173 50E
Åbenrå Denmark 71 A3 55 03N 9 26E
Abeokuta Nigeria 112 F4 7 10N 3 26E
Aberdare National Park Kenya 110 G7 0 30S 37 00E
Aberdeen Hong Kong U.K. 51 B1 22 14N 114 09E
Aberdeen Scotland United Kingdom 68 I9 57 10N 2 04W
Aberdeen Maryland U.S.A. 93 E1 39 31N 76 10W
Aberdeen South Dakota U.S.A. 91 G6 45 28N 98 30W
Aberdeen Washington U.S.A. 90 B6 46 58N 123 49W
Aberystwyth Wales United Kingdom 68 G4 52 25N 4 05W
Abhā Saudi Arabia 54 F2 18 14N 42 31E
Abidjan Côte d'Ivoire 112 E4 5 19N 4 01W
Abilene Texas U.S.A. 90 G3 32 27N 99 45W
Abitibi, Lake Ontario/Québec Canada 93 D3/E3 48 42N 79 45W
Abitibi River Ontario Canada 93 D3 50 00N 81 20W
Abor Hills India 38 A5 28 30N 94 10E
Abra The Philippines 40 B4 16 30N 120 40E
Absaroka Range mts. U.S.A. 90 D6/E5 45 00N 110 00W
Abu Dhabi see Abū Zabī
Abu Durba Egypt 54 N9 28 29N 33 20E
Abu Hamed Sudan 110 F11 19 32N 33 20E
Abuja Nigeria 112 G4 9 10N 7 11E
Abu Kamal Syria 54 F5 34 29N 40 56E
Abu Kebîr Egypt 109 R3 30 44N 31 48E
Abunã Brazil 102 D11 9 41S 65 20W
Abu Tig Egypt 54 D4 27 06N 31 17E
Abū Zabī (Abu Dhabi) United Arab Emirates 55 H3 24 28N 54 25E
Acambaro Mexico 96 D4 20 01N 100 42W
Acaponeta Mexico 96 C4 22 30N 102 25W
Acapulco Mexico 96 E3 16 51N 99 56W
Açari r. Brazil 103 P2 22 50S 43 22W
Acarigua Venezuela 102 D14 9 35N 69 12W
Acatlán Mexico 96 E3 18 12N 98 02W
Acayucán Mexico 96 E3 17 59N 94 58W
Accra Ghana 112 E4 5 33N 0 15W
Aceh admin. Indonesia 42 A4 4 00N 97 00E
Achacachi Bolivia 102 D9 16 01S 68 44W
Achill Island Irish Republic 68 A5 53 55N 10 05W
Achinsk Russia 57 L7 56 20N 90 33E
Acklins Island The Bahamas 97 J4 22 30N 74 30W
Aconcagua mt. Argentina 103 C6 32 40S 70 02W
Acre admin. Brazil 102 C11 8 30S 71 30W
Actaeon Islands Pacific Ocean 81 F1 22 00S 136 00W
Acton England United Kingdom 66 B3 51 31N 0 17W
Ada Oklahoma U.S.A. 91 G3 34 47N 96 41W
Adachi Japan 47 C4 35 46N 139 48E
Adaga r. Spain 72 B3 40 45N 4 45W
Adamawa Mountains Africa 104 7 00N 13 00E
Adam, Mount Falkland Islands 25 M16 51 36S 60 00W
Adam's Bridge India/Sri Lanka 53 D1 10 00N 79 30E
Adana Turkey 54 E6 37 00N 35 19E
Adapazari Turkey 54 D7 40 45N 30 23E
Adare, Cape Antarctica 21 71 30S 170 24E
Adaut Indonesia 43 H2 8 50S 131 20E
Adda r. Italy 73 C2 45 00N 9 00E
Ad Dakhla Western Sahara 112 B7 23 50N 15 58W
Ad Dammām Saudi Arabia 55 H4 26 25N 50 06E
Ad Dawhah (Doha) Qatar 55 H4 25 15N 51 36E
Ad Dilam Saudi Arabia 55 G3 23 59N 47 06E
Ad Dir'īyah Saudi Arabia 55 G3 24 45N 46 32E
Addis Ababa see Ādīs Ābeba
Ad Dīwānīyah Iraq 54 F5 32 00N 44 57E
Adelaide Australia 78 F3 34 56S 138 36E
Adelbert Range mts. Papua New Guinea 45 L4 4 30S 145 00E
Adélie Land see Terre d'Adélie
Aden Yemen Republic 55 G1 12 50N 45 03E
Adirondack Mountains New York U.S.A. 93 F2 43 15N 74 40W
Ādīs Ābeba (Addis Ababa) Ethiopia 110 G9 9 03N 38 42E
Admiralty Islands Papua New Guinea 45 M5/M6 2 00S 147 00E
Adonara i. Indonesia 43 F2 8 30S 123 00E
Adoni India 53 D3 15 38N 77 16E
Adra Spain 72 B2 36 45N 3 01W
Adrar Algeria 112 E8 27 51N 0 19W
Adrian Michigan U.S.A. 93 D2 41 55N 84 01W
Adriatic Sea Mediterranean Sea 74 B3/C3 43 00N 15 00E
Ādwa Ethiopia 110 G10 14 12N 38 56E
Aegean Sea Mediterranean Sea 74 D2/E2 39 00N 24 00E
Ærø i. Denmark 71 B2 54 52N 10 20E
Aewŏl-li South Korea 50 C1 33 29N 126 15E
Afaahiti Tahiti 82 T9 17 43S 149 18W
Afareaitu Tahiti 82 R9 17 33S 149 47W
AFGHANISTAN 55 J5
Afiamulu Western Samoa 82 B11 13 51S 171 45W
Afognak Island Alaska U.S.A. 88 E4 58 10N 152 50W
Afore Papua New Guinea 45 N2 9 10S 148 30E
Afyon Turkey 54 D6 38 46N 30 32E
Agadès Niger 112 G6 17 00N 7 56E
Agadir Morocco 112 D9 30 30N 9 40W
Agalega Islands Seychelles 24 E5 10 00S 56 00E
Agana Guam 80 B4 13 28N 144 45E
Agano r. Japan 46 C2 37 50N 139 30E
Agartala India 53 G4 23 49N 91 15E
Agawa Ontario Canada 89 S2 47 22N 84 37W
Agege Nigeria 109 V3 6 41N 3 24E
Agen France 73 B1 44 12N 0 38E
Ageo Japan 46 L2 35 57N 139 36E
Ago Japan 46 H1 34 20N 136 50E
Agout r. France 73 B1 43 50N 1 50E
Agra India 53 D5 27 09N 78 00E
Agra r. Spain 72 B3 43 00N 2 50W
Agram see Zagreb
Agri r. Italy 74 C3 40 00N 16 00E
Agrigento Italy 74 B2 37 19N 13 35E
Agrinion Greece 74 D2 38 38N 21 25E
Aguadas Colombia 102 B14 5 36N 75 30W
Aguadilla Puerto Rico 97 K3 18 27N 67 08W
Agua Prieta Mexico 96 C6 31 20N 109 32W
Aguascalientes Mexico 96 D4 21 51N 102 18W
Agueda r. Spain 72 A3 40 50N 6 50W
Aguilas Spain 72 B2 37 25N 1 35W
Agulhas Basin Indian Ocean 24 A2 45 00S 20 00E
Agulhas, Cape Republic of South Africa 111 D1 34 50S 20 00E
Agusan r. The Philippines 40 C2 8 00N 125 00E
Ahau Fiji 83 B14 12 30S 177 00E
Ahaus Germany 70 G4 52 04N 7 01E
Ahmadabad India 53 C4 23 03N 72 40E
Ahmadnagar India 53 C3 19 08N 74 48E
Ahmar Mountains Ethiopia 110 H9 9 00N 41 00E
Ahr r. Germany 70 F2 50 00N 6 00E
Ahrensburg Germany 71 B2 53 41N 10 14E
Ahrensfelde Germany 67 G2 52 35N 13 35E
Ahuachapán El Salvador 96 G2 13 57N 89 49W
Ahvāz Iran 55 G5 31 17N 48 43E
Aichi pref. Japan 46 J2 35 00N 137 15E
Ailao Shan mts. China 38 C4 23 00N 102 30E
Ain r. France 73 C2 46 30N 5 30E
Aïn Sefra Algeria 112 E9 32 45N 0 35W
Aïn Témouchent Algeria 72 B2 35 18N 1 09W
Aïr mts. Niger 112 G6 19 10N 8 20E
Airbangis Indonesia 42 A4 0 18N 99 22E
Airdrie Alberta Canada 88 M3 51 20N 114 00W
Aire r. France 70 D1 49 15N 5 00E
Aire r. England United Kingdom 68 J5 53 40N 1 00W
Aire-sur-l'Adour France 73 A1 43 42N 0 15W
Aire-sur-la-Lys France 70 B2 51 40N 2 25E
Airpanas Indonesia 44 A3 7 52S 125 51E
Aisega Papua New Guinea 45 N4 5 44S 148 22E
Aishihik Yukon Territory Canada 88 H5 62 00N 137 30W
Aisne admin. France 70 C1/D1 49 40N 4 00E
Aisne r. France 73 B2 49 30N 3 00E
Aitape Papua New Guinea 45 K5 3 10S 142 17E
Aitutaki i. Pacific Ocean 81 E3 18 52S 159 46W
Aiviekste r. Latvia 69 F2 57 00N 26 40E
Aiwo Nauru 83 L1 0 31S 166 54E
Aix-en-Provence France 73 C1 43 31N 5 27E
Aix-les-Bains France 73 C2 45 41N 5 55E
Aiyion Greece 74 D2 38 15N 22 05E
Aizawl India 38 A6 23 45N 92 45E
Aizu-Wakamatsu Japan 46 C2 37 30N 139 58E
Ajaccio Corsica 73 C1 41 55N 8 43E
Ajax Ontario Canada 93 E2 43 48N 79 00W
Ajdābiyā Libya 110 D14 30 46N 20 14E
Ajegunle Nigeria 109 V3 6 24N 3 24E
Ajlūn Jordan 54 O11 32 20N 35 345E
Ajmer India 53 C5 26 29N 74 40E
Ajo Arizona U.S.A. 90 D3 32 24N 112 51W
Akabira Japan 46 D3 43 40N 141 55E
Akaroa South Island New Zealand 79 B2 43 49S 172 58E
Akashi Japan 46 F1 34 39N 135 00E
Akechi Japan 46 J2 35 19N 137 22E
Akelamo Indonesia 44 B6 0 03S 127 53E
Aketi Zaïre 110 D8 2 42N 23 51E
Akhelöös r. Greece 74 D2 39 00N 21 00E
Akhisar Turkey 74 E2 38 54N 27 50E
Akhlun Mountains Alaska U.S.A. 88 C4/5 60 00N 161 00W
Akhtubinsk Russia 58 F4 48 20N 46 10E
Akimiski Island i. Northwest Territories Canada 89 S3 53 00N 81 00W
Akita Japan 46 D2 39 44N 140 05E
'Akko Israel 54 O11 32 55N 35 04E
Aklavik Northwest Territories Canada 88 I6 68 15N 135 02W
Akmola (Tselinograd) Kazakhstan 59 L5 51 10N 71 28E
Akobo Sudan 110 F9 7 50N 33 05E
Akola India 53 D4 20 49N 77 05E
Akoma Papua New Guinea 45 L3 7 50S 145 02E
Ak'ordat Eritrea 54 E2 15 26N 3745E
Akpatok Island Northwest Territories Canada 89 V5 60 30N 68 00W
Ákra Akritas c. Greece 74 D2 36 43N 21 52E
Ákra Kafirévs c. Greece 74 D2 38 10N 24 35E
Ákra Maléa c. Greece 74 D2 36 27N 23 12E
Akranes Iceland 69 H6 64 19N 22 05W
Ákra Tainaron c. Greece 74 D2 36 23N 22 29E
Akron Ohio U.S.A. 93 D2 41 04N 81 31W
Aksum Ethiopia 54 E1 14 10N 38 45E
Aktyubinsk Kazakhstan 59 H5 50 16N 57 13E
Aku Papua New Guinea 82 A7 6 40S 155 40E
Akureyri Iceland 69 I7 65 41N 18 04W
Akyab see Sittwe
Alabama r. Alabama U.S.A. 91 I3 31 00N 88 00W
Alabama state U.S.A. 91 I3 32 00N 87 00W
Alabat i. The Philippines 40 B3 14 07N 122 00E
Alagoas admin. Brazil 102 J11 9 30S 37 00W
Alagoinhas Brazil 102 J10 12 09S 38 21W
Alagón r. Spain 72 A2 40 00N 6 30W
Alah r. The Philippines 40 B2 6 00N 125 00E
Alajuela Costa Rica 97 H2 10 00N 84 12W
Alakanuk Alaska U.S.A. 88 C5 62 39N 164 48W
Al'Amārah Iraq 55 G5 31 51N 47 10E
Alaminos The Philippines 40 A4 16 11N 119 58E
Alamosa Colorado U.S.A. 90 E4 37 28N 105 54W
Åland is. Finland 69 D3 60 15N 20 00E
Alanya Turkey 54 D6 36 32N 32 02E
Al Artāwīyah Saudi Arabia 55 G4 26 31N 45 21E
Ala Shan mts. China 49 K6/7 40 00N 102 30E
Alaska state U.S.A. 88 D5/F5 63 10N 157 30W
Alaska, Gulf of U.S.A. 88 F4/G4 58 00N 147 00W
Alaska Peninsula Alaska U.S.A. 88 D4 56 30N 159 00W
Alaska Range mts. Alaska U.S.A. 88 E5/G5 62 30N 152 30W
Alatna Alaska U.S.A. 88 E6 66 33N 152 49W
Alaungdaw Kathapa National Park Myanmar 38 A4 22 15N 94 25E
Al'Ayn United Arab Emirates 55 I3 24 10N 55 43E
Alayor Balearic Islands 72 F4 39 56N 4 08E
Alay Range mts. Asia 59 L2 39 00N 70 00E
Albacete Spain 72 B2 39 00N 1 52W
Alba Iulia Romania 75 D2 46 04N 23 33E
ALBANIA 74 C2/D2
Albany Australia 78 B3 34 57S 117 54E
Albany New York U.S.A. 93 F2 42 40N 73 49W
Albany Oregon U.S.A. 90 B5 44 38N 123 07W
Albany River Ontario Canada 89 S3 52 00N 84 00W
Al Başrah Iraq 55 G5 30 30N 47 50E
Al Bayḑā Libya 110 D14 32 00N 21 30E
Alberche r. Spain 72 B3 40 10N 4 45W
Albert France 73 B3 50 00N 2 40E
Alberta province Canada 88 L3 54 00N 117 30W
Albert-Kanaal can. Belgium 70 D3 51 10N 5 00E
Albert, Lake Uganda/Zaïre 110 F8 2 00N 31 00E
Albert Lea Minnesota U.S.A. 92 B2 43 38N 93 16W
Albertville France 73 C2 45 40N 6 24E
Albi France 73 B1 43 56N 2 08E
Al Bi'r Saudi Arabia 54 E4 28 50N 36 16E
Ålborg Denmark 69 B2 57 05N 9 50E
Albuquerque New Mexico U.S.A. 90 E4 35 05N 106 38W
Al Buraymī Oman 55 I3 24 16N 55 48E
Alcalá de Henares Spain 72 B3 40 28N 3 22W
Alcamo Italy 74 B2 37 58N 12 58E
Alcañiz Spain 72 B3 41 03N 0 09W
Alcázar de San Juan Spain 72 B2 39 24N 3 12W
Alcira Spain 72 B2 39 10N 0 27W
Alcoy Spain 72 B2 38 42N 0 29W
Alcudia Balearic Islands 72 E4 39 51N 3 06E
Aldama Mexico 96 E4 22 54N 98 05W
Aldan Russia 57 O7 58 44N 124 22E
Aldan r. Russia 57 P7 59 00N 132 30E
Alderney i. Channel Islands British Isles 68 I1 49 43N 2 12W
Alegrete Brazil 103 F7 29 45S 55 40W
Aleksandrovsk-Sakhalinskiy Russia 57 Q6 50 55N 142 12E
Alençon France 73 B2 48 25N 0 05E
Alenuihaha Channel sd. Hawaiian Islands 23 Y18 20 20N 156 20W
Alert m.s. Northwest Territories Canada 20 80 31N 60 05W
Alès France 73 B1 44 08N 4 05E
Alessándria Italy 74 A3 44 55N 8 37E
Ålesund Norway 69 B3 62 28N 6 11E
Aleutian Basin Pacific Ocean 22 I13 54 00N 178 00W
Aleutian Islands Alaska U.S.A. 88 A3 54 00N 173 00W
Aleutian Range mts. Alaska U.S.A. 88 D4 56 30N 159 00W
Aleutian Ridge Pacific Ocean 22/23 I13 53 55N 178 00W
Alexander Archipelago is. Alaska U.S.A. 88 H4 57 00N 137 30W
Alexander Bay tn. Republic of South Africa 111 C2 28 40S 16 30E
Alexander Island Antarctica 21 71 00S 70 00W
Alexandra Singapore 41 C3 1 18N 103 50E
Alexandra South Island New Zealand 79 A1 45 15S 169 23E
Alexandria Romania 75 E1 43 59N 25 19E
Alexandria Louisiana U.S.A. 91 H3 31 19N 92 29W
Alexandria Virginia U.S.A. 93 E1 38 49N 77 06W
Alexandria see El Iskandarîya
Alexandria Bay tn. New York U.S.A. 93 E2 44 20N 75 55W
Alexandroúpolis Greece 74 E3 40 51N 25 53E
Alfambra r. Spain 72 B3 40 40N 1 00W
Alfiós r. Greece 74 D2 37 00N 22 00E
Alfred Ontario Canada 93 F3 45 33N 74 52W
Al Fuḩayḩīl Kuwait 55 G4 29 07N 47 02E
Algarve geog. reg. Portugal 60 3 30N 8 00W
Algeciras Spain 72 A2 36 08N 5 27W
Alger (Algiers) Algeria 112 F10 36 50N 3 00E
ALGERIA 112 D8/G10
Alghero Italy 74 A3 40 34N 8 19E
Algiers see Alger
Algona Iowa U.S.A. 92 B2 43 04N 94 11W
Al Ḩadīthah Iraq 54 F5 34 06N 42 25E
Alhambra California U.S.A. 95 B3 34 05N 118 10W
Al Ḩarīq Saudi Arabia 55 G3 23 34N 46 35E
Al Ḩasakah Syria 54 F6 36 32N 40 44E
Al Ḩillah Iraq 54 F5 32 28N 44 29E
Al Hoceima Morocco 72 B2 35 14N 3 56W
Al Ḩudaydah Yemen Republic 54 F1 14 50N 42 58E
Al Hufūf Saudi Arabia 55 G4 25 20N 49 34E
Aliákmon r. Greece 74 D3 40 00N 22 00E
Alicante Spain 72 B2 38 21N 0 29W
Alice Texas U.S.A. 91 G2 27 45N 98 06W
Alice Springs tn. Australia 78 E5 23 42S 133 52E
Aligarh India 53 D5 27 54N 78 04E
Aling Kangri mt. China 48 F5 32 51N 81 03E
Alipur India 52 K2 22 32N 88 19E
Alivérion Greece 74 D2 38 24N 24 02E
Aliwal North Republic of South Africa 111 E1 30 42S 26 43E
Al Jahrah Kuwait 55 G4 29 22N 47 40E
Al Jawf Libya 110 D12 24 12N 23 18E
Al Jawf Saudi Arabia 54 E4 29 49N 39 52E
Al Jubayl Saudi Arabia 55 G4 26 59N 49 40E
Aljustrel Portugal 72 A2 37 52N 8 10W
Al Khums Libya 110 B14 32 39N 14 16E
Alkmaar Netherlands 70 D4 52 38N 4 44E
Al Kufrah Oasis Libya 110 D12 24 10N 23 15E
Al Kūt Iraq 55 G5 32 30N 45 51E
Al Kuwayt Kuwait 55 G4 29 20N 48 00E
Al Lādhiqīyah Syria 54 E6 35 31N 35 47E
Allahabad India 53 E5 25 27N 81 50E
Allanmyo Myanmar 38 B3 19 25N 95 13E
Allardyce Harbour tn. Solomon Islands 82 D6 7 45S 158 40E
Allegheny Mountains U.S.A. 93 E1/2 40 00N 79 00W
Allegheny Reservoir U.S.A. 93 E2 42 00N 79 00W
Allende Mexico 96 D5 28 22N 100 50W
Allentown Pennsylvania U.S.A. 93 E2 40 37N 75 30W
Alleppey India 53 D1 9 30N 76 22E
Aller r. Germany 71 A2 52 00N 9 00E
Alliance Nebraska U.S.A. 90 F5 42 08N 102 54W
Allier r. France 73 B2 46 40N 3 00E
Alliston Ontario Canada 93 E2 44 09N 79 51W
Al Līth Saudi Arabia 54 F3 20 10N 40 20E
Alloa Scotland United Kingdom 68 H8 56 07N 3 49W
Alma Québec Canada 93 F3 48 32N 71 41W
Alma Michigan U.S.A. 93 D2 43 23N 84 40W
Alma-Ata Kazakhstan 59 M3 43 19N 76 55E
Almada Portugal 72 A2 38 40N 9 09W
Almadén Spain 72 B2 38 47N 4 50W
Al Madīnah Saudi Arabia 54 E3 24 30N 39 35E
Almalyk Uzbekistan 59 K3 40 50N 69 40E
Al Manāmah Bahrain 55 H4 26 12N 50 38E
Almansa Spain 72 B2 38 52N 1 06W
Almanzora r. Spain 72 B2 37 15N 2 10W
Al Mayādīn Syria 54 F6 35 01N 40 28E
Almelo Netherlands 70 F4 52 21N 6 40E
Almere Netherlands 70 E4 52 22N 5 12E
Almería Spain 72 B2 36 50N 2 26W
Al'met'yevsk Russia 59 G5 54 50N 52 22E
Älmhult Sweden 69 C2 56 32N 14 10E
Al Miqdādīyah Iraq 54 F5 33 58N 44 58E
Almodôvar Portugal 72 A2 37 31N 8 03W
Almonte Ontario Canada 93 E3 45 13N 76 12W
Al Mubarraz Saudi Arabia 55 G4 25 26N 49 37E
Al Mukallā Yemen Republic 55 G1 14 34N 49 09E
Al Mukhā Yemen Republic 54 F1 13 20N 43 16E
Alofi i. Pacific Ocean 80 D3 14 27S 178 05W
Alokan i. Solomon Islands 82 E4 9 10S 159 10E
Along India 38 A5 28 12N 94 50E
Alor Setar Malaysia 42 B5 6 07N 100 21E
Alotau Papua New Guinea 45 O1 10 20S 150 23E
Alpena Michigan U.S.A. 93 D3 45 04N 83 27W
Alpes Maritimes mts. France/Italy 73 C1 44 15N 6 45E
Alpha Ridge Arctic Ocean 20 85 00N 120 00W
Alphen aan den Rijn Netherlands 70 D4 52 08N 4 40E
Alpi Carniche mts. Europe 74 B4 46 00N 13 00E
Alpi Cozie mts. Europe 74 A3 45 00N 8 00E
Alpi Dolomitiche mts. Italy 74 B4 46 00N 12 00E
Alpi Grai mts. Europe 74 C2 45 00N 7 00E
Alpi Lepontine mts. Switzerland 73 C2 46 26N 8 30E
Alpine Texas U.S.A. 90 F3 30 22N 103 40W
Alpi Pennine mts. Italy/Switzerland 74 A4 45 55N 7 30E
Alpi Retiche mts. Switzerland 74 A4/B4 46 25N 9 45E
Alps mts. Europe 74 A4/B4 46 00N 7 30E
Al Qunfudhah Saudi Arabia 54 F2 19 09N 41 07E
Alsdorf Germany 70 F2 50 53N 6 10E
Alta Norway 69 E4 69 57N 23 10E
Altadena California U.S.A. 95 B3 34 12N 118 08W
Altaelv r. Norway 69 E4 69 50N 23 30E
Alta Gracia Argentina 103 E6 31 42S 64 25W
Altai mts. Mongolia 48 H8 47 00N 92 30E
Altamaha r. Georgia U.S.A. 91 J3 32 00N 82 00W
Altamura Italy 74 C3 40 49N 16 34E
Altay China 48 G8 47 48N 88 07E
Altay mts. Russia 57 K6 51 00N 89 00E
Altenburg Germany 71 B2 50 59N 12 27E
Altlandsberg Germany 67 G2 52 34N 1345E
Altmühl r. Germany 71 B1 49 00N 10 00E
Alto da Boa Vista Brazil 103 P2 22 58S 43 17W
Alto Molocue Mozambique 111 G4 15 38S 37 42E
Alton Illinois U.S.A. 92 B1 38 55N 90 10W
Altona Manitoba Canada 92 A3 49 06N 97 35W
Altoona Pennsylvania U.S.A. 93 E2 40 32N 78 32W
Altun Shan mts. China 48 G6 37 30N 86 00E
Altus Oklahoma U.S.A. 90 G3 34 39N 99 21W
Alu i. Solomon Islands 82 A6 7 00S 155 40E
Alva Oklahoma U.S.A. 90 G4 36 48N 98 40W
Al Wajh Saudi Arabia 54 E4 26 16N 32 28E
Alwar India 53 D5 27 32N 76 35E
Alyat Azerbaijan 58 F2 39 57N 49 25E
Amadeus, Lake Australia 78 E5 24 00S 132 30E
Amadi Sudan 110 F9 5 32N 30 20E
Amadjuak Lake Northwest Territories Canada 89 U6 65 00N 71 00W
Amagasaki Japan 46 C1 34 42N 135 23E
Amahai Indonesia 43 G3 3 19S 128 56E
Ama Keng Singapore 41 B4 1 24N 103 24E
Amakusa-shotō is. Japan 46 B1 32 50N 130 05E
Amamapare Irian Jaya Indonesia 44 G4 4 51S 136 44E
Amanab Papua New Guinea 45 J5 3 38S 141 16E
Amapá Brazil 102 G13 2 00N 50 50W
Amapá admin. Brazil 102 G13 2 00N 52 30W
Amarapura Myanmar 38 B4 21 54N 96 01E
Amarillo Texas U.S.A. 90 F4 35 14N 101 50W
Amatsukominato Japan 46 M2 35 08N 140 14E
Amazonas admin. Brazil 102 D12/F12 4 30S 65 00W
Amazon, Mouths of the est. Brazil 102 G13 1 00N 51 00W
Ambala India 53 D6 30 19N 76 49E
Ambarchik Russia 57 S9 69 39N 162 37E
Ambato Ecuador 102 B12 1 18S 78 39W
Amberg Germany 71 B1 49 26N 11 52E
Amblève r. Belgium 70 F2 50 22N 6 10E
Ambon Indonesia 43 G3 3 41S 128 10E
Ambovombe Madagascar 111 I2 25 10S 46 06E
Ambrym i. Vanuatu 83 H5 16 15S 168 10E
Ambunti Papua New Guinea 45 K4 4 12S 142 49E
Amderma Russia 57 I9 66 44N 61 35E
Amdo China 48 H5 32 22N 91 07E
Ameca Mexico 96 D4 20 34N 104 03W
Ameland i. Netherlands 70 E5 53 28N 5 45E
American Falls tn. Idaho U.S.A. 90 D5 42 47N 112 50W
AMERICAN SAMOA 82
Amersfoort Netherlands 70 E4 52 09N 5 23E
Amersham England United Kingdom 66 A3 51 40N 0 38W
Amery Ice Shelf Antarctica 21 70 00S 70 00E
Ames Iowa U.S.A. 92 B2 42 02N 93 33W
Amfípolis Greece 74 D3 40 48N 23 52E
Amga Russia 57 P8 61 51N 131 59E
Amga r. Russia 57 P8 60 00N 130 00E
Amgun' r. Russia 57 P6 52 00N 137 00E
Amherst Nova Scotia Canada 89 W2 45 50N 64 14W
Amherst Virginia U.S.A. 93 E1 37 35N 79 04W
Amherst see Kyaikkami
Amiens France 73 B2 49 54N 2 18E
Amirante Islands Seychelles 24 E6 5 00S 55 00E
Amlia Island Alaska U.S.A. 88 A3 52 05N 173 30W
Amman Jordan 54 O10 31 04N 46 17E
Ammassalik Greenland 89 BB6 65 45N 37 45W
Ammersee l. Germany 71 B1 48 00N 11 00E
Amnat Charoen Thailand 39 B3 15 50N 104 40E
Ampana Indonesia 43 F3 0 54S 121 35E
Amper r. Germany 71 B1 48 00N 11 00E
Amravati India 53 D4 20 58N 77 50E
Amritsar India 53 C6 31 35N 74 56E
Amroha India 53 D5 28 54N 78 29E
Amrum i. Germany 71 A2 54 00N 8 00E
Amstelveen Netherlands 70 D4 52 18N 4 52E
Amsterdam Netherlands 70 D4 52 22N 4 54E

Awash *r.* Ethiopia **110** H10 10 00N 40 00E
Awa-shima *i.* Japan **46** C2 38 40N 139 15E
Awbāri Libya **110** B13 26 35N 12 46E
Axel Heiberg Island Northwest Territories Canada **89** Q8 80 00N 90 00W
Ayabe Japan **46** G2 35 19N 135 16E
Ayaguz Kazakhstan **59** N4 47 59N 80 27E
Ayamonte Spain **72** A2 37 13N 7 24W
Ayan Russia **57** P7 56 29N 138 07E
Ayaviri Peru **102** C10 14 53S 70 35W
Aydin Turkey **74** E2 37 51N 27 51E
Ayers Rock *mt.* Australia **78** E4 25 18S 131 18E
Ayios Nikólaos Greece **74** E2 35 11N 25 43E
Aylmer Ontario Canada **93** D2 42 47N 80 58W
Aylmer Québec Canada **93** E3 45 23N 75 51W
Ayod Sudan **110** F9 8 08N 31 24E
Ayon *i.* Russia **57** S9 69 55N 169 10E
Ayr Scotland United Kingdom **68** G7 55 28N 4 38W
'Ayūnah Saudi Arabia **54** E4 28 06N 35 08E
AZERBAIJAN **58** F3
Azogues Ecuador **102** B12 2 46S 78 56W
Azores *is.* Atlantic Ocean **25** F10 38 30N 28 00W
Azoum *r.* Chad **110** D10 12 00N 21 00E
Azov, Sea of Asia **58** D4 46 00N 36 00E
Azuero, Peninsula de Panama **97** H1 7 40N 81 00W
Azul Argentina **103** F5 36 46S 59 50W
Azurduy Bolivia **102** E9 20 00S 64 29W
Azusa California U.S.A. **95** C3 34 08N 117 54W
Az Zabadānī Syria **54** P11 33 42N 36 03E
Az Zahrān *(Dhahran)* Saudi Arabia **55** H4 26 13N 50 02E

B

Ba Fiji **83** B9 17 34S 177 40E
Baa Indonesia **43** F1 10 44S 123 06E
Baalbek Lebanon **54** P12 34 00N 36 12E
Baarn Netherlands **70** E4 52 13N 5 16E
Babadag *mt.* Turkey **58** F3 37 49N 28 52E
Babahoyo Ecuador **102** B12 1 53S 79 31W
Bab al Mandab *sd.* Red Sea **110** H10 12 30N 47 00E
Babanakira Solomon Islands **82** E4 9 45S 159 50E
Babat Indonesia **42** P7 7 08S 112 08E
Babelsberg Germany **67** E1 52 23N 13 05E
Babelthuap *i.* Pacific Ocean **80** A4 15 00N 135 00E
Babian Jiang *(Song Da, Hitam) r.* China/Vietnam **38** C4 23 30N 101 20E
Babo Irian Jaya Indonesia **44** E5 2 33S 133 25E
Babushkin Russia **56** M2/N2 55 55N 37 44E
Babuyan *i.* The Philippines **40** B4 19 30N 121 57E
Babuyan Channel The Philippines **40** B4 19 00N 121 00E
Babuyan Islands The Philippines **40** B4 19 00N 122 00E
Babylon *hist. site* Iraq **54** F5 32 33N 44 25E
Bacabal Brazil **102** I12 4 15S 44 45W
Bacău Romania **75** E2 46 33N 26 58E
Bac Can Vietnam **37** C4 22 08N 105 49E
Bac Giang Vietnam **37** C4 21 12N 106 10E
Back *r.* Northwest Territories Canada **89** P6 66 00N 97 00W
Backbone Ranges *mts.* Northwest Territories Canada **88** J5 63 30N 127 50W
Bac Lieu *(Vinh Loi)* Vietnam **37** C1 9 17N 105 44E
Bac Ninh Vietnam **37** C4 21 10N 106 04E
Bacolod The Philippines **40** B3 10 38N 122 58E
Baco, Mount The Philippines **40** B3 12 49N 121 11E
Bac Quang Vietnam **37** B4 22 30N 104 52E
Badajoz Spain **72** A2 38 53N 6 58W
Badalona Spain **72** C3 41 27N 2 15E
Baden Austria **75** C2 48 01N 16 14E
Baden Switzerland **73** C2 47 28N 8 19E
Baden-Baden Germany **71** A1 48 45N 8 15E
Baden-Württemberg *admin.* Germany **71** A1 48 00N 9 00E
Badgastein Austria **71** B1 47 07N 13 09E
Bad Hersfeld Germany **71** A2 50 53N 9 43E
Bad Homburg Germany **71** A2 50 13N 8 37E
Bad Honnef Germany **70** G2 50 38N 7 14E
Bad Ischl Austria **71** B1 47 43N 13 38E
Bad Kissingen Germany **71** B2 50 12N 10 05E
Bad Kreuznach Germany **71** A1 49 51N 7 52E
Badli India **52** L4 28 44N 77 09E
Bad Neuenahr-Ahrweiler Germany **70** G2 50 32N 7 06E
Ba Don Vietnam **37** C3 17 45N 106 25E
Ba Dong Vietnam **37** C1 9 45N 106 40E
Bad Reichenhall **71** B1 47 43N 12 53E
Bad Salzuflen Germany **71** A2 52 06N 8 45E
Bad Tölz Germany **71** B1 47 45N 11 34E
Badu Island Australia **45** K1 10 06S 142 09E
Baffin Bay Canada/Greenland **89** V7 72 00N 65 00W
Baffin Island Northwest Territories Canada **89** S7/V6 68 30N 70 00W
Bafoussam Cameroon **112** H4 5 31N 10 25E
Bāfq Iran **55** I5 31 35N 55 21E
Baga *i.* Solomon Islands **82** B6 7 50S 156 33E
Bagé Brazil **103** G6 31 22S 54 06W
Baghdād Iraq **54** F5 33 20N 44 26E
Baghlān Afghanistan **55** K6 36 11N 68 44E
Bago The Philippines **40** B3 10 34N 122 50E
Baguio The Philippines **40** B4 16 25N 120 37E
Bahamas Bank Atlantic Ocean **84** 24 00N 77 00W
BAHAMAS, THE **97** I4
Baharampur India **53** F4 24 00N 88 30E
Bahau Malaysia **42** B4 2 49N 102 24E
Bahaur Indonesia **42** D3 3 18S 114 02E
Bahawalpur Pakistan **53** C5 29 24N 71 47E
Bahia *admin.* Brazil **102** I10 12 00S 42 30W
Bahía Blanca Argentina **103** E5 38 45S 62 15W
Bahía Blanca *b.* Argentina **103** E5 39 00S 61 00W
Bahía de Campeche *b.* Mexico **96** E4/F4 20 00N 95 00W
Bahía Grande *b.* Argentina **103** D2 51 30S 68 00W
Bahra el Manzala Egypt **109** R4 31 18N 31 54E
Bahra el Timsâh *(Lake Timsâh)* Egypt **109** S3 30 34N 32 18E
Bahraich India **53** E5 27 35N 81 36E
BAHRAIN **55** H4
Bahrain, Gulf of The Gulf **55** H4 25 55N 50 30E
Bahr el Abiad *(White Nile) r.* Sudan **110** F10 14 00N 32 20E
Bahr el Arab *r.* Sudan **110** E9 10 00N 27 30E
Bahr el Azraq *(Blue Nile) r.* Sudan **110** F10 13 30N 33 45E
Bahr el Baqar *r.* Egypt **109** S3 30 54N 32 02E
Bahr el Ghazal *r.* Chad **110** C10 14 00N 16 00E
Bahr Faqus *r.* Egypt **109** R3 30 42N 31 42E
Bahr Hadus *r.* Egypt **109** R4 31 01N 31 43E
Bahr Saft *r.* Egypt **109** R3 30 57N 31 48E
Baia Mare Romania **75** D2 47 39N 23 36E
Baicao Ling *mts.* China **38** C5 26 20N 101 30E
Baicheng China **49** O8 45 37N 122 48E
Baidyabati India **52** K3 22 48N 88 20E
Baie-Comeau *tn.* Québec Canada **93** G3 49 12N 68 10W
Baie de l'Allier *b.* New Caledonia **82** X2 21 05S 168 02E
Baie de la Seine *b.* France **73** A2 49 40N 0 30W
Baie de Taravao *b.* Tahiti **82** T9 17 42S 149 17W
Baie d'Opunohu *b.* Tahiti **82** R10 17 30S 149 52W
Baie-du-Poste *tn.* Québec Canada **93** F4 50 20N 73 50W
Baie du Santal *b.* New Caledonia **82** W3 20 50S 167 05E
Baie St. Paul *tn.* Québec Canada **93** F3 47 27N 70 30W
Baie Trinité *tn.* Québec Canada **93** G3 49 25N 67 20W
Bailleul France **70** B2 50 44N 2 44E
Baimuru Papua New Guinea **45** L3 7 34S 144 49E
Baird Mountains Alaska U.S.A. **88** D6 67 30N 160 00W
Baise *r.* France **73** B1 43 55N 0 25E
Bai Thuong Vietnam **37** C3 19 54N 105 25E
Baiti Nauru **83** L2 0 30S 166 56E
Baiwanzhuang China **47** G1 39 55N 116 18E
Baja Hungary **75** C2 46 11N 18 58E
Baja California *p.* Mexico **96** B5 27 30N 113 00W
Baj Baj India **52** J1 22 28N 88 10E
Baker Oregon U.S.A. **90** C5 44 46N 117 50W
Baker Island Pacific Ocean **80** D4 0 12N 176 28W
Baker Lake Northwest Territories Canada **89** Q5 64 00N 95 00W
Baker Lake *tn.* Northwest Territories Canada **89** P5 64 20N 96 10W
Bakersfield California U.S.A. **90** C4 35 25N 119 00W
Baku Azerbaijan **58** F3 40 22N 49 53E
Balabac *i.* The Philippines **40** A2 8 00N 117 00E
Balabac Strait The Philippines/Malaysia **40** A2 8 00N 117 00E
Balaghat India **53** E4 21 48N 80 16E
Balaghat Range *mts.* India **53** D3 18 45N 77 00E
Balakovo Russia **56** G6 52 04N 47 46E
Balama Mozambique **111** G5 13 19S 38 35E
Bālā Morghāb Afghanistan **55** J6 35 34N 63 20E
Balanga The Philippines **40** B3 14 41N 120 33E
Balashikha Russia **58** D6 55 47N 37 59E
Balashov Russia **58** E5 51 31N 43 10E
Balassagyarmat Hungary **75** C2 48 06N 19 17E
Balaton *l.* Hungary **75** C2 47 00N 17 30E
Balboa Panama **97** I2 8 57N 79 33W
Balclutha South Island New Zealand **79** A1 46 14S 169 44E
Bald Eagle Lake Minnesota U.S.A. **92** B3 47 48N 91 32W
Baldwin Park *tn.* California U.S.A. **95** C3 34 05N 117 59W
Balearic Islands Mediterranean Sea **72** C2/3
Balembangan *i.* Malaysia **42** E5 7 15N 116 55E
Balembangan *p.* Malaysia **40** A2 7 15N 116 55E
Balgowlah Australia **79** H2 33 48S 151 16E
Bali *i.* Indonesia **42** R6 8 30S 115 00E
Balikesir Turkey **54** C6 39 37N 27 51E
Balikpapan Indonesia **42** E3 1 15S 116 50E
Balimo Papua New Guinea **45** K2 8 00S 143 00E
Balingen Germany **71** A1 48 17N 8 52E
Balintang Channel The Philippines **40** B4 20 00N 122 00E
Balkan Mountains Europe **60** 43 00N 25 00E
Balkhash Kazakhstan **59** L4 46 50N 74 57E
Balkhash, Lake *see* Ozero Balkhash
Ballarat Australia **78** G2 37 36S 143 58E
Ball Bay Norfolk Island **81** L4 29 03S 167 58E
Ball Bay Reserve Norfolk Island **81** L4 29 02S 167 58E
Balleny Islands Southern Ocean **22** G1 66 30S 1 64E
Bally India **52** K2 22 38N 88 20E
Ballygunge India **52** K2 22 31N 88 20E
Ballymena Northern Ireland United Kingdom **68** E6 54 52N 6 17W
Balmain Australia **79** G2 33 51S 151 11E
Balsas Mexico **96** E3 18 00N 99 44W
Baltic Sea Europe **69** D2 55 15N 17 00E
Baltimore Maryland U.S.A. **93** E1 39 18N 76 38W
Baltrum *i.* Germany **71** A2 53 44N 7 23E
Baluchistan *geog. reg.* Pakistan **52** A5/B5 27 30N 65 00E
Balurin Indonesia **43** F2 8 40S 124 00E
Balut *i.* The Philippines **40** C2 5 25N 125 23E
Bam Iran **55** I4 29 07N 58 20E
Bamaga Australia **45** K1 10 50S 142 25E
Bamako Mali **112** D5 12 40N 7 59W
Bambari Central African Republic **110** D9 5 40N 20 37E
Bamberg Germany **71** B1 49 54N 10 54E
Bamenda Cameroon **112** H4 5 55N 10 09E
Bamingui Bangoran National Park Central African Republic **110** C9/D9 8 00N 20 00E
Banam Cambodia **37** C2 11 20N 105 17E
Banas *r.* India **53** D5 26 00N 75 00E
Ban Ban Laos **37** B3 19 38N 103 32E
Banbury England United Kingdom **68** J4 52 04N 1 20W
Bancroft Ontario Canada **93** E3 45 03N 77 52W
Banda India **53** E5 25 28N 80 20E
Banda Aceh Indonesia **42** A5 5 30N 95 20E
Bandama Blanc *r.* Côte d'Ivoire **112** D4 8 00N 5 45W
Bandanaira Indonesia **44** C4 4 13S 129 50E
Ban Dang Khrien Vietnam **37** C2 11 59N 107 29E
Ban Dan Lan Hoi Thailand **39** A3 17 00N 99 36E
Bandar Abbās Iran **55** I4 27 12N 56 15E
Bandarbeyla Somalia **110** J9 9 30N 50 50E
Bandar-e Lengeh Iran **55** H4 26 34N 54 52E
Bandar-e Torkeman Iran **55** H6 36 55N 54 01E
Bandar Khomeynī Iran **55** G5 30 40N 49 08E
Bandar Seri Begawan Brunei Darussalam **42** D4 4 53N 114 57E
Banda Sea Indonesia **43** G2 5 50S 126 00E
Bandeirantes Beach Brazil **103** P1 23 01S 43 23W
Bandel India **52** K3 22 55N 88 23E
Bandirma Turkey **54** C7 40 21N 27 58E
Bandundu Zaire **111** C7 3 20S 17 24E
Bandung Indonesia **42** N7 6 57S 107 34E
Banff Alberta Canada **88** L3 51 10N 115 34W
Banff National Park Alberta Canada **88** L3 52 00N 116 00W
Banfora Burkina **112** E5 10 36N 4 45W
Bangalore India **53** D2 12 58N 77 35E
Bangassou Central African Republic **110** D8 4 41N 22 48E
Bang Bua Thong Thailand **39** B2 13 55N 100 22E
Banggai Indonesia **43** F3 1 34S 123 33E
Banggi *i.* Malaysia **42** E5 7 15N 117 10E
Banghāzī *(Benghazi)* Libya **110** D14 32 07N 20 04E
Bangil Indonesia **42** Q7 7 34S 112 47E
Bangkalan Indonesia **42** Q7 7 05S 112 44E
Bang Khla Thailand **39** B2 13 43N 101 14E
Bangkinang Indonesia **42** B4 0 21N 101 02E
Bangko Indonesia **42** B3 2 05S 102 20E
Bangkok *(Krung Thep)* Thailand **39** B2 13 44N 100 30E
Bangkok, Bight of Thailand **39** B2 13 00N 100 30E
BANGLADESH **53** F4/G4
Banglang Reservoir Thailand **39** B1 6 00N 101 30E
Bangli Indonesia **42** R6 8 25S 115 25E
Bang Mun Nak Thailand **39** B3 16 02N 100 26E
Bangor Northern Ireland United Kingdom **68** F6 54 40N 5 40W
Bangor Wales United Kingdom **68** G5 53 13N 4 08W
Bangor Maine U.S.A. **93** G2 44 49N 68 47W
Bang Saphan Thailand **39** A2 11 110N 99 33E
Bangued The Philippines **40** B4 17 36N 120 37E
Bangui Central African Republic **110** C8 4 23N 18 37E
Bangweulu, Lake Zambia **111** E5 11 15S 29 45E
Ban Huai Yang Thailand **39** A2 11 38N 99 38E
Baniara Papua New Guinea **45** N2 9 46S 149 51E
Baniyachung Bangladesh **38** A4 24 30N 91 21E
Banja Luka Bosnia-Herzegovina **74** C3 44 47N 17 11E
Banjaran Crocker *mts.* Malaysia **42** E5 5 30N 116 00E
Banjarmasin Indonesia **42** D3 3 22S 114 33E
Banjul The Gambia **112** B5 13 28N 16 39W
Banka India **52** K2 22 36N 88 17E
Banka *i.* Indonesia **42** C3 2 00S 106 00E
Ban Keo Lom Vietnam **37** B4 21 15N 103 14E
Ban Khlung Thailand **39** B2 12 27N 102 12E
Ban Khok Kloi Thailand **39** A1 8 15N 98 18E
Banks Island Vanuatu **83** G8 13 30S 167 30E
Banks Island Northwest Territories Canada **88** K7/L7 72 30N 122 30W
Banks Peninsula South Island New Zealand **79** B2 43 44S 173 00E
Bankstown Australia **79** G2 33 55S 151 02E
Banmauk Myanmar **38** B4 24 26N 95 54E
Ban Me Thuot Vietnam **37** C2 12 41N 108 02E
Ban Mi Thailand **39** B3 15 03N 100 36E
Bann *r.* Northern Ireland United Kingdom **68** E7 54 20N 6 10W
Ban Nang Sata Thailand **39** B1 6 12N 101 12E
Ban Nape Laos **37** C3 18 18N 105 07E
Ban Na San Thailand **39** A1 8 49N 99 20E
Bannu Pakistan **55** L5 33 00N 70 40E
Ban Pak Pat Thailand **39** B3 17 42N 100 37E
Ban Pak Phraek Thailand **39** B1 8 11N 100 10E
Ban Phai Thailand **39** B3 16 03N 102 45E
Ban Phon Laos **37** C3 15 24N 106 43E
Ban Phu Thailand **39** B3 17 41N 102 30E
Ban Pong Thailand **39** A2 13 49N 99 53E
Bansberia India **52** K3 22 57N 88 23E
Banská Bystrica Slovakia **75** C2 48 44N 19 10E
Banstead England United Kingdom **66** C2 51 19N 0 12W
Bantayan *i.* The Philippines **40** B3 11 12N 123 45E
Ban Tha Song Yang Thailand **39** A3 17 33N 97 56E
Bantry Bay Irish Republic **68** B3 51 35N 9 40W
Bantul Indonesia **42** P7 7 56S 110 21E
Ban Xéno Laos **37** C3 16 44N 105 03E
Banyuwangi Indonesia **42** R6 8 12S 114 22E
Baoding China **49** N6 38 54N 115 26E
Baoji China **49** L5 34 23N 107 16E
Bao Loc Vietnam **37** C2 11 33N 107 48E
Baoshan China **38** B5 25 09N 99 11E
Baotou China **49** L7 40 38N 109 59E
Ba'qūbah Iraq **54** F5 33 45N 44 40E
Ba Ra Vietnam **37** C2 11 50N 106 59E
Barabai Indonesia **42** E3 2 38S 115 22E
Barabash Russia **50** E6 43 11N 131 33E
Baraboo Wisconsin U.S.A. **92** C2 43 27N 89 45W
Baracaldo Spain **72** B3 43 17N 2 59W
Barahanagar India **52** K2 22 38N 88 23E
Barahona Dominican Republic **97** J3 18 13N 71 07W
Barail Range India **38** A5 25 20N 93 30E
Barajala Canal India **52** J2 22 35N 88 12E
Barak *r.* India **38** A5 25 20N 93 40E
Bārākpur India **52** K3 22 45N 88 22E
Baral India **52** K1 22 27N 88 22E
Baram *r.* Malaysia **42** D4 3 50N 114 30E
Barangbarang Indonesia **43** F2 6 00S 120 30E
Bārāsat India **52** K2 22 43N 88 26E
Barbacena Brazil **103** I8 21 13S 43 47W
BARBADOS **97** M2
Barbastro Spain **72** C3 42 02N 0 07E
Barbuda *i.* Antigua & Barbuda **97** L3 17 41N 61 48W
Barcaldine Australia **78** H5 23 31S 145 15E
Barcellona Italy **74** B2 38 10N 15 15E
Barcelona Spain **72** C3 41 25N 2 10E
Barcelona Venezuela **102** E15 10 08N 64 43W
Barcelonnette France **73** C1 44 24N 6 40E
Barcelos Brazil **102** E12 0 59S 62 58W
Barcoo *r.* Australia **78** G5 23 30S 144 00E
Barcs Hungary **75** C2 45 58N 17 30E
Barddhamān India **53** F4 23 20N 88 00E
Bardu *r.* Norway **69** D4 68 48N 18 22E
Bareilly India **53** D5 28 20N 79 24E
Barents Sea Arctic Ocean **20** 75 00N 40 00E
Barga China **53** E6 30 51N 81 20E
Bari Italy **74** C3 41 07N 16 52E
Ba Ria Vietnam **37** C2 10 24N 107 07E
Bariga Nigeria **109** V3 6 32N 3 28E
Barinas Venezuela **102** C14 8 36N 70 15W
Barisal Bangladesh **53** G4 22 41N 90 20E
Bariti, Lake India **52** K3 22 48N 88 26E
Barito *r.* Indonesia **42** D3 2 00S 114 45E
Barking England United Kingdom **66** D3 51 33N 0 06E
Barkly-Tableland *geog. reg.* Australia **78** F6 17 30S 137 00E
Bar-le-Duc France **73** C2 48 46N 5 10E
Barlee, Lake Australia **78** B4 28 30S 120 00E
Barletta Italy **74** C3 41 20N 16 17E
Barnaul Russia **57** K6 53 21N 83 45E
Barnes England United Kingdom **66** C2 51 28N 0 15W
Barnes Ice Cap Northwest Territories Canada **89** U7 70 10N 74 00W
Barnet England United Kingdom **66** C3 51 39N 0 12W
Barneveld Netherlands **70** E4 52 08N 5 35E
Barnstaple England United Kingdom **68** G3 51 05N 4 04W
Barora Fa *i.* Solomon Islands **82** D6 7 30S 158 16E
Barpeta India **36** A7 26 20N 91 02E
Barquisimeto Venezuela **102** D15 10 03N 69 18W
Barra *i.* Scotland United Kingdom **68** D9 57 00N 7 25W
Barra da Tijuca Brazil **103** P1 23 00S 43 20W
Barra do Corba Brazil **102** H11 5 30S 45 12W
Barrancabermeja Colombia **102** C14 7 06N 73 54W
Barrancas Venezuela **102** E14 8 45N 62 13W
Barrancones Point Trinidad and Tobago **96** T10 10 30N 61 28W
Barranjoey Head *c.* Australia **79** H3 33 35S 151 20E
Barranquilla Colombia **102** C15 11 10N 74 50W
Barre Vermont U.S.A. **93** F2 44 13N 72 31W
Barreiras Brazil **102** I10 12 09S 44 58W
Barreiro Portugal **72** A2 38 40N 9 05W
Barrhead Alberta Canada **88** M3 54 10N 114 22W
Barrie Ontario Canada **93** E2 44 22N 79 42W
Barrier Reef Papua New Guinea **45** P1 11 45S 153 00E
Barrow Alaska U.S.A. **88** D7 71 16N 156 50W
Barrow *r.* Irish Republic **68** D4 52 55N 7 00W
Barrow-in-Furness England United Kingdom **68** H6 54 07N 3 14W
Barrow Island Australia **78** B5 21 00S 115 00E
Barrow, Point Alaska U.S.A. **88** D7 71 05N 156 00W
Barry Wales United Kingdom **68** H3 51 24N 3 18W
Barrys Bay *tn.* Ontario Canada **93** E3 45 30N 77 41W
Barstow California U.S.A. **90** C3 34 55N 117 01W
Barthelemy Pass Laos/Vietnam **37** B3 19 50N 104 40E
Bartlesville Oklahoma U.S.A. **91** G4 36 44N 95 59W
Barton Vermont U.S.A. **93** F2 44 44N 72 12W
Barung *i.* Indonesia **42** Q6 8 30S 113 00E
Basalt Island Hong Kong U.K. **51** C1 22 19N 114 21E
Basdorf Germany **67** F2 52 44N 13 27E
Basel Switzerland **73** C2 47 33N 7 36E
Basiano Indonesia **43** F3 1 40S 123 30E
Basilan *i.* The Philippines **40** B2 6 00N 122 00E
Basildon England United Kingdom **68** L3 51 34N 0 25W
Basingstoke England United Kingdom **68** J3 51 16N 1 05W
Baskunchak Russia **58** F4 48 14N 46 44E
Bassas da India *i.* Mozambique Channel **111** G3 22 00S 40 00E
Bassein Myanmar **38** A3 16 46N 94 45E
Bassein *r.* Myanmar **38** A3 16 00N 94 20E
Basse Terre Trinidad and Tobago **96** T9 10 07N 61 17W
Basse Terre *i.* Lesser Antilles **97** L3 16 00N 61 20W
Bass Strait Australia **78** H1/2 40 00S 145 00E
Bastia Corsica France **73** C1 42 14N 9 26E
Bastogne Belgium **70** E2 50 00N 5 43E
Bastrop Louisiana U.S.A. **91** H3 32 49N 91 54W
Bata Equatorial Guinea **112** G3 1 51N 9 49E
Batakan Indonesia **42** D3 4 03S 114 39E
Batala India **53** D6 31 48N 75 17E
Batan *i.* The Philippines **40** B5 20 25N 121 58E
Batanagar India **52** K2 22 30N 88 14E
Batang China **49** J5 30 02N 99 01E
Batangafo Central African Republic **110** C9 7 27N 18 11E
Batangas The Philippines **40** B3 13 46N 121 01E
Batanghari *r.* Indonesia **42** B3 1 20S 103 30E
Batan Islands The Philippines **40** B5 20 00N 122 00E
Batavia New York U.S.A. **93** E2 43 00N 78 11W
Bate Bay Australia **79** G1 34 03S 151 11E
Bates, Mount Norfolk Island **81** K5 29 00S 167 56E
Bath Jamaica **97** R7 17 57N 76 22W
Bath England United Kingdom **68** I3 51 23N 2 22W
Batha *r.* Chad **110** C10 13 00N 19 00E
Bathsheba Barbados **96** V12 13 12N 59 32W
Bathurst Australia **78** H3 33 27S 149 35E
Bathurst New Brunswick Canada **89** V2 47 37N 65 40W
Bathurst, Cape Northwest Territories Canada **88** J7 70 31N 127 53W
Bathurst Inlet Northwest Territories Canada **88** N6 66 49N 108 00W
Bathurst Island Australia **78** E7 12 00S 130 00E
Bathurst Island Northwest Territories Canada **89** P8 76 00N 100 00W
Batiki *i.* Fiji **83** D9 17 47S 179 10E
Batna Algeria **112** G10 35 34N 6 10E
Batnavni Vanuatu **83** H6 15 38S 168 08E
Batong Group Thailand **39** A1 6 30N 99 30E
Baton Rouge Louisiana U.S.A. **91** H3 30 30N 91 10W
Batroûn Lebanon **54** O12 36 16N 35 40E
Battambang Cambodia **37** B2 13 06N 103 13E
Battle Creek *tn.* Michigan U.S.A. **92** C2 42 20N 85 21W
Battle Harbour *tn.* Newfoundland Canada **89** X3 51 16N 55 36W
Batumi Georgia **58** E3 41 37N 41 36E
Batu Pahat Malaysia **42** B4 1 50N 102 56E
Baturaja Indonesia **42** B3 4 10S 104 10E
Baturetno Indonesia **42** P6 8 00S 110 54E
Bat Yam Israel **54** O10 32 01N 34 45E
Baubau Indonesia **43** F2 5 30S 122 37E
Bauchi Nigeria **112** G5 10 16N 9 50E
Bau Island Fiji **83** C9 17 55S 178 37E
Baukau Indonesia **43** G2 8 30S 126 28E
Baulkham Hills Australia **79** F2/G2 33 46S 151 00E
Bauru Brazil **103** H8 22 19S 49 07W
Bautzen Germany **71** B2 51 11N 14 29E
Bavaria *see* Bayern
Bawdwin Myanmar **38** B4 23 06N 97 18E
Bawe Irian Jaya Indonesia **44** F5 2 59S 134 43E
Bawean *i.* Indonesia **42** Q8 5 50S 112 45E
Bayamo Cuba **97** I4 20 23N 76 39W
Bayawan The Philippines **40** B2 9 21N 122 47E
Baybay The Philippines **40** B3 10 40N 124 54E
Bay City Michigan U.S.A. **93** D2 43 35N 83 52W
Bay City Texas U.S.A. **91** G2 28 59N 96 00W
Baydhabo Somalia **110** H8 3 08N 43 34E
Bayerische Alpen *mts.* Germany **71** B1 47 00N 11 00E
Bayerische Wald *geog. reg.* Germany **71** B1 49 00N 13 00E
Bayern *(Bavaria) admin.* Germany **71** B1 49 00N 12 00E
Bayeux France **73** A2 49 16N 0 42W
Bayfield Barbados **96** W12 13 10N 59 25W
Baykal, Lake *see* Ozero Baykal
Baykonyr Kazakhstan **59** K4 47 50N 66 03E
Bay of Plenty North Island New Zealand **79** C3 37 48S 177 12E
Bayombong The Philippines **40** B4 16 27N 121 10E
Bayonne France **73** A1 43 30N 1 28W
Bayonne New Jersey U.S.A. **94** B1 40 39N 74 07W
Bayo Point The Philippines **40** B3 10 24N 121 57E
Bayreuth Germany **71** B1 49 27N 11 35E
Bay Ridge *tn.* New York U.S.A. **94** B1 40 37N 74 02W
Baytown Texas U.S.A. **91** H2 29 43N 94 59W
Bayugan The Philippines **40** C2 8 44N 125 43E
Baza Spain **72** B2 37 30N 2 45W
Bazar-Dyuzi *mt.* Azerbaijan **58** F3 41 14N 47 50E

Bondoc Peninsula The Philippines **40** B3 13 00N 122 00E
Bondowoso Indonesia **42** Q7 7 54S 113 50E
Bongor Chad **110** C10 10 18N 15 20E
Bong Son *(Hoai Nhon)* Vietnam **37** C2 14 24N 109 00E
Bonifacio Corsica **73** C1 41 23N 9 10E
Bonifacio, Strait of Corsica/Sardinia **73** C1 41 20N 8 45E
Bonn Germany **71** A2 50 44N 7 06E
Bonny, Bight of *b.* West Africa **112** G3 2 10N 7 30E
Bonthe Sierra Leone **112** C4 7 32N 12 30W
Bontoc The Philippines **40** B4 17 07N 120 58E
Boorama Somalia **110** H9 9 56N 43 13E
Boosaaso Somalia **110** I10 11 18N 49 10E
Boothia, Gulf of Northwest Territories Canada **89** R6 69 00N 88 00W
Boothia Peninsula Northwest Territories Canada **89** Q7 70 30N 94 30W
Boot Reefs Papua New Guinea **45** L1 10 00S 144 45E
Bor Sudan **110** F9 6 18N 31 34E
Borås Sweden **56** C2 57 44N 12 55E
Bordeaux France **73** A1 44 50N 0 34W
Borden Peninsula Northwest Territories Canada **89** S7 73 00N 82 30W
Borehamwood England United Kingdom **66** B3 51 40N 0 16W
Borgholm Sweden **69** D2 56 51N 16 40E
Borgsdorf Germany **67** F2 52 44N 13 17E
Borikhan Laos **37** B3 18 35N 103 44E
Borisoglebsk Russia **58** E5 51 23N 42 02E
Borisov Belarus **75** E3 54 09N 28 30E
Borken Germany **70** F3 51 50N 6 52E
Borkum Germany **71** A2 53 35N 6 40E
Borkum *i.* Germany **71** A2 53 00N 6 00E
Borlänge Sweden **69** D3 60 29N 15 25E
Bormida di Spigno *r.* Italy **73** C1 44 17N 8 14E
Borneo *i.* Indonesia/Malaysia **42** D4 1 00N 113 00E
Bornholm *i.* Denmark **69** C2 55 02N 15 00E
Borongan The Philippines **40** C3 11 38N 125 27E
Borough Green England United Kingdom **66** D2 51 17N 0 19E
Borūjerd Iran **55** G5 33 55N 48 48E
Borzya Russia **57** N6 50 24N 116 35E
Bose China **36** D6 24 00N 106 30E
Bosna *r.* Bosnia-Herzegovina **74** C3 45 00N 18 00E
BOSNIA-HERZEGOVINA 74 C3/4
Bosnik Irian Jaya Indonesia **44** G6 1 09S 136 14E
Bōsō-hantō Japan **46** M2
Bosphorous *sd.* Europe/Asia **60** 41 00N 29 00E
Bossangoa Central African Republic **110** C9 6 27N 17 21E
Bosso Niger **112** H5 13 43N 13 19E
Boston England United Kingdom **68** K4 52 29N 0 01W
Boston Massachusetts U.S.A. **93** F2 42 20N 71 05W
Boston Mountains Arkansas U.S.A. **91** H4 36 00N 94 00W
Botafogo Brazil **103** Q2 22 57S 43 11W
Botany Australia **79** G2 33 58S 151 12E
Botany Bay Australia **79** G2 34 04S 151 08E
Bothnia, Gulf of Finland/Sweden **69** D3 61 00N 19 10E
Botoşani Romania **75** E2 47 44N 26 41E
Botrange *sum.* Belgium **70** F2 50 30N 6 05E
BOTSWANA 111 D3/E3
Bottrop Germany **71** A2 51 31N 6 55E
Bötzow Germany **67** E2 52 40N 13 07E
Bouaké Côte d'Ivoire **112** E4 7 42N 5 00W
Bouar Central African Republic **110** C9 5 58N 15 35E
Bouârfa Morocco **112** E9 32 30N 1 59W
Boucherville Québec Canada **93** F3 45 00N 73 00W
Boufarik Algeria **72** C2 36 36N 2 54E
Bougainville Island Papua New Guinea **45** Q3 6 15S 155 00E
Bougainville Strait Papua New Guinea **82** B6 8 00S 156 00E
Bougouni Mali **112** D5 11 25N 7 28W
Bougzoul Algeria **72** C2 35 42N 2 51E
Bouillon Belgium **70** E1 49 47N 5 04E
Boulder Colorado U.S.A. **90** E5 40 02N 105 16W
Boulogne-Billancourt France **67** A2/B2 48 50N 2 15E
Boulogne-sur-Mer France **73** B3 50 43N 1 37E
Bouloupari New Caledonia **82** V2 21 50S 166 04E
Bouma Fiji **83** E10 16 50S 179 56W
Boung Long Cambodia **37** C2 13 45N 107 00E
Boun Tai Laos **37** B4 21 26N 102 00E
Bounty Islands Pacific Ocean **80** C1 7 45S 179 05E
Bourail New Caledonia **82** U2 21 34S 165 29E
Bourem Mali **112** E6 16 59N 0 20W
Bourg-en-Bresse France **73** C2 46 12N 5 13E
Bourges France **73** B2 47 05N 2 23E
Bourke Australia **78** H3 30 09S 145 59E
Bournemouth England United Kingdom **68** J2 50 43N 1 54W
Bouroumba Vanuatu **83** H5 16 42S 168 08E
Bou Saâda Algeria **112** F10 35 10N 4 09E
Bousso Chad **110** C10 10 32N 16 45E
Bouvet Island Southern Ocean **25** I1 54 26S 3 24E
Bowen Australia **78** H5 20 00S 148 10E
Bowling Green Kentucky U.S.A. **92** C1 37 00N 86 29W
Bowling Green Missouri U.S.A. **92** B1 39 21N 91 11W
Bowling Green Ohio U.S.A. **93** D2 41 22N 83 40W
Bowman North Dakota U.S.A. **90** F6 46 11N 103 26W
Bowutu Mountains Papua New Guinea **45** M3 7 45S 147 00E
Box Hill England United Kingdom **66** B2 51 16N 0 13W
Boxmeer Netherlands **70** E3 51 39N 5 57E
Boxtel Netherlands **70** E3 51 36N 5 20E
Boyne *r.* Irish Republic **68** E5 53 40N 6 35W
Boyoma Falls Zaïre **110** E8 0 18N 25 30E
Bozeman Montana U.S.A. **90** D6 45 40N 111 00W
Bozoum Central African Republic **110** C9 6 16N 16 22E
Brabant *admin.* Belgium **70** D2 50 45N 4 30E
Brač *i.* Croatia **74** C3 43 00N 16 00E
Braddell Heights *tn.* Singapore **41** D4 1 21N 103 53E
Bradenton Florida U.S.A. **91** J2 27 29N 82 33W
Bradford England United Kingdom **68** J5 53 48N 1 45W
Bradford Pennsylvania U.S.A. **93** E2 41 57N 78 39W
Brady Texas U.S.A. **90** G3 31 08N 99 22W
Braga Portugal **72** A3 41 32N 8 26W
Bragança Brazil **102** H12 1 02S 46 46W
Bragança Portugal **72** A3 41 47N 6 46W
Brahmapur India **53** E3 19 21N 84 51E
Brahmaputra *r.* Asia **53** G5 26 40N 93 00E
Brăila Romania **75** E2 45 17N 27 58E
Braine l'Alleud Belgium **70** D2 50 41N 4 22E
Brainerd Minnesota U.S.A. **92** B3 46 20N 94 10W
Brampton Ontario Canada **93** E2 43 42N 79 46W
Brandenburg Germany **71** B2 52 25N 12 34E
Brandenburg *admin.* Germany **71** B2 53 00N 13 00E
Brandon Manitoba Canada **89** P2 49 50N 99 57W
Brandon Vermont U.S.A. **93** F2 43 47N 73 05W
Brantford Ontario Canada **93** D2 43 09N 80 17W
Brasileia Brazil **102** D10 10 59S 68 45W
Brásilia Brazil **102** H9 15 45S 47 57W
Brasov Romania **75** E2 45 39N 25 35E
Brasschaat Belgium **70** D3 51 17N 4 30E
Brassey Range *mts.* Malaysia **40** A2 5 40N 117 50E
Bratislava Slovakia **75** C2 48 10N 17 10E
Bratsk Russia **57** M7 56 20N 101 50E
Bratsk Vodokhranilishche *res.* Russia **57** M7 56 00N 102 00E
Brattleboro Vermont U.S.A. **93** F2 42 51N 75 36W
Braunau Austria **71** B1 48 16N 13 03E
Braunschweig Germany **71** B2 52 15N 10 30E
Brawley California U.S.A. **90** C3 32 59N 115 30W
Bray Irish Republic **68** E5 53 12N 6 06W
BRAZIL 102 G10
Brazil Basin Atlantic Ocean **25** F5/6 10 00S 26 00W
Brazilian Highlands Brazil **98** 10 00S 50 00W
Brazil Plateau Brazil **98** 20 00S 45 00W
Brazos *r.* Texas U.S.A. **91** G3 32 00N 97 00W
Brazzaville Congo **112** I2 4 14S 15 14E
Brdy *mts.* Czech Republic **71** B1 49 00N 14 00E
Brea Reservoir California U.S.A. **95** C2 33 54N 117 56W
Brebes Indonesia **42** O7 6 54S 109 00E
Breckenridge Minnesota U.S.A. **92** A3 46 14N 96 35W
Brecon Beacons *mts.* Wales United Kingdom **68** H3 51 53N 3 30W
Breda Netherlands **70** D3 51 35N 4 46E
Bredy Russia **59** J5 52 23N 60 16E
Bregenz Austria **71** A1 47 31N 9 46E
Breidha Fjördur *b.* Iceland **69** H7 65 15N 23 00W
Brekstad Norway **69** B3 63 50N 9 50E
Bremen Germany **71** A2 53 05N 8 48E
Bremen *admin.* Germany **71** A2 53 00N 9 00E
Bremerhaven Germany **71** A2 53 33N 8 35E
Bremerton Washington U.S.A. **90** B6 47 34N 122 40W
Brenham Texas U.S.A. **91** G3 30 09N 96 24W
Brenner Pass Austria/Italy **75** B2 47 02N 11 32E
Brent *bor.* England United Kingdom **66** B3 51 34N 0 17W
Brentwood England United Kingdom **66** E3 51 38N 0 18E
Brescia Italy **74** B4 45 33N 10 13E
Brest Belarus **75** D3 52 08N 23 40E
Brest France **73** A2 48 23N 4 30W
Brewerton New York U.S.A. **93** E2 43 15N 76 09W
Brezhnev see Neberezhnyye Chelny
Bria Central African Republic **110** D9 67 32N 22 00E
Briançon France **73** C1 44 53N 6 39E
Brickfield Trinidad and Tobago **96** T9 10 20N 61 16W
Bridgeport Connecticut U.S.A. **93** F2 41 12N 73 12W
Bridgeton New Jersey U.S.A. **93** E1 39 26N 75 14W
Bridgetown Barbados **96** V12 13 06N 59 37W
Bridgwater England United Kingdom **68** H3 51 08N 3 00W
Brie-Comte-Robert France **67** C1 48 41N 2 37E
Brienz Switzerland **73** C2 46 46N 8 02E
Brieselang Germany **67** E2 52 36N 13 00E
Briey France **73** C2 49 15N 5 57E
Brig Switzerland **73** C2 46 19N 8 00E
Brigham City Utah U.S.A. **90** D5 41 30N 112 02W
Brighton England United Kingdom **68** K2 50 50N 0 10W
Brighton Beach *tn.* New York U.S.A. **94** C1 40 34N 73 58W
Brignoles France **73** C1 43 25N 6 03E
Brindisi Italy **74** C3 40 37N 17 57E
Brisbane Australia **78** I4 27 30S 153 00E
Bristol England United Kingdom **68** I3 51 27N 2 35W
Bristol Bay Alaska U.S.A. **88** D4 57 30N 159 00W
Bristol Channel United Kingdom **68** H3 51 20N 3 50W
British Columbia *province* Canada **88** J4 56 50N 125 30W
British Mountains U.S.A./Canada **88** G6 65 40N 142 30W
Britt Ontario Canada **93** D3 45 46N 80 35W
Brittany Peninsula France **60** 48 00N 4 00W
Brive-la-Gailliarde France **73** B2 45 09N 1 32E
Brno Czech Republic **75** C2 49 13N 16 40E
Brockton Massachusetts U.S.A. **93** F2 42 06N 71 01W
Brockville Ontario Canada **93** E2 44 35N 75 44W
Brodeur Peninsula Northwest Territories Canada **89** R7 72 00N 87 30W
Brody Ukraine **58** B5 50 05N 25 08E
Broer Ruys, Cape Greenland **20** 73 30N 20 20W
Broken Bridge Creek Norfolk Island **81** L5 29 01S 167 57E
Broken Hill *tn.* Australia **78** G3 31 57S 141 30E
Broken Ridge Indian Ocean **24** I3 30 00S 93 00E
Bromley *bor.* England United Kingdom **66** D2 51 31N 0 01W
Brønnøysund Norway **69** C4 65 38N 12 15E
Brooke's Point *tn.* The Philippines **40** A2 8 50N 117 52E
Brookings South Dakota U.S.A. **92** A2 44 19N 96 47W
Brooklyn New York U.S.A. **94** C1 40 41N 73 57W
Brooks Alberta Canada **88** M3 50 35N 111 54W
Brooks Range *mts.* Alaska U.S.A. **88** E6/G6 67 55N 155 00W
Brookvale Australia **79** H2 33 46S 151 16E
Brookville Pennsylvania U.S.A. **93** E2 41 10N 79 06W
Broome Australia **78** C6 17 58S 122 15E
Browning Montana U.S.A. **90** D6 48 33N 113 00W
Brown's Town Jamaica **97** Q8 18 28N 77 22W
Browns Valley *tn.* Minnesota U.S.A. **92** A3 45 35N 96 50W
Brownsville Texas U.S.A. **91** G2 25 54N 97 30W
Brownwood Texas U.S.A. **90** G3 31 42N 98 59W
Bruay-en-Artois France **73** B3 50 29N 2 33E
Bruce Mines *tn.* Ontario Canada **93** D3 46 19N 83 48W
Bruce Peninsula Ontario Canada **93** D2/3 45 00N 81 20W
Bruchsal Germany **71** A1 49 07N 8 35E
Bruges see Brugge
Brugg Switzerland **73** C2 47 29N 8 13E
Brugge *(Bruges)* Belgium **70** C3 51 13N 3 14E
Brühl Germany **70** F2 50 50N 6 55E
Brunei Bay Brunei Darussalam/Malaysia **40** A2 5 05N 115 20E
BRUNEI DARUSSALAM 42 D4
Brunoy France **67** C1 48 40N 2 31E
Brunssum Netherlands **70** E2 50 57N 5 59E
Brunswick Georgia U.S.A. **91** J3 31 09N 81 30W
Brunswick Maine U.S.A. **93** G2 43 55N 69 59W
Brussel see Bruxelles
Brussels see Bruxelles
Bruxelles *(Brussel, Brussels)* Belgium **70** D2 50 50N 4 21E
Bryan Texas U.S.A. **91** G3 30 41N 96 24W
Bryansk Russia **56** F6 53 15N 34 09E
Brzeg Poland **75** C3 50 52N 17 27E
Bua Fiji **83** C10 16 49S 178 39E
Buada Lagoon Nauru **83** L1 0 31S 166 55E
Bü Ağri Daği *(Mt. Ararat) mt.* Turkey **54** F6 39 44N 44 15E
Buala Solomon Islands **82** E5 8 11S 159 37E
Bua Yai Thailand **39** B3 15 35N 102 25E
Buca Fiji **83** D10 16 39S 179 51E
Bucaramanga Colombia **102** C14 7 08N 73 10W
Bucas Grande *i.* The Philippines **40** C2 9 38N 125 58E
Buchanan Liberia **112** C4 5 57N 10 02W
Bucharest see Bucureşti
Bucholz Germany **67** F2 51 25N 6 45E
Buckingham Québec Canada **93** E3 45 35N 75 25W
Buckinghamshire *co.* England United Kingdom **66** A3 51 50N 0 50W
Buckow Germany **67** F1 52 24N 1324E
Bucks Point Reserve Norfolk Island **81** L4 29 02S 167 59E
Bucksport Maine U.S.A. **93** G2 44 35N 68 47W
Bucureşti *(Bucharest)* Romania **75** E1 44 25N 26 07E
Budapest Hungary **75** C2 47 30N 19 03E
Budjala Zaïre **110** C8 2 38N 19 48E
Buea Cameroon **112** G3 4 09N 9 13E
Buena Park *tn.* California U.S.A. **95** B2 33 52N 118 02W
Buenaventura Colombia **102** B13 3 54N 77 02W
Buenaventura Mexico **96** C5 29 50N 107 30W
Buenos Aires Argentina **103** F6 34 40S 58 30W
Buenos Aires, Lake Argentina/Chile **103** C3 47 00S 72 00W
Buffalo New York U.S.A. **93** E2 42 52N 78 55W
Buffalo Wyoming U.S.A. **90** E5 44 21N 106 40W
Buffalo Lake Northwest Territories Canada **88** L5 60 40N 115 30W
Buffalo Narrows *tn.* Saskatchewan Canada **88** N4 55 52N 108 28W
Buff Bay *tn.* Jamaica **97** R8 18 18N 76 40W
Bugsuk *i.* The Philippines **40** A2 8 15N 117 17E
Bugul'ma Russia **59** G5 54 32N 52 46E
Buheirat-Murrat-el-Kubra *(Great Bitter Lake) l.* Egypt **109** S2 30 22N 32 22E
Buheirat-Murrat-el-Sughra *(Little Bitter Lake) l.* Egypt **109** T2 30 14N 32 33E
Buin Papua New Guinea **45** Q3 6 52S 155 42E
Bujumbura Burundi **111** E7 3 22S 29 19E
Bukachacha Russia **57** N6 53 00N 116 58E
Buka Island Papua New Guinea **45** Q4 5 15S 154 35E
Bukama Zaïre **111** E6 9 13S 25 52E
Bukatatonoa Reefs Fiji **83** F8 18 15S 178 25W
Bukavu Zaïre **110** E7 2 30S 28 50E
Bukhara Uzbekistan **59** J2 39 47N 64 26E
Bukit Batok Singapore **41** B4 1 21N 103 45E
Bukit Gombak *hill* Singapore **41** C4 1 22N 103 45E
Bukit Liangpran *hill* Indonesia **42** D4 1 04N 114 22E
Bukit Mandai Singapore **41** C4 1 25N 103 46E
Bukit Mertajam Malaysia **39** B1 5 21N 100 27E
Bukit Panjang Singapore **41** C4 1 23N 103 46E
Bukit Panjang Singapore **41** C4 1 23N 103 46E
Bukit Paya *mt.* Indonesia **42** D3 0 31S 112 37E
Bukit Timah Singapore **41** B4 1 22N 103 44E
Bukit Timah *hill* Singapore **41** C4 1 21N 103 47E
Bukittinggi Indonesia **42** B3 0 18S 100 20E
Bukoba Tanzania **110** F7 1 19S 31 49E
Bula Indonesia **43** H3 3 07S 130 27E
Bula Papua New Guinea **45** J2 9 15S 141 15E
Bulan The Philippines **40** B3 12 40N 123 53E
Bulandshahr India **53** D5 28 30N 77 49E
Bulawayo Zimbabwe **111** E3 20 10S 28 43E
BULGARIA 74 D3/E3
Bulileka Fiji **83** D10 16 27S 179 29E
Bulim Singapore **41** B4 1 22N 103 43E
Buliya *i.* Fiji **83** C8 18 50S 178 33E
Buller *r.* South Island New Zealand **79** B2 41 50S 171 35E
Bull Shoals Lake U.S.A. **91** H4 36 00N 93 00W
Bulolo Papua New Guinea **45** M3 7 13S 146 35E
Buluan, Lake The Philippines **40** B2 6 40N 124 50E
Bulukumba Indonesia **43** F2 5 35N 120 13E
Bulun Russia **57** O10 70 45N 127 20E
Bumba Zaïre **110** D8 2 10N 22 30E
Bumba Bum *mt.* Myanmar **38** B5 26 45N 97 16E
Bumbora Reserve Norfolk Island **81** K4 29 03S 167 56E
Bumbulan Indonesia **43** F4 0 31N 122 04E
Bunabufi Papua New Guinea **45** L4 4 36S 145 32E
Bunama Papua New Guinea **45** O1 10 10S 151 05E
Bunbury Australia **78** B3 33 20S 115 34E
Bundaberg Australia **78** I5 24 50S 152 21E
Bundeena Australia **79** G1 34 06S 151 07E
Bung Boraphet *l.* Thailand **39** B3 15 45N 100 30E
Bung Kan Thailand **39** B3 18 20N 103 41E
Bungo-suidō *sd.* Japan **46** B1 33 00N 132 30E
Bunia Zaïre **110** F8 1 33N 30 13E
Buntok Indonesia **42** D3 1 45S 114 47E
Buol Indonesia **43** F4 0 50N 121 30E
Buona Vista Singapore **41** C3 1 17N 103 47E
Bura Kenya **110** G7 1 06S 39 58E
Buran Darat *i.* Singapore **41** D2 1 15N 103 51E
Burauen The Philippines **40** B3 10 58N 124 56E
Buraydah Saudi Arabia **54** F4 26 20N 43 59E
Burbank California U.S.A. **95** A3 34 10N 118 25W
Burco Somalia **108** O9 9 31N 45 33E
Burdur Turkey **54** D6 37 44N 30 17E
Bure *r.* England United Kingdom **68** M4 52 47N 1 20E
Bureya *r.* Russia **57** P6 52 00N 133 00E
Būr Fu'ad Egypt **109** S4 31 50N 32 19E
Burg Germany **71** B2 52 17N 11 51E
Burgas Bulgaria **74** E3 42 30N 27 29E
Burgos Spain **72** B3 42 21N 3 41W
Burhanpur India **53** D4 21 18N 76 08E
Burias *i.* The Philippines **40** B3 13 00N 123 00E
Buri Khali India **52** J1 22 30N 88 10E
Buri Ram Thailand **39** B2 14 59N 103 09E
BURKINA 112 E5
Burk's Falls *tn.* Ontario Canada **93** E3 45 37N 79 25W
Burlington Ontario Canada **93** E2 43 19N 79 48W
Burlington Colorado U.S.A. **90** F4 39 17N 102 17W
Burlington Iowa U.S.A. **92** B2 40 50N 91 07W
Burlington Vermont U.S.A. **93** F2 44 28N 73 14W
Burlington West Virginia U.S.A. **93** E1 39 20N 78 56W
Burlington Wisconsin U.S.A. **92** C2 42 41N 88 17W
BURMA see MYANMAR
Burnie Australia **78** H1 41 03S 145 55E
Burnt Pine Norfolk Island **81** K4 29 02S 167 57E
Burquin China **59** O4 47 44N 86 55E
Bursa Turkey **54** C7 40 12N 29 04E
Būr Safâga Egypt **110** F13 25 43N 33 55E
Būr Taufiq Egypt **109** T1 29 57N 32 34E
BURUNDI 111 E7
Burwell Nebraska U.S.A. **90** G5 41 48N 99 09W
Busa, Mount The Philippines **40** B2 6 07N 124 41E
Būshehr Iran **55** H4 28 57N 50 52E
Bushey England United Kingdom **66** B3 51 39N 0 22W
Busira *r.* Zaïre **110** C7 1 00S 20 00E
Bussum Netherlands **70** E4 52 16N 5 09E
Busto Arsizio Italy **74** A4 45 37N 8 51E
Busuanga *i.* The Philippines **40** B3 12 00N 120 00E
Buta Zaïre **110** D8 2 49N 24 50E
Butare Rwanda **110** E7 2 35S 29 44E
Butaritari *i.* Pacific Ocean **80** C4 3 10N 172 45E
Bute *i.* Scotland United Kingdom **68** F7 55 50N 5 05W
Buthidaung Myanmar **38** A4 20 50N 92 35E
Butler Pennsylvania U.S.A. **93** E2 40 51N 79 55W
Butovo Russia **56** M1 55 30N 37 32E
Butte Montana U.S.A. **90** D6 46 00N 112 31W
Butterworth Malaysia **42** B5 5 24N 100 22E
Butt of Lewis *c.* Scotland United Kingdom **68** E10 58 30N 6 20W
Butuan The Philippines **40** C2 8 56N 125 31E
Buulobarde Somalia **110** I8 3 50N 45 33E
Buxtehude Germany **71** A2 53 29N 9 42E
Buzău Romania **75** E2 45 09N 26 49E
Bwagaoia Papua New Guinea **45** P1 10 39S 152 48E
Bydgoszcz Poland **75** C3 53 16N 18 00E
Byelorussia see BELARUS
Byfleet England United Kingdom **66** B2 51 21N 0 29W
Bygland Norway **69** B2 58 50N 7 49E
Bylot Island Northwest Territories Canada **89** T7 73 30N 79 00W
Byron, Cape Solomon Islands **83** M3 10 40S 166 09E
Byrranga Mountains Russia **57** L10 75 00N 100 00E
Bytom Poland **75** C3 50 21N 18 51E

C

Cabanatuan The Philippines **40** B4 15 30N 120 58E
Cabano Québec Canada **93** G3 47 40N 68 56W
Cabimas Venezuela **102** C15 10 26N 71 27W
Cabinda *admin.* Angola **111** B6 5 30S 12 20E
Cabo Brazil **102** J11 8 16S 35 00W
Cabo Blanco *c.* Costa Rica **97** G1 9 36N 85 06W
Cabo Caballeria *c.* Balearic Islands **72** F5 40 05N 4 05E
Cabo Catoche *c.* Mexico **97** G4 21 38N 87 08W
Cabo Corrientes *c.* Colombia **102** B14 5 29N 77 36W
Cabo Corrientes *c.* Mexico **96** C4 20 25N 105 42W
Cabo d'Artrutx *c.* Balearic Islands **72** E4 39 55N 3 49E
Cabo de Barberia *c.* Balearic Islands **72** D4 38 40N 1 20E
Cabo de Cala Figuera *c.* Balearic Islands **72** E4 39 27N 2 31E
Cabo de Creus *c.* Spain **72** C3 42 19N 3 19E
Cabo de Formentor *c.* Balearic Islands **72** E4 39 58N 3 13E
Cabo de Gata *c.* Spain **72** B2 36 44N 2 10W
Cabo de Hornos *(Cape Horn) c.* Chile **103** D1 56 00S 67 15W
Cabo de la Nao *c.* Spain **72** C2 38 44N 0 14E
Cabo Delgado *c.* Mozambique **111** H5 10 45S 40 45E
Cabo de Palos *c.* Spain **72** B2 37 38N 0 40W
Cabo de Peñas *c.* Spain **72** A3 43 39N 5 50W
Cabo de Salinas *c.* Balearic Islands **72** E4 39 16N 3 04E
Cabo de São Vicente *c.* Portugal **72** A2 37 01N 8 59W
Cabo de Tortosa *c.* Spain **72** C3 40 44N 0 54E
Cabo Dos Bahías *c.* Argentina **103** D4 45 00S 65 30W
Cabo Espichel *c.* Portugal **72** A2 38 24N 9 13W
Cabo Falso *c.* Mexico **96** B4 22 50N 110 00W
Cabo Finisterre *c.* Spain **72** A3 42 52N 9 16W
Cabo Freu *c.* Balearic Islands **72** E4 39 45N 3 27E
Cabo Gracias á Dios *c.* Nicaragua **97** H3 15 00N 83 10W
Cabo Guardafui see Raas Caseyr
Cabo Orange *c.* Brazil **102** G13 4 25N 51 32W
Cabo Ortegal *c.* Spain **72** A3 43 46N 7 54W
Cabora Bassa Dam Mozambique **111** F4 16 00S 33 00E
Caborca Mexico **96** B6 30 42N 112 10W
Cabo San Juan *c.* Argentina **103** E2 54 45S 63 46W
Cabo Santa Elena *c.* Costa Rica **97** G2 10 54N 85 56W
Cabot Strait Nova Scotia/Newfoundland Canada **89** W2 47 10N 59 30W
Cabo Vírgenes *c.* Argentina **103** D2 52 20S 68 00W
Cabrera *i.* Balearic Islands **72** E4 39 00N 2 59E
Cabriel *r.* Spain **72** B2 39 20N 1 15W
Čačak Serbia Yugoslavia **74** D3 43 54N 20 22E
Cáceres Brazil **102** F9 16 05S 57 40W
Cáceres Spain **72** A2 39 29N 6 23W
Cachoeira Brazil **102** J10 12 35S 38 59W
Cachoeira do Sol Brazil **103** G7 30 03S 52 52W
Cachoeiro de Itapemirim Brazil **103** I8 20 51N 41 07W
Cadig Mountains The Philippines **40** B3 14 00N 122 00E
Cádiz Spain **72** A2 36 32N 6 18W
Cadiz The Philippines **40** B3 10 57N 123 18E
Cádiz, Gulf of Spain **72** A2 36 30N 7 15W
Caen France **73** A2 49 11N 0 22W
Caernarfon Wales United Kingdom **68** G5 53 08N 4 16W
Cagayan *r.* The Philippines **40** B4 17 00N 123 30E
Cagayan de Oro The Philippines **40** B2 8 29N 124 40E
Cagayan Islands The Philippines **40** B2 9 00N 121 00E
Cagayan Sulu The Philippines **42** E5 6 00N 119 00E
Cagayan Sulu *(Pulau Mapin) i.* The Philippines **40** A2 7 00N 118 28E
Cágliari Italy **74** A2 39 13N 9 08E
Caguas Puerto Rico **97** K3 18 41N 66 04W
Caha Mountains Irish Republic **68** B3 51 40N 9 40W
Cahors France **73** B1 44 28N 0 26E
Caicos Passage *sd.* West Indies **97** J4 22 20N 72 30W
Cairngorms *mts.* Scotland United Kingdom **68** H9 57 10N 3 30W
Cairns Australia **78** H6 16 51S 145 43E
Cairo Illinois U.S.A. **92** C1 37 01N 89 09W
Cairo see El Qâ'hira
Cajamarca Peru **102** B11 7 09S 78 32W
Cajàzeiras Brazil **102** J11 6 52S 38 31W
Caju Brazil **103** Q2 22 53S 43 13W
Cakau Matacucu *reef* Fiji **83** E10 16 06S 179 38W

Diahot *r.* New Caledonia **82** T3 20 20S 164 20E
Diamantina Brazil **102** I9 18 17S 43 37W
Diamantina *r.* Australia **78** G5 24 00S 142 00E
Diamantina Fracture Zone Indian Ocean **24** J3/K3
Dian Chi *l.* China **38** C4 24 50N 102 45E
Dibang *r.* India **38** B5 28 25N 95 45E
Dibrugarh India **53** G5 27 29N 94 56E
Dickinson North Dakota U.S.A. **90** F6 46 54N 102 48W
Diego Martin Trinidad and Tobago **96** S10 10 48N 61 34W
Diekirch Luxembourg **70** F1 49 52N 6 10E
Diemel *r.* Germany **71** A2 52 00N 9 00E
Dien Bien Phu Vietnam **37** B4 21 23N 103 02E
Dien Chau Vietnam **37** C3 19 00N 105 30E
Diepholz Germany **71** A2 52 37N 8 22E
Dieppe France **73** B2 49 55N 1 05E
Diest Belgium **70** E2 50 58N 5 03E
Digboi India **38** B5 27 22N 95 34E
Digby Nova Scotia Canada **89** V1 44 37N 65 47W
Digne France **73** C1 44 05N 6 14E
Digos The Philippines **40** C2 6 45N 125 23E
Digul *r.* Irian Jaya Indonesia **44** J3 7 30S 140 15E
Dihang *r.* India **38** B5 28 10N 95 10E
Dijon France **73** C2 47 20N 5 02E
Diksmuide Belgium **70** B3 51 02N 2 52E
Dikson Russia **57** K10 73 32N 80 39E
Dikwa Nigeria **112** H5 12 01N 13 55E
Dili *(Oekusi)* Indonesia **43** G2 8 33S 125 34E
Di Linh Vietnam **37** C2 11 38N 108 07E
Dillingham Alaska U.S.A. **88** D4 59 03N 158 30W
Dillons Bay *tn.* Vanuatu **83** H3 18 48S 169 00E
Dimapur India **38** A5 25 54N 93 45E
Dimashq *(Damascus)* Syria **54** P11 33 30N 36 19E
Dimitrovgrad Bulgaria **74** E3 42 03N 25 34E
Dimitrovgrad Russia **58** F5 54 14N 49 37E
Dinagat The Philippines **40** C2 9 57N 125 56E
Dinagat *i.* The Philippines **40** C2 10 15N 125 00E
Dinaig The Philippines **40** B2 7 10N 124 10E
Dinajpur Bangladesh **53** F5 25 38N 88 44E
Dinan France **73** A2 48 27N 2 02W
Dinant Belgium **70** D2 50 16N 4 55E
Dinara Planina *(Dinaric Alps) mts.* Europe **74** C3 44 00N 17 00E
Dinard France **73** A2 48 38N 2 03W
Dinaric Alps *see* Dinara Planina
Dindigul India **53** D2 10 23N 78 00E
Dingalen Bay The Philippines **40** B4 15 00N 121 00E
Dingle Bay Irish Republic **68** A4 52 05N 10 15W
Dingwall Scotland United Kingdom **68** G9 57 35N 4 29W
Dinh Lap Vietnam **37** C4 21 32N 107 06E
Dinkel *r.* Europe **70** G4 52 00N 7 00E
Din, Mount Papua New Guinea **45** K4 5 30S 142 50E
Dinslaken Germany **70** F3 51 34N 6 43E
Dintel Mark *r.* Netherlands **70** D3 51 35N 4 25E
Diphu India **38** A5 25 50N 93 25E
Dipolog The Philippines **40** B2 8 34N 123 23E
Dir Pakistan **53** C7 35 12N 71 54E
Dirē Dawa Ethiopia **110** H9 9 35N 41 50E
Disappointment, Lake Australia **78** C5 23 00S 123 00E
Discovery Bay Hong Kong U.K. **51** B1 22 18N 114 02E
Discovery Bay *tn.* Hong Kong U.K. **51** B1 22 18N 114 01E
Disko *i.* Greenland **89** Y6 70 00N 54 00W
Disko Bugt *b.* Greenland **89** Y6 69 00N 54 00W
Dispur India **38** A5 26 03N 91 52E
Ditan China **47** G1 39 58N 116 24E
Diu India **52** C4 20 41N 71 03E
Diuata Mountains The Philippines **40** C2 9 00N 126 00E
Divinópolis Brazil **102** I8 20 08S 44 55W
Divriği Turkey **54** E6 39 23N 38 06E
Dixon Entrance *sd.* U.S.A./Canada **88** I3 54 00N 132 30W
Diyarbakir Turkey **54** F6 37 55N 40 14E
Djambala Congo **112** H2 2 32S 14 43E
Djaul Island Papua New Guinea **45** Q5 2 58S 150 50E
Djelfa Algeria **112** F9 34 43N 3 14E
DJIBOUTI **54** F1
Djibouti Djibouti **54** F1 11 35N 43 11E
Djougou Benin **112** F4 9 40N 1 47E
Dnepr *r.* Europe **56** F5 47 30N 33 00E
Dneprodzerzhinsk Ukraine **58** C4 48 30N 34 37E
Dnepropetrovsk Ukraine **58** C4 48 29N 35 00E
Dnestr *r.* Moldova **75** E2 47 30N 28 30E
Doberai Peninsula *(Vogelkop)* Irian Jaya Indonesia **44** E6 1 00S 132 15E
Dobo Indonesia **43** H2 5 48S 134 13E
Dobreta-Turnu-Severin Romania **75** D1 44 36N 22 39E
Dobrich *(Tolbukhin)* Bulgaria **74** E3 43 34N 27 51E
Dobrogea *geog. reg.* Romania **75** E1 44 00N 29 00E
Dodecanese *see* Dhodhekánisos
Dodge City Kansas U.S.A. **90** F4 37 45N 100 02W
Dodgeville Wisconsin U.S.A. **92** B2 42 57N 90 08W
Dodoma Tanzania **111** G6 6 10S 35 40E
Doetinchem Netherlands **70** F3 51 58N 6 17E
Dogai Coring *l.* China **53** F6 34 30N 89 00E
Dōgo *i.* Japan **46** B2 36 20N 133 15E
Dogura Papua New Guinea **45** O1 10 05S 150 05E
Doha *see* Ad Dawhah
Dohazari Bangladesh **38** A4 22 11N 92 03E
Doi *i.* Fiji **83** F6 20 39S 178 42W
Doi Inthanon *mt.* Thailand **39** A3 18 35N 98 29E
Doi Saket Thailand **39** A3 18 51N 99 11E
Dokkum Netherlands **70** F5 53 20N 6 00E
Dolak Island *see* Pulau Yos Sudarso
Dolbeau Québec Canada **93** F3 48 52N 72 15W
Dôle France **73** C2 47 05N 5 30E
Dolit Indonesia **44** B6 0 13S 127 40E
Dollard *b.* Netherlands/Germany **70** G5 53 20N 7 15E
Dolo Ethiopia **110** H8 4 11N 42 03E
Dolphin, Cape Falkland Islands **25** M16 51 15S 58 55W
Do Luong Vietnam **37** C3 19 00N 105 10E
Domažlice Czech Republic **71** B1 49 27N 12 56E
Dombas Norway **69** B3 62 05N 9 07E
DOMINICA **97** L3
DOMINICAN REPUBLIC **97** K3
Don *r.* Russia **56** G6 50 00N 41 00E
Don *r.* England United Kingdom **68** J5 53 37N 1 02W
Don *r.* Scotland United Kingdom **68** I9 57 15N 2 55W
Donau *(Danube) r.* Germany/Austria **71** B1 48 00N 10 00E
Donauwörth Germany **71** B1 48 44N 10 48E
Don Benito Spain **72** A2 38 57N 5 52W
Doncaster England United Kingdom **68** J5 53 32N 1 07W
Donegal Irish Republic **68** C6 54 39N 8 07W
Donegal Bay Irish Republic **68** C6 54 30N 8 30W
Donegal Mountains Irish Republic **68** C6/D7 55 00N 8 05W
Donetsk Ukraine **58** D4 48 00N 37 50E
Dongba China **47** H1 39 58N 116 35E
Dongchuan China **49** K4 26 07N 103 05E
Dongen Netherlands **70** D3 51 38N 4 56E
Dongfang China **37** C3 19 11N 108 40E
Donggala Indonesia **43** E3 0 30S 119 40E
Donggou China **50** B4 39 52N 124 08E
Dong Ha Vietnam **37** C3 16 47N 107 09E
Dong Hoi Vietnam **37** C3 17 32N 106 35E
Dongkalang Indonesia **43** F4 0 12N 120 07E
Dongola Sudan **110** F11 19 10N 30 27E
Dongou Congo **112** I3 2 02N 18 02E
Dong Phraya Yen *(Phetchabun Range) mts.* Thailand **39** B3 16 30N 101 30E
Dong Trieu Vietnam **37** C4 21 04N 106 31E
Dønna *i.* Norway **69** C4 66 05N 12 30E
Donnacona Québec Canada **93** F3 46 41N 71 45W
Dongting Hu *l.* China **49** M4 29 00N 112 30E
Door Peninsula Wisconsin U.S.A. **92** C2/3 45 00N 87 00W
Dora Báltea *r.* Italy **73** C2 45 00N 7 00E
Dora Riparia *r.* Italy **73** C2 45 00N 7 00E
Dorchester England United Kingdom **73** A3 50 43N 2 26W
Dordogne *r.* France **73** B1 44 55N 0 30E
Dordrecht Netherlands **70** D3 51 48N 4 40E
Dore *r.* France **73** B2 45 40N 3 30E
Dori *r.* Afghanistan **55** K5 31 20N 65 00E
Dorion Ontario Canada **92** C3 48 49N 88 33W
Dorking England United Kingdom **66** B1 51 14N 0 20W
Dormagen Germany **70** F3 51 06N 6 50E
Dornbirn Austria **75** A2 47 25N 9 46E
Dornoch Firth *est.* Scotland United Kingdom **68** H9 57 55N 3 55W
Dorsten Germany **70** F3 51 38N 6 58E
Dortmund Germany **71** A2 51 32N 7 27E
Dosso Niger **112** F5 13 03N 3 10E
Dothan Alabama U.S.A. **91** I3 31 12N 85 25W
Douai France **73** B3 50 22N 3 05E
Douala Cameroon **112** G3 4 04N 9 43E
Douarnenez France **73** A2 48 05N 4 20W
Double Island Hong Kong U.K. **51** C3 22 31N 114 08E
Doubs *r.* France **73** C2 47 20N 6 25E
Douglas Isle of Man British Isles **68** G6 54 09N 4 29W
Douglas Alaska U.S.A. **88** I4 58 15N 134 24W
Douglas Arizona U.S.A. **90** E3 31 21N 109 34W
Doullens France **73** B3 50 09N 2 21E
Dourados Brazil **103** G8 22 09S 54 52W
Douro *(Duero) r.* Portugal/Spain **72** A3 41 00N 8 30W
Dover England United Kingdom **68** M3 51 08N 1 19E
Dover Delaware U.S.A. **93** E1 39 10N 75 32W
Dover New Hampshire U.S.A. **93** F2 43 12N 70 55W
Dover Foxcroft Maine U.S.A. **93** G3 45 12N 69 16W
Dover, Strait of *(Pas de Calais)* English Channel **68** M2 51 00N 1 20W
Dovrefjell *mts.* Norway **69** B3 62 15N 9 10E
Downey California U.S.A. **95** B2 33 56N 118 25W
Dōzen *is.* Japan **46** B2 36 05N 133 00E
Drachten Netherlands **70** F5 53 07N 6 06E
Dragan *l.* Sweden **69** D3 64 05N 15 20E
Dragons Mouths, The *(Bocas del Dragons)* Trinidad and Tobago **96** S10 10 37N 61 50W
Draguignan France **73** C1 43 32N 6 28E
Drakensberg *mts.* Republic of South Africa **111** E1/2 30 00S 28 00E
Drake Passage *sd.* Southern Ocean **103** C1/E1 58 00S 66 00W
Dráma Greece **74** D3 41 10N 24 11E
Drammen Norway **69** C2 59 45N 10 15E
Drancy France **67** B2 48 55N 2 28E
Drau *r.* Austria **75** B2 46 00N 14 00E
Draveil France **67** B1 48 40N 2 25E
Drenthe *admin.* Netherlands **70** F4 52 55N 6 45E
Dresden Germany **71** B2 51 03N 13 45E
Dreux France **73** B2 48 44N 1 23E
Drewitz Germany **67** E1 52 20N 13 08E
Drin *r.* Albania **74** C3/D3 42 00N 20 00E
Drina *r.* Europe **74** C3 43 30N 15 19E
Drogheda Irish Republic **68** E5 53 43N 6 21W
Drôme *r.* France **73** C1 44 50N 5 00E
Dronning Maud Land *(Queen Maud Land) geog. reg.* Antarctica **21** 73 00S 10 00E
Dronten Netherlands **70** E4 53 21N 5 41E
Drua *i.* Fiji **83** D10 16 12S 179 38E
Drueulu New Caledonia **82** W3 20 55S 167 05E
Drumheller Alberta Canada **88** M3 51 28N 112 40W
Drummond Island Michigan U.S.A. **93** D3 46 00N 84 00W
Drummondville Québec Canada **93** F3 45 52N 72 30W
Drummoyne Australia **79** G2 33 51S 151 09E
Drumsite *tn.* Christmas Island **81** R2 10 26S 105 41E
Druzhba Kazakhstan **49** F8 45 18N 82 29E
Dryden Ontario Canada **92** B3 49 48N 92 48W
Dry Fork *r.* Missouri U.S.A. **92** B1 38 00N 91 00W
Dschang Cameroon **112** H4 5 28N 10 02E
Dubawnt Lake Northwest Territories Canada **89** O5 68 15N 102 00W
Dubayy United Arab Emirates **55** I4 25 14N 55 17E
Dubbo Australia **78** H3 32 16S 148 41E
Dublin Irish Republic **68** E5 53 20N 6 15W
Dublin Georgia U.S.A. **91** J3 32 31N 82 54W
Dubno Ukraine **58** B5 50 28N 25 40E
Dubrovnik Croatia **74** C3 42 40N 18 07E
Dubuque Iowa U.S.A. **92** B2 42 31N 90 41W
Ducie Island Pitcairn Islands **23** N5 24 40S 124 48W
Duc Pho Vietnam **37** C2 14 56N 108 55E
Dudelange Luxembourg **70** F1 49 28N 6 05E
Dudinka Russia **57** K9 69 27N 86 13E
Dudley England United Kingdom **68** I4 52 30N 2 05W
Duero *(Douro) r.* Spain/Portugal **72** A3 41 25N 6 30W
Duff Islands Solomon Islands **83** N4 9 53S 167 08E
Dugi Otok *i.* Croatia **74** B3/C3 44 00N 15 00E
Duisberg Germany **71** A2 51 26N 6 45E
Duiveland *i.* Netherlands **70** C3 51 37N 4 00E
Dukou China **38** C5 26 34N 101 44E
Dülmen Germany **70** G3 51 49N 7 17E
Duluth Minnesota U.S.A. **92** B3 46 45N 92 10W
Dumaguete The Philippines **40** B2 9 20N 123 18E
Dumai Indonesia **42** B4 1 39N 101 28E
Dumaran *i.* The Philippines **40** A3 10 00N 120 00E
Dumbéa New Caledonia **82** V1 22 10S 166 30E
Dum Dum India **52** K2 22 37N 88 24E
Dumfries Scotland United Kingdom **68** H7 55 04N 3 37W
Dumont d'Urville *r.s.* Antarctica **21** 66 40S 140 01E
Dumyât *(Damietta)* Egypt **109** R4 31 26N 31 48E
Duna *(Danube) r.* Hungary **75** C2 46 00N 19 00E
Dunarea *(Danube) r.* Romania **75** E1 44 00N 28 00E
Dunaújváros Hungary **75** C2 47 00N 18 55E
Dunav *(Danube) r.* Serbia/Bulgaria **74** D3 45 00N 20 00E
Duncan Oklahoma U.S.A. **91** G3 34 30N 97 57W
Duncan Passage Andaman Islands **38** A2 11 10N 92 30E
Duncansby Head *c.* Scotland United Kingdom **68** H10 58 39N 3 02W
Duncombe Bay Norfolk Island **81** K5/6 29 00S 167 55E
Dundalk Irish Republic **68** E6 54 01N 6 25W
Dundas Ontario Canada **93** E2 43 16N 79 57W
Dundas *(Uummannaq)* Greenland **89** V8 76 30N 68 58W
Dundee Scotland United Kingdom **68** I8 56 28N 3 00W
Dunedin South Island New Zealand **79** B1 45 53S 170 30E
Dunfermline Scotland United Kingdom **68** H8 56 04N 3 29W
Dunkerque *(Dunkirk)* France **73** B3 51 02N 2 23E
Dunkirk France *see* Dunkerque
Dunkirk New York U.S.A. **93** E2 42 29N 79 21W
Dún Laoghaire Irish Republic **68** E5 53 17N 6 08W
Duong Dong Vietnam **37** B2 10 15N 103 58E
Duque de Caxias Brazil **103** P2 22 46S 43 18W
Dural Australia **79** G3 33 41S 151 02E
Durance *r.* France **73** C1 43 50N 5 15E
Durand Wisconsin U.S.A. **92** B2 44 37N 91 56W
Durango Mexico **96** D4 24 01N 104 40W
Durango Colorado U.S.A. **90** E4 37 16N 107 53W
Durant Oklahoma U.S.A. **91** G3 33 59N 96 24W
Durazno Uruguay **103** F6 33 22S 56 31W
Durban Republic of South Africa **111** F2 29 53S 31 00E
Düren Germany **71** A2 50 48N 6 30E
Durgapur India **53** F4 24 47N 87 44E
Durgāpur India **52** J1 22 47N 87 44E
Durg-Bhilai India **53** E4 21 12N 81 20E
Durham England United Kingdom **68** J6 54 47N 1 34W
Durham North Carolina U.S.A. **91** K4 36 00N 78 54W
Durrës Albania **74** C3 41 18N 19 28E
Dushan China **36** D7 25 50N 107 31E
Dushanbe Tajikistan **59** K2 38 38N 68 51E
Düsseldorf Germany **71** A2 51 13N 6 47E
Dutch Harbor *tn.* Alaska U.S.A. **88** B3 53 55N 166 36W
Duyun China **49** L4 26 16N 107 29E
Dyke Ackland Bay Papua New Guinea **45** N2 8 50S 148 45E
Dzerzhinsk Belarus **58** B5 53 40N 27 01E
Dzhambul Kazakhstan **59** L3 42 50N 71 25E
Dzhetygara Kazakhstan **59** J5 52 14N 61 10E
Dzhezkazgan Kazakhstan **59** K4 47 44N 67 42E
Dzhugdzhur Range *mts.* Russia **57** P7 57 00N 137 00E
Dzungarian Basin *see* Junggar Pendi
Dzungarian Gate *pass* Kazakhstan/China **59** N4 45 00N 83 00E

E

Eagle Alaska U.S.A. **88** G5 64 46N 141 20W
Eagle Lake Maine U.S.A. **93** G3 46 00N 69 00W
Eagle Pass *tn.* Texas U.S.A. **90** F2 28 44N 100 31W
Ealing *bor.* Greater London England United Kingdom **66** B3 51 31N 0 18W
East Antarctica *geog. reg.* Antarctica **21**
Eastbourne England United Kingdom **68** L2 50 46N 0 17E
East Cape North Island New Zealand **79** C3 37 41S 178 33E
East Caroline Basin Pacific Ocean **22** E8 4 00N 148 00E
East China Sea China/Japan **49** P5 32 00N 126 00E
East End Point Phillip Island **81** L1 29 07S 167 57E
Easter Island Pacific Ocean **23** P5 27 05S 109 20W
Easter Island Fracture Zone Pacific Ocean **23** Q5/R5 24 00S 100 00W
Eastern Fields *reef* Papua New Guinea **45** L2 10 05S 145 40E
Eastern Ghats *mts.* India **53** D2/E3 15 00N 80 00E
Eastern Sayan *mts.* Russia **57** L6 53 00N 97 30E
East Falkland Falkland Islands **25** M15/16 52 00S 58 50W
East Fork White River Indiana U.S.A. **92** C1 39 00N 87 00W
East Frisian Islands *see* Ostfriesische Inseln
East Grand Forks *tn.* Minnesota U.S.A. **92** A3 47 56N 96 59W
East Hills *tn.* Australia **79** G2 33 58S 150 59E
East Horsley England United Kingdom **66** B2 51 16N 0 26W
East Kilbride Scotland United Kingdom **68** G7 55 46N 4 10W
East Lamma Channel Hong Kong U.K. **51** B1 22 14N 114 08E
East Liverpool Ohio U.S.A. **93** D2 40 38N 80 36W
East London Republic of South Africa **111** E1 33 00S 27 54E
East Los Angeles California U.S.A. **95** B3 34 02N 118 12W
Eastmain Québec Canada **89** T3 52 10N 78 30W
East Marianas Basin Pacific Ocean **22** F9 13 00N 153 00E
Easton Maryland U.S.A. **93** E1 38 46N 76 05W
Easton Pennsylvania U.S.A. **93** E2 40 41N 75 13W
East Pacific Basin Pacific Ocean **23** K9 16 00N 153 00E
East Pacific Ridge Pacific Ocean **23** O5 20 00S 113 00W
East Pacific Rise Pacific Ocean **23** P9 13 00N 103 00W
East Rift Valley East Africa **110** G8/9 6 00N 37 00E
East River New York U.S.A. **94** B1 40 43N 74 00W
East St. Louis Illinois U.S.A. **92** B1 38 34N 90 04W
East Siberian Sea Arctic Ocean **20** 72 00N 165 00E
Eastwood Australia **79** G2 33 48S 151 05E
Eaton Wash Reservoir California U.S.A. **95** B3 34 10N 118 05W
Eau Claire *tn.* Wisconsin U.S.A. **92** B2 44 50N 91 30W
Eauripik-New Guinea Rise Pacific Ocean **22** E8 2 00N 142 00E
Ebensburg Pennsylvania U.S.A. **93** E2 40 28N 78 44W
Eberswalde-Finow Germany **71** B2 52 50N 13 53E
Ebinur Hu *l.* China **48** F7 45 00N 83 00E
Ebolowa Cameroon **112** H3 2 56N 11 11E
Ebro *r.* Spain **72** C3 41 00N 0 30E
Ebute Metta Nigeria **109** V3 6 27N 3 28E
Ech Cheliff Algeria **112** F10 36 05N 1 15E
Echo Bay *tn.* Northwest Territories Canada **88** L6 65 50N 117 30W
Echternach Luxembourg **70** F1 49 49N 6 25E
Ecija Spain **72** A2 37 33N 5 04W
Eckernförde Germany **71** A2 54 28N 9 50E
Écouen France **67** B3 49 01N 2 22E
ECUADOR **102** B12
Edam Netherlands **70** E4 52 30N 5 02E
Ed Damer Sudan **110** F11 17 37N 33 59E
Ed Debba Sudan **110** F11 18 02N 30 56E
Eddyville Kentucky U.S.A. **92** C1 37 03N 88 02W
Ede Netherlands **70** E4 52 03N 5 40E
Edéa Cameroon **112** H3 3 47N 10 13E
Eden *r.* England United Kingdom **68** I6 54 50N 2 45W
Eder *r.* Germany **71** A2 51 00N 9 00E
Edgewood Maryland U.S.A. **93** E1 39 25N 76 18W
Edgware England United Kingdom **66** B3 51 36N 0 16W
Édhessa Greece **74** D3 40 48N 22 03E
Edinboro Pennsylvania U.S.A. **93** D2 41 53N 80 08W
Edinburgh Scotland United Kingdom **68** H7 55 57N 3 13W
Edirne Turkey **74** E3 41 40N 26 34E
Edmonton Alberta Canada **88** M3 53 34N 113 25W
Edmonton England United Kingdom **66** C3 51 37N 0 04W
Edmunston New Brunswick Canada **93** G3 47 22N 68 20W
Edogawa Japan **47** C3 35 41N 139 51E
Edremit Turkey **74** E2 39 34N 27 01E
Edward, Lake Zaïre/Uganda **110** E7 0 30S 29 00E
Edwards Plateau Texas U.S.A. **90** F3 31 00N 100 00W
Edward VII Land *geog. reg.* Antarctica **21** 75 00S 150 00W
Eeklo Belgium **70** C3 51 11N 3 34E
Eems *(Ems) est.* Netherlands/Germany **70** F5 53 25N 6 55E
Éfaté *(Vaté) i.* Vanuatu **83** H4 17 40S 168 25E
Eger Hungary **75** D2 47 53N 20 28E
Egeria Point Christmas Island **81** P1 10 31S 105 32E
Egham England United Kingdom **66** A2 51 26N 0 34W
Egholo Solomon Islands **82** C5 8 26S 157 24E
Egmont, Cape North Island New Zealand **79** B3 39 17S 173 45E
Egmont, Mount *(Mount Taranaki)* North Island New Zealand **79** B3 39 18S 174 04E
Egridir Gölü *l.* Turkey **54** D6 37 52N 30 51E
EGYPT **110** E13/F13
Eichwalde Germany **67** G1 52 23N 13 37E
Eifel *plat.* Germany **71** A2 50 00N 7 00E
Eigg *i.* Scotland United Kingdom **68** E8 56 55N 6 10W
Eight Degree Channel Indian Ocean **53** C1 8 00N 73 30E
Eighty Mile Beach Australia **78** C6 19 00S 121 00E
Einbeck Germany **71** A2 51 49N 9 53E
Eindhoven Netherlands **70** E3 51 26N 5 30E
Eisenach Germany **71** B2 50 59N 10 19E
Eisenhüttenstadt Germany **71** B2 52 10N 14 42E
Ekibastuz Kazakhstan **59** M5 51 50N 75 10E
Ekubu Fiji **83** B8 18 30S 177 39E
El Aaiún *see* Laayoune
El Arco Mexico **96** B5 28 00N 113 25W
El 'Arîsh Egypt **54** N10 31 08N 33 48E
Elat Israel **54** O9 29 33N 34 57E
Elato *i.* Micronesia **80** B4 8 00N 145 00E
Elâziğ Turkey **54** E6 38 41N 39 14E
El Bahr el Saghîr Egypt **109** R4 31 38N 31 39E
El Ballâh Egypt **109** S3 30 47N 32 19E
El Banco Colombia **102** C14 9 04N 73 59W
Elbasan Albania **74** D3 41 07N 20 05E
El Bayadh Algeria **112** F9 33 40N 1 00E
Elbe *(Labe) r.* Germany **71** B2 53 00N 9 00E
Elbert, Mount Colorado U.S.A. **90** E4 39 05N 106 27W
Elbeuf France **73** B2 49 17N 1 01E
Elblag Poland **75** C3 54 10N 19 25E
El'brus *mt.* Russia **58** E3 43 21N 42 29E
Elburg Netherlands **70** E4 52 27N 5 50E
Elburz Mountains Iran **55** H6 36 15N 51 00E
El Callao Venezuela **102** E14 7 18N 61 50W
El Cap Egypt **109** S3 30 55N 32 23E
El Centro California U.S.A. **90** C3 32 47N 115 33W
El Cerro del Aripo *mt.* Trinidad and Tobago **96** T10 10 49N 61 14W
Elche Spain **72** B2 38 16N 0 41W
Elda Spain **72** B2 38 29N 0 47W
El Dorado Arkansas U.S.A. **91** H3 33 12N 92 40W
El Dorado Kansas U.S.A. **91** G4 37 51N 96 52W
Eldoret Kenya **110** G8 0 31N 35 17E
Elektrostal' Russia **58** D6 55 46N 38 30E
Elephant Island South Shetland Islands **103** F0 62 00S 55 00W
Eleuthera *i.* The Bahamas **97** I5 25 05N 76 30W
El Faiyûm Egypt **110** F13 29 19N 30 50E
El Fasher Sudan **110** E10 13 37N 25 22E
El Ferrol del Caudillo Spain **72** A3 43 29N 8 14W
El Firdân Egypt **109** S3 30 42N 32 20E
El Fuerte Mexico **96** C5 26 28N 108 35W
Elgin Scotland United Kingdom **68** H9 57 39N 3 20W
Elgin Illinois U.S.A. **92** C2 42 03N 88 19W
El Gîza Egypt **110** F13 30 01N 31 12E
El Golea Algeria **112** F9 30 35N 2 51E
Elgon, Mount Uganda/Kenya **110** F8 1 07N 34 35E
Eliase Indonesia **43** H2 8 21S 130 48E
Elido Insurgentes Mexico **90** D2 25 00N 110 45W
El Iskandarîya *(Alexandria)* Egypt **110** E14 31 13N 29 55E
Elista Russia **56** G5 46 18N 44 14E
Elizabeth Australia **78** F3 34 45S 138 39E
Elizabeth New Jersey U.S.A. **94** B1 40 39N 74 13W
Elizabeth City North Carolina U.S.A. **91** K4 36 18N 76 16W
Elizabethtown Kentucky U.S.A. **92** C1 37 41N 85 51W
El Jadida Morocco **112** D9 33 19N 8 35W
El Jafr Jordan **54** O10 30 16N 36 11E
Elk Poland **75** D3 53 51N 22 20E
Elk City Oklahoma U.S.A. **90** G4 34 25N 99 26W
El Khârga Egypt **110** F13 25 27N 30 32E
Elkhart Indiana U.S.A. **92** C2 41 52N 85 56W
Elkhorn Wisconsin U.S.A. **92** C2 42 40N 88 34W
Elkhorn *r.* Nebraska U.S.A. **91** G5 42 00N 98 00W
Elkins West Virginia U.S.A. **93** E1 38 56N 79 53W
Elko Nevada U.S.A. **90** C5 40 50N 115 46W
Elk River West Virginia U.S.A. **93** D1 38 00N 81 00W
Elk River *tn.* Minnesota U.S.A. **92** B3 45 19N 93 31W

Fort Pierce Florida U.S.A. **91** J2 27 28N 80 20W
Fort Portal Uganda **110** F8 0 40N 30 17E
Fort Providence Northwest Territories Canada **88** L5 61 03N 117 40W
Fort Randall Alaska U.S.A. **88** C4 55 10N 162 47W
Fort Resolution Northwest Territories Canada **88** M5 61 10N 113 39W
Fort Rupert Québec Canada **93** E4 51 30N 79 45W
Fort St. John British Columbia Canada **88** K4 56 14N 120 55W
Fort Saskatchewan Alberta Canada **88** M3 53 42N 113 12W
Fort Scott Kansas U.S.A. **92** B1 37 52N 94 43W
Fort Severn Ontario Canada **89** R4 56 00N 87 40W
Fort Simpson Northwest Territories Canada **88** K5 61 46N 121 15W
Fort Smith Northwest Territories Canada **88** M5 60 01N 111 55W
Fort Smith Arkansas U.S.A. **91** H4 35 22N 94 27W
Fort Stockton Texas U.S.A. **90** F3 30 54N 102 54W
Fort Sumner New Mexico U.S.A. **90** F3 34 27N 104 16W
Fort Vermilion Alberta Canada **88** L4 58 22N 115 59W
Fort Walton Beach *tn.* Florida U.S.A. **91** I3 30 25N 86 38W
Fort Ware British Columbia Canada **88** J4 57 26N 124 41W
Fort Wayne Indiana U.S.A. **92** C2 41 05N 85 08W
Fort William Scotland United Kingdom **68** F8 56 49N 5 07W
Fort Worth Texas U.S.A. **91** G3 32 45N 97 20W
Fort Yukon Alaska U.S.A. **88** F6 66 35N 145 20W
Foshan China **49** M3 23 03N 113 08E
Fosna *geog. reg.* Norway **69** C3 64 00N 10 30E
Fotuha'a *i.* Tonga **83** B3 19 50S 174 38W
Fougères France **73** A2 48 21N 1 12W
Foula *i.* Scotland United Kingdom **68** I12 60 08N 2 05W
Foulwind, Cape South Island New Zealand **79** B2 41 45S 171 28E
Foumban Cameroon **112** H4 5 43N 10 50E
Fountain Valley *tn.* California U.S.A. **95** B1 33 41N 117 58W
Fourmies France **73** B3 50 01N 4 03E
Four Mountains, Islands of the Alaska U.S.A. **88** A3 53 00N 172 00W
Four Roads *tn.* Trinidad and Tobago **96** S10 10 42N 61 33W
Fouta Djallon *geog. reg.* Guinea **112** C5 12 00N 13 10W
Foveaux Strait South Island New Zealand **79** A1 46 42S 167 59E
Fox *r.* Wisconsin U.S.A. **92** C2 44 00N 88 00W
Foxe Basin *b.* Northwest Territories Canada **89** T6 66 20N 79 00W
Foxe Channel Northwest Territories Canada **89** S6 65 00N 81 00W
Foxe Peninsula Northwest Territories Canada **89** T5/6 65 00N 76 00W
Fox Islands Alaska U.S.A. **88** B3 58 20N 169 10W
Foyle Northern Ireland United Kingdom **68** D6 54 40N 7 30W
Foz do Iguaçú Argentina **103** G7 25 33S 54 31W
Frameries Belgium **70** C2 50 25N 3 54E
Franca Brazil **102** H8 20 33S 47 27W
FRANCE 73
Francis Case, Lake South Dakota U.S.A. **90** G5 43 00N 99 00W
Francistown Botswana **111** E3 21 11S 27 32E
Franeker Netherlands **70** E5 53 11N 5 33E
Frankenthal Germany **71** A1 49 32N 8 22E
Frankfield Jamaica **97** Q8 18 08N 77 22W
Frankfort Kentucky U.S.A. **92** D1 38 11N 84 53W
Frankfurt am Main Germany **71** A2 50 06N 8 41E
Frankfurt an der Oder Germany **71** B2 52 20N 14 32E
Fränkische Alb *mts.* Germany **71** B1 49 00N 11 00E
Franklin New Hampshire U.S.A. **93** F2 43 26N 71 42W
Franklin Pennsylvania U.S.A. **93** E2 41 24N 79 49W
Franklin Canyon Reservoir California U.S.A. **95** A3 34 05N 118 25W
Franklin D. Roosevelt Lake Washington U.S.A. **90** C6 48 05N 118 15W
Fraser *r.* British Columbia Canada **88** K3 52 00N 122 00W
Fraserburgh Scotland United Kingdom **68** I9 57 42N 2 00W
Frederick Maryland U.S.A. **93** E1 39 25N 77 25W
Fredericksburg Virginia U.S.A. **93** E1 38 18N 77 30W
Fredericktown Missouri U.S.A. **92** B1 37 33N 90 19W
Fredericton New Brunswick Canada **89** V2 45 57N 66 40W
Frederikshåb Greenland **89** Z5 62 05N 49 30W
Frederikshavn Denmark **69** C2 57 28N 10 33E
Fredersdorf Germany **67** G2 52 31N 13 44E
Fredrikstad Norway **69** C2 59 20N 10 50E
Freeport Illinois U.S.A. **92** C2 42 17N 89 38W
Freeport Nova Scotia Canada **89** V1 44 17N 66 19W
Freeport The Bahamas **91** K2 26 30N 78 42W
Freeport Texas U.S.A. **91** G2 28 56N 95 20W
Freetown Sierra Leone **112** C4 8 30N 13 17W
Freiberg Germany **71** B2 50 55N 13 21E
Freiberger Mulde *r.* Germany **71** B2 51 00N 13 00E
Freiburg im Breisgau Germany **71** A1 48 00N 7 52E
Freising Germany **71** B1 48 24N 11 45E
Freital Germany **71** B2 51 00N 13 40E
Fréjus France **73** C1 43 26N 6 44E
Fremantle Australia **78** B3 32 07S 115 44E
Fremont Nebraska U.S.A. **92** A2 41 26N 96 30W
Fremont Ohio U.S.A. **93** D2 41 21N 83 08W
French Guiana *territory* France **102** G13 5 00N 53 00W
Frenchman Fork *r.* U.S.A. **90** F5 40 00N 103 00W
French Polynesia Pacific Ocean **81** E3/F3 21 00S 150 00W
French's Forest *tn.* Australia **79** G3 33 45S 151 14E
Fresnillo Mexico **96** D4 23 10N 102 54W
Fresno California U.S.A. **90** C4 36 41N 119 47W
Fribourg Switzerland **73** C2 46 50N 7 10E
Friedrichshafen Germany **71** A1 47 39N 9 29E
Friedrichshagen Germany **67** G1 52 27N 13 38E
Friedrichshain Germany **67** F2 52 32N 13 26E
Friesland *admin.* Netherlands **70** E5 53 00N 6 00E
Frobisher Bay Northwest Territories Canada **89** V5 62 15N 65 00W
Frobisher Bay *tn. see* Iqaluit
Frohavet *sd.* Norway **69** B3 63 55N 9 10E
Frohnau Germany **67** F2 52 38N 13 19E
Frome England United Kingdom **73** A3 51 14N 2 20W
Frontera Mexico **96** F3 18 32N 92 39W
Frosinone Italy **74** B3 41 38N 13 22E
Frøya *i.* Norway **69** B3 63 45N 8 45E
Frunze *see* Bishkek
Fua'amotu Tonga **83** D1 21 16S 175 08W
Fuchū Japan **47** B3 35 40N 139 29E
Fuertaventura *i.* Canary Islands **112** C8 28 25N 14 00W
Fuga *i.* The Philippines **40** B4 18 54N 121 22E
Fuji Japan **46** C2 35 10N 138 37E
Fuji-Hakone-Izu National Park Japan **46** K2 35 28N 138 47E
Fujinomiya Japan **46** C2 35 16N 138 33E
Fujioka Japan **46** L3 36 15N 139 03E
Fuji-san *mt.* Japan **46** C2 35 23N 138 42E
Fujisawa Japan **47** B2 35 20N 139 29E
Fukaya Japan **46** L3 36 12N 139 17E
Fukuchiyama Japan **46** G2 35 19N 135 08E
Fukui Japan **46** C2 36 04N 136 12E
Fukui *pref.* Japan **46** G2 35 30N 135 40E
Fukuoka Japan **46** B1 33 39N 130 21E
Fukushima Japan **46** D2 37 44N 140 28E
Fukuyama Japan **46** B1 34 29N 133 21E
Fulaga *i.* Fiji **83** F7 19 10S 178 39W
Fulda Germany **71** A2 50 33N 9 41E
Fulda *r.* Germany **71** A2 51 00N 9 00E
Fullerton Trinidad and Tobago **96** S9 10 05N 61 54W
Fullerton California U.S.A. **95** C2 33 53N 117 55W
Fullerton Reservoir California U.S.A. **95** C2 33 54N 117 54W
Fulton New York U.S.A. **93** E2 43 20N 76 26W
Funabashi Japan **46** L2 35 42N 139 59E
Funafuti Atoll Pacific Ocean **80** C3 8 30S 179 12E
Funakoshi Japan **47** B2 35 18N 139 34E
Funchal Madeira **112** B9 32 40N 16 55W
Fundy, Bay of New Brunswick/Nova Scotia Canada **89** V1 45 00N 66 00W
Fuqing China **51** F8 25 43N 119 21E
Furneaux Group *is.* Australia **78** H1 45 00S 148 00E
Furona Solomon Islands **82** E5 8 05S 159 05E
Fürstenfeldbruck Germany **71** B1 48 10N 11 15E
Fürstenwalde Germany **71** B2 52 22N 14 04E
Fürth Germany **71** B1 49 28N 11 00E
Furukawa Japan **46** D2 38 34N 140 56E
Fushun China **49** O7 41 50N 123 54E
Fusi Western Samoa **82** B11 13 52S 171 36W
Fusong China **50** C6 42 15N 127 20E
Füssen Germany **71** B1 47 35N 10 43E
Fustic Barbados **96** V13 13 18N 59 43W
Fu Tau Fan Chau *i.* Hong Kong U.K. **51** D2 22 20N 114 21E
Futtsu Japan **46** L2 35 13N 139 53E
Futuna Atoll Pacific Ocean **80** D3 14 25S 178 20W
Fuxian Hu *l.* China **38** C4 24 30N 102 55E
Fuxin China **49** O7 42 04N 121 39E
Fuyuan China **38** C5 25 41N 104 20E
Fuzhou China **49** N4 26 09N 119 17E
Fyn *i.* Denmark **69** C2 55 30N 10 00E

G

Gaalkacyo Somalia **110** I9 6 47N 47 12E
Gabas *r.* France **73** A1 43 30N 0 15W
Gabès Tunisia **112** H9 33 52N 10 06E
GABON 112 H2/3
Gaborone Botswana **111** E3 24 45S 25 55E
Gabrovo Bulgaria **74** E3 42 52N 25 19E
Gadag India **53** D3 15 26N 75 42E
Gadsden Alabama U.S.A. **91** I3 34 00N 86 00W
Gaeta Italy **74** B3 41 13N 13 36E
Gafsa Tunisia **112** G9 34 28N 8 43E
Gag *i.* Irian Jaya Indonesia **44** C6 0 25S 129 53E
Gagarin Russia **56** L1 55 40N 37 27E
Gagnoa Côte d'Ivoire **112** D4 6 04N 5 55W
Gaillard Cut Panama Canal **97** Y2 9 05N 79 40W
Gainesville Florida U.S.A. **91** J2 29 37N 82 21W
Gainesville Texas U.S.A. **91** G3 33 09N 97 38W
Gairdner, Lake Australia **78** F3 32 50S 136 00E
Galana *r.* Kenya **110** G7 3 30S 34 30E
Galapagos Rise Pacific Ocean **23** R6 12 00S 87 00W
Galashiels Scotland United Kingdom **68** I7 55 37N 2 49W
Galați Romania **75** E2 45 27N 28 02E
Galeão Brazil **103** Q2 22 49S 43 14W
Galela Indonesia **43** G4 1 50N 127 49E
Galeota Point Trinidad and Tobago **96** U9 10 09N 60 00W
Galera Point Trinidad and Tobago **96** U10 10 49N 60 54W
Galesburg Illinois U.S.A. **92** B2 40 58N 90 22W
Galeton Pennsylvania U.S.A. **93** E2 41 43N 77 39W
Galilee, Sea of *see* Lake Tiberias
Galina Point Jamaica **97** R8 18 24N 76 58W
Gallego *r.* Spain **72** B3 41 55N 0 56W
Gallipoli Italy **74** C3 40 03N 17 59E
Gallipoli Turkey *see* Gelibolu
Gallipolis Ohio U.S.A. **93** D1 38 49N 82 14W
Gallup New Mexico U.S.A. **90** E4 32 32N 108 46W
Galston Australia **79** G3 33 39S 151 03E
Galty Mountains Irish Republic **68** C4 52 20N 8 10W
Galveston Texas U.S.A. **91** H2 29 17N 94 48W
Galway Irish Republic **68** B5 53 16N 9 03W
Galway Bay Irish Republic **68** B5 53 15N 9 15W
Gamagōri Japan **46** J1 34 49N 137 15E
Gambell Alaska U.S.A. **88** A5 63 46N 171 45W
Gambia *r.* Senegal/The Gambia **112** C5 13 45N 13 15W
GAMBIA, THE 112 B5
Gambier Islands Pitcairn Islands **81** F2 23 10S 135 00W
Gamboa Panama **97** Y2 9 08N 79 42W
Gananoque Ontario Canada **93** E2 44 21N 76 11W
Gancheng China **37** C3 18 55N 108 41E
Gand *see* Gent
Gandak *r.* India **53** E5 26 30N 84 30E
Gander Newfoundland Canada **89** Y2 49 00N 54 15W
Ganga *(Ganges) r.* India **53** F4 25 00N 87 00E
Ganga, Mouths of the *est.* Bangladesh/India **53** F4 21 30N 89 00E
Ganganagar India **53** C5 29 54N 73 56E
Gangaw Myanmar **38** A4 22 11N 94 09E
Gangaw Range *mts.* Myanmar **38** B4 24 00N 96 00E
Gangdisê Shan *mts.* China **49** F5 31 00N 82 30E
Gangtok India **53** F5 27 20N 88 39E
Gani Indonesia **43** G3 1 00S 128 00E
Ganzhou China **49** M4 25 45N 114 51E
Gao Mali **112** E6 16 19N 0 09W
Gao Xian China **38** C5 28 28N 104 38E
Gap France **73** C1 44 33N 6 05E
Garanhuns Brazil **102** J11 8 53S 36 28W
Garbsen Germany **71** A2 52 25N 9 36E
Gard *r.* France **73** B1 44 05N 4 20E
Gardena California U.S.A. **95** A2 33 53N 118 19W
Garden City Kansas U.S.A. **90** F4 37 57N 100 54W
Garden City New York U.S.A. **94** D1 40 43N 73 39W
Garden Grove California U.S.A. **95** C2 33 48N 117 52W
Gardēz Afghanistan **55** K5 33 37N 69 07E
Gardner Island *see* Nikumaroro
Garfield New Jersey U.S.A. **94** B2 40 52N 74 05W
Garissa Kenya **110** G7 0 27S 39 39E
Gariya India **52** K1 22 27N 88 23E
Garland Texas U.S.A. **91** G3 32 55N 96 37W
Garmisch-Partenkirchen Germany **71** B1 47 30N 11 05E
Garnet Point Phillip Island **81** K1 29 08S 167 56E
Garonne *r.* France **73** A1 44 45N 0 15E
Garoua Cameroon **112** H4 9 17N 13 22E
Garove Island Papua New Guinea **45** N4 4 40S 149 30E
Garry Lake Northwest Territories Canada **89** O6 66 20N 100 00W
Gartempe *r.* France **73** B2 46 10N 1 10E
Garulia India **52** K3 22 49N 88 23E
Garut Indonesia **42** N7 7 15S 107 55E
Gary Indiana U.S.A. **92** C2 41 34N 87 20W
Garyarsa China **53** E6 31 46N 80 21E
Garzón Colombia **102** B13 2 14N 75 37W
Gasconade *r.* Missouri U.S.A. **92** B1 38 00N 92 00W
Gascoyne *r.* Australia **78** A5 25 00S 114 00E
Gasherbrum *mts.* Kashmir **53** D7 35 46N 76 38E
Gaspar Grande *i.* Trinidad and Tobago **96** S10 10 40N 61 39W
Gaspé Québec Canada **89** W2 48 50N 64 30W
Gata, Cape Cyprus **54** N12 34 40N 33 01E
Gateshead England United Kingdom **68** J6 54 58N 1 35W
Gatineau Québec Canada **93** E3 45 29N 75 40W
Gatún Panama **97** Y2 9 16N 79 55W
Gatún Lake Panama **97** Y2 9 15N 79 50W
Gatun Locks Panama **97** Y2 9 16N 79 55W
Gau *i.* Fiji **83** D8 18 00S 179 16E
Gaua *(Santa Maria) i.* Vanuatu **83** G7 14 15S 167 30E
Gauhati India **53** G5 26 10N 91 45E
Gávdhos *i.* Greece **74** D1 34 00N 24 00E
Gave d'Oloron *r.* France **73** A1 43 15N 0 40W
Gave du Pau *r.* France **73** A1 43 20N 0 30W
Gävle Sweden **56** D3 60 41N 17 10E
Gaya India **53** F4 24 48N 85 00E
Gaylord Michigan U.S.A. **93** D3 45 02N 84 41W
Gaza Israel **54** O10 31 30N 34 28E
Gaza Strip *territory* Israel **54** O10 31 28N 34 05E
Gazelle Peninsula Papua New Guinea **45** P4 4 30S 152 15E
Gaziantep Turkey **54** E6 37 04N 37 21E
Gbarnga Liberia **112** D4 7 02N 9 26W
Gdańsk Poland **75** C3 54 22N 18 41E
Gdańsk, Gulf of Baltic Sea **75** C3 54 00N 19 00E
Gdynia Poland **75** C3 54 31N 18 30E
Gebel el Tîh *p.* Egypt **54** N9/O9 29 30N 33 45E
Gebel Katherîna *hill* Egypt **54** N9 28 30N 33 57E
Gebel Mûsa *(Mount Sinai)* Egypt **54** N9 28 32N 33 59E
Gedaref Sudan **110** G10 14 01N 35 24E
Gediz *r.* Turkey **54** C6 38 40N 27 30E
Geel Belgium **70** D3 51 10N 5 00E
Geelong Australia **78** G2 38 10S 144 26E
Gejiu China **49** K3 23 25N 103 05E
Gela Italy **74** B2 37 04N 14 15E
Gelderland *admin.* Netherlands **70** E4/F4 52 05N 6 10E
Geldern Germany **70** F3 51 31N 6 19E
Geldrop Netherlands **70** E3 51 25N 5 34E
Geleen Netherlands **70** E2 50 58N 5 45E
Gelibolu *(Gallipoli)* Turkey **74** E3 40 25N 26 41E
Gelsenkirchen Germany **71** A2 51 30N 7 05E
Gembloux Belgium **70** D2 50 34N 4 42E
Gemsbok National Park Botswana **111** D2 26 00S 21 00E
Genalē *r.* Ethiopia **110** H9 6 00N 40 00E
Gendringen Netherlands **70** F3 51 53N 6 24E
Geneina Sudan **110** D10 13 27N 22 30E
General Belgrano II *r.s.* Antarctica **21** 77 52S 34 37W
General Bernardo O'Higgins *r.s.* Antarctica **21** 63 19S 57 54W
General San Martin *r.s.* Antarctica **21** 68 08S 67 06W
General Santos The Philippines **40** C2 6 05N 125 15E
Geneva Switzerland *see* Genève
Geneva New York U.S.A. **93** E2 42 53N 76 59W
Geneva, Lake *see* Lac Léman
Genève *(Geneva)* Switzerland **73** C2 46 13N 6 09E
Gengma China **38** B4 23 31N 99 28E
Genil *r.* Spain **72** B2 37 20N 4 45W
Genk Belgium **70** E2 50 58N 5 30E
Gennevilliers France **67** B2 48 56N 2 17E
Genoa *see* Genova
Genova *(Genoa)* Italy **74** A3 44 24N 8 56E
Gent *(Gand)* Belgium **70** C3 51 02N 3 42E
Genyem Indonesia **45** J5 2 38S 140 26E
George *r.* Québec Canada **89** V4 58 00N 65 30W
George Island Falkland Islands **25** M15 52 20S 59 45W
Georges River Australia **79** F2 33 57S 150 57E
Georgetown Guyana **102** F14 6 46N 58 10W
Georgetown Malaysia **42** B5 5 25N 100 20E
Georgetown Delaware U.S.A. **93** E1 38 43N 75 05W
Georgetown South Carolina U.S.A. **91** K3 33 23N 79 18W
George VI Sound Antarctica **21** 72 00S 67 00W
George V Land *geog. reg.* Antarctica **21** 70 00S 150 00E
Gheorghe Gheorghiu-Dej Romania **75** E2 46 17N 26 45E
GEORGIA 58 E3/F3
Georgia *state* U.S.A. **91** J3 33 00N 83 00W
Georgian Bay Ontario Canada **93** D2/3 45 00N 81 00W
Georgina *r.* Australia **78** F5 22 00S 137 00E
Georg von Neumayer *r.s.* Antarctica **21** 70 37S 8 22W
Gera Germany **71** B2 50 51N 12 11E
Gera *r.* Germany **71** B2 50 00N 10 00E
Geraardsbergen Belgium **70** C2 50 47N 3 53E
Geraldton Australia **78** A4 28 49S 144 36E
Geraldton Ontario Canada **92** C3 49 44N 86 59W
GERMANY 71 A1/B2
Gerona Spain **72** C3 41 59N 2 49E
Gerrards Cross England United Kingdom **66** A3 51 35N 0 34W
Getafe Spain **72** B3 40 18N 3 44W
Gettysburg Pennsylvania U.S.A. **93** E1 39 50N 77 16W
Getz Ice Shelf Antarctica **21** 75 00S 120 00W
Geylang Singapore **41** D3 1 19N 103 53E
Geylang River Singapore **41** D3 1 18N 103 53E
Geylang Serai Singapore **41** D3 1 19N 103 54E
Ghadāmis Libya **110** A14 30 08N 9 30E
Ghaghara *r.* India **53** E5 26 20N 83 30E
Ghaghe *i.* Solomon Islands **82** D6 7 23S 158 14E
GHANA 112 E4
Ghanzi Botswana **111** D3 21 42S 21 39E
Ghardaïa Algeria **112** F9 32 20N 3 40E
Gharyān Libya **110** B14 32 10N 13 01E
Ghāt Libya **110** B12 24 58N 10 11E
Ghatere Solomon Islands **82** E6 7 50S 159 08E
Ghaziabad India **53** D5 28 39N 77 26E
Ghazni Afghanistan **55** K5 33 33N 68 26E
Ghisonaccia Corsica **73** C1 42 01N 9 24E
Gia Nghia Vietnam **37** C2 11 59N 107 42E
Gia Rai Vietnam **37** C1 9 14N 105 28E
Gibraltar *territory* U.K. **72** A2 36 09N 5 21W
Gibraltar, Strait of Spain/Morocco **72** A2 35 58N 5 30W
Gibson Desert Australia **78** C5 25 00S 123 00E
Gīdolē Ethiopia **110** G9 5 38N 37 28E
Gien France **73** B2 47 41N 2 37E
Giessen Germany **71** A2 50 35N 8 42E
Gifu Japan **46** H2 35 27N 136 46E
Gifu *pref.* Japan **46** H2 35 30N 136 50E
Gigüela *r.* Spain **72** B2 39 40N 3 15W
Gijón Spain **72** A3 43 32N 5 40W
Gila *r.* U.S.A. **90** D3 33 00N 114 00W
Gila Bend Arizona U.S.A. **90** D3 32 56N 112 42W
Gilbert *r.* Australia **78** G6 17 00S 142 30E
Gilbert Islands Pacific Ocean **80** C3/4 0 00 173 00E
Gilgit Kashmir **53** C7 35 54N 74 20E
Gilimanuk Indonesia **42** R6 8 12S 114 27E
Gillam Manitoba Canada **89** Q4 56 25N 94 45W
Gillette Wyoming U.S.A. **90** E5 44 18N 105 30W
Gillingham England United Kingdom **68** L3 51 24N 0 33E
Gimli Manitoba Canada **92** A4 50 39N 97 00W
Gimpu Indonesia **43** E3 2 00S 119 50E
Gineifa Egypt **109** S2 30 12N 32 26E
Gingoog The Philippines **40** C2 8 50N 125 08E
Gīnīr Ethiopia **110** H9 7 06N 40 40E
Gippsland *geog. reg.* Australia **78** H2 37 30S 147 00E
Girardot Colombia **102** C13 4 19N 74 47W
Girga Egypt **110** F13 26 17N 31 58E
Gironde *r.* France **73** A2 45 30N 0 45W
Gisborne North Island New Zealand **79** C3 38 40S 178 01E
Giurgiu Romania **75** E1 43 53N 25 58E
Givet Belgium **70** E2 50 08N 4 49E
Gizhiga Russia **57** S8 62 00N 160 34E
Gizo *i.* Solomon Islands **82** B5 8 04S 156 45E
Gizo Strait Solomon Islands **82** B5 8 10S 156 40E
Gjirokastër Albania **74** D3 40 05N 20 10E
Gjoa Haven *tn.* Northwest Territories Canada **89** P6 68 39N 96 09W
Glace Bay *tn.* Nova Scotia Canada **89** X2 46 11N 59 58W
Glacier National Park Montana U.S.A. **90** D6 48 50N 114 00W
Gladbeck Germany **70** F3 51 34N 6 59E
Gladesville Australia **79** G2 33 50S 151 08E
Gladstone Australia **78** I5 23 52S 151 16E
Glåma *r.* Norway **69** C3 60 15N 12 00E
Glan The Philippines **40** C2 5 49N 125 11E
Glarner Alpen *mts.* Switzerland **73** C2 46 50N 9 00E
Glasgow Scotland United Kingdom **68** G7 55 53N 4 15W
Glauchau Germany **71** B2 50 48N 12 32E
Glazov Russia **59** G6 58 09N 52 42E
Glenboro Manitoba Canada **92** A3 49 35N 99 20W
Glendale California U.S.A. **95** B3 34 09N 118 20W
Glendora California U.S.A. **95** C3 34 07N 117 53W
Glen Grove *tn.* New York U.S.A. **94** D2 40 52N 73 38W
Glen Ridge *tn.* New Jersey U.S.A. **94** B2 40 47N 74 13W
Glens Falls *tn.* New York U.S.A. **93** F2 43 17N 73 41W
Glenwood Iowa U.S.A. **92** A2 41 04N 95 46W
Glienicke Germany **67** F2 52 39N 13 19E
Gliwice Poland **75** C3 50 20N 18 40E
Globe Arizona U.S.A. **90** D3 33 23N 110 48W
Głogów Poland **75** C3 51 40N 16 06E
Gloucester Ontario Canada **93** E3 45 16N 75 39W
Gloucester Papua New Guinea **45** N4 5 30S 148 40E
Gloucester England United Kingdom **68** I3 51 53N 2 14W
Glovertown Newfoundland Canada **89** Y2 48 40N 54 03W
Gmunden Austria **71** B1 47 56N 13 48E
Gniezno Poland **75** C3 52 32N 17 32E
Goa, Damān & Diu *admin.* India **53** C3 15 00N 74 00E
Goalpara India **53** G5 26 10N 90 38E
Gobabis Namibia **111** C3 22 30S 18 58E
Gobe Papua New Guinea **45** N2 9 05S 148 06E
Gobi Desert Mongolia **49** J7/L7 48 30N 100 00E
Goch Germany **71** A2 51 40N 6 10E
Go Cong Vietnam **37** C2 10 22N 106 41E
Godāvari *r.* India **53** D3/E3 19 00N 80 00E
Goderich Ontario Canada **93** D2 43 43N 81 43W
Godhavn *see* Qeqertarsuaq
Godhra India **53** C4 22 49N 73 40E
Gods Lake Manitoba Canada **89** Q3 54 40N 94 20W
Godthåb *(Nuuk)* Greenland **89** Y5 64 10N 51 40W
Godwin Austen *see* K2
Goes Netherlands **70** C3 51 30N 3 54E
Goiânia Brazil **102** H9 16 43S 49 18W
Goiás Brazil **102** G9 15 57S 50 07W
Goiás *admin.* Brazil **102** H10 12 30S 48 00W
Goias Massif *hills* South America **98** 15 00S 53 00W
Gojō Japan **46** G1 34 21N 135 42E
Gökçeada *i.* Turkey **74** E2 40 00N 25 00E
Golaghat India **36** A7 26 30N 93 59E
Golan Heights *territory* Israel **54** O11 33 00N 35 50E
Gold Coast *tn.* Australia **78** I4 27 59S 153 22E
Golden Bay South Island New Zealand **79** B2 40 40S 172 49E
Goldsboro North Carolina U.S.A. **91** K4 35 23N 78 00W
Goldsworthy Australia **78** B5 20 20S 119 31E
Golfe de Gabès *g.* Tunisia **112** H9 34 20N 10 30E
Golfe de St-Malo *g.* France **73** A2 48 55N 2 30W
Golfe du Lion *g.* France **73** B1 43 10N 4 00E
Golfo de California *g.* Mexico **96** B5 27 00N 111 00W
Golfo de Guayaquil *g.* Ecuador **102** A12 3 00S 81 30W
Golfo de Honduras *g.* Caribbean Sea **96/97** G3 17 00N 87 30W

Hamilton Ontario Canada **93** E2 43 15N 79 50W
Hamilton North Island New Zealand **79** C3 37 47S 175 17E
Hamilton Ohio U.S.A. **93** D1 39 23N 84 33W
Hamilton Inlet Newfoundland Canada **89** X3 54 18N 57 42W
Hamm Germany **71** A2 51 40N 7 49E
Hammerdal Sweden **69** D3 63 35N 15 20E
Hammerfest Norway **69** E5 70 40N 23 44E
Hammersmith *bor.* England United Kingdom **66** C2 51 30N 0 14W
Hamminkeln Germany **70** F3 51 43N 6 36E
Hammond Indiana U.S.A. **92** C2 41 36N 87 30W
Hampstead Heath England United Kingdom **66** C3 51 34N 0 10W
Hampton Virginia U.S.A. **93** E1 37 02N 76 23W
Ham Tan Vietnam **37** C2 10 39N 107 47E
Hamuku Irian Jaya Indonesia **44** F5 3 23S 135 09E
Hanazono Japan **46** G1 34 09N 135 31E
Hancock New York U.S.A. **93** E2 41 58N 75 17W
Handa Japan **46** H1 34 52N 136 57E
Handan China **49** M6 36 35N 114 31E
Hang Ha Po Hong Kong U.K. **51** B2 22 27N 114 08E
Hang Hau Hong Kong U.K. **51** C1 22 18N 114 16E
Hang Hau Tsuen Hong Kong U.K. **51** A2 22 28N 113 59E
Hango Finland **69** E2 50 50N 23 00E
Hangzhou China **49** O5 30 18N 120 07E
Hanna Alberta Canada **88** M3 51 38N 111 56W
Hannibal Missouri U.S.A. **92** B1 39 41N 91 20W
Hanno Japan **46** L2 35 52N 139 19E
Hannover Germany **71** A2 52 23N 9 44E
Hannut Belgium **70** E2 50 40N 5 05E
Hanöbukten *b.* Sweden **69** C2 55 50N 14 30E
Hanoi Vietnam **37** C4 21 01N 105 52E
Hanover Ontario Canada **93** D2 44 10N 81 03W
Hanover New Hampshire U.S.A. **93** F2 43 42N 71 17W
Hanover Pennsylvania U.S.A. **93** E1 39 47N 76 59W
Hao *i.* Pacific Ocean **81** E3 18 04S 141 00W
Haora India **52** K2 22 35N 88 19E
Happy Land *tn.* Vanuatu **83** J3 18 55S 169 05E
Happy Valley Hong Kong U.K. **51** C1 22 16N 114 11E
Happy Valley-Goose Bay *tn.* Newfoundland Canada **89** W3 53 15N 60 20W
Hapsu North Korea **50** D5 41 12N 128 48E
Haql Saudi Arabia **54** D4 29 14N 34 56E
Harad Saudi Arabia **55** G3 24 12N 49 12E
Harare Zimbabwe **111** F4 17 50S 31 03E
Harbin China **49** P8 45 45N 126 41E
Harbor Beach *tn.* Michigan U.S.A. **93** D2 43 51N 83 40W
Harbour Breton *tn.* Newfoundland Canada **89** X2 47 29N 55 50W
Harbours, Bay of Falkland Islands **25** M15 52 30S 59 30W
Hardangerfjorden *fj.* Norway **69** B2 59 45N 5 20E
Hardangervidda *plat.* Norway **69** B3 60 10N 7 00E
Hardenberg Netherlands **70** F4 52 34N 6 38E
Harderwijk Netherlands **70** E4 52 21N 5 37E
Harefield England United Kingdom **66** B3 51 36N 0 28W
Härer Ethiopia **110** H9 9 20N 42 10E
Hargeysa Somalia **110** H9 9 31N 44 02E
Haridwar India **53** D5 29 58N 78 09E
Harima-nada *sea* Japan **46** B1 34 30N 134 30E
Haringey *bor.* England United Kingdom **66** C3 51 35N 0 07W
Hari Rud *r.* Afghanistan **55** J5 34 00N 64 00E
Harlem New York U.S.A. **94** B2 40 48N 73 56W
Harlingen Netherlands **70** E5 53 10N 5 25E
Harlingen Texas U.S.A. **91** G2 26 12N 97 43W
Härnösand Sweden **69** D3 62 37N 17 55E
Harper Liberia **112** D3 4 25N 7 43W
Harricanaw River Québec Canada **93** E4 50 00N 79 50W
Harrington Harbour *tn.* Québec Canada **89** X3 50 31N 59 30W
Harris *i.* Scotland United Kingdom **68** D9 57 50N 6 55W
Harrisburg Illinois U.S.A. **92** C1 37 40N 88 10W
Harrisburg Pennsylvania U.S.A. **93** E2 40 17N 76 54W
Harrisonburg Virginia U.S.A. **93** E1 38 27N 78 54W
Harrisonville Missouri U.S.A. **92** B1 38 04N 94 21W
Harrisville Michigan U.S.A. **93** D2 44 41N 83 19W
Harrogate England United Kingdom **68** J6 54 00N 1 33W
Harrow *bor.* Greater London England United Kingdom **66** B3 51 34N 0 20W
Hart Michigan U.S.A. **92** C2 43 43N 86 22W
Hartford Connecticut U.S.A. **93** F2 41 00N 72 00W
Hartland Point England United Kingdom **68** G3 51 02N 4 31W
Hartlepool England United Kingdom **68** J6 54 41N 1 13W
Harwich England United Kingdom **68** M3 51 57N 1 17E
Haryana *admin.* India **53** D5 29 20N 75 30E
Harz *mts.* Europe **71** B2 52 00N 10 00E
Hasaki Japan **46** M2 35 46N 140 50E
Hase *r.* Germany **71** A2 52 00N 8 00E
Hashima Japan **46** H2 35 19N 136 43E
Hashimoto Japan **46** G1 34 19N 135 33E
Hassan India **53** D2 13 01N 76 03E
Hasselt Belgium **70** E2 50 56N 5 20E
Hassi Messaoud Algeria **112** G9 31 52N 5 43E
Hastings Barbados **96** V12 13 05N 59 36W
Hastings England United Kingdom **68** L2 50 51N 0 36E
Hastings Minnesota U.S.A. **92** B2 44 43N 92 50W
Hastings Nebraska U.S.A. **91** G5 40 37N 98 22W
Ha Tien Vietnam **37** B2 10 24N 104 30E
Ha Tinh Vietnam **37** C3 18 21N 105 55E
Hat Lek Thailand **39** B2 11 38N 102 54E
Ha Tsuen Hong Kong U.K. **51** A2 22 26N 113 59E
Hattiesburg Mississippi U.S.A. **91** I3 31 20N 89 19W
Hat Yai Thailand **39** B1 7 00N 100 25E
Hatzfeldhafen Papua New Guinea **45** L4 4 26S 145 11E
Haud *geog. reg.* Africa **110** H9/I9 8 00N 50 00E
Haugesund Norway **69** B2 59 25N 5 16E
Hauhui Solomon Islands **82** F4 9 18S 161 06E
Haung *(Heung) r.* Laos/Thailand **37** B3 17 45N 101 20E
Haukivesi *l.* Finland **69** F3 62 10N 28 30E
Hauraha Solomon Islands **82** G3 10 47S 161 55E
Hauraki Gulf North Island New Zealand **79** B3/C3 36 38S 175 04E
Hausruck *mts.* Austria **71** B1 47 00N 14 00E
Haut Atlas *mts.* Morocco **112** D9 30 45N 6 50W
Hautes Fagnes *moor* Belgium **70** F2 50 29N 6 08E
Hauteurs de Gatine *hills* France **73** A2 46 38N 0 38W
Hauts de Meuse *hills* France **73** C2 49 15N 5 20E
Hauz Khas India **52** L4 28 34N 77 11E
Havana *see* La Habana
Havel *r.* Germany **71** B2 52 00N 12 00E
Havelkanal *can.* Germany **67** E2 52 38N 13 02E
Havelock Ontario Canada **93** E2 44 26N 77 53W
Haveluloto Tonga **83** D1 21 08S 175 14W
Haverhill Massachusetts U.S.A. **93** F2 42 47N 71 07W
Havering *bor.* England United Kingdom **66** D3 51 34N 0 14E
Havre Montana U.S.A. **90** E6 48 34N 109 40W
Hawaii *i.* Hawaiian Islands **23** Z17 19 50N 157 50W
Hawaiian Islands Pacific Ocean **22/23** I10/K10 25 00N 166 00W
Hawaiian Ridge Pacific Ocean **23** J10 23 00N 166 00W
Hawea, Lake South Island New Zealand **79** A2 44 28S 169 17E
Hawera North Island New Zealand **79** B3 39 35S 174 17E
Hawick England United Kingdom **68** I7 55 25N 2 47W
Hawke Bay North Island New Zealand **79** C3 39 23S 177 12E
Hawkesbury Ontario Canada **89** U2 45 36N 74 38W
Hawthorne California U.S.A. **95** A2 33 54N 118 21W
Hawthorne New Jersey U.S.A. **94** B2 40 57N 74 10W
Hay *r.* Alberta/Northwest Territories Canada **88** L5 61 00N 115 30W
Hayama Japan **47** B2 35 16N 139 35E
Haycock *i.* Solomon Islands **82** C6 7 30S 157 40E
Hayes England United Kingdom **66** B3 51 31N 0 25W
Hayes *r.* Manitoba Canada **89** Q4 56 00N 94 00W
Hayes *see* Halvø
Hay River *tn.* Northwest Territories Canada **88** L5 60 51N 115 42W
Hayward Wisconsin U.S.A. **92** B3 46 02N 91 26W
Hazard Kentucky U.S.A. **93** D1 37 14N 83 11W
Hazebrouck France **70** B2 50 43N 2 32E
Hazelton British Columbia Canada **88** J4 55 16N 127 18W
Headstone Point Norfolk Island **81** K4 29 02S 167 55E
Headstone Reserve Norfolk Island **81** K4 29 02S 167 55E
Heard Island Indian Ocean **24** G1 53 07S 73 20E
Hearst Ontario Canada **93** D3 49 42N 83 40W
Heart *r.* North Dakota U.S.A. **90** F6 47 00N 102 00W
Heathcote Australia **79** G1 34 05S 151 00E
Hebi China **49** M6 35 57N 114 08E
Hebron Jordan **54** O10 31 32N 35 06E
Hecate Strait British Columbia Canada **88** I3 53 00N 131 00W
Hechi China **36** D6 24 39N 108 02E
Hechuan China **49** L5 30 02N 106 5E
Heda Japan **46** K1 34 58N 138 46E
Hedesundafjärdarna *l.* Sweden **69** D3 60 20N 17 00E
Heemstede Netherlands **70** D4 52 21N 4 37E
Heerenveen Netherlands **70** E4 52 57N 5 55E
Heerhugowaard Netherlands **70** D4 52 40N 4 50E
Heerlen Netherlands **70** E2 50 53N 5 59E
Hefei China **49** N5 31 55N 117 18E
Hegang China **49** Q8 47 36N 130 30E
Hegura-jima *i.* Japan **46** C2 37 52N 136 56E
Heidelberg Germany **71** A1 49 25N 8 42E
Heidenheim Germany **71** B1 48 41N 10 10E
Heilbronn Germany **71** A1 49 08N 9 14E
Hei Ling Chau *i.* Hong Kong U.K. **51** B1 22 15N 114 02E
Heilong Jiang *see* Amur
Heiloo Netherlands **70** D4 52 36N 4 43E
Heinze Chaung *b.* Myanmar **38** B2 14 45N 97 00E
Heist op den Berg Belgium **70** D3 51 05N 4 44E
Hekla *mt.* Iceland **69** I6 64 00N 19 41W
Hekou China **49** K3 22 30N 104 00E
Helan Shan *mts.* China **49** L6 38 00N 106 00E
Helchteren Belgium **70** E3 51 03N 5 23E
Helena Montana U.S.A. **90** D6 46 35N 112 00W
Helen Reef Caroline Islands **43** H4 2 43N 131 46E
Helgeland *geog. reg.* Norway **69** C4 64 45N 13 00E
Heligoland Bight *b.* Germany **71** A2 54 00N 8 00E
Hellendoorn Netherlands **70** F4 52 23N 6 27E
Hellersdorf Germany **67** G2 52 32N 13 35E
Hellevoetsluis Netherlands **70** D3 51 49N 4 08E
Hellín Spain **72** B2 38 31N 1 43W
Helmand *r.* Afghanistan **55** J5 30 00N 62 30E
Helmond Netherlands **70** E3 51 28N 5 40E
Helong China **50** D6 42 38N 128 58E
Helsingborg Sweden **69** C2 56 03N 12 43E
Helsinki *(Helsingfors)* Finland **69** E3 60 08N 25 00E
Hempstead New York U.S.A. **94** D1 40 41N 73 39W
Henares *r.* Spain **72** B3 40 45N 3 10W
Henderson Kentucky U.S.A. **92** C1 37 49N 87 35W
Henderson Nevada U.S.A. **90** D4 36 01N 115 00W
Hendon England United Kingdom **66** C3 51 35N 0 14W
Heng-ch'un Taiwan **51** G5 22 03N 120 45E
Hengduan Shan *mts.* China **38** B5 28 00N 98 30E
Hengelo Netherlands **70** F4 52 16N 6 46E
Hengyang China **49** M4 26 58N 112 31E
Henningsdorf *admin.* Germany **67** E2 52 39N 13 08E
Henrietta Maria, Cape Ontario Canada **89** S4 55 00N 82 30W
Henryetta Oklahoma U.S.A. **91** G4 35 27N 96 00W
Henzada Myanmar **38** B3 17 36N 95 26E
Hepu China **37** C4 21 37N 109 11E
Heqing China **38** C5 26 35N 100 13E
Herāt Afghanistan **55** J5 34 20N 62 12E
Hérault *r.* France **73** B1 43 50N 3 30E
Herblay France **67** A2 48 59N 2 10E
Hereford England United Kingdom **68** I4 52 04N 2 43W
Herentals Belgium **70** D3 51 11N 4 50E
Herford Germany **71** A2 52 07N 8 40E
Herisau Switzerland **71** A1 47 23N 9 17E
Hermel Lebanon **54** P12 34 25N 36 23E
Hermit Islands Papua New Guinea **45** L6 1 30S 145 15E
Hermon, Mount Lebanon/Syria **54** O11 33 24N 35 50E
Hermosillo Mexico **96** B5 29 15N 110 59W
Herne Germany **70** G3 51 32N 7 12E
Herning Denmark **69** B2 56 08N 8 59E
Hernodorf Germany **67** F2 52 38N 13 18E
Herstal Belgium **70** E2 50 40N 5 38E
Hertfordshire *co.* England United Kingdom **66** C3 51 50N 0 05W
Hervey *i.* Pacific Ocean **81** E3 19 21S 158 58W
Hessen *admin.* Germany **71** A2 50 00N 9 00E
Heung *(Haung) r.* Laos/Thailand **37** B3 17 45N 101 20E
Hezhang China **38** C5 27 08N 104 48E
Hibbing Minnesota U.S.A. **92** B3 47 25N 92 55W
Hickory North Carolina U.S.A. **91** J4 35 44N 81 23W
Hidaka Japan **46** F2 35 29N 134 44E
Hidalgo Mexico **96** E4 24 16N 99 28W
Hidalgo del Parral Mexico **96** C5 26 58N 105 40W
Hienghène New Caledonia **82** T3 20 40S 164 54E
Higashi-Matsuyama Japan **46** L3 36 02N 139 25E
Higashi-Murayama Japan **47** A4 35 46N 139 28E
Higashi-Ōsaka Japan **46** G1 34 40N 135 35E
Higashi-suidō *sd.* Japan **46** A1 34 10N 130 00E
Highgate Jamaica **97** R8 18 16N 76 53W
High Island Hong Kong U.K. **51** D2 22 21N 114 21E
High Island Reservoir Hong Kong U.K. **51** D2 22 22N 114 20E
High Level *tn.* Alberta Canada **88** L4 58 10N 117 20W
High Point *tn.* North Carolina U.S.A. **91** K4 35 58N 80 00W
High Veld *mts.* Republic of South Africa **111** E2 28 00S 28 00E
Hiiumaa *i.* Estonia **69** E2 58 55N 22 30E
Hikami Japan **46** F2 35 12N 135 00E
Hikone Japan **46** H2 35 17N 136 13E
Hila Indonesia **43** G2 7 36S 127 25E
Hildesheim Germany **71** A2 52 09N 9 58E
Hillaby, Mount Barbados **96** V12 13 12N 59 35W
Hillingdon *bor.* England United Kingdom **66** B3 51 32N 0 27W
Hillsboro Ohio U.S.A. **93** D1 39 12N 83 37W
Hilo Hawaiian Islands **23** Z17 19 42N 155 04W
Hilversum Netherlands **70** E4 52 14N 5 10E
Himachal Pradesh *admin.* India **53** D6 32 00N 77 30E
Himalaya *mts.* Asia **53** D6/G5
Himeji Japan **46** B1 34 50N 134 40E
Hims Syria **54** E5 34 42N 36 40E
Hindu Kush *mts.* Afghanistan **55** K6 35 00N 70 00E
Hinigaran The Philippines **40** B3 10 17N 122 51E
Hinnøya *i.* Norway **69** D4 68 35N 15 50E
Hirado *i.* Japan **50** D1 33 20N 129 30E
Hirakata Japan **46** G1 34 45N 135 35E
Hirakud Reservoir India **53** E4 21 40N 83 40E
Hiratsuka Japan **46** L2 35 20N 139 19E
Hirosaki Japan **46** D3 40 34N 140 28E
Hirson France **73** B2 49 56N 4 05E
Hiroshima Japan **46** B1 34 23N 132 27E
Hisai Japan **46** H1 34 42N 136 28E
Hisar India **53** D5 29 10N 75 45E
Hisiu Papua New Guinea **45** M2 9 02S 146 48E
Hispaniola *i.* West Indies **97** J3 18 00N 70 00W
Hitachi Japan **46** D2 36 35N 140 40E
Hitiaa Tahiti **82** T9 17 35S 149 17W
Hitra *i.* Norway **69** B3 63 37N 8 46E
Hiu *i.* Vanuatu **83** F8 13 07S 166 34E
Hiva Hoa *i.* Pacific Ocean **81** F3 9 45S 139 00W
Hjørring Denmark **69** B2 57 28N 9 59E
Hkakabo Razi *mt.* Myanmar **38** B5 28 17N 97 46E
Hnathalo New Caledonia **82** W3 20 48S 167 18E
Ho Ghana **112** F4 6 38N 0 38E
Hoa Binh Vietnam **37** C4 20 49N 105 20E
Hoa Da Vietnam **37** C2 11 13N 108 34E
Hoai Nhon *see* Bong Son
Hobart Australia **78** H1 42 54S 147 18E
Hoboken New Jersey U.S.A. **94** B1 40 44N 74 02W
Hobyo Somalia **110** I9 5 20N 48 30E
Ho Chi Minh *(Saigon)* Vietnam **37** C2 10 46N 106 43E
Ho Chung Hong Kong U.K. **51** C2 22 22N 114 14E
Hódmezovásárhely Hungary **75** D2 46 26N 20 21E
Hodogaya Japan **47** B2 35 26N 139 36E
Hoek van Holland Netherlands **70** D4 51 59N 4 08E
Hoeryŏng North Korea **50** D6 42 29N 129 45E
Hof Germany **71** B2 50 19N 11 56E
Höfn Iceland **69** I6 64 16N 15 10W
Hofsjökull *ice cap* Iceland **69** I6 64 45N 18 45W
Hofu Japan **46** B1 34 02N 131 34E
Hoggar *mts.* Algeria **112** G7 23 45N 6 00E
Hog Harbour *tn.* Vanuatu **83** G6 15 10S 167 08E
Hohe Acht *mt.* Germany **70** G2 50 22N 7 00E
Hohe Rhön *hills* Germany **71** A2/B2 50 00N 10 00E
Hohe Tauern *mts.* Austria **71** B1 47 00N 13 00E
Hohhot China **49** M7 40 49N 117 37E
Hoi An Vietnam **37** C3 15 55N 108 29E
Hoi Ha Hong Kong U.K. **51** C2 22 28N 114 20E
Hokitika South Island New Zealand **79** B2 42 43S 170 58E
Hokkaidō *i.* Japan **46** D3 43 30N 143 00E
Hokota Japan **46** M3 36 10N 141 30E
Holetown Barbados **96** V12 13 11N 59 38W
Holguín Cuba **97** I4 20 54N 76 15W
Holland *tn.* Michigan U.S.A. **92** C2 42 46N 86 06W
Holland Village Singapore **41** C3 1 19N 103 48E
Hollick-Kenyon Plateau Antarctica **21** 77 00S 100 00W
Hollis Reservoir Trinidad and Tobago **96** T10 10 42N 61 11W
Hollywood California U.S.A. **95** A3 34 05N 118 21W
Hollywood Reservoir California U.S.A. **95** A3 34 07N 118 20W
Holsteinborg Greenland **89** Y6 66 55N 53 30W
Holston *r.* U.S.A. **91** J4 37 00N 82 00W
Ho-lung Taiwan **51** G7 24 37N 120 46E
Holy Cross Alaska U.S.A. **88** D5 62 10N 159 53W
Holyhead Wales United Kingdom **68** G5 53 19N 4 38W
Holy Island England United Kingdom **68** J7 55 41N 1 48W
Holy Island Wales United Kingdom **68** G5 53 16N 4 39W
Holyoke Massachusetts U.S.A. **93** F2 42 12N 72 37W
Ho Man Tin Hong Kong U.K. **51** B1 22 19N 114 10E
Homburg Germany **71** A1 49 20N 7 20E
Home Bay Northwest Territories Canada **89** V6 69 00N 67 00W
Homer Alaska U.S.A. **88** E4 59 40N 151 37W
Homestead Florida U.S.A. **91** J2 25 29N 80 29W
Homonhon *i.* The Philippines **40** C3 10 45N 125 41E
Hon Chong Vietnam **37** B2 10 25N 104 30E
Honda Colombia **102** C14 5 15N 74 50W
Honda Bay The Philippines **40** A2 10 00N 119 00E
HONDURAS **96/97** G2
Hone Manitoba Canada **89** O4 56 20N 101 15W
Hon Gai Vietnam **37** C4 20 57N 107 06E
Hong Kah Singapore **41** B4 1 21N 103 43E
Hong Kong *i.* Hong Kong U.K. **51** B1/C1 22 10N 114 10E
Hong Kong *territory* U.K. **49** M3 23 00N 114 00E
Hong Lok Yuen Hong Kong U.K. **51** B2 22 27N 114 09E
Hongsŏng South Korea **50** C3 36 36N 126 41E
Honguedo Passage *(Détroit d'Honguedo) sd.* Québec Canada **89** W2 49 30N 64 20W
Hongwŏn North Korea **50** C5 40 00N 127 56E
Honiara Solomon Islands **82** E4 9 28S 159 57E
Honjō Japan **46** L3 36 16N 139 09E
Hon Lon *i.* Vietnam **37** C2 12 36N 109 22E
Honokaa Hawaiian Islands **23** Z18 20 04N 155 27W
Honolulu Hawaiian Islands **23** Y18 21 19N 157 50W
Hon Quan *(An Loc)* Vietnam **37** C2 11 40N 106 35E
Hon Rai *i.* Vietnam **37** B1 9 47N 104 33E
Honshū *i.* Japan **46** C2 37 15N 139 00E
Hon Tre *i.* Vietnam **37** C2 12 12N 109 19E
Hood, Mount Oregon U.S.A. **90** B6 45 24N 121 41W
Hood Point Papua New Guinea **45** M1 10 10S 145 45E
Hoofdorp Netherlands **70** D4 52 18N 4 41E
Hoogeveen Netherlands **70** F4 52 43N 6 29E
Hoogezand Netherlands **70** F5 53 10N 6 45E
Hook England United Kingdom **66** B2 51 17N 0 58W
Hoolehua Hawaiian Islands **23** Y18 21 11N 157 06W
Hooper Bay *tn.* Alaska U.S.A. **88** B5 61 29N 166 10W
Hoorn Netherlands **70** E4 52 38N 5 03E
Ho-pang Myanmar **38** B4 23 20N 98 40E
Hope Barbados **96** V13 13 20N 59 36W
Hope British Columbia Canada **88** K2 49 21N 121 28W
Hopes Advance, Cape Québec Canada **89** V5 61 00N 69 40W
Hopkinsville Kentucky U.S.A. **91** I4 36 50N 87 30W
Ho Pui Hong Kong U.K. **51** B2 22 24N 114 04E
Hormuz, Strait of The Gulf **55** I4 26 35N 56 30E
Hornavan *l.* Sweden **69** D4 66 15N 17 40E
Hornchurch England United Kingdom **66** D3 51 34N 0 13E
Hornsby Australia **79** G3 33 42S 151 06E
Horsens Denmark **69** B2 55 53N 9 53E
Horsham Australia **78** G2 36 45S 142 15E
Hoskins Papua New Guinea **45** O4 5 30S 150 27E
Hospet India **53** D3 15 16N 76 20E
Hospitalet Spain **72** C3 41 21N 2 06E
Hotan China **48** E6 37 07N 79 57E
Hotan He *r.* China **48** F6 37 07N 79 57E
Hoting Sweden **69** D3 64 08N 16 15E
Hot Springs *tn.* Arkansas U.S.A. **91** H3 34 30N 93 02W
Houaïlou New Caledonia **82** U2 21 18S 165 33E
Houamuang Laos **37** B4 20 00N 104 00E
Houayxay Laos **37** B4 20 15N 100 29E
Hougang Singapore **41** D4 1 22N 103 54E
Houghton Michigan U.S.A. **92** C3 47 06N 88 34W
Houma China **49** M6 35 36N 111 15E
Houma Tonga **83** D1 21 10S 175 18W
Houma Louisiana U.S.A. **91** H2 29 35N 90 44W
Houma Toloa *c.* Tonga **83** D1 21 16S 175 08W
Hounslow *bor.* England United Kingdom **66** B2 51 28N 0 21W
Houston Texas U.S.A. **91** G2 29 45N 95 25W
Hovd Mongolia **48** H8 48 00N 91 43E
Hövsgöl Nuur *l.* Mongolia **49** K9 51 00N 100 30E
Howar *r.* Sudan **110** E11 17 00N 25 00E
Howe, Cape Australia **78** H2 37 20S 149 59E
Howe, Point Norfolk Island **81** K6 28 59S 167 55E
Howland Island Pacific Ocean **80** D4 0 48N 176 38W
Höxter Germany **71** A2 51 47N 9 22E
Hoy *i.* Scotland United Kingdom **68** H10 58 48N 3 20W
Hoya Japan **47** B3 35 44N 139 34E
Hoyerswerda Germany **71** B2 51 28N 14 17E
Hradec Králové Czech Republic **75** C3 50 13N 15 50E
Hron *r.* Slovakia **75** C2 48 00N 18 00E
Hsenwi Myanmar **38** B4 23 16N 97 59E
Hsi-hseng Myanmar **38** B4 20 07N 97 17E
Hsin-tien Taiwan **51** H7 24 57N 121 32E
Hsin-ying Taiwan **51** G6 23 18N 120 18E
Hsipaw Myanmar **38** B4 22 32N 97 12E
Hua Bon *see* Cheo Reo
Huacho Peru **102** B10 11 05S 77 36W
Hua Hin Thailand **39** A2 12 56N 99 58E
Huaide China **49** O7 43 30N 124 48E
Huai Luang Reservoir Thailand **39** B3 17 20N 102 35E
Huainan China **49** N5 32 41N 117 06E
Huai Yot Thailand **39** A1 7 49N 99 49E
Huaiji China **36** E6 24 03N 112 06E
Huajuápan de León Mexico **96** E3 17 50N 97 48W
Hua-lien Taiwan **51** H6 23 58N 121 35E
Huambo Angola **111** C5 12 44S 15 47E
Huamuang Laos **37** B4 20 02N 104 00E
Huancayo Peru **102** B10 12 05S 75 12W
Huang Hai *see* Yellow Sea
Huang He *r.* China **49** M6 38 00N 111 00E
Huangshi China **49** N5 30 13N 115 05E
Huanuco Peru **102** B11 9 55S 76 11W
Hua-p'ing Hsü *i.* Taiwan **51** H8 25 26N 121 57E
Huaráz Peru **102** B11 9 33S 77 31W
Huascaran *mt.* Peru **102** B11 9 08S 77 36W
Huashixia China **49** J6 35 13N 99 12E
Huatabampo Mexico **90** E2 26 49N 109 40W
Huat Choe Singapore **41** B4 1 20N 103 41E
Huch'ang North Korea **50** C5 41 23N 127 04E
Huddersfield England United Kingdom **68** J5 53 39N 1 47W
Hudson Bay Canada **89** R5 60 00N 89 00W
Hudson Bay *tn.* Saskatchewan Canada **89** O3 52 45N 102 45W
Hudson Strait Northwest Territories/Québec Canada **89** U5 62 00N 70 00W
Hue Vietnam **37** C3 16 28N 107 35E
Huelva Spain **72** A2 37 15N 6 56W
Huelva *r.* Spain **72** A2 37 50N 6 30W
Huesca Spain **72** B3 42 08N 0 25W
Huevos *i.* Trinidad and Tobago **96** S10 10 47N 61 11W
Hughenden Australia **78** G5 20 50S 144 10E
Hugli *r.* India **52** J2 22 30N 88 14E
Hugli-Chinsurah India **52** K3 22 54N 88 23E
Hugo Oklahoma U.S.A. **91** G3 34 01N 95 31W
Hŭich'ŏn North Korea **50** C5 40 06N 126 20E
Huili China **38** C5 26 40N 102 20E
Huisne *r.* France **73** B2 48 15N 0 40E
Huixtla Mexico **96** F3 15 09N 92 30W
Huize China **38** C5 26 26N 103 22E
Huizen Netherlands **70** E4 52 17N 5 15E
Huizhou China **49** M3 23 08N 114 28E
Hukawng Valley Myanmar **38** B5 26 35N 96 45E
Hula Papua New Guinea **45** M1 10 05S 147 45E
Hull Québec Canada **93** E3 45 26N 75 45W
Hull Island *see* Orona
Hulst Netherlands **70** D3 51 17N 4 03E
Humaitá Brazil **102** E11 7 33S 63 01W
Humber *r.* England United Kingdom **68** K5 53 40N 0 10W
Humboldt Saskatchewan Canada **88** N3 52 12N 105 07W
Humboldt *mt.* New Caledonia **82** V2 21 55S 166 29E
Humboldt *r.* Nevada U.S.A. **90** C5 41 00N 118 00W

Humboldt Glacier Greenland **20** 79 40N 64 00W
Hunchun China **50** E6 42 55N 130 28E
Hunga i. Tonga **83** B4 18 40S 174 07W
Hunga Ha'apia i. Tonga **83** A2 20 33S 175 25W
Hungarian Basin Europe **60** 47 00N 20 00E
HUNGARY 75 C2/D2
Hunga Tonga i. Tonga **83** A2 20 32S 175 25W
Hung Hom Hong Kong U.K. **51** C1 22 18N 114 11E
Hŭngnam North Korea **50** C4 39 49N 127 40E
Hung Yen Vietnam **37** C4 20 38N 106 05E
Hunjiang China **49** P7 41 54N 126 23E
Hunsrück mts. Germany **71** A1 50 00N 7 00E
Hunte r. Germany **71** A2 53 00N 8 00E
Hunter, Point Norfolk Island **81** L4 29 03S 167 57E
Hunter's Bay Myanmar **38** A3 20 00N 93 15E
Hunter Trench Pacific Ocean **22** H5 23 00S 175 00E
Huntingdon Québec Canada **93** F3 45 05N 74 11W
Huntington Indiana U.S.A. **92** C2 40 54N 85 30W
Huntington West Virginia U.S.A. **93** D1 38 24N 82 26W
Huntington Beach tn. California U.S.A. **95** B1 33 40N 118 00W
Huntly North Island New Zealand **79** C3 37 34S 175 10E
Huntsville Ontario Canada **93** E3 45 20N 79 13W
Huntsville Alabama U.S.A. **91** I3 34 44N 86 35W
Huntsville Texas U.S.A. **91** G3 30 43N 95 34W
Hun Yeang Singapore **41** E4 1 22N 103 55E
Huong Thuy Vietnam **37** C3 16 22N 107 43E
Huon Gulf Papua New Guinea **45** M3 6 55S 147 15E
Huon Peninsula Papua New Guinea **45** M3 6 15S 147 30E
Hurghada Egypt **110** F13 27 17N 33 47E
Huron South Dakota U.S.A. **92** A2 44 22N 98 12W
Huron, Lake Canada/U.S.A. **93** D2/3 45 00N 83 00W
Hurstville Australia **79** G2 33 58S 151 06E
Hürth Germany **70** F2 50 52N 6 51E
Húsavik Iceland **69** I7 66 03N 17 17W
Husn Jordan **54** O11 32 29N 35 53E
Husum Germany **71** A2 54 29N 9 04E
Hutchinson Kansas U.S.A. **91** G4 38 03N 97 56W
Hutjena Papua New Guinea **45** Q4 5 25S 154 38E
Huu Lung Vietnam **37** C4 21 00N 106 00E
Huy Belgium **70** E2 50 32N 5 14E
Huzhou China **49** O5 30 56N 120 04E
Hvar i. Croatia **74** C3 43 00N 17 00E
Hwange Zimbabwe **111** E4 18 22S 26 29E
Hwange National Park Zimbabwe **111** E4 19 00S 26 00E
Hyderabad India **53** D3 17 22N 78 26E
Hyderabad Pakistan **52** B5 25 23N 68 24E
Hyesan North Korea **50** D5 41 25N 128 12E
Hykenhpa Myanmar **38** B5 27 48N 97 30E
Hyōgo pref. Japan **46** F2/G1 35 00N 135 00E
Hythe Alberta Canada **88** L4 55 18N 119 33W
Hyvinkää Finland **69** E3 60 37N 24 50E

I

Ialomiţa r. Romania **75** E1 44 00N 27 00E
Iamara Papua New Guinea **45** K2 8 27S 142 58E
Iaşi Romania **75** E2 47 09N 27 38E
Iba The Philippines **40** A4 15 20N 119 59E
Ibadan Nigeria **112** F4 7 23N 3 56E
Ibagawa Japan **46** H2 35 32N 136 31E
Ibagué Colombia **102** B13 4 25N 75 20W
Ibaraki Ibaraki Japan **46** M3 36 17N 140 25E
Ibaraki Osaka Japan **46** G1 34 50N 135 34E
Ibaraki pref. Japan **46** M3 36 10N 140 00E
Ibarra Ecuador **102** B13 0 23N 78 05W
Ibb Yemen Republic **54** F1 14 03N 44 10E
Ibbenbüren Germany **71** A2 52 17N 7 44E
Iberian Peninsula Europe **104** 40 00N 5 00W
Iberville Québec Canada **93** F3 45 18N 73 15W
Ibi Nigeria **112** G4 8 11N 9 44E
Ibi-gawa r. Japan **46** H2 35 34N 136 30E
Ibiza Balearic Islands **72** D4 38 54N 1 26E
Ibiza i. Balearic Islands **72** D4 39 00N 1 20E
Ibotirama Brazil **102** I10 12 13S 43 12W
Ibrī Oman **55** I3 23 15N 56 35E
Ica Peru **102** B10 14 02S 75 48W
Icacos Trinidad and Tobago **96** S9 10 04N 61 55W
Icacos Point Trinidad and Tobago **96** S9 10 41N 61 42W
ICELAND 69 I6
Ichalkaranji India **53** C3 16 40N 74 33E
Ichāpur India **52** K3 22 48N 88 22E
Ichihara Japan **46** M2 35 32N 140 04E
Ichikawa Japan **47** C3 35 45N 139 55E
Ichinomiya Aichi Japan **46** H2 35 18N 136 48E
Ichinomiya Ōsaka Japan **46** F1 34 25N 134 47E
Idaho state U.S.A. **90** D5 44 00N 115 00W
Idaho Falls tn. Idaho U.S.A. **90** D5 43 30N 112 01W
Idar-Oberstein Germany **71** A1 49 43N 7 19E
Iddo Nigeria **109** V3 6 25N 3 27E
Idfu Egypt **110** F12 24 58N 32 50E
Idi Indonesia **42** A5 4 57N 97 44E
Idre Sweden **69** C3 61 52N 12 45E
Ieper (Ypres) Belgium **70** B2 50 51N 2 53E
Igan Malaysia **42** D4 2 50N 111 42E
Igarka Russia **57** K9 67 31N 86 33E
Igbobi Nigeria **109** V3 6 32N 3 27E
Iglesias Italy **74** A2 39 19N 8 32E
Ignace Ontario Canada **92** B3 49 26N 91 40W
Iguaçu r. Brazil **103** P3 22 44S 43 16W
Iguala Mexico **96** E3 18 21N 99 31W
Iguape Brazil **103** H8 24 37S 47 30W
Iguatu Brazil **102** J11 6 22S 39 20W
Ihosy Madagascar **111** I3 22 23S 46 09E
Ihu Papua New Guinea **45** L3 7 52S 145 22E
Iida Japan **46** C2 35 32N 137 48E
Iisalmi Finland **69** F3 63 34N 27 08E
IJmuiden Netherlands **70** D4 52 27N 4 37E
IJssel r. Netherlands **70** F4 52 40N 6 10E
IJsselmeer l. Netherlands **70** E4 52 50N 5 15E
Ijuw Nauru **83** M2 0 30S 166 57E
Ijzer (Yser) r. Belgium **70** B3 51 03N 2 50E
Ikaría i. Greece **74** E2 37 00N 26 00E
Ikeja Nigeria **109** V3 6 37N 3 25E
Ikela Zaïre **110** D7 1 06S 23 06E
Iki i. Japan **46** A1 33 50N 129 40E
Ikoyi Nigeria **109** W3 6 23N 3 32E
Ikuno Japan **46** F2 35 12N 134 46E
Ikuta Japan **47** B3 35 36N 139 34E
Ilagan The Philippines **40** B4 17 07N 121 53E
Ilagan r. The Philippines **40** B4 17 00N 122 00E
I-lan Taiwan **51** H7 24 45N 121 44E
Île Amsterdam i. Indian Ocean **24** G3 37 56S 77 40E
Île Art i. New Caledonia **82** S4 19 45S 163 39E
Île Baaba i. New Caledonia **82** S3 20 05S 163 55E
Île Balabio i. New Caledonia **82** T3 20 05S 164 15E
Île Beautemps Beaupré i. New Caledonia **82** V3 20 25S 166 02E
Ilebo Zaïre **111** D7 4 20S 20 35E
Île d'Anticosti i. Québec Canada **89** W2 49 20N 62 30W
Île de Groix i. France **73** A2 47 38N 3 26W
Ile de Jerba i. Tunisia **112** H9 33 40N 11 00E
Île de l'Europa i. Mozambique Channel **111** H3 22 20S 40 20E
Île de Noirmoutier i. France **73** A2 47 00N 2 15W
Île de Ré i. France **73** A2 46 10N 1 26W
Île des Pins (Kunyé) i. New Caledonia **82** W1 22 35S 167 30E
Île d'Oléron i. France **73** A2 45 55N 1 16W
Île d'Ouessant i. France **73** A2 48 28N 5 05W
Île Ducos i. New Caledonia **82** V1 22 00S 166 01E
Île Dudun i. New Caledonia **82** W2 21 21S 167 44E
Île d'Yeu i. France **73** A2 46 43N 2 20W
Île Grimault i. New Caledonia **82** T2 21 22S 165 00E
Île Hugon i. New Caledonia **82** V1 22 03S 166 01E
Île Huo i. New Caledonia **82** W2 21 15S 167 36E
Île Huon i. New Caledonia **82** U5 18 00S 162 58E
Ilek r. Kazakhstan/Russia **59** H5 51 00N 57 00E
Île Leliogat i. New Caledonia **82** W2 21 08S 167 32E
Île Neba i. New Caledonia **82** S3 20 10S 163 55E
Île Nie i. New Caledonia **82** W2 21 19S 167 35E
Île Ouen i. New Caledonia **82** V1 22 25S 166 49E
Île Pam i. New Caledonia **82** T3 20 15S 164 18E
Île Pentecôte see Pentecost Island
Île Pott i. New Caledonia **82** S4 19 35S 163 35E
Île St. Paul i. Indian Ocean **24** G3 38 44S 77 30E
Îles Belep is. New Caledonia **82** S4 19 45S 163 35E
Îles Chesterfield is. Pacific Ocean **78** J6 19 00S 153 30E
Îles Crozet is. Indian Ocean **24** E2 46 27S 52 00E
Îles Daos is. New Caledonia **82** S4 19 50S 163 40E
Îles de Hoorn is. Pacific Ocean **80** D3 12 00S 179 00W
Îles de la Madeleine is. Québec Canada **89** W2 48 00N 63 00W
Îles d'Hyères is. France **73** C1 43 10N 6 25E
Ilesha Nigeria **112** F4 7 39N 4 38E
Îles Kerguelen is. Indian Ocean **24** F2 49 30S 69 30E
Îles Kerkenah is. Tunisia **74** B1 34 50N 11 30E
Îles Loyauté (Loyalty Islands) is. New Caledonia **82** V3/X2 21 00S 167 00E
Îles Wallis is. Pacific Ocean **80** D3 13 16S 176 15W
Île Tiga i. New Caledonia **82** W2 21 08S 167 50E
Île Toupéti i. New Caledonia **82** V2 21 20S 166 26E
Île Walpole i. New Caledonia **82** X1 22 35S 168 55E
Île Yandé i. New Caledonia **82** S3 20 05S 163 49E
Ilford England United Kingdom **66** D3 51 33N 0 06E
Ilha Bazaruto i. Mozambique **111** G3 21 40S 35 30E
Ilha de Marajó i. Brazil **102** G12 1 30S 50 00W
Ilha de Paquetá i. Brazil **103** Q2 22 46S 43 07W
Ilha do Fundão i. Brazil **103** Q2 22 52S 43 13W
Ilha do Governador i. Brazil **103** Q2 22 47S 43 13W
Ilha do Pai i. Brazil **103** Q2 22 59S 43 05W
Ilha Fernando de Noronha i. Brazil **102** K12 3 50S 32 25W
Ilhéus Brazil **102** J10 14 50S 39 06W
Ili r. Asia **59** M3 44 00N 78 00E
Iliamna Lake Alaska U.S.A. **88** D4 59 30N 155 30W
Iligan The Philippines **40** B2 8 12N 124 13W
Iligan Bay The Philippines **40** B2 8 00N 124 00E
Ilikurangi North Island New Zealand **79** C3 37 30S 177 40E
Illana Bay The Philippines **40** B2 7 00N 123 00E
Illapel Chile **103** C6 31 40S 71 13W
Iller r. Germany **71** B1 47 00N 10 00E
Illinois r. Illinois U.S.A. **92** B2 40 00N 90 00W
Illinois state U.S.A. **92** B2/C2 40 00N 89 00W
Illizi Algeria **112** G8 26 45N 8 30E
Il'men l. Russia **56** F7 58 00N 31 30E
Ilmenau Germany **71** B2 50 41N 10 55E
Ilmenau r. Germany **71** B2 53 00N 10 00E
Iloilo The Philippines **40** B3 10 41N 122 33E
Ilorin Nigeria **112** F4 8 32N 4 34E
Ilupeju Nigeria **109** V3 6 35N 3 25E
Ilwaki Indonesia **43** G2 7 40S 126 20E
Imabari Japan **46** B1 34 04N 132 59E
Imari Japan **50** D1 33 18N 129 51E
Imatra Finland **69** F3 61 14N 28 50E
Imazu Japan **46** H2 35 25N 136 01E
Īmī Ethiopia **110** H9 6 28N 42 10E
Imjin r. North Korea/South Korea **50** C3/4 38 00N 127 00E
Imperatriz Brazil **102** H11 5 32S 47 28W
Imperia Italy **74** A3 43 53N 8 03E
Impfondo Congo **112** I3 1 36N 18 00E
Imphal India **53** G4 24 47N 93 55E
Imsil South Korea **50** C2 35 37N 127 14E
Imuran Bay The Philippines **40** A3 10 00N 119 00E
Inakona Solomon Islands **82** F4 9 54S 160 28E
Inanwatan Irian Jaya Indonesia **44** E5 2 06S 132 08E
Inarijärvi l. Finland **69** F4 69 15N 27 30E
Inca Balearic Islands **72** E4 39 43N 2 54E
Ince Burun c. Turkey **58** C3 42 05N 34 55E
Inch'ŏn South Korea **50** C3 37 30N 126 38E
Indalsälven r. Sweden **69** D3 63 00N 16 30E
Indawgyi Lake Myanmar **38** B5 25 00N 96 20E
Independence Kansas U.S.A. **92** A1 37 13N 95 43W
Independence Missouri U.S.A. **92** B1 39 04N 94 27W
Independence Fjord Greenland **20** 82 00N 30 00W
Inderagiri r. Indonesia **42** B3 0 30S 103 00E
INDIA 52 B4/F4
Indiana Pennsylvania U.S.A. **93** E2 40 39N 79 11W
Indiana state U.S.A. **92** C1/2 40 00N 86 00W
Indian-Antarctic Ridge Southern Ocean **22** C2 51 00S 124 00E
Indianapolis Indiana U.S.A. **92** C1 39 45N 86 10W
Indian Ocean 24
Indigirka r. Russia **57** Q9 70 00N 147 30E
Indispensable Strait Solomon Islands **82** F5 9 00S 160 20E
INDONESIA 42-43
Indore India **53** D4 22 42N 75 54E
Indramayu Indonesia **42** O7 6 22S 108 20E
Indravati r. India **53** E3 19 00N 81 30E
Indre r. France **73** B2 46 50N 1 25E
Indus r. Pakistan **52** B5/C6 26 00N 68 00E
Indus, Mouths of the est. Pakistan **52** B4 24 00N 67 00E
Inebolu Turkey **58** C3 41 57N 33 45E
Ingersoll Ontario Canada **93** D2 43 03N 80 53W
Ingham Australia **78** H6 18 35S 146 12E
Inglewood California U.S.A. **95** A2 33 58N 118 22W
Ingolstadt Germany **71** B1 48 46N 11 27E
Inhambane Mozambique **111** G3 23 51S 35 29E
Inle Lake Myanmar **38** B4 20 40N 96 55E
Inn r. Europe **71** B1 48 00N 12 00E
Inner Hebrides is. Scotland United Kingdom **68** E8 56 45N 6 45W
Inner Mongolia Autonomous Region see Nei Mongol Zizhiqu
Innherad geog. reg. Norway **69** C3 63 50N 12 00E
Innisfail Australia **78** H6 17 30S 146 00E
Innisfail Alberta Canada **88** M3 52 01N 113 59W
Innsbruck Austria **75** B2 47 17N 11 25E
Inongo Zaïre **110** C7 1 55S 18 20E
Inowrocław Poland **75** C3 52 49N 18 12E
In Salah Algeria **112** F8 27 20N 2 03E
Insein Myanmar **38** B3 16 54N 96 08E
Inta Russia **57** I9 66 04N 60 01E
Interlaken Switzerland **73** C2 46 42N 7 52E
Interview Island Andaman Islands **38** A2 12 55N 92 45E
Inubō-zaki c. Japan **46** D2 35 41N 140 52E
Inukjuak Québec Canada **89** T4 58 40N 78 15W
Inuvik Northwest Territories Canada **88** I6 68 16N 133 40W
Inuyama Japan **46** H2 35 22N 136 56E
Invercargill South Island New Zealand **79** A1 46 25S 168 22E
Inverness Nova Scotia Canada **89** W2 46 14N 61 19W
Inverness Scotland United Kingdom **68** G9 57 28N 4 15W
Ioánnina Greece **74** D2 39 40N 20 51E
Ioma Papua New Guinea **45** M2 8 20S 147 51E
Iona i. Scotland United Kingdom **68** E8 56 19N 6 25W
Ionian Islands see Iónioi Nísoi
Ionian Sea Mediterranean Sea **74** C2 38 00N 27 00E
Iónioi Nísoi (Ionian Islands) is. Greece **74** C2/D2 39 00N 20 00E
Íos i. Greece **74** E2 36 00N 25 00E
Iowa r. U.S.A. **92** B2 42 00N 92 00W
Iowa state U.S.A. **92** B2 42 00N 94 00W
Iowa City Iowa U.S.A. **92** B2 41 39N 91 31W
Ipanema Brazil **103** Q2 22 59S 43 13W
Ipanema Beach Brazil **103** Q2 23 00S 43 14W
Ipatinga Brazil **102** I9 19 32S 42 30W
Ipiales Colombia **102** B13 0 52N 77 38W
Ipoh Malaysia **42** B4 4 36N 101 05E
Ipswich England United Kingdom **68** M4 52 04N 1 10E
Ipu Brazil **102** I12 4 32S 40 44W
Iqaluit (Frobisher Bay) Northwest Territories Canada **89** V5 63 45N 68 30W
Iquique Chile **102** C8 20 15S 70 08W
Iquitos Peru **102** C12 3 51S 73 13W
Irago-suidō sd. Japan **46** H1 34 27N 137 00E
Irajá Brazil **103** P2 22 50S 43 19W
Iraklion Greece **74** E2 35 20N 25 08E
IRAN 55 H5
Irānshahr Iran **55** J4 27 15N 60 41E
Irapuato Mexico **96** D4 20 40N 101 30W
IRAQ 54 F5
Irbid Jordan **54** O11 32 33N 35 51E
Irecê Brazil **102** I10 11 22S 41 51W
Iri South Korea **50** C2 35 55N 126 57E
Irian Jaya admin. Indonesia **44** E5-H3 3 00S 133 00E
Iriga The Philippines **40** B3 13 26N 123 24E
Iringa Tanzania **111** G6 7 49S 35 39E
Iriri r. Brazil **102** G12 5 00S 54 50W
IRISH REPUBLIC 68 C5
Irish Sea British Isles **68** F5 53 30N 5 30W
Irkutsk Russia **57** M6 52 18N 104 15E
Irois Bay Trinidad and Tobago **96** S9 10 09N 61 45W
Iron Bottom Sound Solomon Islands **82** E4 9 10S 159 50E
Iron Gate see Portile de Fier
Iron Knob tn. Australia **78** F3 32 44S 137 08E
Iron Mountain tn. Michigan U.S.A. **92** C3 45 51N 88 03W
Ironwood Michigan U.S.A. **92** B3 46 25N 90 08W
Iroquois Falls tn. Ontario Canada **93** D3 48 47N 80 41W
Irosin The Philippines **40** B3 12 41N 124 01E
Irrawaddy admin. Myanmar **38** A3/B3 16 55N 95 00E
Irrawaddy r. Myanmar **38** B3 19 40N 95 10E
Irrawaddy, Mouths of the est. Myanmar **38** A3/B3 15 40N 94 30E
Irún Spain **72** B3 43 20N 1 48W
Irvine Hill Christmas Island **81** R2 10 26S 105 41E
Irving Texas U.S.A. **91** G3 32 49N 96 57W
Irvington New Jersey U.S.A. **94** A1 40 44N 74 15W
Isabela The Philippines **40** B2 6 44N 121 58E
Ísafjördur Iceland **69** H7 66 05N 23 08W
Isangel Vanuatu **83** J2 19 32S 169 16E
Isar r. Germany **71** B1 47 00N 11 00E
Ise Japan **46** H1 34 29N 136 41E
Isère r. France **73** C2 45 17N 5 47E
Iserlohn Germany **71** A2 51 23N 7 42E
Ise shima National Park Japan **46** H1 34 25N 136 50E
Iset' r. Russia **59** K6 56 30N 65 00E
Ise-wan b. Japan **46** H1 34 50N 136 40E
Iseyin Nigeria **112** F4 7 59N 3 40E
Ishikan r. Japan **46** D3 43 20N 141 45E
Ishikari-wan b. Japan **46** D3 43 30N 141 00E
Ishim Russia **59** K6 56 21N 69 30E
Ishim r. Russia **57** I7 54 00N 68 00E
Ishimskaya Step geog. reg. Kazakhstan/Russia **59** L5 54 00N 71 00E
Ishinomaki Japan **46** D2 38 25N 141 18E
Ishioka Japan **46** M3 36 11N 140 16E
Isiro Zaïre **110** E8 2 50N 27 40E
Iskenderun Turkey **54** E6 36 37N 36 08E
Iskŭr r. Bulgaria **74** D3 43 30N 24 00E
Isla Asinara i. Italy **74** A3 41 00N 8 00E
Isla de Chiloé i. Chile **103** C4 42 30S 74 00W
Isla de Coiba i. Panama **97** H1 7 40N 82 00W
Isla de Cozumel i. Mexico **97** G4 20 30N 87 00W
Isla de la Juventud i. Cuba **97** H4 22 00N 82 30W
Isla d'Elba i. Italy **74** B3 42 00N 10 00E
Isla del Coco (Cocos Islands) i. Costa Rica **23** R8 5 33N 87 00W
Isla de los Estados i. Argentina **103** E2 55 00S 64 00W
Isla de Patos i. Venezuela **96** S10 10 38N 61 51W
Isla Dragonera i. Balearic Islands **72** E4 39 35N 2 19E
Isla Grande de Tierra del Fuego i. Chile/Argentina **103** D2 54 00S 67 30W
Islamabad Pakistan **53** C6 33 40N 73 08E
Isla Margarita i. Venezuela **97** L2 11 30N 64 00W
Island Beach New Jersey U.S.A. **93** F1 40 00N 74 00W
Island Lake Manitoba Canada **89** Q3 53 50N 94 00W
Island Park tn. New York U.S.A. **94** D1 40 36N 73 39W
Islands, Bay of North Island New Zealand **79** B3 35 13S 174 12E
Isla San Ambrosio i. Chile **103** B7 26 28S 79 53W
Isla San Felix i. Chile **103** A7 26 23S 80 05W
Islas de la Bahia is. Honduras **97** G3 16 40N 86 00W
Islas Galapagos is. Pacific Ocean **23** Q7 0 05S 90 00W
Islas Juan Fernández is. Chile **103** B6 33 30S 78 00W
Islas Marias is. Mexico **96** C4 22 00N 107 00W
Islas Revillagigedo is. Pacific Ocean **96** B3 19 00N 112 30W
Islay i. Scotland United Kingdom **68** E7 55 48N 6 12W
Isle r. France **73** B2 45 02N 0 02E
Isle of Man British Isles **68** G6 54 15N 4 30W
Isle of Wight co. England United Kingdom **68** J2 50 40N 1 20W
Isle Royale i. Michigan U.S.A. **92** C3 48 00N 89 00W
Isle Royale National Park Michigan U.S.A. **92** C3 48 00N 89 00W
Islington bor. England United Kingdom **66** C3 51 33N 0 06W
Ismâ'ilîya Egypt **109** S3 30 36N 32 16E
Isna Egypt **54** D4 25 16N 32 30E
Isogo Japan **47** B2 35 23N 139 37E
Isoka Zambia **111** F5 10 09S 32 39E
Isola Lipari is. Italy **74** B2 38 00N 14 00E
Isolo Nigeria **109** V3 6 32N 3 23E
ISRAEL 54 O10
Issoire France **73** B2 45 33N 3 15E
Issyk-Kul' (Rybach'ye) Kirgyzstan **59** M3 42 28N 76 09E
Istanbul Turkey **54** C7 41 02N 28 57E
Isthme de Taravao ist. Tahiti **82** T9 17 43S 149 19W
Istmo de Tehuantepec ist. Mexico **96** F3 17 20N 93 10W
Istres France **73** B1 43 30N 4 59E
Itabaiana Brazil **102** J10 10 42S 37 37W
Itabashi Japan **47** B4 35 46N 139 39E
Itabuna Brazil **102** J10 14 48S 39 18W
Itacoatiara Brazil **102** F12 3 06S 58 22W
Itagüi Colombia **102** B14 6 13N 75 40W
Itaituba Brazil **102** F12 4 15S 55 56W
Itajaí Brazil **103** H7 26 50S 48 39W
Itako Japan **46** M2 35 57N 140 31E
ITALY 74 A4/C2
Itanagar India **38** A5 27 02N 93 38E
Itapipoca Brazil **102** J12 3 29S 39 35W
Itaqui Brazil **103** F7 29 10S 56 30W
Itarsi India **53** D4 22 39N 77 48E
Itbayat The Philippines **40** B5 20 47N 121 52E
Ithaca New York U.S.A. **93** E2 42 26N 76 30W
Itō Japan **46** L1 34 58N 139 04E
Ittoqqortoormiit (Scoresbysund) sd. Greenland **20** 70 30N 22 45W
Itui r. Brazil **102** C11 5 30S 71 00W
Itzehoe Germany **71** A2 53 56N 9 32E
Iva Western Samoa **82** A11 13 41S 172 09W
Ivano-Frankovsk Ukraine **58** A4 48 40N 24 40E
Ivanovo Russia **56** G7 57 00N 41 00E
Ivdel' Russia **56** I8 60 45N 60 30E
IVORY COAST see CÔTE D'IVOIRE
Ivry-sur-Seine France **67** B2 48 48N 2 24E
Ivujivik Québec Canada **89** T5 62 25N 77 54W
Iwai Japan **46** L3 36 02N 139 53E
Iwaki Japan **46** D2 37 03N 140 58E
Iwakuni Japan **46** B1 34 10N 132 09E
Iwamizawa Japan **46** D3 43 12N 141 47E
Iwanai Japan **46** D3 43 01N 140 32E
Iwo Nigeria **112** F4 7 38N 4 11E
Ixtaccihuati mt. Mexico **96** E3 19 11N 98 38W
Ixtepec Mexico **96** E3 16 32N 95 10W
Iyo-nada b. Japan **46** B1 33 50N 132 00E
Izegem Belgium **70** C2 50 55N 3 13E
Izhevsk (Ustinov) Russia **56** H7 56 49N 53 11E
Izhma r. Russia **56** H8 64 00N 54 00E
Izmail Ukraine **75** E2 45 20N 28 48E
Izmir Turkey **54** C6 38 25N 27 10E
Izmit Turkey **54** C7 40 47N 29 55E
Izra' Syria **54** P11 32 52N 36 15E
Izuhara Japan **50** D2 34 12N 129 18E
Izumi Japan **46** G1 34 29N 135 25E
Izu-shotō is. Japan **46** C1 34 20N 139 20E

J

Jabal Akhdar mt. Oman **55** I3 24 00N 56 30E
Jabal al Akhdar mts. Libya **110** D14 33 00N 22 00E
Jābal as Sawdā' mts. Libya **110** B13/C13 29 00N 15 00E
Jabalpur India **53** D4 23 10N 79 59E
Jablonec Czech Republic **75** C3 50 44N 15 10E
Jaboatão Brazil **102** J11 8 05S 35 00W
Jaca Spain **72** B3 42 34N 0 33W
Jacarepagua Brazil **103** P2 22 57S 43 21W
Jackman Maine U.S.A. **93** F3 45 37N 70 16W
Jackson Barbados **96** V12 13 09N 59 40W
Jackson Michigan U.S.A. **93** D2 42 15N 84 24W
Jackson Mississippi U.S.A. **91** H3 32 20N 90 11W
Jackson Ohio U.S.A. **93** D1 39 03N 82 40W
Jackson Tennessee U.S.A. **91** I4 35 37N 88 50W
Jackson Wyoming U.S.A. **90** D5 43 28N 110 45W
Jackson Head South Island New Zealand **79** A2 43 58S 168 37E
Jackson Heights tn. New York U.S.A. **94** B2 40 45N 73 52W
Jacksonville Florida U.S.A. **91** J3 30 20N 81 40W
Jacksonville Illinois U.S.A. **92** B1 39 44N 90 14W
Jacksonville North Carolina U.S.A. **91** K3 34 45N 77 26W
Jacksonville Beach tn. Florida U.S.A. **91** J3 30 18N 81 24W
Jacmel Haiti **97** J3 18 18N 72 32W
Jacobabad Pakistan **52** B5 28 16N 68 30E
Jacobina Brazil **102** I10 11 13S 40 30W
Jacobs Rock Norfolk Island **81** J5 29 01S 167 55W
Jacques-Cartier Passage sd. Québec Canada **89** W3 50 00N 64 00W
Jaén Spain **72** B2 37 46N 3 48W
Jagdalpur India **53** E3 19 04N 82 05E
Jagst r. Germany **71** A1 49 00N 9 00E
Jahrom Iran **55** H4 28 29N 53 32E
Jaipur India **53** D5 26 53N 75 50E
Jaisalmer India **55** L4 26 52N 70 55E
Jakarta Indonesia **42** N7 6 08S 106 45E
Jakobshavn Greenland **89** Y6 69 10N 51 05W
Jakobstad Finland **69** E3 63 40N 22 42E
Jalālābād Afghanistan **55** L5 34 26N 70 25E
Jalan Kayu Singapore **41** D4 1 24N 103 54E
Jalapa Enriquez Mexico **96** E3 19 32N 96 56W
Jalgaon India **53** D4 21 01N 75 39E
Jalna India **53** D3 19 50N 75 58E

128

Kasaragod India **53** C2 12 30N 74 59E
Kasavu Fiji **83** C9 17 58S 178 31E
Kasempa Zambia **111** E5 13 28S 25 48E
Kasese Uganda **110** F8 0 10N 30 06E
Kaset Wisai Thailand **39** B3 15 40N 103 38E
Kāshān Iran **55** H5 33 59N 51 35E
Kashi China **48** E6 39 29N 76 02E
Kashihara Japan **46** G1 34 28N 135 46E
Kashima Japan **46** M2 35 58N 140 39E
Kashiwa Japan **46** L2 35 51N 139 58E
Kashiwazaki Japan **46** C2 37 22N 138 33E
Kashmir *see* Jammu & Kashmir
Kaskö Finland **69** E3 62 23N 21 10E
Kas Kong Cambodia **37** B2 11 29N 103 10E
Kasli Russia **59** J6 55 54N 60 45E
Kásos Greece **74** E2 35 00N 28 00E
Kassala Sudan **110** G11 15 24N 36 30E
Kassel Germany **71** A2 51 18N 9 30E
Kasserine Tunisia **74** A2 35 13N 8 43E
Kastamonu Turkey **58** C3 41 22N 33 47E
Kastoria Greece **74** D3 40 33N 21 15E
Kasugai Japan **46** H2 35 15N 136 57E
Kasukabe Japan **46** L3 35 59N 139 45E
Kasumiga-ura *l.* Japan **46** M3 36 03N 140 20E
Kasur Pakistan **53** C6 31 07N 74 30E
Kataba Zambia **111** E4 16 02S 25 03E
Katafaga *i.* Fiji **83** F9 17 31S 178 42W
Katase Japan **47** A2 35 18N 139 30E
Katchall *i.* Nicobar Islands **36** A3 7 30N 93 30E
Kateríni Greece **74** D3 40 15N 22 30E
Katha Myanmar **38** B4 24 11N 96 20E
Katherine Australia **78** E7 14 29S 132 20E
Kathiawar *p.* India **52** C4 21 10N 71 00E
Kat Hing Wai Hong Kong U.K. **51** B2 22 26N 114 03E
Kathmandu Nepal **53** F5 27 42N 85 19E
Katihar India **53** F5 25 33N 87 34E
Katong Singapore **41** D3 1 19N 103 55E
Katowice Poland **75** C3 50 15N 18 59E
Katrineholm Sweden **69** D2 58 59N 16 15E
Katsina Ala Nigeria **112** G4 7 10N 9 30E
Katsuura Japan **46** M2 35 10N 140 20E
Kattakurgan Uzbekistan **59** K2 39 54N 66 13E
Kattegat *sd.* Denmark/Sweden **69** C2 57 00N 11 00E
Katun' *r.* Russia **59** O5 51 30N 86 00E
Katwijk aan Zee Netherlands **70** D4 52 12N 4 24E
Kau Indonesia **43** G4 1 15N 127 50E
Kauai *i.* Hawaiian Islands **23** X18-19 22 00N 159 30W
Kauai Channel *sd.* Hawaiian Islands **23** X18 21 45N 158 50W
Kaufbeuren Germany **71** B1 47 53N 10 37E
Kaukkwe Hills Myanmar **38** B4 24 45N 97 20E
Kaula *i.* Hawaiian Islands **23** W18 21 35N 160 40W
Kaulakahi Channel *sd.* Hawaiian Islands **23** X18 21 58N 159 50W
Kaulsdorf Germany **67** G1 52 29N 13 34E
Kaunas Lithuania **69** E1 54 52N 23 55E
Kaura Namoda Nigeria **112** G5 12 39N 6 38E
Kau Sai Chau *i.* Hong Kong U.K. **51** C2 22 22N 114 19E
Kau-ye Kyun *i.* Myanmar **38** B2 11 00N 98 30E
Kau Yi Chau Hong Kong U.K. **51** B1 22 17N 114 04E
Kavajë Albania **74** C3 41 11N 19 33E
Kavála Greece **74** D3 40 56N 24 25E
Kavaratti Island India **53** C2 10 32N 72 43E
Kavieng Papua New Guinea **45** O5 2 34S 150 48E
Kawa Myanmar **38** B3 17 04N 96 30E
Kawachi-Nagano Japan **46** G1 34 24N 135 32E
Kawagoe Japan **46** L2 35 55N 139 30E
Kawaguchi Japan **46** L2 35 47N 139 44E
Kawaihae Hawaiian Islands **23** Z18 20 02N 155 05W
Kawang Myanmar **38** B5 27 45N 97 42E
Kawasaki Japan **47** C3 35 30N 139 45E
Kawawa Japan **47** B3 35 31N 139 33E
Kawawachikamach *see* Schefferville
Kawerau North Island New Zealand **79** C3 38 05S 176 42E
Kawkareik Myanmar **38** B3 16 33N 98 18E
Kawlin Myanmar **38** B4 23 48N 95 41E
Kawthaung Myanmar **38** B1 10 01N 98 32E
Kaya Burkina **112** E5 13 04N 1 09W
Kayah State *admin.* Myanmar **38** B3 19 15N 97 30E
Kayan Myanmar **38** B3 16 54N 96 35E
Kayan *r.* Indonesia **42** E4 2 50N 116 20E
Kayeli Indonesia **44** B5 3 25S 127 07E
Kayes Mali **112** C5 14 26N 11 28W
Kayseri Turkey **54** E6 38 42N 35 28E
Kayuagung Indonesia **42** B3 3 18S 104 53E
Kazach'ye Russia **57** P10 70 46N 136 15E
KAZAKHSTAN **59** H4/O4
Kazakh Upland Kazakhstan **59** L5 47 00N 75 00E
Kazan' Russia **56** G7 55 45N 49 10E
Kazanlŭk Bulgaria **74** E3 42 37N 25 23E
Kazbek *mt.* Georgia **58** E3 42 42N 44 30E
Kāzerūn Iran **55** H4 29 35N 51 40E
Kazym *r.* Russia **57** I8 63 00N 67 30E
Kéa *i.* Greece **74** D2 37 00N 24 00E
Kearney Nebraska U.S.A. **90** G5 40 42N 99 04W
Kearny New Jersey U.S.A. **94** B2 40 45N 74 07W
Kebumen Indonesia **42** O7 7 40S 109 41E
Kecskemét Hungary **75** C2 46 56N 19 43E
Kediri Indonesia **42** Q7 7 45S 112 01E
Keele *r.* Northwest Territories Canada **88** J5 64 15N 126 00W
Keene New Hampshire U.S.A. **93** F2 42 55N 72 17W
Keetmanshoop Namibia **111** C2 26 36S 18 08E
Keewatin Ontario Canada **92** B3 49 47N 94 30W
Kefallinia *i.* Greece **74** D2 38 00N 20 00E
Kefamenanu Indonesia **43** F2 9 31S 124 29E
Keflavik Iceland **69** H6 64 01N 22 35W
Kehl Germany **71** A1 48 35N 7 50E
Keihoku Japan **46** G2 35 09N 135 37E
Kei Ling Ha Lo Wai Hong Kong U.K. **51** C2 22 25N 114 16E
Kei Lun Wai Hong Kong U.K. **51** A2 22 24N 113 58E
Keitele *l.* Finland **69** F3 63 10N 26 24E
Keiyasi Fiji **83** B9 17 55S 177 45E
Keketa Papua New Guinea **45** K3 6 48S 143 38E
K'elafo Ethiopia **110** H9 5 37N 44 10E
Kelefesia *i.* Tonga **83** B2 20 30S 174 45W
Kelkit *r.* Turkey **54** E7 40 20N 37 40E
Kells Irish Republic **68** E5 53 44N 6 53W
Kelowna British Columbia Canada **88** L2 49 50N 119 29W
Kelsey Bay *tn.* British Columbia Canada **88** J3 50 22N 125 29W
Kemerovo Russia **57** K7 55 25N 86 05E
Kemi Finland **69** E4 65 46N 24 34E
Kemijärvi *l.* Finland **69** F4 66 42N 27 30E
Kemijöki *r.* Finland **69** F4 66 00N 25 00
Kempenland *(Campines) admin.* Belgium **70** E3 51 08N 5 22E
Kemp Land *geog. reg.* Antarctica **21** 65 00S 60 00E
Kempten Germany **71** B1 47 44N 10 19E
Kemptville Ontario Canada **93** E3 45 01N 75 39W
Kemsing England United Kingdom **66** D2 51 18N 0 14E
Kenai Alaska U.S.A. **88** E5 60 35N 151 19W
Kendal England United Kingdom **68** I6 54 20N 2 45W
Kendari Indonesia **43** F3 3 57S 122 36E
Kendawangan Indonesia **42** D3 2 32S 110 13E
Kenema Sierra Leone **112** C4 7 57N 11 11W
Kengtung Myanmar **38** B4 21 15N 99 40E
Keningau Malaysia **42** E5 5 21N 116 11E
Kénitra Morocco **112** D9 34 20N 6 34W
Kennebunk Maine U.S.A. **93** F2 43 24N 70 33W
Kennedy Peak Myanmar **38** A4 23 35N 93 48E
Kennedy Town Hong Kong U.K. **51** B1 22 17N 114 07E
Kenora Ontario Canada **92** B3 49 47N 94 26W
Kenosha Wisconsin U.S.A. **92** C2 42 34N 87 50W
Kensington *bor.* England United Kingdom **66** C3 51 29N 0 10W
Kent England United Kingdom **66** D2 51 15N 0 09E
Kenthurst Australia **79** F3 33 40S 151 01E
Kenting National Park Taiwan **51** G5 22 00N 120 50E
Kenton Ohio U.S.A. **93** D2 40 38N 83 38W
Kent Peninsula Northwest Territories Canada **89** N6 68 30N 106 00W
Kentucky *r.* Kentucky U.S.A. **92** D1 38 00N 85 00W
Kentucky *state* U.S.A. **91** I4 37 00N 85 00W
Kentucky Lake Kentucky U.S.A. **92** C1 37 00N 88 00W
KENYA **110** G7/G8
Kenya, Mount *see* Kirinyaga
Keokuk Iowa U.S.A. **92** B2 40 23N 91 25W
Keo Nua Pass Laos/Vietnam **37** C3 18 00N 105 00E
Kepi Irian Jaya Indonesia **44** H3 6 34S 139 22E
Keppel Harbour Singapore **41** C3 1 16N 103 50E
Kepulauan Alor *is.* Indonesia **44** A2 8 15S 124 30E
Kepulauan Anambas *is.* Indonesia **42** C4 3 00N 106 20E
Kepulauan Aru *is.* Indonesia **43** H2 6 00S 134 30E
Kepulauan Asia *is.* Indonesia **43** H4 1 15N 131 15E
Kepulauan Ayu *is.* Indonesia **43** H4 0 45N 131 15E
Kepulauan Babar *is.* Indonesia **43** G2 7 50S 129 30E
Kepulauan Banda *is.* Indonesia **43** G3 4 45S 129 45E
Kepulauan Banggai *is.* Indonesia **43** F3 1 30S 123 00E
Kepulauan Banyak *is.* Indonesia **42** A4 2 00N 97 20E
Kepulauan Barat Daya *is.* Indonesia **43** G2 7 15S 127 00E
Kepulauan Batu *is.* Indonesia **42** A3 0 18S 98 29E
Kepulauan Gorong *i.* Indonesia **44** D4 4 00S 131 25E
Kepulauan Kai *is.* Indonesia **43** H2 5 30S 132 30E
Kepulauan Kangean *is.* Indonesia **42** R7 7 00S 115 30T
Kepulauan Karimata *is.* Indonesia **42** C3 1 25S 108 50E
Kepulauan Karimunjawa *is.* Indonesia **42** P8 5 50S 110 30E
Kepulauan Laut Kecil *is.* Indonesia **42** E3 4 50S 116 00E
Kepulauan Leti *is.* Indonesia **43** G2 8 15S 127 45E
Kepulauan Lingga *is.* Indonesia **42** B3 0 10S 104 30E
Kepulauan Lucipara *is.* Indonesia **44** B4 5 15S 127 45E
Kepulauan Maluku *(Moluccas)* Indonesia **43** G3 4 00S 127 00E
Kepulauan Mapia *is.* Indonesia **43** H4 1 10N 134 25E
Kepulauan Masalembu *is.* Indonesia **42** R8 5 30S 114 20E
Kepulauan Mentawai *is.* Indonesia **42** A3 2 00S 99 00E
Kepulauan Natuna Selatan *is.* Indonesia **42** C4 2 50N 109 00E
Kepulauan Obi *is.* Indonesia **44** B6 1 30S 127 30E
Kepulauan Riau *is.* Indonesia **42** B4 0 30N -4 30E
Kepulauan Sabalana *is.* Indonesia **42** E2 6 40S 119 00E
Kepulauan Sangir *is.* Indonesia **43** G4 3 00N 125 30E
Kepulauan Sermata *i.* Indonesia **43** G2 8 13S 128 55E
Kepulauan Sula *is.* Indonesia **43** G3 1 50S 124 50E
Kepulauan Talaud *is.* Indonesia **43** G4 4 00N 127 00E
Kepulauan Tambelan *is.* Indonesia **42** C4 1 00N 107 25E
Kepulauan Tanimbar *is.* Indonesia **43** H2 7 30S 131 30E
Kepulauan Tayandu *is.* Indonesia **43** H2 5 30S 132 00E
Kepulauan Tengah *is.* Indonesia **42** E2 7 20S 118 00E
Kepulauan Tongian *is.* Indonesia **43** F3 0 30S 122 00E
Kepulauan Tukangbesi *is.* Indonesia **43** F2 5 30S 123 30E
Kepulauan Watubela *is.* Indonesia **44** D4 4 45S 131 30E
Kerala *admin.* India **53** D2 10 10N 76 30E
Keravat Papua New Guinea **45** P4 4 20S 152 00E
Kerch' Ukraine **58** D4 45 22N 36 27E
Kerema Papua New Guinea **45** L3 7 59S 145 46E
Keren Eritrea **110** G11 15 46N 38 30E
Kerguelen Plateau Indian Ocean **24** G1/H1 55 00S 80 00E
Kerikeri North Island New Zealand **79** B3 35 14S 173 57E
Kerki Turkmenistan **59** K2 37 53N 65 10E
Kérkira Greece **74** C2 39 00N 19 00E
Kérkira *(Corfu) i.* Greece **74** C2 39 00N 19 00E
Kerkrade Netherlands **70** F2 50 52N 6 04E
Kermadec Islands Pacific Ocean **80** D2 30 00S 178 30W
Kermadec Trench Pacific Ocean **22** I4 33 00S 177 00W
Kermān Iran **55** I5 30 18N 57 05E
Kermānshāh Iran **55** G5 34 19N 47 04E
Kerme Körfezi *b.* Turkey **74** E2 37 00N 27 00E
Kerpen Germany **70** F2 50 52N 6 42E
Kerrville Texas U.S.A. **90** G3 30 03N 99 09W
Kerulen *r.* Mongolia **49** M8 47 30N 112 30E
Kesagami Lake Ontario Canada **93** D4 50 00N 80 00W
Keşan Turkey **74** E3 40 52N 26 37E
Ket' Russia **59** O6 58 30N 86 30E
Ket' *r.* Russia **57** K7 58 30N 86 30E
Ketam Channel Singapore **41** E4 1 24N 103 57E
Ketapang Indonesia **42** C3 1 50S 109 59E
Ketchikan Alaska U.S.A. **88** I4 55 25N 131 40W
Ketrzyn Poland **75** D3 54 05N 21 24E
Kettering Ohio U.S.A. **93** D1 39 42N 84 11W
Kewanee Illinois U.S.A. **92** C2 41 14N 89 56W
Kewaunee Wisconsin U.S.A. **92** C2 44 27N 87 31W
Keweenaw Bay Wisconsin U.S.A. **92** C3 47 00N 88 00W
Keweenaw Peninsula Michigan U.S.A. **92** C3 47 00N 88 00W
Key West Florida U.S.A. **91** J1 24 34N 81 48W
Khabarovsk Russia **57** P5 48 32N 135 08E
Khalîg el Tîna Egypt **109** T4 31 08N 32 36E
Khalkidhikí *p.* Greece **74** D3 40 30N 23 00E
Khalkís Greece **74** D2 38 28N 23 36E
Khambhat India **53** C4 22 19N 72 39E
Khambhat, Gulf of India **53** C4 20 30N 72 00E
Khammam India **53** E3 17 16N 80 13E
Khammouan *(Thakhek)* Laos **37** B3 17 22N 104 50E
Khānābad Afghanistan **55** K6 36 42N 69 08E
Khānaqīn Iraq **55** G5 34 22N 45 22E
Khandwa India **53** D4 21 49N 76 23E
Khanh Hung *see* Soc Trang
Khaniá Greece **74** D2 35 31N 24 01E
Khanty-Mansiysk Russia **57** I8 61 01N 69 00E
Khān Yūnis Israel **54** O10 31 21N 34 18E
Khao Laem Reservoir Thailand **39** A2/A3 14 50N 98 30E
Khao Luang *mt.* Thailand **39** A1 8 28N 99 40E
Khao Soi Dao Tai *mt.* Thailand **39** B2 12 53N 102 11E
Khao Yai National Park Thailand **39** B2 14 20N 101 30E
Kharagpur India **53** F4 22 23N 87 22E
Kharan Pakistan **52** B5 28 32N 65 26E
Khardah India **52** K2 22 43N 88 20E
Khārg Island Iran **55** H4 29 14N 50 20E
Khar'kov Ukraine **58** D4 50 00N 36 15E
Khartoum Sudan **110** F11 15 33N 32 35E
Khasan Russia **50** E6 42 28N 130 48E
Khāsh Iran **55** J4 28 14N 61 15E
Khash *r.* Afghanistan **55** J5 31 30N 62 30E
Khashm el Girba Sudan **54** E1 14 59N 35 59E
Khasi Hills India **38** A5 25 30N 92 20E
Khaskovo Bulgaria **74** E3 41 57N 25 32E
Khatanga Russia **57** M10 71 59N 102 31E
Khatanga *r.* Russia **57** M10 72 30N 102 30E
Khatib Bongsu River Singapore **41** D5 1 26N 103 51E
Khemisset Morocco **112** D9 33 50N 6 03W
Khemmarat Thailand **39** C3 16 03N 105 16E
Khe Sanh Vietnam **37** C3 16 37N 106 50E
Kheta *r.* Russia **57** L10 71 30N 95 00E
Khilok *r.* Russia **57** M6 51 00N 107 30E
Khimki Russia **56** L2 55 51N 37 28E
Khimki-Khovrino Russia **56** L2 55 51N 37 30E
Khimki Reservoir Russia **56** L2 55 49N 37 29E
Khíos Greece **74** E2 38 23N 26 07E
Khíos *i.* Greece **74** E2 38 00N 26 00E
Khiva Uzbekistan **59** J3 41 25N 60 49E
Khlong Thom Thailand **39** A1 7 52N 99 05E
Khmel'nitsky Ukraine **58** B4 49 25N 26 59E
Khodzheyli Uzbekistan **59** H3 42 25N 59 25E
Khok Samrong Thailand **39** B3 15 06N 100 45E
Kholayarvi Russia **69** F4 67 07N 28 50E
Kholmsk Russia **57** Q5 47 02N 142 03E
Không Laos **37** C2 14 08N 105 50E
Khôngxédôn Laos **37** C3 15 35N 105 57E
Khon Kaen Thailand **39** B3 16 25N 102 50E
Khoper Russia **58** E5 50 20N 42 00E
Khorat *see* Nakhon Ratchasima
Khorat Plateau Thailand **39** B3 16 00N 103 30E
Khorochevo Russia **56** L2 55 46N 37 30E
Khorog Tajikistan **59** L2 37 22N 71 32E
Khorramābad Iran **55** G5 33 29N 48 21E
Khorramshahr Iran **55** G5 30 25N 48 09E
Khouribga Morocco **112** D9 32 54N 6 57W
Khrebet Kopat Dag *canal* Turkmenistan **59** H2 39 50N 56 00E
Khrishnapur Canal India **52** K2 22 34N 88 23E
Khujand *(Leninabad)* Kirgyzstan **59** K3 40 20N 69 55E
Khu Khan Thailand **39** B2 14 37N 104 12E
Khulna Bangladesh **53** F4 22 49N 89 34E
Khwae Noi *r.* Thailand **39** A2 14 30N 99 00E
Khwae Yai *r.* Thailand **39** A2 14 20N 99 20E
Khyber Pass Afghanistan/Pakistan **55** L5 34 06N 71 05E
Kiantajärvi *l.* Finland **69** F4 65 02N 29 00E
Kibobo Islets Fiji **83** E9 17 01S 179 00W
Kibombo Zaïre **111** E7 3 58S 25 54E
Kiel Germany **71** B2 54 20N 10 08E
Kiel Bay Europe **71** B2 54 00N 10 00E
Kielce Poland **75** D3 50 51N 20 39E
Kieta Papua New Guinea **45** Q3 6 15S 155 37E
Kiev *see* Kiyev
Kigali Rwanda **110** F7 1 56S 30 04E
Kigoma Tanzania **111** E7 4 52S 29 36E
Kii-Nagashima Japan **46** H1 34 11N 136 19E
Kii-sanchi *mts.* Japan **46** G1 34 15N 135 50E
Kii-suidō *sd.* Japan **46** B1 34 00N 134 45E
Kikinda Serbia Yugoslavia **74** D4 45 50N 20 30E
Kikladhes *(Cyclades) is.* Greece **74** D2/E2 37 00N 25 00E
Kikori Papua New Guinea **45** L3 7 25S 144 13E
Kikori *r.* Papua New Guinea **45** K3 6 50S 143 55E
Kikwit Zaïre **111** C6 5 02S 18 51E
Kila Kila Papua New Guinea **45** M2 9 31S 147 10E
Kilanea Hawaiian Islands **23** W19 22 05N 159 35W
Kilchu North Korea **50** D5 40 55N 129 21E
Kilimanjaro *mt.* Tanzania **110** G7 3 04S 37 22E
Kilkenny Irish Republic **68** D4 52 39N 7 15W
Kilkis Greece **74** D3 40 59N 22 52E
Killarney Irish Republic **68** B4 52 03N 9 30W
Killarney Manitoba Canada **89** P2 49 12N 99 40W
Killeen Texas U.S.A. **91** G3 31 08N 97 44W
Kilmarnock Scotland United Kingdom **68** G7 55 36N 4 30W
Kiltan Island India **53** C2 11 30N 73 00E
Kilwa Masoko Tanzania **111** G6 8 55S 39 31E
Kilyos Turkey **74** E3 41 14N 29 02E
Kimbe Papua New Guinea **45** O4 5 36S 150 10E
Kimbe Bay Papua New Guinea **45** O4 5 15S 150 30E
Kimberley British Columbia Canada **88** L2 49 40N 115 58W
Kimberley Republic of South Africa **111** D2 28 45S 24 46E
Kimberley Plateau Australia **78** D6 17 30S 126 00E
Kimberling City Missouri U.S.A. **92** B1 36 40N 93 25W
Kimch'aek *see* Sŏngjin
Kimch'ŏn South Korea **50** D3 36 07N 128 08E
Kimitsu Japan **46** L2 35 19N 139 53E
Kinabatangan *r.* Malaysia **40** A2 5 20N 118 00E
Kinbasket Lake British Columbia Canada **88** L3 51 57N 118 02W
Kincardine Ontario Canada **93** D2 44 11N 81 38W
Kindersley Saskatchewan Canada **88** N3 51 27N 109 08W
Kindia Guinea **112** C5 10 03N 12 49W
Kindu Zaïre **111** E7 3 00S 25 56E
Kineshma Russia **58** E6 57 28N 42 08E
King George Bay Falkland Islands **25** L16 51 50S 61 00W
King George Island Antarctica **21** 60 00S 60 00W
King George Island South Shetland Islands **103** F0 62 00S 58 00W
King George's Reservoir England United Kingdom **66** C3 51 41N 0 05W
King Island Australia **78** G2 40 00S 144 00E
Kingissepp *see* Kuressaare
Kingman Arizona U.S.A. **90** D4 35 12N 114 02W
Kingman Reef Pacific Ocean **81** D3 6 27N 162 24W
King Sejong *r.s.* Antarctica **21** 62 13S 58 47W
Kingsgrove Australia **79** G2 33 58S 151 09E
Kings Langley England United Kingdom **66** B3 51 43N 0 28W
King's Lynn Norfolk England United Kingdom **68** L4 52 45N 0 24E
King Sound Australia **78** C6 16 00S 123 00E
Kings Point *tn.* New York U.S.A. **94** C2 40 49N 73 45W
Kingsport Tennessee U.S.A. **91** J4 36 33N 82 34W
Kingston Ontario Canada **93** E2 44 14N 76 30W
Kingston Jamaica **97** R7 17 58N 76 48W
Kingston Norfolk Island **81** L4 29 03S 167 57E
Kingston New York U.S.A. **93** F2 41 55N 74 00W
Kingston Common Reserve Norfolk Island **81** K4 29 03S 167 57E
Kingston upon Hull England United Kingdom **68** K5 53 45N 0 20W
Kingston-upon-Thames England United Kingdom **66** B2 51 25N 0 18W
Kingstown St. Vincent and The Grenadines **97** L2 13 12N 61 14W
Kingsville Ontario Canada **93** D2 42 02N 82 44W
Kingsville Texas U.S.A. **91** G2 27 32N 97 53W
King William Island Northwest Territories Canada **89** P6 69 00N 97 30W
Kinkala Congo **112** G2 4 18S 14 49E
Kino *r.* Japan **46** G1 34 15N 135 30E
Kinshasa Zaïre **111** C7 4 18S 15 18E
Kinu Myanmar **38** B4 22 47N 95 36E
Kinzig *r.* Germany **71** A2 50 00N 9 00E
Kioa Fiji **83** D10 16 14S 179 07E
Kiparissiakós Kólpos *g.* Greece **74** D2 37 00N 21 00E
Kipili Tanzania **111** F6 7 30S 30 39E
Kirakira Solomon Islands **82** G3 10 30S 161 55E
Kirensk Russia **57** M7 57 45N 108 02E
KIRGHIZIA *see* KIRGYZSTAN
Kirghiz Step *geog. reg.* Kazakhstan **58/59** F4/K4
KIRGYZSTAN *(KIRGHIZIA)* **59** L3/M3
KIRIBATI **80** D3
Kirikiri Nigeria **109** V3 6 22N 3 22E
Kirikkale Turkey **54** D6 39 51N 33 32E
Kirinyaga *(Mount Kenya) mt.* Kenya **110** G7 0 10S 37 19E
Kirkağaç Turkey **74** E2 39 06N 27 40E
Kirkcaldy Fife Scotland United Kingdom **68** H8 56 07N 3 10W
Kirkcudbright Scotland United Kingdom **68** G6 54 50N 4 03W
Kirkland Lake *tn.* Ontario Canada **93** D3 48 10N 80 02W
Kirklareli Turkey **74** E3 41 45N 27 12E
Kirksville Missouri U.S.A. **92** B2 40 12N 92 35W
Kirkūk Iraq **54** F6 35 28N 44 26E
Kirkwall Orkney Islands Scotland United Kingdom **68** I10 58 59N 2 58W
Kirov Russia **56** G7 58 00N 49 38E
Kirov *r.* Russia **58** G6 58 00N 50 50E
Kirovabad *see* Gyandzha
Kirovakan Armenia **58** E3 40 49N 44 30E
Kirovograd Ukraine **58** C4 48 31N 32 15E
Kirti Nagar India **52** L4 28 39N 77 09E
Kiruna Sweden **69** E4 67 53N 20 15E
Kiryū Japan **46** C2 36 26N 139 18E
Kisangani Zaïre **110** E8 0 33N 25 14E
Kisar *i.* Indonesia **44** B2 8 05S 127 12E
Kisarazu Japan **47** C2 35 22N 139 55E
Kiselevsk' Russia **59** O5 54 01N 86 41E
Kishiwada Japan **46** G1 34 28N 135 22E
Kiskunfélegyháza Hungary **75** C2 46 42N 19 52E
Kiskunhalas Hungary **75** C2 46 26N 19 29E
Kislovodsk Russia **58** E3 43 56N 42 44E
Kismaayo Somalia **110** H7 0 25S 42 31E
Kisumu Kenya **110** F7 0 08S 34 47E
Kita Japan **47** B4 35 46N 139 43E
Kita-Kyūshū Japan **46** B1 33 52N 130 49E
Kitami Japan **46** D3 43 51N 143 54E
Kita-ura Japan **46** M3 36 02N 140 33E
Kitchener Ontario Canada **93** D2 43 27N 80 30W
Kíthira *i.* Greece **74** D2 36 00N 23 00E
Kíthnos *i.* Greece **74** D2 37 00N 24 00E
Kitimat British Columbia Canada **88** J3 54 05N 128 38W
Kitridge Point Barbados **96** W12 13 08N 59 22W
Kittanning Pennslylvania U.S.A. **93** E2 40 49N 79 31W
Kittery Maine U.S.A. **93** F2 43 05N 70 45W
Kitwe Zambia **111** E5 0 08S 30 30E
Kitzbühel Austria **75** B2 47 27N 12 23E
Kitzbühler Alpen *mts.* Austria **71** B1 47 00N 12 00E
Kitzingen Germany **71** B1 49 45N 10 11E
Kiu Lom Reservoir Thailand **39** A3 18 35N 99 35E
Kiunga Papua New Guinea **45** J3 6 10S 141 15E
Kivu, Lake Zaïre/Rwanda **110** E7 2 00S 29 00E
Kiwai Island Papua New Guinea **45** K2 8 35S 143 25E
Kiyev *(Kiev)* Ukraine **58** C5 50 25N 30 30E
Kiyose Japan **47** B4 35 46N 139 32E
Kızıl Irmak *r.* Turkey **54** D7 40 30N 34 00E
Kizlyar Russia **58** F3 43 51N 46 43E
Kizu-gawa *r.* Japan **46** G1 34 50N 135 55E
Kizyl Arvat Turkmenistan **59** H2 39 00N 56 23E
Kladar Irian Jaya Indonesia **44** G2 8 24S 137 48E
Kladno Czech Republic **75** B3 50 10N 14 07E
Kladow Germany **67** E1 52 27N 13 08E
Klaeng Thailand **39** B2 12 46N 101 39E
Klagenfurt Austria **75** B2 46 38N 14 20E
Klaipėda Lithuania **69** E2 55 43N 21 07E
Klamath *r.* U.S.A. **90** B5 42 00N 123 00W
Klamath Falls *tn.* Oregon U.S.A. **90** B5 42 14N 121 47W
Klamono Irian Jaya Indonesia **44** D6 1 08S 131 28E
Klang Malaysia **42** B4 3 03N 101 25E
Klarälven *r.* Sweden **69** C3 60 45N 13 00E
Klaten Indonesia **42** P7 7 40S 110 32E
Klatovy Czech Republic **75** B2 49 24N 13 17E
Kleinmachnow Germany **67** E1/F1 52 24N 13 13E
Klerksdorp Republic of South Africa **111** E2 26 52S 26 39E
Kleve Germany **71** A2 51 47N 6 11E
Kłodzko Poland **75** C3 50 28N 16 40E
Klöfta Norway **69** C3 60 04N 11 06E
Kluane National Park Yukon Territory Canada **88** H5 60 30N 139 00W
Kluang Malaysia **42** B4 2 01N 103 19E
Klyazma *r.* Russia **58** E6 56 00N 42 00E
Klyuchevskaya Sopka *mt.* Russia **57** S7 56 03N 160 38E
Kmagha Solomon Islands **82** E5 8 20S 159 44E
Knokke-Heist Belgium **70** C3 51 21N 3 19E
Knossós *hist. site* Greece **54** C6 35 18N 25 10E
Knox Indiana U.S.A. **92** C2 41 17N 86 37W
Knoxville Iowa U.S.A. **92** B2 41 26N 93 05W

Knoxville Tennessee U.S.A. **91** J4 36 00N 83 57W
Kobe Indonesia **43** G4 0 30N 127 56E
Kōbe Japan **46** G1 34 40N 135 12E
København *(Copenhagen)* Denmark **69** C2 55 43N 12 34E
Kobi Indonesia **44** C5 2 59S 129 54E
Koblenz Germany **71** A2 50 21N 7 36E
Kobuk *r.* Alaska U.S.A. **88** D6 67 00N 157 30W
Koca *r.* Turkey **74** E2 39 00N 27 00E
Kŏch'ang South Korea **50** C2 35 39N 127 59E
Ko Chang *i.* Thailand **39** B2 12 00N 102 20E
Koch Bihār India **53** F5 26 18N 89 32E
Kōchi Japan **46** B1 33 33N 133 32E
Kochubey Russia **58** F3 44 25N 46 33E
Kodaira Japan **47** A3 35 44N 139 28E
Kodiak Alaska U.S.A. **88** E4 57 49N 152 30W
Kodiak Island Alaska U.S.A. **88** E4 57 20N 153 40W
Kodok Sudan **110** F9 9 51N 32 07E
Koforidua Ghana **112** E4 6 01N 0 12W
Kofu Japan **46** C2 35 42N 138 34E
Koga Japan **46** L3 36 12N 139 42E
Koganei Japan **47** B3 35 42N 139 30E
Kohat Pakistan **53** C6 33 37N 71 30E
Kohima India **53** G5 25 40N 94 08E
Koh-i-Mazar *mt.* Afghanistan **55** K5 32 3ON 66 23E
Kohinggo *i.* Solomon Islands **82** C5 8 10S 157 20E
Koh Kong *i.* Cambodia **37** B2 11 25N 103 00E
Kohoku Japan **47** B3 35 30N 139 39E
Koh Rong *i.* Cambodia **37** B2 10 30N 104 00E
Kohtla-Järve Estonia **69** F2 59 28N 27 20E
Kohung South Korea **50** C2 34 30N 127 10E
Kojŏ North Korea **50** C4 38 54N 127 55E
Kokand Uzbekistan **59** L3 40 33N 70 55E
Kokas Irian Jaya Indonesia **44** E5 2 45S 132 26E
Kokawa Japan **46** G1 34 16N 135 24E
Kokchetav Kazakhstan **59** K5 53 18N 69 25E
Kokenau Irian Jaya Indonesia **44** G4 4 46S 136 33E
Ko Khram Yai *i.* Thailand **39** B2 13 10N 100 50E
Kokkola Finland **69** E3 62 45N 30 06E
Kokoda Papua New Guinea **45** M2 8 52S 147 44E
Kokomo Indiana U.S.A. **92** C2 40 30N 86 09W
Kokopo Papua New Guinea **45** P4 4 18S 152 17E
Koksoak *r.* Québec Canada **89** V4 58 00N 69 00W
Ko Kut *i.* Thailand **39** B2 11 40N 102 32E
Ko Ladang *i.* Thailand **39** A1 6 30N 99 17E
Kolaka Indonesia **43** F3 4 04S 121 38E
Kola Peninsula Russia **56** F9 67 30N 37 30E
Kolar Gold Fields *tn.* India **53** D2 12 54N 78 16E
Kolbano Indonesia **44** A1 10 02S 124 31E
Kolding Denmark **69** B2 55 29N 9 30E
Kolguyev *i.* Russia **56** G9 69 00N 49 30E
Kolhapur India **53** C3 16 40N 74 20E
Kolín Czech Republic **75** C3 50 02N 15 11E
Köln *(Cologne)* Germany **71** A2 50 56N 6 57E
Kołobrzeg Poland **75** C3 54 10N 15 35E
Kolombangara *i.* Solomon Islands **82** C6 8 00S 157 10E
Kolomna Russia **58** D6 55 05N 38 45E
Kolomyya Ukraine **58** A4 48 31N 25 00E
Kolonga Tonga **83** D1 21 07S 175 05W
Kolovai Tonga **83** D1 21 05S 175 20W
Kolpashevo Russia **57** K7 58 21N 82 59E
Kolpino Russia **58** C6 59 44N 30 39E
Kolvereid Norway **69** C3 64 53N 11 35E
Kolwezi Zaïre **111** E5 10 45S 25 25E
Kolyma *r.* Russia **57** R9 66 30N 152 00E
Kolyma (Gydan) Range *mts.* Russia **57** R8 63 00N 160 00E
Kolyma Lowland Russia **57** R9 69 00N 155 00E
Komae Japan **47** B3 35 38N 139 36E
Komaki Japan **46** H2 35 18N 136 54E
Komandorskiye Ostrova *is.* Russia **22** G13 55 00N 166 30E
Komárno Slovakia **75** C2 47 46N 18 05E
Komatsu Japan **46** C2 36 25N 136 27E
Kommunarsk Ukraine **58** D4 48 30N 38 47E
Komo *i.* Fiji **83** F8 18 42S 178 38W
Komotiní Greece **74** E3 41 06N 25 25E
Kompong Cham Cambodia **37** C2 11 59N 105 26E
Kompong Chhnang Cambodia **37** B2 12 16N 104 39E
Kompong Kleang Cambodia **37** B2 13 07N 104 08E
Kompong Som Cambodia **37** B2 10 38N 103 28E
Kompong Speu Cambodia **37** B2 11 25N 104 32E
Kompong Sralao Cambodia **37** C2 14 11N 105 50E
Kompong Thom Cambodia **37** B2 12 42N 104 52E
Kompong Trabek Cambodia **37** C2 13 07N 105 17E
Komsomol'sk-na-Amure Russia **57** P6 50 32N 136 59E
Konda *r.* Russia **59** K7 60 00N 65 00E
Kondūz Afghanistan **55** K6 36 45N 68 51E
Koné New Caledonia **82** T2 21 04S 164 50E
Kong Christian X Land *geog. reg.* Greenland **89** CC8 75 00N 27 30W
Konghur Shan *mt.* China **59** M2 39 00N 75 10E
Kongju South Korea **50** C3 36 28N 127 03E
Kongkemul *mt.* Indonesia **42** E4 1 55N 116 04E
Kong Krailat Thailand **39** A3 16 55N 100 00E
Kongolo Zaïre **111** E6 5 20S 27 00E
Kong Oscars Fjord Greenland **89** EE7 72 30N 23 00W
Kon Plong Vietnam **37** C2 14 36N 108 23E
Königswinter Germany **70** G2 50 41N 7 11E
Königs Wusterhausen Germany **67** G1 52 18N 13 37E
Konin Poland **75** C3 52 12N 18 12E
Konnagar India **52** K2 22 42N 88 20E
Konos Papua New Guinea **45** O5 3 09S 151 47E
Konosha Russia **56** G8 60 58N 40 08E
Konotop Ukraine **58** C5 51 15N 33 14E
Konstantinovka Ukraine **58** D4 48 33N 37 45E
Konstanz Germany **71** A1 47 40N 9 10E
Kontum Vietnam **37** C2 14 23N 108 00E
Kontum Plateau Vietnam **37** C2 14 00N 108 00E
Konya Turkey **54** D6 37 51N 32 30E
Konz Germany **70** F1 49 42N 6 35E
Kootenay Lake British Columbia Canada **88** L3 50 00N 117 15W
Kopano Papua New Guinea **45** M5 2 10S 146 55E
Köpenick Germany **67** G1 52 27N 13 36E
Koper Slovenia **74** B4 45 31N 13 44E
Kopeysk Russia **59** J6 55 08N 61 39E
Ko Phaluai *i.* Thailand **39** A1 9 30N 99 40E
Ko Phangan *i.* Thailand **39** A1/B1 9 45N 100 00E
Ko Phra Thong *i.* Thailand **39** A1 9 05N 98 18E
Ko Phuket *i.* Thailand **39** A1 8 00N 98 20E
Ko Rawi *i.* Thailand **39** A1 6 31N 99 10E
Korbach Germany **71** A2 51 16N 8 53E
Korçë Albania **74** D3 40 38N 20 44E
Korčula *i.* Croatia **74** C3 43 00N 17 00E
Korea Bay China/North Korea **49** O6 39 00N 124 00E
Korea Strait Japan/South Korea **50** D2 33 00N 129 00E
Korhogo Côte d'Ivoire **112** D4 9 22N 5 31W
Korido Irian Jaya Indonesia **44** F6 0 46S 135 34E
Korim Irian Jaya Indonesia **44** G6 0 55S 136 08E
Korinthiakós Kólpos *g.* Greece **74** D2 38 00N 22 00E
Kórinthos Greece **74** D2 37 56N 22 55E
Kōriyama Japan **46** D2 37 23N 140 22E
Korla China **48** G7 41 48N 86 10E
Koro *i.* Fiji **83** D9 17 20S 179 25E
Koroba Papua New Guinea **45** K4 5 46S 142 48E
Korolevu Fiji **83** B8 18 15S 177 43E
Koronadal The Philippines **40** B2 6 30N 124 53E
Koror Palau Islands **80** A4 7 21N 134 31E
Koro Sea Fiji **83** D9/E9 18 00S 180 00
Korosten' Ukraine **58** B5 51 00N 28 30E
Korotasere Fiji **83** D10 16 35S 179 35E
Korovou Fiji **83** C9 17 49S 178 32E
Koroynitu *mt.* Fiji **83** B9 17 40S 177 35E
Korsakov Russia **57** Q5 46 36N 142 50E
Kortrijk *(Courtrai)* Belgium **70** C2 50 50N 3 17E
Koryak Range *mts.* Russia **57** T8 62 00N 170 00E
Kos *i.* Greece **74** E2 36 00N 27 00E
Ko Samui *i.* Thailand **39** A1/B1 9 30N 100 00E
Kosciusko, Mount Australia **78** H2 36 28S 148 17E
Koshigaya Japan **46** L2 35 54N 139 47E
Košice Slovakia **75** D2 48 44N 21 15E
Kosŏng North Korea **50** D4 38 36N 128 21E
Kosrae *i.* Pacific Ocean **80** C4 8 00N 178 00E
Kosti Sudan **110** F10 13 11N 32 28E
Kostroma Russia **56** G7 57 46N 40 59E
Kostrzyn Poland **75** B3 52 35N 14 40E
Ko Surin Nua *i.* Thailand **39** A1 9 25N 97 55E
Koszalin Poland **75** C3 54 10N 16 10E
Kota India **53** D5 25 11N 75 58E
Kotaagung Indonesia **42** B2 5 30S 104 39E
Kotabaru Kalimantan Indonesia **42** E3 3 15S 116 15E
Kotabaru Sumatera Indonesia **42** B3 1 08S 101 40E
Kota Belud Malaysia **40** A2 6 22N 116 28E
Kota Bharu Malaysia **42** B5 6 08N 102 14E
Kotabumi Indonesia **42** B3 4 52S 104 59E
Kota Kinabalu Malaysia **42** E5 5 59N 116 04E
Kotamobagu Indonesia **43** F4 0 46N 124 21E
Ko Tao *i.* Thailand **39** A2 10 05N 99 50E
Ko Tarutao *i.* Thailand **39** A1 6 35N 99 40E
Köthen Germany **71** B2 51 46N 11 59E
Kotka Finland **69** F3 60 26N 26 55E
Kotlas Russia **56** G8 61 15N 46 35E
Kōtō Japan **47** C3 35 40N 139 49E
Kotri Pakistan **52** B5 25 22N 68 18E
Kotto *r.* Central African Republic **110** D9 7 00N 22 30E
Kotu *i.* Tonga **83** B3 19 55S 174 50W
Kotu Group Tonga **83** B2/3 20 00S 174 50W
Kotuy *r.* Russia **57** M9 67 30N 102 00E
Kotzebue Alaska U.S.A. **88** C6 66 51N 162 40W
Kotzebue Sound Alaska U.S.A. **88** C6 66 40N 162 20W
Kouaoua New Caledonia **82** U2 21 23S 165 50E
Koudougou Burkina **112** E5 12 15N 2 23W
Koulamoutou Gabon **112** H2 1 12S 12 29E
Koulen Cambodia **37** B2 13 49N 104 43E
Koulikoro Mali **112** D5 12 55N 7 31W
Koumac New Caledonia **82** T3 20 32S 164 20E
Koumra Chad **110** C9 8 56N 17 32E
Kounradskiy Kazakhstan **59** L4 46 58N 74 59E
Kourou French Guiana **102** G14 5 08N 52 37W
Kouroutetapo Vanuatu **83** F8 13 25S 166 41E
Kouvola Finland **69** F3 60 54N 26 45E
Kovel' Ukraine **58** A5 51 12N 24 48E
Kovrov Russia **58** E6 56 23N 41 21E
Kovzha *r.* Russia **58** D7 61 00N 37 00E
Kowloon Hong Kong U.K. **51** B1 22 19N 114 11E
Kowloon City Hong Kong U.K. **51** C2 22 20N 114 11E
Kowloon Peak Hong Kong U.K. **51** C2 22 20N 114 13E
Kowŏn North Korea **50** C4 39 25N 127 15E
Ko Yao Yai *i.* Thailand **39** A1 7 58N 98 35E
Koyukuk *r.* Alaska U.S.A. **88** E6 66 00N 154 00W
Kozáni Greece **74** D3 40 18N 21 48E
Kpalimé Togo **112** F4 6 55N 0 44E
Krabi Thailand **39** A1 8 04N 98 52E
Kra Buri Thailand **39** A2 10 25N 98 48E
Kragujevac Serbia Yugoslavia **74** D3 44 01N 20 55E
Kra, Isthmus of Myanmar/Thailand **39** A2 10 20N 99 00E
Krakatau *i.* Indonesia **42** M8 6 11S 105 26E
Krakor Cambodia **37** B2 12 31N 104 12E
Kraków Poland **75** C3 50 03N 19 55E
Kraljevo Serbia Yugoslavia **74** D3 43 44N 20 41E
Kramatorsk Ukraine **58** D4 48 43N 37 33E
Kranj Slovenia **74** B4 46 15N 14 20E
Kranji Singapore **41** C5 1 26N 103 45E
Kranji Reservoir Singapore **41** B5 1 26N 103 44E
Krasieo Reservoir Thailand **39** A2 14 50N 99 35E
Krasnodar Russia **56** F5 45 02N 39 00E
Krasnoyarsk Russia **57** L7 56 05N 92 46E
Krasnoyarskoye Vodokhranilishche *res.* Russia **59** P5/6 55 00N 91 00E
Krasny Stroitel Russia **56** M1 55 31N 37 08E
Krasnyy Kut Russia **58** F5 50 58N 47 00E
Krasnyy Luch Ukraine **58** D4 48 10N 39 00E
Kratie Cambodia **37** C2 12 30N 106 03E
Krau Irian Jaya Indonesia **44** H5 2 45S 139 35E
Krefeld Germany **71** A1 51 20N 6 32E
Kremenchug Ukraine **58** C4 49 03N 33 25E
Kremenchugskoye Vodokhranilishche *res.* Ukraine **58** C4 49 30N 32 30E
Krems Austria **75** C2 48 25N 15 36E
Kreuzberg Germany **67** F2 52 30N 13 24E
Kribi Cameroon **112** G3 2 56N 9 56E
Krim *(Crimea)* *p.* Ukraine **58** C3/4 46 00N 34 00E
Krishna *r.* India **53** D3 16 00N 79 00E
Kristiansand Norway **69** B2 58 08N 8 01E
Kristianstad Sweden **69** C2 56 02N 14 10E
Kristiansund Norway **69** B3 63 06N 7 58E
Kríti *(Crete)* *i.* Greece **74** D2/E2 35 00N 25 00E
Krivoy Rog Ukraine **58** C4 47 55N 33 24E
Krk *i.* Croatia **74** B3/B4 45 00N 14 00E
Krong *r.* Laos/Vietnam **37** C2 12 50N 107 55E
Krong Koh Kong Cambodia **37** B2 11 33N 103 00E
Kronshtadt Russia **69** G3 60 00N 29 40E
Krosno Poland **75** D2 49 40N 21 46E
Kruger National Park Republic of South Africa **111** F2/F3 24 00S 32 00E
Krugersdorp Republic of South Africa **111** E2 26 06S 27 46E
Krui Indonesia **42** B2 5 13S 103 56E
Kru Kru Papua New Guinea **45** J5 2 45S 141 27E
Krung Thep *see* Bangkok
Kruševaç Serbia Yugoslavia **74** D3 43 34N 21 20E
Krušnéhory *see* Erzbebirge
Ksar El Boukhari Algeria **112** F10 35 55N 2 47E
Ksar-el-Kebir Morocco **72** A1 35 04N 5 56W
Kuala Bedengan Malaysia **42** D4 3 00N 112 00E
Kuala Belait Brunei Darussalam **42** D4 4 27N 114 48E
Kuala Dungun Malaysia **42** B4 4 47N 103 25E
Kualakapuas Indonesia **42** D3 3 00S 114 22E
Kuala Kerai Malaysia **39** B1 5 33N 101 12E
Kuala Lipis Malaysia **42** B4 4 12N 102 02E
Kuala Lumpur Malaysia **42** B4 3 09N 101 42E
Kuala Terengganu Malaysia **42** B5 5 20N 103 09E
Kuala Tomani Malaysia **42** E4 4 51N 115 52E
Kuamut *r.* Malaysia **40** A2 5 00N 116 00E
Kuandang Indonesia **43** F4 0 50N 123 00E
Kuandian China **50** B5 40 45N 124 46E
Kuangfu Taiwan **51** H6 23 40N 121 25E
Kuantan Malaysia **42** B4 3 48N 103 19E
Kuata *i.* Fiji **83** B9 17 21S 177 08E
Kubiri Japan **47** B1 35 13N 139 42E
Kubuna Papua New Guinea **45** M2 8 48S 146 42E
Kubutambahan Indonesia **42** R6 8 04S 115 10E
Kuching Malaysia **42** D4 1 35N 110 21E
Kudat Malaysia **42** E5 6 54N 116 50E
Kudus Indonesia **42** P7 6 46S 110 48E
Kufar Indonesia **44** D5 3 34S 130 47E
Kuhumo Finland **69** F3 64 04N 29 30E
Kui Papua New Guinea **45** M3 7 30S 147 16E
Kui Buri Thailand **39** A2 12 01N 99 49E
Kuito Angola **111** C5 12 25S 16 56E
Kujūkuri-hama *beach* Japan **40** M2 35 30N 140 30E
Kujū-san *mt.* Japan **46** B1 33 07N 131 14E
Kukës Albania **74** D3 42 05N 20 24E
Kuki Japan **46** L3 36 03N 139 41E
Kukipi Papua New Guinea **45** M2 8 11S 146 09E
Kukunda Solomon Islands **82** B5 8 00S 157 00E
Kula Gulf Solomon Islands **82** C5 8 05S 157 10E
Kuldiga Latvia **69** E2 56 58N 21 58E
Kulmbach Germany **71** B2 50 06N 11 28E
Kulumadau Papua New Guinea **45** P2 9 05S 152 43E
Kulundinskaya Step' *geog. reg.* Kazakhstan/Russia **59** M5/N5 52 00N 80 00E
Kŭm *r.* South Korea **50** C3 36 00N 126 45E
Kuma *r.* Russia **56** G4 45 00N 45 00E
Kumagaya Japan **46** L3 36 09N 139 22E
Kumairi *(Leninakan)* Armenia **58** E3 40 47N 43 49E
Kumamoto Japan **46** B1 32 50N 130 42E
Kumanovo Macedonia (Former Yugoslav Republic) **74** D3 42 07N 21 40E
Kumasi Ghana **112** E4 6 45N 1 35W
Kumba Cameroon **112** G3 4 39N 9 26E
Kumbakonam India **53** D2 10 59N 79 24E
Kumbe Irian Jaya Indonesia **44** J2 8 21S 140 12E
Kŭmch'ŏn North Korea **50** C4 38 11N 126 25E
Kŭmhwa South Korea **50** C4 38 12N 127 28E
Kumi South Korea **50** D3 36 06N 128 22E
Kŭmnyŏng South Korea **50** C1 33 32N 126 44E
Kumon Range Myanmar **38** B5 26 00N 97 20E
Kumukahi, Cape Hawaiian Islands **23** Z17 19 30N 154 50W
Kumul *see* Hami
Kunashir *i.* Russia **46** E3 44 30N 146 20E
Kundiawa Papua New Guinea **45** L3 6 00S 144 57E
Kungrad Uzbekistan **59** H3 43 06N 58 54E
Kunhing Myanmar **38** B4 21 20N 98 26E
Kuningan Indonesia **42** O7 7 02S 108 30E
Kuning Sea *(Huang Hai)* China **50** B3 35 30N 122 30E
Kunlong Myanmar **38** B4 23 21N 98 39E
Kunlun Shan *mts.* China **48** F6/G6 36 30N 85 00E
Kunming China **49** K4 25 04N 102 41E
Kunming Hu *l.* China **47** F1 40 00N 116 15E
Kunsan South Korea **50** C2 35 57N 126 42E
Kunti, River India **52** K3 22 55N 88 20E
Kuntsevo Russia **56** L1 55 43N 37 25E
Kunua Papua New Guinea **45** Q4 5 49S 154 48E
Kununurra Australia **78** D6 15 42S 128 50E
Kunyé *see* Île des Pins
Kuopio Finland **69** F3 62 54N 27 40E
Kupa *r.* Croatia **74** C4 45 30N 15 00E
Kupang Indonesia **43** F1 10 13S 123 38E
Kupiano Papua New Guinea **45** N1 10 06S 148 12E
Kur *i.* Indonesia **44** D4 5 21S 131 59E
Kura *r.* Azerbaijan **58** E3 41 00N 47 30E
Kurashiki Japan **46** B1 34 36N 133 43E
Kurchum *r.* Kazakhstan **59** N4 49 00N 85 00E
Kure Japan **46** B1 34 14N 132 32E
Kuressaare *(Kingissepp)* Estonia **69** E2 59 22N 28 40E
Kureyka *r.* Russia **57** L9 67 30N 91 00E
Kurgan Russia **56** I7 55 30N 65 20E
Kuria Muria Islands Oman **55** I2 17 30N 56 00E
Kurihama Japan **47** B1 35 12N 139 41E
Kurikka Finland **69** E3 62 36N 22 25E
Kuril Islands Russia **22** F12 50 00N 155 00E
Kuril Ridge Pacific Ocean **22** F12 47 50N 152 00E
Kuril Trench Pacific Ocean **22** F12 45 40N 154 00E
Ku-ring-gai Chase National Park Australia **79** G3 33 40S 151 00E
Kurnell Australia **79** G1 34 01S 151 12E
Kurnool India **53** D3 15 51N 78 01E
Kursk Russia **56** F6 51 45N 36 14E
Kurtalan Turkey **58** E2 37 58N 41 36E
Kurume Japan **46** B1 33 20N 130 29E
Kusatsu Japan **46** G2 35 02N 135 59E
Kushida-gawa *r.* Japan **46** H1 34 23N 136 15E
Kushiro Japan **46** D3 42 58N 144 24E
Kushka Afghanistan **55** J6 35 14N 62 15E
Kushva Russia **59** H6 58 20N 59 48E
Kuskokwim Bay Alaska U.S.A. **88** C4 58 50N 164 00W
Kuskokwim Mountains Alaska U.S.A. **88** D5 62 00N 158 00W
Kuskokwim *r.* Alaska U.S.A. **88** C5 61 30N 160 45W
Kusŏng North Korea **50** B4 39 57N 125 20E
Kustanay Kazakhstan **59** J5 53 15N 63 40E
Kütahya Turkey **54** C6 39 25N 29 56E
Kutaisi Georgia **58** E3 42 15N 42 44E
Kutno Poland **75** C3 52 13N 19 20E
Kuto New Caledonia **82** W1 22 40S 167 28E
Kuujjuaq Québec Canada **89** V4 58 25N 68 55W
Kuujjuarapik Québec Canada **89** T4 55 15N 77 41W
Kuusamo Finland **69** F4 65 57N 29 15E
Kuvango Angola **111** C5 14 27S 16 20E
Kuwaé *see* Tongoa
KUWAIT **55** G4
Kuwana Japan **46** H2 35 04N 136 40E
Kuybyshev *see* Samara
Kuybyshev Forest Russia **56** M2 55 50N 37 45E
Kuytun China **48** F7 44 30N 85 00E
Kuzbass *geog. reg.* Russia **59** O5/6 55 00N 87 00E
Kuzey Anadolu Kağlari *mts.* Turkey **54** E7 41 15N 36 20E
Kuz'minki Russia **56** M1/N1 55 41N 37 45E
Kwai Chung Hong Kong U.K. **51** B2 22 22N 114 07E
Kwajalein Atoll Pacific Ocean **80** C4 96 15N 167 30E
Kwangju South Korea **50** C2 35 07N 126 52E
Kwangmyong South Korea **50** C3 37 26N 126 53E
Kwango *r.* Zaïre **111** C6 6 00S 17 00E
Kwangyang South Korea **50** C2 35 01N 127 32E
Kwan Tei Hong Kong U.K. **51** B3 22 31N 114 09E
Kwatisore Irian Jaya Indonesia **44** F5 3 18S 134 50E
Kwekwe *(Que Que)* Zimbabwe **111** E4 18 55S 29 49E
Kwethluk Alaska U.S.A. **88** C5 60 46N 161 34W
Kwigillingok Alaska U.S.A. **88** C4 59 50N 163 10W
Kwikila Papua New Guinea **45** M2 9 51S 147 43E
Kwilu *r.* Zaïre **111** C6 6 00S 19 00E
Kwun Tong Hong Kong U.K. **51** C1 22 18N 114 13E
Kwu Tung Hong Kong U.K. **51** B3 22 30N 114 06E
Kyaikkami *(Amherst)* Myanmar **38** B3 16 04N 97 34E
Kyaiklat Myanmar **38** B3 16 25N 95 42E
Kyaikto Myanmar **38** B3 17 16N 97 01E
Kyangin Myanmar **38** B3 18 20N 95 15E
Ky Anh Vietnam **37** C3 18 03N 106 20E
Kyaukme Myanmar **38** B4 22 30N 97 02E
Kyaukpadaung Myanmar **38** B4 20 50N 95 08E
Kyaukpyu Myanmar **38** A3 19 27N 93 33E
Kyaukse Myanmar **38** B4 21 33N 96 06E
Kyauktaw Myanmar **38** A4 20 48N 93 00E
Kyaunggon Myanmar **38** B3 17 04N 95 12E
Kyawkku Myanmar **38** B4 21 49N 96 56E
Kyeintali Myanmar **38** A3 18 00N 94 29E
Kyle of Lochalsh Scotland United Kingdom **68** F9 57 17N 5 43W
Kyoga, Lake Uganda **110** F8 2 00N 34 00E
Kyoga-misaki *c.* Japan **46** C2 35 48N 135 12E
Kyŏmip'o North Korea **50** B4 38 55N 125 50E
Kyŏngju South Korea **50** D2 35 52N 129 15E
Kyŏngsan South Korea **50** D2 35 46N 128 42E
Kyŏngsŏng North Korea **50** D5 41 38N 129 39E
Kyōto Japan **46** G2 35 02N 135 45E
Kyōto *pref.* Japan **46** G2 35 00N 135 30E
Kyronjöki *r.* Finland **69** E3 63 00N 21 30E
Ky Son Vietnam **37** B3 19 40N 104 00E
Kyugok Myanmar **38** B4 24 02N 98 05E
Kyungon Myanmar **38** B3 19 00N 96 25E
Kyūshū *i.* Japan **46** B1 32 20N 131 00E
Kyūshū-Palau Ridge Pacific Ocean **22** D9/D10 15 00N 135 00E
Kyustendil Bulgaria **74** D3 42 26N 22 40E
Kyzyl Russia **57** L6 51 45N 94 28E
Kzyl-Orda Kazakhstan **59** K3 44 25N 65 28E

L

Laascaanood Somalia **110** I9 8 35N 46 55E
La Asunción Venezuela **97** L2 11 06N 63 53W
Laayoune *(El Aaiún)* Western Sahara **112** C8 27 10N 13 11W
Labasa Fiji **83** D10 16 25S 179 24E
la Baule-Escoublac France **73** A2 47 18N 2 22W
Labé Guinea **112** C5 11 17N 12 11W
Labe *see* Elbe
Labo The Philippines **40** B3 14 09N 122 52E
Labrador *geog. reg.* Newfoundland Canada **89** W3 54 00N 63 00W
Labrador Basin Atlantic Ocean **25** B12/C12 58 00N 50 00W
Labrador City Newfoundland Canada **89** V3 52 54N 66 50W
Labrador Sea Canada/Greenland **89** X4 59 00N 56 00W
Lábrea Brazil **102** E11 7 20S 64 46W
La Brea Trinidad and Tobago **96** S9 10 14N 61 37W
Labuan *i.* Malaysia **42** E5 5 20N 115 15E
Labuha Indonesia **43** G3 0 35S 127 28E
Labuhan Indonesia **42** M7 6 25S 105 49E
Labuhanbajo Indonesia **43** E2 8 33S 119 55E
Labuhanbilik Indonesia **42** B4 2 30N 100 10E
Labuk *r.* Malaysia **40** A2 6 00N 117 00E
Labuk Bay Malaysia **40** A2 6 05N 117 50E
Labutta Myanmar **38** A3 16 10N 94 45E
Labytnangi Russia **57** I9 66 43N 66 28E
Lac Alaotra *l.* Madagascar **111** I4 17 30S 54 00E
Lac à l'Eau Claire *l.* Québec Canada **89** U4 56 20N 74 30W
La Canada California U.S.A. **95** B3 34 12N 118 12W
Lac Bienville *l.* Québec Canada **89** U4 55 30N 73 00W
Lac de la Fôret d'Orient *l.* France **73** B2 48 15N 4 20E
Lac de Neuchâtel *l.* Switzerland **73** C2 46 45N 6 40E
Lac du Bonnet *tn.* Manitoba Canada **92** A4 50 16N 96 03W
Lac du Der-Chantecoq *l.* France **73** B2 48 35N 4 45E
La Ceiba Honduras **97** G3 15 45N 86 45W
Lac Fitri *l.* Chad **110** C10 13 00N 17 30E
la Chaux-de-Fonde Switzerland **73** C2 47 07N 6 51E
Lachlan *r.* Australia **78** G3 33 30S 145 30E
La Chorrera Panama **97** Y1 8 51N 79 46W
Lachute Québec Canada **93** F3 45 39N 74 21W
la Ciotat France **73** C1 43 10N 5 36E
Lac Joseph *l.* Newfoundland Canada **89** V3 52 30N 65 15W
Lackawanna New York U.S.A. **93** E2 42 49N 78 49W
Lac la Martre *tn.* Northwest Territories Canada **88** L5 63 00N 117 30W
Lac la Ronge *l.* Saskatchewan Canada **88** N4 55 10N 105 00W
Lac Léman *(Lake Geneva)* *l.* Switzerland **73** C2 46 20N 6 20E
Lac Mai-Ndombe *l.* Zaïre **110** C7 2 00S 18 20E
Lac Manouané *l.* Québec Canada **93** F4 51 00N 71 00W
Lac Matagami *l.* Ontario Canada **93** E3 47 54N 81 35W
Lac Minto *l.* Québec Canada **89** T4 57 35N 75 00W
Lac Mistassini *l.* Québec Canada **89** U3 51 00N 73 20W
Lac Moero *see* Mweru, Lake
Lacolle Québec Canada **93** F3 45 04N 73 22W
La Coruña *(Corunna)* Spain **72** A3 43 22N 8 24W
Lac Payne *l.* Québec Canada **89** U4 59 25N 74 00W
La Cresenta California U.S.A. **95** B3 34 13N 118 14W
La Crosse Wisconsin U.S.A. **92** B2 43 48N 91 04W
Lac St.-Jean *l.* Québec Canada **93** F3 48 00N 72 00W
Lac Seul *l.* Ontario Canada **89** O3 50 20N 92 00W
Lacul Razelm *l.* Romania **75** E1 45 00N 29 00E
Ladakh Range *mts.* Kashmir **53** D6 34 30N 78 30E
la Défense France **67** A2 48 53N 2 14E
Ladoga, Lake *see* Ladozhskoye Ozero
Ladozhskoye Ozero *(Lake Ladoga)* *l.* Russia **56** F8 61 00N 30 00E

Ladysmith British Columbia Canada **88** K2 48 57N 123 50W
Ladysmith Republic of South Africa **111** E2 28 34S 29 47E
Ladysmith Wisconsin U.S.A. **92** B3 45 27N 91 07W
Lae Papua New Guinea **45** M3 6 45S 147 00E
Laedalsøyri Norway **69** B3 61 05N 7 15E
Laena *i.* Solomon Islands **82** C6 7 20S 157 35E
La Esmeralda Venezuela **102** D13 3 11N 65 33W
Lafayette Indiana U.S.A. **92** C2 40 25N 86 54W
Lafayette Louisiana U.S.A. **91** H3 30 12N 92 18W
La Fé Cuba **97** H4 22 02N 84 15W
la Flèche France **73** A2 47 42N 0 04W
la'Foa New Caledonia **82** U2 21 40S 165 52E
Lågen *r.* Norway **69** B3 61 40N 9 45E
Laghouat Algeria **112** F9 33 49N 2 55E
Lago Argentino *l.* Argentina **103** C2 50 10S 72 30W
Lago da Tijuca *l.* Brazil **103** P2 22 59S 43 22W
Lago de Chapala *l.* Mexico **96** D4 20 05N 103 00W
Lago de Maracaibo *l.* Venezuela **102** C14 9 50N 71 30W
Lago de Marapendi *l.* Brazil **103** Q2 23 00S 43 20W
Lago de Nicaragua *l.* Nicaragua **97** G2 11 50N 86 00W
Lago de Piratininga *l.* Brazil **103** Q2 22 57S 43 05W
Lago de Poopó *l.* Bolivia **102** D9 18 30S 67 20W
Lago di Bolsena *l.* Italy **74** B3 42 00N 12 00E
Lago di Como *l.* Italy **74** A4 46 00N 9 00E
Lago di Garda *l.* Italy **74** B4 45 00N 10 00E
Lago do Jacarepaguá *l.* Brazil **103** P2 22 58S 43 23W
Lago Maggiore *l.* Italy **74** A4 46 00N 8 00E
Lagonoy Gulf The Philippines **40** B3 13 00N 124 00E
Lago Rodrigo de Freitas *l.* Brazil **103** Q2 22 58S 43 13W
Lagos Nigeria **112** F4 6 27N 3 28E
Lagos Portugal **72** A2 37 05N 8 40W
Lagos Island *tn.* Nigeria **109** V3 6 24N 3 28E
Lagos Lagoon Nigeria **109** W3 6 30N 3 33E
Lago Titicaca *l.* Peru/Bolivia **102** C9/D9 16 00S 69 30W
La Grande Oregon U.S.A. **90** C6 45 21N 118 05W
La Grande 2, Réservoir Québec Canada **89** T3 54 00N 77 00W
La Grande 3, Réservoir Québec Canada **89** U3 54 10N 72 30W
La Grande Rivière *r.* Québec Canada **89** U3 54 00N 74 00W
La Grange Georgia U.S.A. **91** I3 33 02N 85 02W
La Guaira Venezuela **102** D15 10 38N 66 55W
Laguna Brazil **103** H7 28 29S 48 45W
Laguna Caratasca *l.* Honduras **97** H3 15 05N 84 00W
Laguna de Bay *l.* The Philippines **40** B3 14 00N 121 00E
Laguna de Perlas *l.* Nicaragua **97** H2 12 30N 83 30W
Laguna Madre *l.* Mexico **96** E4 25 00N 98 00W
Laguna Mar Chiquita *l.* Argentina **103** E6 30 30S 62 30W
Lagunillas Venezuela **102** C15 10 07N 71 16W
La Habana *(Havana)* Cuba **97** H4 23 07N 82 25W
La Habra California U.S.A. **95** C2 33 56N 117 59W
Lahad Datu Malaysia **42** E5 5 01N 118 20E
Lahaina Hawaiian Islands **23** Y18 20 23N 156 40W
Lahn *r.* Germany **71** A2 50 00N 8 00E
Lahore Pakistan **53** C6 31 34N 74 22E
Lahr Germany **71** A1 48 21N 7 52E
Lahti Finland **69** F3 61 00N 25 40E
Lai Chau Vietnam **37** B4 22 04N 103 10E
Lai Chi Chong Hong Kong U.K. **51** C2 22 27N 114 17E
Lai Chi Wo Hong Kong U.K. **51** C3 22 32N 114 15E
Lais Indonesia **42** B3 3 30S 102 02E
Lajes Brazil **103** G7 27 48S 50 20W
Lajpat Nagar India **52** M4 28 34N 77 15E
La Junta Colorado U.S.A. **90** F4 37 59N 103 34W
Lakao *i.* Solomon Islands **83** N4 9 55S 167 10E
Lakeba *i.* Fiji **83** F8 18 10S 178 49W
Lakeba Passage Fiji **83** F9 18 00S 178 40W
Lake Charles *tn.* Louisiana U.S.A. **91** H3 30 13N 93 13W
Lake City Michigan U.S.A. **92** C2 44 22N 85 12W
Lake Harbour *tn.* Northwest Territories Canada **89** V5 62 50N 69 50W
Lakeland *tn.* Florida U.S.A. **91** J2 28 02N 81 59W
Lake Murray *tn.* Papua New Guinea **45** J3 6 35S 141 28E
Lakeport California U.S.A. **90** B4 39 04N 122 56W
Lake River *tn.* Ontario Canada **89** S3 54 30N 82 30W
Lakeview Oregon U.S.A. **90** B5 42 13N 120 21W
Lakewood California U.S.A. **95** B2 33 49N 118 08W
Lakewood Ohio U.S.A. **93** D2 41 29N 81 50W
Lakor *i.* Indonesia **44** C2 8 18S 128 09E
Lakota North Dakota U.S.A. **92** A3 48 02N 98 20W
Lak Sao Laos **37** B3 18 12N 104 59E
Laksefjord *fj.* Norway **69** F5 70 40N 26 30E
Lakselv Norway **69** E5 70 03N 24 55E
Lakshadweep *admin.* India **53** C1 9 30N 73 00E
Laliki Indonesia **43** G2 7 41S 126 22E
Lalinda Vanuatu **83** H5 16 20S 168 05E
La Línea de la Concepción Spain **72** A2 36 10N 5 21W
Lalitpur India **53** D4 24 42N 78 24E
Lalona *i.* Tonga **83** B2 20 21S 174 32W
la Louvrière Belgium **70** D2 50 29N 4 12E
La Mancha *admin.* Spain **72** B2 39 10N 2 45W
Lamap *(Port Sandwich)* Vanuatu **83** G5 16 25S 167 48E
Lamar Colorado U.S.A. **90** F4 38 04N 102 37W
Lamari *r.* Papua New Guinea **45** L3 6 45S 145 30E
Lambaréné Gabon **112** H2 0 41S 10 13E
Lambert Glacier Antarctica **21** 73 00S 70 00E
Lambeth *bor.* England United Kingdom **66** C2 51 30N 0 07W
Lamboukouti Vanuatu **83** H5 16 53S 168 34E
Lam Chi *r.* Thailand **39** B3 16 15N 102 40E
Lamdesar Indonesia **44** D3 7 15S 131 57E
Lamego Portugal **72** A3 41 05N 7 49W
Lamen Vanuatu **83** H5 16 37S 168 09E
Lami Fiji **83** C8 18 06S 178 25E
Lamía Greece **74** D2 38 55N 22 26E
Lamitan The Philippines **40** B2 6 39N 122 09E
Lamlam Irian Jaya Indonesia **44** D6 0 05S 130 44E
Lamma Island Hong Kong U.K. **51** B1 22 12N 114 08E
Lammermuir Hills Scotland United Kingdom **68** I7 55 50N 2 45W
Lam Nam Chi *r.* Thailand **39** B2 14 50N 103 20E
Lamon Bay The Philippines **40** B3 14 00N 122 00E
Lamongan Indonesia **42** Q7 7 05S 112 26E
Lampang Thailand **39** A3 18 16N 99 30E
Lam Pao Reservoir Thailand **39** B3 16 40N 103 25E
Lampazos Mexico **96** D5 27 00N 100 30W
Lampedusa *i.* Italy **74** B2 35 00N 12 00E
Lamphun Thailand **39** A3 18 36N 99 02E
Lampung *admin.* Indonesia **42** B2/C2 4 30S 105 00E
Lam San Singapore **41** B4 1 22N 103 43E
Lam Si Bai *r.* Thailand **39** B3 15 30N 104 40E
Lam Tei Hong Kong U.K. **51** A2 22 25N 113 59E
Lamu Kenya **110** H7 2 17S 40 54E
Lanai *i.* Hawaiian Islands **23** Y18 20 50N 156 55W
Lanai City Hawaiian Islands **23** Y18 20 50N 156 56W
Lanao, Lake The Philippines **40** B2 8 00N 124 00E
Lanbi Kyun *i.* Myanmar **38** B2 10 58N 98 10E
Lancang Jiang *r.* China **49** J5 30 00N 98 00E
Lancaster England United Kingdom **68** I6 54 03N 2 48W
Lancaster California U.S.A. **90** C3 34 42N 118 09W
Lancaster New Hampshire U.S.A. **93** F2 44 29N 71 34W
Lancaster Ohio U.S.A. **93** D1 39 43N 82 37W
Lancaster Pennsylvania U.S.A. **93** E2 40 01N 76 19W
Lancaster Sound Northwest Territories Canada **89** R7 74 00N 87 30W
Landau Germany **71** A1 49 12N 8 07E
Landerneau France **73** A2 48 27N 4 16W
Landes *geog. reg.* France **73** A1 44 15N 1 00E
Landfall Island Andaman Islands **38** A2 13 40N 93 00E
Landgraaf Netherlands **70** F2 50 55N 6 02E
Landianchang China **47** F1 39 58N 116 17E
Land's End *c.* England United Kingdom **68** F2 50 03N 5 44W
Landshut Germany **71** B1 48 31N 12 10E
Landskrona Sweden **69** C2 55 53N 12 50E
La Nga *r.* Vietnam **37** C2 11 20N 107 50E
Langdon North Dakota U.S.A. **92** A3 48 46N 98 21W
Langeland *i.* Denmark **71** B2 55 00N 10 00E
Langeoog *i.* Germany **71** A2 53 00N 7 00E
Langer See *l.* Germany **67** G1 52 24N 13 36E
Langjökull *ice cap* Iceland **69** H6 64 45N 20 00W
Langkawi *i.* Myanmar **39** A1 6 25N 99 40E
Langon France **73** A1 44 33N 0 14W
Langøy *i.* Norway **69** C4 68 45N 15 00E
Langres France **73** C2 47 53N 5 20E
Langsa Indonesia **42** A4 4 28N 97 59E
Lang Son Vietnam **37** C4 21 50N 106 45E
Lang Suan Thailand **39** A1 9 55N 99 01E
Langtao Myanmar **38** B5 27 16N 97 39E
Lan Hsü *i.* Taiwan **51** H5 22 04N 121 32E
Lannion France **73** A2 48 44N 3 27W
L'Annonciation Québec Canada **93** F3 46 24N 74 52W
Lanping China **38** B5 26 19N 99 20E
Lansdowne House *tn.* Ontario Canada **89** R3 52 05N 88 00W
L'Anse Michigan U.S.A. **92** C3 46 45N 88 27W
Lansing Michigan U.S.A. **93** D2 42 44N 85 34W
Lantau Channel Hong Kong U.K. **51** A1 22 11N 113 52E
Lantau Island Hong Kong U.K. **51** A1 22 15N 113 56E
Lantau Peak Hong Kong U.K. **51** A1 22 15N 113 55E
Lanzarote *i.* Canary Islands **112** C8 29 00N 13 38W
Lanzhou China **49** K6 36 01N 103 45E
Laoag The Philippines **40** B4 18 14N 120 36E
Laoang The Philippines **40** C3 12 35N 125 02E
Laobie Shan *mts.* China **38** B4 24 00N 99 30E
Lao Cai Vietnam **37** B4 22 30N 103 57E
Laon France **73** B2 49 34N 3 37E
La Oroya Peru **102** B10 11 36S 75 54W
LAOS **37** B3/C2
La Paz Bolivia **102** D9 16 30S 68 10W
La Paz Mexico **96** B4 24 10N 110 17W
La Perouse Australia **79** G2/H2 33 59S 151 14E
La Pesca Mexico **96** E4 23 46N 97 47W
La Plata Argentina **103** F5 34 52S 57 55W
Lappajärvi *l.* Finland **69** E3 63 13N 23 40E
Lappland *geog. reg.* Finland/Sweden **69** E4 67 30N 20 05E
Laprairie Québec Canada **93** F3 45 24N 73 30W
Laptev Sea Arctic Ocean **20** O10 76 00N 125 00E
Laptev Strait Russia **57** Q10 73 00N 141 00E
Lapua Finland **69** E3 62 57N 23 00E
La Puebla Balearic Islands **72** E4 39 46N 3 01E
La Puente California U.S.A. **95** C3 34 01N 117 58W
Lapu-Lapu The Philippines **40** B3 10 18N 123 58E
L'Aquila Italy **74** B3 42 22N 13 24E
Lār Iran **55** H4 27 42N 54 19E
Larache Morocco **112** D10 35 12N 6 10W
Laramie Wyoming U.S.A. **90** E5 41 20N 105 38W
Larantuka Indonesia **43** F2 8 20S 123 00E
Laredo Texas U.S.A. **90** G2 27 32N 99 22W
La Rioja Argentina **103** D7 29 26S 66 50W
Lárisa Greece **74** D2 39 38N 22 25E
Larkana Pakistan **52** B5 27 32N 68 18E
Larnaca Cyprus **54** D5 34 54N 33 29E
Larne Northern Ireland United Kingdom **68** F6 54 51N 5 49W
la Roche New Caledonia **82** X2 21 27S 168 05E
la Roche-en-Ardenne Belgium **70** E2 50 11N 5 35E
la Rochelle France **73** A2 46 10N 1 10W
la Roche-sur-Yon France **73** A2 46 40N 1 25W
La Romana Dominican Republic **97** K3 18 27N 68 57W
Larsen Ice Shelf Antarctica **21** 67 00S 62 00W
La Salle Illinois U.S.A. **92** C2 41 20N 89 06W
Las Cruces New Mexico U.S.A. **90** E3 32 18N 106 47W
Lasem Indonesia **42** P7 6 42S 111 30E
La Serena Chile **103** C7 29 54S 71 18W
la Seyne-sur-Mer France **73** C1 43 06N 5 53E
Lashio Myanmar **38** B4 22 58N 97 48E
Las Marismas *geog. reg.* Spain **72** A2 36 55N 6 00W
Las Palmas Canary Islands **112** B8 28 08N 15 27W
La Spezia Italy **74** A3 44 07N 9 48E
L'Assomption Québec Canada **93** F3 45 48N 73 27W
Last Mountain Lake Saskatchewan Canada **88** N3 51 40N 106 55W
Las Vegas Nevada U.S.A. **90** C4 36 10N 115 10W
Las Vegas New Mexico U.S.A. **90** E4 35 36N 105 15W
Latacunga Ecuador **102** B12 0 58S 78 36W
Late *i.* Tonga **83** B4 18 49S 174 40W
Latina Italy **74** B3 41 28N 12 53E
la Tontouta New Caledonia **82** V1 22 00S 166 15E
La Tuque Québec Canada **93** F3 47 26N 72 47W
Latur India **53** D3 18 24N 76 34E
LATVIA **69** F2
Lau Papua New Guinea **45** O4 5 51S 151 20E
Laucala *i.* Fiji **83** E10 16 46S 179 42W
Lauf Germany **71** B1 49 30N 11 16E
Launceston Australia **78** H1 41 25S 147 07E
Launglon Myanmar **38** B2 13 59N 98 08E
Laurel Mississippi U.S.A. **91** I3 31 41N 89 09W
Lausanne Switzerland **73** C2 46 32N 6 39E
Laut *i.* Indonesia **42** C4 4 40N 107 50E
Laut *i.* Indonesia **42** E3 3 30S 116 20E
Lautem Indonesia **44** B2 8 24S 126 56E
Lautoka Fiji **83** B9 17 36S 177 28E
Lauzon Québec Canada **93** F3 46 49N 71 10W
Laval France **73** A2 48 04N 0 45W
Lavanggu Solomon Islands **82** F2 11 42S 160 15E
La Vega Dominican Republic **97** J3 19 15N 70 33W
Laverton Australia **78** C4 28 49S 122 25E
La Victoria Venezuela **102** D15 10 16N 67 21W
Lawang Indonesia **42** Q7 7 50S 112 40E
Lawksawk Myanmar **38** B4 21 13N 96 50E
Lawndale California U.S.A. **95** A2 33 52N 118 21W
Lawrence Kansas U.S.A. **91** G4 38 58N 95 15W
Lawrence Massachusetts U.S.A. **93** F2 42 41N 71 12W
Lawton Oklahoma U.S.A. **90** G3 34 36N 98 25W
Lay *r.* France **73** A2 46 32N 1 15W
Laylá Saudi Arabia **55** G3 22 16N 46 45E
Laysan *i.* Hawaiian Islands **22** I10 25 46N 171 44W
Lea *r.* England United Kingdom **66** C3 51 40N 0 05W
Leach Cambodia **37** B2 12 18N 103 51E
Leamington Ontario Canada **93** D2 42 03N 82 35W
Lear *i.* Vanuatu **83** G8 13 31S 167 20E
Leatherhead England United Kingdom **66** B2 51 18N 0 20W
Lebak The Philippines **40** B2 6 30N 124 02E
LEBANON **54** O11/P12
Lebanon Missouri U.S.A. **91** H4 37 40N 92 40W
Lebanon New Hampshire U.S.A. **93** F2 43 39N 72 17W
Lebanon Pennsylvania U.S.A. **93** E2 40 21N 76 25W
le Blanc France **73** B2 46 38N 1 04E
le Blanc-Mesnil France **67** B2 48 56N 2 28E
Lebu Chile **103** C5 37 38S 73 43W
Lecce Italy **74** C3 40 21N 18 11E
Lech *r.* Europe **71** B1 48 00N 11 00E
Lechtaler Alpen *mts.* Austria **71** B1 47 00N 10 00E
le Creusot France **73** B2 46 48N 4 27E
Ledong China **37** C3 18 43N 109 09E
Leduc Alberta Canada **88** M3 53 17N 113 30W
Lee *r.* Irish Republic **68** C3 51 50N 8 50W
Leech Lake Minnesota U.S.A. **92** B3 47 00N 94 00W
Leeds England United Kingdom **68** J5 53 50N 1 35W
Leer Germany **71** A2 53 14N 7 27E
Leerdam Netherlands **70** E3 51 53N 5 05E
Leeuwarden Netherlands **70** E5 53 12N 5 48E
Leeuwin, Cape Australia **78** B3 34 24S 115 09E
Leeward Islands Lesser Antilles **97** L3 17 30N 64 00W
Leganés Spain **72** B3 40 20N 3 4WE
Legaspi The Philippines **40** B3 13 10N 123 45E
Legnica Poland **75** C3 51 12N 16 10E
Leh Kashmir **53** D6 34 09N 77 35E
le Havre France **73** B2 49 30N 0 06E
Leicester England United Kingdom **68** J4 52 38N 1 05W
Leichhardt Australia **79** G2 33 53S 151 09E
Leiden Netherlands **70** D4 52 10N 4 30E
Leidschendam Netherlands **70** D4 52 05N 4 24E
Leie *r.* Belgium **70** C2 50 50N 3 20E
Leine *r.* Germany **71** A2 52 00N 10 00E
Leipzig Germany **71** B2 51 20N 12 25E
Leiria Portugal **72** A2 39 45N 8 49W
Leitre Papua New Guinea **45** J5 2 52S 141 42E
Leizhou Bandao *p.* China **49** M3 21 00N 110 00E
Lek *r.* Netherlands **70** D3 51 48N 4 47E
Lekkous *r.* Morocco **72** A1 35 00N 5 40W
Leksula Indonesia **44** B5 3 46S 126 35E
Leli *i.* Solomon Islands **82** G5 8 45S 161 04E
Lelystad Netherlands **70** E4 52 32N 5 29E
le Mans France **73** B2 48 00N 0 12E
Lemgo Germany **71** A2 52 02N 8 54E
Lemmer Netherlands **70** E4 52 50N 5 43E
Lemyethna Myanmar **38** B3 17 36N 95 08E
Lena *r.* Russia **57** O9 70 00N 125 00E
Lengshuijiang China **36** E7 27 40N 111 26E
Leninabad *see* Khojand
Leninakan *see* Kumairi
Leningrad *see* St. Petersburg
Lenino Russia **56** M1 55 35N 37 10E
Leninogorsk Kazakhstan **59** N5 50 23N 83 32E
Leninsk-Kuznetskiy Russia **57** K6 54 44N 86 13E
Lenkoran' Azerbaijan **58** F2 38 45N 48 50E
Lennoxville Québec Canada **93** F3 45 22N 71 51W
Lens France **73** B3 50 26N 2 50E
Lensk Russia **57** N8 60 48N 114 55E
Lenya *r.* Myanmar **38** B2 11 00N 98 55E
Leoben Austria **75** C2 47 23N 15 06E
León Mexico **96** D4 21 10N 101 42W
León Spain **72** A3 42 35N 5 34W
Leon *r.* Texas U.S.A. **91** G3 32 00N 98 00W
Leonard Murray Mountains Papua New Guinea **45** K3 7 00S 143 30E
Leone American Samoa **82** 14 21S 170 47W
Leonora Australia **78** C4 28 54S 121 20E
Lepel' Belarus **75** E3 54 48N 28 40E
le Puy France **73** B2 45 03N 3 53E
le Raincy France **67** C2 48 54N 2 32E
Léré Chad **110** B9 9 41N 14 17E
Lérida *(Lleida)* Spain **72** C3 41 37N 0 38E
Lerwick Scotland United Kingdom **68** J12 60 09N 1 09W
Les Cayes Haiti **97** J3 18 15N 73 46W
Les Coudreaux France **67** C2 48 54N 2 36E
Lesiaceva Point Fiji **83** D10 16 50S 179 17E
Les Îles Belcher *is.* Northwest Territories Canada **89** T4 56 00N 79 30W
Leskovac Serbia Yugoslavia **74** D3 43 00N 21 57E
LESOTHO **111** E2
les Pétroglyphes New Caledonia **82** V2 21 38S 166 01E
les Sables-d'Olonne France **73** A2 46 30N 1 47W
Lesse Belgium **70** E2 50 10N 5 10E
Lesser Antilles *is.* West Indies **97** K2/L3
Lesser Slave Lake Alberta Canada **88** L4 55 25N 115 30W
Lessines Belgium **70** C2 50 43N 3 50E
les Ulis France **67** A1 48 41N 2 11E
Lésvos *i.* Greece **74** E2 39 00N 26 00E
Leszno Poland **75** C3 51 51N 16 35E
Letha Range Myanmar **38** A4 23 30N 93 30E
Lethbridge Alberta Canada **88** M2 49 43N 112 48W
Leti *i.* Indonesia **44** B2 8 10S 127 40E
Leticia Colombia **102** C12 4 09S 69 57W
le Touquet-Paris-Plage France **73** B3 50 13N 1 36E
Letpadan Myanmar **38** B3 17 46N 95 45E
le Tréport France **73** B3 50 04N 1 22E
Letsok-aw Kyun *i.* Myanmar **38** B2 11 30N 98 15E
Leulumoega Western Samoa **82** B11 13 49S 171 53W
Leuven *(Louvain)* Belgium **70** D2 50 53N 4 42E
Levádhia Greece **74** D2 38 26N 22 53E
Lévêque, Cape Australia **78** C6 16 25S 122 55E
Leverkusen Germany **71** A2 51 02N 6 59E
Levice Slovakia **75** C2 48 14N 18 35E
Levin North Island New Zealand **79** C2 40 37S 175 17E
Lévis Québec Canada **93** F3 46 47N 71 12W
Levkás *i.* Greece **74** D2 38 00N 20 00E
Levuka Fiji **83** C9 17 42S 178 50E
Lewe Myanmar **38** B3 19 40N 96 04E
Lewes Delaware U.S.A. **93** E1 38 47N 75 09W
Lewis *i.* Scotland United Kingdom **68** F10 58 15N 6 30W
Lewisburg Pennsylvania U.S.A. **93** E2 40 58N 76 55W
Lewisham *bor.* England United Kingdom **66** C2 51 27N 0 00
Lewis Pass South Island New Zealand **79** B2 42 23S 172 24E
Lewiston Idaho U.S.A. **90** C6 46 25N 117 00W
Lewiston Maine U.S.A. **93** F2 44 08N 70 14W
Lewiston New York U.S.A. **93** E2 43 11N 79 03W
Lewistown Montana U.S.A. **90** E6 47 04N 109 26W
Lewistown Pennsylvania U.S.A. **93** E2 40 37N 77 36W
Lexington Kentucky U.S.A. **93** D1 38 03N 84 30W
Lexington Virginia U.S.A. **93** E1 37 47N 79 27W
Lexington Park Maryland U.S.A. **93** E1 38 15N 76 28W
Leyte *i.* The Philippines **40** B3/C3 11 00N 125 00E
Leyte Gulf The Philippines **40** C3 11 00N 125 00E
Lezhë Albania **74** C3 41 47N 19 39E
Lhasa China **48** H4 29 41N 91 10E
Lhazê China **48** G4 29 08N 87 43E
Lhokseumawe Indonesia **42** A5 5 09N 97 09E
Li Thailand **39** A3 17 48N 98 58E
Lianga The Philippines **40** C2 8 38N 126 05E
Liangwang Shan *mts.* China **38** C5 25 30N 103 20E
Lian Xian China **36** E6 24 48N 112 26E
Lianyungang China **49** N5 34 37N 119 10E
Liaoyang China **49** O7 41 16N 123 12E
Liaoyuan China **49** P7 42 53N 125 10E
Liard *r.* British Columbia/Northwest Territories Canada **88** J4 61 55N 122 30W
Libenge Zaïre **110** C8 3 39N 18 39E
Liberal Kansas U.S.A. **90** F4 37 03N 100 56W
Liberec Czech Republic **75** C3 50 48N 15 05E
LIBERIA **112** C4/D4
Liberty New York U.S.A. **93** F2 41 47N 74 46W
Libourne France **73** A1 44 55N 0 14W
Libreville Gabon **112** G3 0 30N 9 25E
LIBYA **110** B13/D13
Libyan Desert North Africa **110** E12/D13 25 00N 25 00E
Libyan Plateau Egypt **110** E14 31 00N 26 00E
Lichinga Mozambique **111** G5 13 19S 35 13E
Lichtenberg Germany **67** G2 52 32N 13 30E
Lichtenrade Germany **67** F1 52 23N 13 22E
Licking *r.* Kentucky U.S.A. **93** D1 38 00N 84 00W
Lida Belarus **75** E3 53 50N 25 19E
Lidcombe Australia **79** G2 33 52S 151 03E
LIECHTENSTEIN **73** C2
Liège Belgium **70** E2 50 38N 5 35E
Liège *admin.* Belgium **70** E2 50 30N 5 45E
Lienz Austria **75** B2 46 51N 12 50E
Liepāja Latvia **69** E2 56 30N 21 00E
Lier Belgium **70** D3 51 08N 4 35E
Liestal Switzerland **73** C2 47 29N 7 43E
Lifou *i.* New Caledonia **82** W3 21 00S 167 10E
Lifuka *i.* Tonga **83** B3 19 50S 174 22W
Ligao The Philippines **40** B3 13 14N 123 33E
Ligurian Sea Mediterranean Sea **74** A3 44 00N 9 00E
Lihir Group *is.* Papua New Guinea **45** P5 3 10S 152 30E
Lihue Hawaiian Islands **23** X18 21 59N 159 23W
Lijiang China **38** C5 26 51N 100 18E
Likasi Zaïre **111** E5 10 58S 26 47E
Liku Indonesia **32** D4 1 47N 109 19E
Likupang Indonesia **43** G4 1 40N 125 05E
Lille France **73** B3 50 39N 3 05E
Lillehammer Norway **69** C3 61 06N 10 27E
Lilongwe Malawi **111** F5 13 58S 33 49E
Liluah India **52** K2 22 37N 88 20E
Lima Peru **102** B10 12 06S 8 40W
Lima Ohio U.S.A. **93** D2 40 43N 84 06W
Lima *r.* Portugal **72** A3 42 00N 8 30W
Limassol Cyprus **54** D5 34 04N 33 03E
Limburg Germany **71** A2 50 23N 8 04E
Limburg *admin.* Belgium **70** E2 50 55N 5 20E
Limburg *admin.* Netherlands **70** E3 51 32N 5 45E
Lim Chu Kang Singapore **41** B4 1 24N 103 41E
Limeira Brazil **103** H8 22 34S 47 25W
Limerick Irish Republic **68** C4 52 04N 8 38W
Limfjorden *sd.* Denmark **69** B2 57 00N 8 50E
Limnos *i.* Greece **74** E2 39 00N 25 00E
Limoges France **73** B2 45 50N 1 15E
Limón Costa Rica **97** H2 10 00N 83 01W
Limoux France **73** B1 43 03N 2 13E
Limpopo *r.* Southern Africa **111** F3 22 30S 32 00E
Limu *i.* Tonga **83** B2 20 02S 174 29W
Linapacan *i.* The Philippines **40** A3 11 00N 120 00E
Linares Mexico **96** E4 24 54N 99 38W
Linares Spain **72** B2 38 05N 3 38W
Lincang China **38** C4 23 56N 100 16E
Lincoln England United Kingdom **68** K5 53 14N 0 33W
Lincoln Maine U.S.A. **93** G3 45 23N 68 30W
Lincoln Nebraska U.S.A. **92** A2 40 49N 96 41W
Lincoln Wolds *hills* England United Kingdom **68** K5 53 25N 0 05W
Linden Guyana **102** F14 5 59N 58 19W
Linden New Jersey U.S.A. **94** B1 40 37N 74 13W
Lindenberg Germany **67** G2 52 37N 13 31E
Lindfield Australia **79** G2 33 47S 151 10E
Lindis Pass South Island New Zealand **79** A2 44 35S 169 39E
Lindsay Ontario Canada **93** E2 44 21N 78 44W
Line Islands Kiribati **81** D3/E2 0 00 160 00W
Lingao China **37** C3 19 59N 109 41E
Lingayen The Philippines **40** B4 16 02N 120 14E
Lingayen Gulf The Philippines **40** B4 16 00N 120 00E
Lingen Germany **71** A2 52 32N 7 19E
Lingga *i.* Indonesia **42** B3 0 10S 104 40E
Ling Tong Mei Hong Kong U.K. **51** B2 22 29N 114 06E
Linhares Brazil **102** J9 19 22S 40 04W
Linh Cam Vietnam **37** C3 18 31N 105 35E
Linjiang China **50** C5 41 45N 126 56E
Linköping Sweden **69** D2 58 25N 15 35E
Linsell Sweden **69** C3 62 10N 13 50E
Linstead Jamaica **97** Q8 18 08N 77 02W
Linton North Dakota U.S.A. **90** F6 46 17N 100 14W
Linxia China **49** K6 35 31N 103 08E
Linz Austria **75** B2 48 19N 14 18E
Lion Rock *mt.* Hong Kong U.K. **51** C2 22 21N 114 11E
Lioppa Indonesia **44** B3 7 41S 126 01E
Lipa The Philippines **40** B3 13 57N 121 10E
Lipe Solomon Islands **83** M3 10 20S 166 15E
Lipetsk Russia **56** F6 52 37N 39 36E
Lippe *r.* Germany **70** G3 51 00N 7 00E
Lippstadt Germany **71** A2 51 41N 8 20E
Lisas, Point Trinidad and Tobago **96** T9 10 22N 61 37W
Lisboa *(Lisbon)* Portugal **72** A2 38 44N 9 08W
Lisbon Portugal *see* Lisboa
Lisbon North Dakota U.S.A. **92** A3 46 28N 97 30W

Mahalapye Botswana **109** K3 23 05S 26 52E
Mahanadi *r.* India **53** E4 21 00N 84 00E
Maharashtra *admin.* India **53** C3/D3 19 30N 75 00E
Maharepa Tahiti **82** R10 17 28S 149 47W
Maha Sarakham Thailand **39** B3 16 08N 103 21E
Mahaxai Laos **37** C3 17 28N 105 18E
Mahdia Tunisia **74** B2 35 29N 11 03E
Mahia Peninsula North Island New Zealand **79** C3 39 10S 177 53E
Mahina Tahiti **82** T9 17 29S 149 27W
Mahlow Germany **67** F1 52 22N 13 24E
Mahón Balearic Islands **72** F4 39 54N 4 15E
Mahrauli India **52** L4 28 30N 77 11E
Maia American Samoa **82** F12 14 14S 169 25W
Maibang Indonesia **43** F2 8 08S 124 33E
Maidstone England United Kingdom **68** L3 51 17N 0 32E
Maiduguri Nigeria **112** H5 11 53N 13 16E
Maikala Range *mts.* India **53** E4 22 30N 81 30E
Main *r.* Germany **71** A2 50 00N 8 00E
Main Channel Ontario Canada **93** D3 45 00N 82 00W
Maingkwan Myanmar **38** B5 26 20N 96 37E
Mainit, Lake The Philippines **40** C2 9 00N 125 00E
Mainland *i.* Orkney Islands Scotland United Kingdom **68** H11 59 00N 3 15W
Mainland *i.* Shetland Islands Scotland United Kingdom **68** J12 60 15N 1 20W
Maintirano Madagascar **111** H4 18 01S 44 03E
Mainz Germany **71** A1 50 00N 8 16E
Mai Po Lo Wai Hong Kong U.K. **51** B2 22 29N 114 03E
Maiquetía Venezuela **102** D15 10 38N 66 59W
Maiskhal *i.* Bangladesh **38** A4 21 36N 91 53E
Maisons-Lafitte France **67** A2 48 57N 2 09E
Maitland Australia **78** I3 32 33S 151 33E
Maitland Range Malaysia **40** A1-2 5 00N 116 40E
Maitri *r.s.* Antarctica **21** 70 37S 8 22E
Maizuru Japan **46** G2 35 30N 135 20E
Majene Indonesia **42** E3 3 33S 118 59E
Maji Ethiopia **110** G9 6 12N 35 32E
Majiuqiao China **47** H1 39 45N 116 33E
Majorca *see* Mallorca
Majuro Pacific Ocean **80** C4 7 05N 171 08E
Makabe Japan **46** M3 36 15N 140 05E
Makale Indonesia **43** E3 3 06S 119 53E
Makassar Strait *sd.* Indonesia **42** E3 0 00 119 00E
Makaw Myanmar **38** B5 26 28N 96 40E
Makeni Sierra Leone **112** C4 8 57N 12 02W
Makeyevka Ukraine **58** D4 48 01N 38 00E
Makgadikgadi Salt Pan Botswana **111** E3 21 00S 26 00E
Makhachkala Russia **56** G4 42 59N 47 30E
Maki Irian Jaya Indonesia **44** F5 3 18S 134 13E
Makkah *(Mecca)* Saudi Arabia **54** E3 21 26N 39 49E
Makkovik Newfoundland Canada **89** X4 55 09N 59 10W
Makó Hungary **75** D2 46 11N 20 30E
Makodroga *i.* Fiji **83** C9 17 24S 179 01E
Makogai *i.* Fiji **83** C9 17 26S 178 59E
Makoku Gabon **112** H3 0 38N 12 47E
Makran *geog. reg.* Iran/Pakistan **55** J4 25 55N 61 30E
Makung *(Penghu)* Taiwan **51** F6 23 35N 119 33E
Makurdi Nigeria **112** G4 7 44N 8 35E
Malabar Coast India **53** C2/D1 12 00N 74 00E
Malabo Equatorial Guinea **112** G3 3 45N 8 48E
Malacca, Strait of *(Selat Melaka)* Indonesia **42** B4 4 00N 100 00E
Málaga Spain **72** B2 36 43N 4 25W
Malaita Solomon Islands **82** F5/G4 9 00S 161 00E
Malakal Sudan **110** F9 9 31N 31 40E
Malake Fiji **83** C9 17 20S 178 09E
Malakobi *i.* Solomon Islands **82** D6 7 20S 158 00E
Malakula Vanuatu **83** G5 16 20S 167 30E
Malam Papua New Guinea **45** K2 8 45S 142 46E
Malalamai Papua New Guinea **45** M4 5 49S 146 44E
Malang Indonesia **42** Q7 7 59S 112 45E
Malanje Angola **111** C6 9 32S 16 20E
Malao Vanuatu **83** F6 15 10S 166 49E
Mälaren *(Lake Mälar) l.* Sweden **69** D2 59 30N 17 00E
Malartic Québec Canada **93** E3 48 09N 78 09W
Malatya Turkey **54** E6 38 22N 38 18E
Malau Fiji **83** D10 16 24S 179 23E
MALAWI **111** F5
Malawi, Lake *see* Nyasa Lake
Malaya *see* Peninsular Malaysia
Malaybalay The Philippines **40** C2 8 09N 125 07E
MALAYSIA **42** B5-E5
Malbork Poland **75** C3 54 02N 19 01E
Maldegem Belgium **70** C3 51 12N 3 27E
Malden Island Pacific Ocean **81** E3 4 03S 154 59W
MALDIVES **24** G7
Maldonado Uruguay **103** G6 34 57S 54 59W
Malegaon India **53** C4 20 32N 74 38E
Malema Mozambique **111** G5 14 57S 37 25E
Malevangga Solomon Islands **82** B7 6 40S 156 28E
MALI **112** D5/F6
Mali *i.* Fiji **83** D10 16 28S 179 21E
Mali Hka *r.* Myanmar **38** B5 26 00N 97 40E
Mali Kyun *i.* Myanmar **38** B2 13 10N 98 10E
Malili Indonesia **43** F3 2 38S 121 06E
Malima *i.* Fiji **83** E9 17 07S 179 13W
Malindang, Mount The Philippines **40** B2 8 12N 123 40E
Malines *see* Mechelen
Malin Head *c.* Irish Republic **68** D7 55 30N 7 20W
Malipo China **37** B4 23 09N 104 45E
Mallaig Scotland United Kingdom **68** F9 57 00N 5 50W
Mallawi Egypt **54** D4 27 44N 30 50E
Mallorca *(Majorca) i.* Balearic Islands **72** E4 39 50N 2 30E
Malmédy Belgium **70** F2 50 26N 6 02E
Malmesbury Republic of South Africa **111** C1 33 28S 18 43E
Malmö Sweden **69** C2 55 35N 13 00E
Malo Solomon Islands **8** L3 10 40S 165 45E
Malo *i.* Vanuatu **83** G6 15 40S 167 10E
Maloelap Atoll Pacific Ocean **80** C4 8 45N 171 00E
Malolo *i.* Fiji **83** B9 17 45S 177 10E
Malolo Barrier Reef Fiji **83** B9 17 49S 177 09E
Malolos The Philippines **40** B3 14 51N 120 49E
Malom Papua New Guinea **45** O5 3 15S 151 55E
Malone New York U.S.A. **93** F2 44 52N 74 19W
Malonga Zaïre **111** D5 10 26S 23 10E
Måløy Norway **69** B3 61 57N 5 06E
Malpelo *i.* Colombia **102** A13 4 00N 81 35W
MALTA **74** B2
Malta Montana U.S.A. **90** E6 48 22N 107 51W
Malta *i.* Mediterranean Sea **74** B2 35 00N 14 00E
Ma Lui Shui Hong Kong U.K. **51** C2 22 25N 114 12E
Maluku *(Moluccas) admin.* Indonesia **43** G3 2 00S 127 00E
Malu'u Solomon Islands **82** F5 8 20S 160 40E
Malviya Nagar India **52** L4 28 32N 77 12E
Mamanuku-i-cake Group Fiji **83** B9 17 30S 177 05E
Mamaroneck New York U.S.A. **94** D2 40 57N 73 43W
Mamba Japan **46** K3 36 07N 138 54E
Mambasa Zaïre **110** E8 1 20N 29 05E
Mamberamo *r.* Indonesia **33** 2 00S 138 00E
Mamburao The Philippines **40** B3 13 13N 120 39E
Mamié New Caledonia **82** V1 22 02S 166 55E
Mamonovo Russia **58** A5 54 30N 19 59E
Mamuju Indonesia **42** E3 2 41S 118 55E
Man Côte d'Ivoire **112** D4 7 31N 7 37W
Mana *i.* Fiji **83** B9 17 40S 177 09E
Manacapuru Brazil **102** E12 3 16S 60 37W
Manacor Balearic Islands **72** E4 39 35N 3 12E
Manado Indonesia **43** F4 1 32N 124 55E
Managua Nicaragua **97** G2 12 06N 86 18W
Manali India **53** D6 32 12N 77 06E
Manam Island Papua New Guinea **45** L4 4 15S 144 15E
Manatuto Indonesia **44** A2 8 31S 126 00E
Manau Papua New Guinea **45** M2 8 02S 148 00E
Manaus Brazil **102** F12 3 06S 60 00W
Manchester England United Kingdom **68** I5 53 30N 2 15W
Manchester Kentucky U.S.A. **93** D1 37 09N 83 46W
Manchester New Hampshire U.S.A. **93** F2 42 59N 71 28W
Manchester Tennessee U.S.A. **91** I4 35 29N 86 04W
Mandal Norway **69** B2 58 02N 7 30E
Mandalay Myanmar **38** B4 21 57N 96 04E
Mandalay *admin.* Myanmar **38** B4 21 10N 95 30E
Mandaue The Philippines **40** B3 10 21N 123 57E
Mandeville Jamaica **97** Q8 18 02N 77 31W
Mandvi India **52** B4 22 50N 69 25E
Mandya India **53** D2 12 34N 76 55E
Manfredonia Italy **74** C3 41 37N 15 55E
Mangai Papua New Guinea **45** O5 2 49S 151 09E
Mangaia *i.* Pacific Ocean **81** E2 21 56S 157 56W
Mangalore India **53** C2 12 54N 74 51E
Manggar Indonesia **42** C3 2 52S 108 13E
Manggautu Solomon Islands **82** E1 11 38S 159 58E
Manggawitu Irian Jaya Indonesia **44** E4 4 13S 133 30E
Mangin Range Myanmar **38** B4 24 30N 95 50E
Mango *i.* Tonga **83** B2 20 20S 174 53W
Mangoky *r.* Madagascar **111** H3 22 00S 45 00E
Mangui China **49** O9 52 05N 122 17E
Manhasset New York U.S.A. **94** D2 40 48N 73 41W
Manhattan Kansas U.S.A. **92** A1 39 11N 96 35W
Manhattan New York U.S.A. **94** C2 40 48N 73 58W
Manhattan Beach *tn.* California U.S.A. **95** A2 33 53N 118 24W
Mania *r.* Madagascar **111** I4 19 30S 50 30E
Manica Mozambique **111** F4 18 56S 32 52E
Manicoré Brazil **102** E11 5 48S 61 16W
Manicouagan Québec Canada **89** V3 50 40N 68 45W
Manicouagan *r.* Québec Canada **93** G3/4 50 00N 69 00W
Manihiki *i.* Pacific Ocean **81** D3 10 24S 161 01W
Manikpur India **52** J2 22 32N 88 12E
Manila The Philippines **40** B3 14 37N 120 58E
Manila Bay The Philippines **40** B3 14 00N 121 00E
Manipur *admin.* India **53** G4 24 30N 94 00E
Manipur *r.* India/Myanmar **38** A4 23 55N 93 35E
Manisa Turkey **74** E2 38 36N 27 29E
Manistee Michigan U.S.A. **92** C2 44 14N 86 20W
Manistee *r.* Michigan U.S.A. **92** C2 45 00N 85 00W
Manistique Michigan U.S.A. **92** C2 45 58N 86 17W
Manitoba *province* Canada **89** P4 55 15N 100 00W
Manitoba, Lake Manitoba Canada **89** P3 50 30N 98 15W
Manitoulin Island Ontario Canada **93** D3 46 00N 82 00W
Manitowoc Wisconsin U.S.A. **92** C2 44 04N 87 40W
Maniwaki Québec Canada **93** E3 46 22N 75 58W
Manizales Colombia **102** B14 5 03N 75 32W
Manjra *r.* India **53** D3 18 30N 76 00E
Man Kam To Hong Kong U.K. **51** B3 22 32N 114 07E
Mankato Minnesota U.S.A. **92** B2 44 10N 94 00W
Manly Australia **79** H2 33 48S 151 17E
Manna Indonesia **42** B3 4 29S 102 55E
Mannar, Gulf of India/Sri Lanka **53** D1 8 30N 79 00E
Mannheim Germany **71** A1 49 30N 8 28E
Manning Alberta Canada **88** L4 56 53N 117 39W
Manning Strait Solomon Islands **82** C6 7 20S 158 00E
Manokwari Irian Jaya Indonesia **44** F6 0 53S 134 05E
Manono *i.* Western Samoa **82** A11 13 50S 172 06W
Manoron Myanmar **38** B2 11 36N 99 02E
Manotick Ontario Canada **93** E3 45 10N 75 45W
Manpojin North Korea **50** C5 41 06N 126 24E
Manra *(Sydney Island) i.* Pacific Ocean **80** D3 4 30S 171 30W
Manresa Spain **72** C3 41 43N 1 50E
Mansa Zambia **111** E5 11 10S 28 52E
Mansel Island Northwest Territories Canada **89** T5 62 00N 80 00W
Mansfield Ohio U.S.A. **93** D2 40 46N 82 31W
Mansfield Pennsylvania U.S.A. **93** E2 41 47N 77 05W
Manta Ecuador **102** A12 0 59S 80 44W
Mantalingajan, Mount The Philippines **40** A2 8 50N 117 43E
Mantarara Indonesia **44** A6 1 50S 125 03E
Mantes-la-Jolie France **73** B2 48 59N 1 43E
Mantova Italy **74** B4 45 10N 10 47E
Manua Islands American Samoa **82** F12 14 14S 169 28W
Manukau North Island New Zealand **79** B3 37 00S 174 52E
Manukau Harbour North Island New Zealand **79** B3 37 02S 174 43E
Manus Island Papua New Guinea **45** M6 2 00S 147 00E
Manyoni Tanzania **111** F6 5 46S 34 50E
Manzanares Spain **72** B2 39 00N 3 23W
Manzanilla Bay Trinidad and Tobago **96** T9/10 10 40N 61 55W
Manzanilla Point Trinidad and Tobago **96** T10 10 31N 61 01W
Manzanillo Cuba **97** I4 20 21N 77 21W
Manzanillo Mexico **96** D3 19 00N 104 20W
Manzhouli China **49** N8 46 36N 117 28E
Maoming China **49** M3 21 50N 110 56E
Ma On Shan Hong Kong U.K. **51** C2 22 26N 114 13E
Ma On Shan *mt.* Hong Kong U.K. **51** C2 22 24N 114 16E
Maotou Shan *mt.* China **38** C4 24 22N 100 46E
Mapi Irian Jaya Indonesia **44** H3 7 06S 139 23E
Mapi *r.* Irian Jaya Indonesia **44** H3 6 30S 139 35E
Maple Creek *tn.* Saskatchewan Canada **88** N2 49 55N 109 28W
Maprik Papua New Guinea **45** K5 3 38S 143 02E
Maputo Mozambique **111** F2 25 58S 32 35E
Marabá Brazil **102** H11 5 23S 49 10W
Marabo *i.* Fiji **83** F8 18 59S 178 50W
Maracaibo Venezuela **102** C15 10 44N 71 37W
Maracay Venezuela **102** D15 10 20N 67 28W
Maradi Niger **112** G5 13 29N 7 10E
Marais Poitevin *marsh* France **73** A2 46 22N 1 06W
Marakei *i.* Pacific Ocean **80** C4 2 00N 173 25E
Maramasike *(Small Malaita) i.* Solomon Islands **82** G4 9 30S 161 30E
Maramba *(Livingstone)* Zambia **111** E4 17 50S 25 53E
Marang Malaysia **42** B5 5 12N 103 12E
Maranhão *admin.* Brazil **102** H11 5 20S 46 00W
Marapa *i.* Solomon Islands **82** F4 9 50S 160 50E
Marathon Ontario Canada **92** C3 48 44N 86 23W
Maraval Trinidad and Tobago **96** T10 10 42N 61 31W
Maravovo Solomon Islands **82** E4 9 21S 159 37E
Marawi The Philippines **40** B2 7 59N 124 16E
Marbella Spain **72** B2 36 31N 4 53W
Marble Bar *tn.* Australia **78** B5 21 16S 119 45E
Marble Canyon *tn.* Arizona U.S.A. **90** D4 36 50N 111 38W
Marburg Germany **71** A2 50 49N 8 36E
Marche-en-Famenne Belgium **70** E2 50 13N 5 21E
Marchfield Barbados **96** W12 13 07N 59 29W
Marcus Island Pacific Ocean **22** F10 24 30N 157 30E
Mardan Pakistan **53** C6 34 14N 72 05E
Mar del Plata Argentina **103** F5 38 00S 57 32W
Mardin Turkey **54** F6 37 19N 40 43E
Maré *i.* New Caledonia **82** W2/X2 21 30S 168 00E
Margai Caka *l.* China **53** F7 35 00N 87 00E
Margat *r.* The Philippines **40** B4 17 00N 121 00E
Margate England United Kingdom **68** M3 51 24N 1 24E
Margilan Uzbekistan **59** L3 40 30N 71 45E
Maria *i.* Pacific Ocean **81** E2 23 00S 155 00W
Maria Elena Chile **103** D8 22 18S 69 40W
Marianas Trench Pacific Ocean **22** E9 16 00N 147 30E
Mariani India **38** A5 26 39N 94 18E
Marian Lake *tn.* Northwest Territories Canada **88** L5 62 55N 115 55W
Mariánské Lázně Czech Republic **71** B1 49 48N 12 45E
Maria van Diemen, Cape North Island New Zealand **79** B4 34 29S 172 39E
Maribor Slovenia **74** C4 46 34N 15 38E
Marie Byrd Land *geog. reg.* Antarctica **21** 77 00S 130 00W
Mariehamn Finland **69** D3 60 05N 19 55E
Mariental Namibia **111** C3 24 36S 17 59E
Marietta Ohio U.S.A. **93** D1 39 26N 81 27W
Marignane France **73** C1 43 25N 5 12E
Marijampole *(Kapsukas)* Lithuania **69** E1 54 31N 23 20E
Marília Brazil **103** G8 22 13S 49 58W
Marina del Rey California U.S.A. **95** A2 33 58N 118 28W
Marina East Singapore **41** D3 1 17N 103 53E
Marina South Singapore **41** D3 1 17N 103 52E
Marinduque *i.* The Philippines **40** B3 13 20N 122 00E
Marinette Wisconsin U.S.A. **92** C3 45 06N 87 38W
Maringá Brazil **103** G8 23 26S 52 02W
Marion Illinois U.S.A. **92** C1 37 42N 88 58W
Marion Indiana U.S.A. **92** C2 40 33N 85 40W
Marion Ohio U.S.A. **93** D2 40 35N 83 08W
Marion, Lake South Carolina U.S.A. **91** J3 33 00N 80 00W
Mariscal Estigarribia Paraguay **103** E8 22 03S 60 35W
Mariu Indonesia **45** J2 8 40S 140 37E
Mariupol *(Zhdanov)* Ukraine **58** D4 47 05N 37 34E
Mariveles The Philippines **40** B3 14 26N 120 29E
Marjayoun Lebanon **54** O11 33 22N 35 34E
Mark *r.* Belgium **70** D3 51 45N 4 45E
Marka Somalia **110** H8 1 42N 44 47E
Markerwaard Netherlands **70** E4 52 35N 5 15E
Markha *r.* Russia **57** N8 64 00N 12 30E
Markham *r.* Papua New Guinea **45** M3 6 30S 146 15E
Markovo Russia **57** T8 64 40N 170 24E
Marl Germany **71** A2 51 38N 7 06E
Marly-le-Roi France **67** A2 48 52N 2 05E
Marmande France **73** B1 44 30N 0 10E
Marmara, Sea of Turkey **54** C7 15 40N 28 10E
Marne *r.* France **73** B2 49 00N 5 00E
Maroantsetra Madagascar **111** I4 15 23S 49 44E
Maroko Nigeria **109** W3 6 21N 3 32E
Maroni *r.* Surinam **102** G13 4 00N 54 30W
Maros Indonesia **43** E3 4 59S 119 35E
Maroua Cameroon **112** H5 10 35N 14 20E
Maroubra Australia **79** G2/H2 33 57S 151 15E
Marquesas Islands Pacific Ocean **81** E3 10 00S 137 00W
Marquette Michigan U.S.A. **92** C3 46 33N 87 23W
Marrakech Morocco **112** D9 31 49N 8 00W
Marrickville Australia **79** G2 33 55S 151 09E
Marsabit Kenya **110** G8 2 20N 37 59E
Marsala Italy **74** B2 37 48N 12 27E
Marseille France **73** C1 43 18N 5 22E
Marshall Missouri U.S.A. **92** B1 39 06N 93 11W
MARSHALL ISLANDS **80** C4
Marshalltown Iowa U.S.A. **92** B2 42 05N 92 54W
Marshfield Wisconsin U.S.A. **92** B2 44 40N 90 11W
Marsh Harbour The Bahamas **91** K2 26 31N 77 05W
Martaban Myanmar **38** B3 16 32N 97 35E
Martaban, Gulf of Myanmar **38** B3 16 15N 96 40E
Martapura Indonesia **42** D3 3 31S 114 45E
Martha's Vineyard *i.* Massachusetts U.S.A. **93** F2 41 00N 70 00W
Martigny Switzerland **73** C2 46 07N 7 05E
Martigues France **73** C1 43 24N 5 03E
Martinique *i.* Lesser Antilles **97** L2 14 30N 61 00W
Martin Lake Alabama U.S.A. **91** I3 33 00N 86 00W
Martinsburg West Virginia U.S.A. **93** E1 39 28N 77 59W
Martinsville Indiana U.S.A. **92** C1 39 25N 86 25W
Martinsville Virginia U.S.A. **91** K4 36 43N 79 53W
Martin Vaz *i.* Atlantic Ocean **25** F4 21 00S 27 30W
Marton North Island New Zealand **79** C2 40 05S 175 23E
Marum, Mount Vanuatu **83** H5 16 15S 168 08E
Marunga Papua New Guinea **45** P4 4 58S 152 13E
Marutea *i.* Pacific Ocean **81** E3 17 00S 143 10W
Marvejols France **73** B1 44 33N 3 18E
Marwitz Germany **67** E2 52 44N 13 08E
Mary Turkmenistan **59** J2 37 42N 61 54E
Maryborough Australia **78** I4 25 32S 152 36E
Maryland *state* U.S.A. **93** E1 39 00N 77 00W
Marysville California U.S.A. **90** B4 39 10N 121 34W
Marysville Ohio U.S.A. **93** D2 40 13N 83 22W
Masada *see* Mezada
Masamasa *i.* Solomon Islands **82** B7 6 50S 156 10E
Masan South Korea **50** D2 35 10N 128 35E
Masapun Indonesia **44** B3 7 46S 126 39E
Masaya Nicaragua **97** G2 11 59N 86 03W
Masbate The Philippines **40** B3 12 21N 123 36E
Mascara Algeria **72** C2 35 20N 0 09E
Mascarene Basin Indian Ocean **24** E5 15 00S 55 00E
Mascot Australia **79** G2 33 56S 151 12E
Masela *i.* Indonesia **44** C2 8 07S 129 51E
Maseru Lesotho **111** E2 29 19S 27 29E
Mashhad Iran **55** I6 36 16N 59 34E
Masin Irian Jaya Indonesia **44** H3 6 09S 139 25E
Masindi Uganda **110** F8 1 41N 31 45E
Masirah *i.* Oman **55** I3 20 25N 58 40E
Mason City Iowa U.S.A. **92** B2 43 10N 93 10W
Masqat Oman **55** I3 23 37N 58 38E
Massachusetts *state* U.S.A. **93** F2 42 00N 72 00W
Massachusetts Bay U.S.A. **93** F2 42 00N 70 00W
Masseik Belgium **70** E3 51 08N 5 48E
Massena New York U.S.A. **93** F2 44 56N 74 57W
Massey Ontario Canada **93** D3 46 13N 82 06W
Massif Central *mts.* France **73** B1/2 45 00N 3 30E
Massif de la Vanoise *mts.* France **73** C2 45 20N 6 20E
Massif de L'Isola *mts.* Madagascar **111** H3/I3 23 00S 45 00E
Massif de l'Ouarsenis *mts.* Algeria **72** C2 36 00N 2 00E
Massif des Bongos *mts.* Central African Republic **110** D9 9 00N 23 00E
Massif des Ecrins *mts.* France **73** C1 45 00N 6 00E
Massif de Tsaratanana *mts.* Madagascar **111** I5 14 00S 49 00E
Massy France **67** B1 48 44N 2 17E
Masterton North Island New Zealand **79** C2 40 57S 175 39E
Masuda Japan **46** B1 34 42N 131 51E
Masuku Gabon **112** H2 1 40S 13 31E
Masvingo Zimbabwe **111** F3 20 05S 30 50E
Matacawa Levu *i.* Fiji **83** B10 16 59S 177 20E
Matachel *r.* Spain **72** A2 38 40N 6 00W
Matadi Zaïre **111** B6 5 50S 13 32E
Matagalpa Nicaragua **97** G2 12 52N 85 58W
Matagami Québec Canada **93** E3 49 45N 77 45W
Mataiéa Tahiti **82** T8 17 47S 149 24W
Matamoros Mexico **96** D5 25 33N 103 51W
Matamoros Mexico **96** E5 25 50N 97 31W
Matane Québec Canada **93** F3 48 50N 67 31W
Matanzas Cuba **97** H4 23 04N 81 35W
Mataram Indonesia **42** E2 8 36S 116 07E
Mataró Spain **72** C3 41 32N 2 27E
Mataura South Island New Zealand **79** A1 46 12S 168 52E
Mataura *r.* South Island New Zealand **79** A1 45 45S 168 50E
Matautu Western Samoa **82** B11 13 57S 171 55W
Matehuala Mexico **96** D4 23 40N 100 40W
Matelot Trinidad and Tobago **96** T10 10 49N 61 07W
Matera Italy **74** C3 40 40N 16 37E
Mateur Tunisia **74** A2 37 03N 9 40E
Mathura India **53** D5 27 30N 77 42E
Mati The Philippines **40** C2 6 59N 126 12E
Mato Grosso *admin.* Brazil **102** F10 14 00S 56 00W
Mato Grosso *tn.* Brazil **102** F9 15 05S 59 57W
Mato Grosso do Sul *admin.* Brazil **102** F8/9 20 00S 55 00W
Matong Papua New Guinea **45** O4 5 35S 151 46E
Matopo Hills Zimbabwe **111** E3 21 00S 28 30E
Matosinhos Portugal **72** A3 41 08N 8 45W
Maṭraḥ Oman **55** I3 23 31N 58 18E
Matsudo Japan **47** C4 35 46N 139 54E
Matsue Japan **46** B2 35 29N 133 04E
Matsumoto Japan **46** C2 36 18N 137 58E
Matsusaka Japan **46** H1 34 33N 136 31E
Matsuyama Japan **46** B1 33 50N 132 47E
Mattagami River Ontario Canada **93** D3 50 00N 82 00W
Mattawa Ontario Canada **93** E3 46 19N 78 42W
Matterhorn *mt.* Switzerland **73** C2 45 59N 7 39E
Mattice Ontario Canada **93** D3 49 36N 83 16W
Mattoon Illinois U.S.A. **92** C1 39 29N 88 21W
Matu Solomon Islands **82** L3 10 40S 166 00E
Matua Indonesia **42** D3 3 30S 111 00E
Matuku *i.* Fiji **83** D7 19 11S 179 45E
Matura Trinidad and Tobago **96** T10 10 40N 61 04W
Matura Bay Trinidad and Tobago **96** T10 10 40N 61 04W
Maturin Venezuela **102** E14 9 45N 63 10W
Matveyevskoye Russia **56** L1 55 42N 37 30E
Maubara Indonesia **43** G2 8 39S 125 19E
Maubeuge France **73** B3 50 17N 3 58E
Ma-ubin Myanmar **38** B3 16 44N 95 37E
Maués Brazil **102** F12 3 22S 57 38W
Maui *i.* Hawaiian Islands **23** Y18 21 00N 156 30W
Maulvi Bazar Bangladesh **38** A4 24 30N 91 48E
Maumere Indonesia **43** F2 8 35S 122 13E
Mauna Kea *mt.* Hawaiian Islands **23** Z17 19 50N 155 25W
Mauna Loa *vol.* Hawaiian Islands **23** Z17 19 28N 155 35W
Mauriche National Park Québec Canada **93** F3 46 30N 74 00W
MAURITANIA **112** C6/D7
MAURITIUS **24** E4
Ma Wan *i.* Hong Kong U.K. **51** B2 22 21N 114 03E
Ma Wan Chung Hong Kong U.K. **51** A1 22 17N 113 56E
Mawchi Myanmar **38** B3 19 00N 96 30E
Mawlaik Myanmar **38** A4 23 40N 94 26E
Mawson *r.s.* Antarctica **21** 67 36S 62 52E
Maya *i.* Indonesia **42** C3 0 50S 109 40E
Mayaguana *i.* The Bahamas **97** J4 22 30N 72 40W
Mayagüez Puerto Rico **97** K3 18 13N 67 09W
Mayaro Bay Trinidad and Tobago **96** U9 10 07N 61 00W
Mayen Germany **70** G2 50 19N 7 14E
Mayenne France **73** A2 48 18N 0 37W
Mayenne *r.* France **73** A2 47 45N 0 50W
Maykop Russia **56** G4 44 37N 40 48E
Maymyo Myanmar **38** B4 22 05N 96 33E
Mayo Yukon Territory Canada **88** H5 63 34N 135 52W
Mayo *i.* Indonesia **42** E2 8 00S 117 30E
Mayon *mt.* The Philippines **40** B3 13 15N 123 42E
Mayotte *i.* Indian Ocean **111** I5 13 00S 45 00E
May Pen Jamaica **97** Q7 17 58N 77 15W
Mayraira Point The Philippines **40** B4 18 37N 120 50E
Maysville Kentucky U.S.A. **93** D1 38 38N 83 46W
Mayu *r.* Myanmar **38** A4 20 45N 92 40E
Mayumba Gabon **112** H2 3 23S 10 38E
Mayville North Dakota U.S.A. **92** A3 47 30N 97 20W
Mazabuka Zambia **111** E4 15 50S 27 47E
Mazamet France **73** B1 43 29N 2 22E
Mazār-e Sharīf Afghanistan **55** K6 36 42N 67 06E
Mazatenango Guatemala **96** F2 14 31N 91 30W
Mazatlán Mexico **96** C4 23 11N 106 25W

Montmirail France 73 B2 48 52N 3 34E
Montmorency France 67 B2 48 59N 2 19E
Montmorillon France 73 B2 46 26N 0 52E
Monto Australia 78 I5 24 53S 151 06E
Montpelier Vermont U.S.A. 93 F2 44 16N 72 34W
Montpellier France 73 B1 43 36N 3 53E
Montréal Québec Canada 93 F3 45 32N 73 36W
Montreux Switzerland 73 C2 46 27N 6 55E
Montrose Colorado U.S.A. 90 E4 38 29N 107 53W
Montrouge France 67 B2 48 49N 2 19E
Monts d'Ambaza mts. France 73 B2 46 00N 1 30E
Monts d'Arrés mts. France 73 A2 48 20N 3 50W
Monts d'Auvergne mts. France 73 B2 45 30N 2 50E
Monts de Tébessa mts. Algeria/Tunisia 74 A2 35 00N 8 00E
Monts du Cantal mts. France 73 B2 45 04N 2 45E
Montserrat i. Lesser Antilles 97 L3 16 45N 62 14W
Monts Nimba mts. Guinea/Liberia 112 D4 7 39N 8 30W
Monts Otish mts. Québec Canada 89 U3 52 30N 70 20W
Monywa Myanmar 38 B4 22 05N 95 12E
Monza Italy 74 A4 45 35N 9 16E
Moora Australia 78 B3 30 40S 116 01E
Mooréa i. Pacific Ocean 81 E3 17 30S 149 50W
Mooréa i. Tahiti 82 R9 17 30S 149 50W
Moore, Lake Australia 78 B4 30 00S 117 30E
Moorhead Minnesota U.S.A. 92 A3 46 51N 96 44W
Moosehead Lake Minnesota U.S.A. 93 G3 46 51N 96 44W
Moose Hill tn. Ontario Canada 92 C3 48 14N 89 26W
Moose Jaw Saskatchewan Canada 88 N3 50 23N 105 35W
Mooselook-megantic Lake Maine U.S.A. 93 F2 45 00N 70 00W
Moose River Ontario Canada 93 D4 51 00N 81 00W
Moose River tn. Ontario Canada 93 D4 50 48N 81 18W
Moosonee Ontario Canada 93 D4 51 18N 80 39W
Mopti Mali 112 E5 14 29N 4 10W
Mora Sweden 69 C3 61 00N 14 30E
Moradabad India 53 D5 28 50N 78 45E
Morant Bay tn. Jamaica 97 R7 17 53N 76 25W
Morant Point Jamaica 97 R7 17 55N 76 12W
Morava r. Europe 75 C2 48 00N 17 00E
Moray Firth est. Scotland United Kingdom 68 H9 57 45N 3 45W
Morcenx France 73 A1 44 02N 0 55W
Morden Manitoba Canada 92 A3 49 12N 98 05W
Moreau r. South Dakota U.S.A. 90 F6 45 00N 102 00W
Moree Australia 78 H4 29 29S 149 53E
Morehead Papua New Guinea 45 J2 8 40S 141 36E
Morehead Kentucky U.S.A. 93 D1 38 11N 83 27W
Morelia Mexico 96 D3 19 40N 101 11W
Morenci Arizona U.S.A. 90 E3 33 05N 109 22W
Moresby Island British Columbia Canada 88 I3 52 30N 131 50W
Mörfelden Walldorf Germany 71 A1 49 58N 8 35E
Morgantown West Virginia U.S.A. 93 E1 39 38N 79 57W
Mori Japan 46 D3 42 07N 140 33E
Morioka Japan 46 D2 39 43N 141 08E
Moriyama Japan 46 G2 35 05N 135 59E
Morlaix France 73 A2 48 35N 3 50W
Morobe Papua New Guinea 45 M3 7 45S 147 37E
MOROCCO 112 D9/E9
Morogoro Tanzania 111 G6 6 49S 37 40E
Moro Gulf The Philippines 40 B2 7 00N 123 00E
Morón Cuba 97 I4 22 08N 78 39W
Morondava Madagascar 111 H3 20 19S 44 17E
Moroni Comoros 111 H5 11 40S 43 16E
Moroto Uganda 110 F8 2 32N 34 41E
Morozaki Japan 46 H1 34 41N 136 58E
Morrinsville North Island New Zealand 79 C3 37 39S 175 32E
Morris Manitoba Canada 92 A3 49 22N 97 21W
Morris Jesup, Cape Greenland 20 83 20N 33 00W
Morris Reservoir California U.S.A. 95 C3 33 11N 117 53W
Moruga Trinidad and Tobago 96 T9 10 06N 61 17W
Moruga r. Trinidad and Tobago 96 T9 10 06N 61 15W
Morvan mts. France 73 B2 47 10N 4 00E
Moscos Islands Myanmar 38 B2 14 10N 97 48E
Moscow Russia see Moskva
Moscow Idaho U.S.A. 90 C6 46 44N 117 00W
Mosel r. Germany 71 A2 50 00N 7 00E
Moselle admin. France 70 F1 49 15N 6 15E
Moselle r. France 73 C2 48 30N 6 00E
Moses Lake tn. Washington U.S.A. 90 C6 47 09N 119 20W
Mosgiel South Island New Zealand 79 B1 45 53S 170 21E
Moshi Tanzania 110 G7 3 21S 37 19E
Mosjøen Norway 69 C4 65 50N 13 10E
Moskva r. Russia 56 M1 55 36N 37 45E
Moskva (Moscow) Russia 56 F7 55 45N 37 42E
Mosman Australia 79 G2 33 50S 151 14E
Moso i. Vanuatu 83 H4 17 34S 168 13E
Moss Norway 69 C2 59 26N 10 41E
Mossoró Brazil 102 J11 5 10S 37 18W
Most Czech Republic 75 B3 50 31N 13 39E
Mostaganem Algeria 112 F10 35 45N 0 05E
Mostar Bosnia-Herzegovina 74 C3 43 20N 17 50E
Móstoles Spain 72 B3 40 19N 3 53W
Mosul Iraq 54 F6 36 21N 43 08E
Mosŭlp'o South Korea 50 C1 33 20N 126 17E
Mota i. Vanuatu 83 G8 13 49S 167 40E
Motherwell Scotland United Kingdom 68 G7 55 48N 3 59W
Motril Spain 72 B2 36 45N 3 31W
Motueka South Island New Zealand 79 B2 41 07S 173 01E
Moturiki i. Fiji 83 C9 17 46S 178 45E
Mouding China 38 C5 25 19N 101 37E
Mouila Gabon 112 H2 1 50S 11 02E
Mouleingyun Myanmar 38 B3 16 25N 95 16E
Moulins France 73 B2 47 00N 3 48E
Moulmein Myanmar 38 B3 16 30N 97 39E
Moundou Chad 110 C9 8 35N 16 01E
Mo'unga'one i. Tonga 83 B3 19 44S 174 30W
Moung Roesser Cambodia 37 B2 13 30N 103 00E
Mountain Village Alaska U.S.A. 88 C5 62 09N 163 49W
Mount Darwin tn. Zimbabwe 111 F4 16 45S 31 39E
Mount Gambier tn. Australia 78 G2 37 51S 140 50E
Mount Hagen tn. Papua New Guinea 45 L4 5 54S 114 13E
Mount Isa tn. Australia 78 F5 20 50S 139 29E
Mount Magnet tn. Australia 78 B4 28 06S 117 50E
Mount Morgan tn. Australia 78 I5 23 40S 150 25E
Mount Pleasant tn. Michigan U.S.A. 92 D2 43 36N 84 46W
Mount Vernon tn. Illinois U.S.A. 92 C1 38 19N 88 52W
Mount Vernon tn. New York U.S.A. 94 B2 40 45N 73 49W
Mount Whitney National Park California U.S.A. 90 C4 36 30N 118 30W
Mourne Mountains Northern Ireland United Kingdom 68 E6 54 05N 6 05W
Mouscron Belgium 70 C2 50 44N 3 14E
Moutong Indonesia 43 F4 0 30N 121 15E
Moy r. Irish Republic 68 C5 53 55N 8 55W
Moyale Kenya 110 G8 3 31N 39 04E
Moyingyi Reservoir Myanmar 38 B3 17 35N 96 35E
Moyobamba Peru 102 B11 6 04S 76 56W
MOZAMBIQUE 111 F3/G5
Mozambique Basin Indian Ocean 24 C3 35 00S 40 00E
Mozambique Channel Mozambique/Madagascar 111 H4 18 00S 42 00E
Mozyr' Belarus 75 E3 52 02N 29 10E
Mpanda Tanzania 111 F6 6 21S 31 01E
Mtwara Tanzania 111 H5 10 17S 40 11E
Mu New Caledonia 82 W2 21 05S 167 25E
Mu'a Tonga 83 D1 21 11S 175 07W
Muang Cambodia 37 B2 13 46N 103 33E
Muang Et Laos 37 B4 20 47N 104 02E
Muang Ham Laos 37 B4 20 19N 104 01E
Muang Hat Hin Laos 37 B4 22 05N 102 13E
Muang Hun Xieng Hung Laos 37 B4 21 37N 102 20E
Muang Kasi Laos 37 B3 19 15N 102 17E
Muang Khoa Laos 37 B4 19 38N 103 32E
Muang Ngoi Laos 37 B4 20 43N 102 42E
Muang Gnommarat Laos 37 C3 17 33N 105 13E
Muang Ou Tai Laos 37 B4 22 06N 101 46E
Muang Pa Laos 37 B3 18 32N 101 36E
Muang Paklay Laos 37 B3 18 16N 101 26E
Muang Phalan Laos 37 C3 16 39N 105 36E
Muang Phin Laos 37 C3 16 32N 106 05E
Muang Sing Laos 37 B4 21 10N 101 06E
Muang Souy Laos 37 B3 19 32N 102 54E
Muang Thadua Laos 37 B3 19 24N 101 49E
Muang Xai Laos 37 B4 20 46N 102 03E
Muang Xon Laos 37 B4 20 29N 103 28E
Muar Malaysia 42 B4 2 02N 102 33E
Muarabadak Indonesia 42 E3 0 20S 117 30E
Muarabeliti Indonesia 42 B3 3 17S 103 02E
Muarabungo Indonesia 42 B3 1 28S 102 06E
Muaraenim Indonesia 42 B3 3 40S 103 48E
Muarajuloi Indonesia 42 D3 0 30S 114 00E
Muarakaman Indonesia 42 E3 0 20S 116 00E
Muaralakitan Indonesia 42 B3 2 46S 103 22E
Muarasipongi Indonesia 42 A4 0 30N 99 50E
Muaratembesi Indonesia 42 B3 1 40S 103 08E
Muarateweh Indonesia 42 D3 0 58S 114 52E
Muchinga Mountains Zambia 111 F5 12 30S 32 30E
Muda r. Malaysia 39 B1 5 57N 100 40E
Mudanjiang China 49 P7 44 36N 129 42E
Mudon Myanmar 38 B3 16 17N 97 40E
Mufulira Zambia 111 E5 12 30S 28 12E
Mugang China 37 C4 23 27N 105 19E
Müggelheim Germany 67 G1 52 24N 13 40E
Mu Gia Pass Laos/Vietnam 37 C3 17 30N 106 00E
Muğla Turkey 54 C6 37 13N 28 22E
Mugutira Irian Jaya Indonesia 44 E5 2 12S 133 00E
Muhammad Qol Sudan 54 E3 20 53N 37 09E
Mühlhausen Germany 71 B2 51 13N 10 28E
Mui Bai Bung c. Vietnam 37 B1 8 30N 104 45E
Mui Ke Ga c. Vietnam 37 C2 10 40N 108 02E
Mui Nam Tram c. Vietnam 37 C3 15 30N 108 50E
Mui Ron Ma c. Vietnam 37 C3 18 07N 106 27E
Mui Wo Hong Kong U.K. 51 A1 22 16N 113 59E
Mui Yen c. Vietnam 37 C2 13 43N 109 13E
Mukdahan Thailand 39 B3 16 31N 104 43E
Mukomuko Indonesia 42 B3 2 35S 101 07E
Mulde r. Germany 71 B2 51 00N 12 00E
Mulegé Mexico 96 B5 26 54N 112 00W
Mulgrave Nova Scotia Canada 89 W2 45 36N 61 25W
Mulhacén mt. Spain 72 B2 37 04N 3 19W
Mülheim an der Ruhr Germany 70 F3 51 25N 6 50E
Mulhouse France 73 C2 47 45N 7 21E
Muli China 38 C5 27 59N 101 21E
Mull i. Scotland United Kingdom 68 F8 56 25N 6 00W
Mullingar Irish Republic 68 D5 53 32N 7 20W
Mull of Galloway c. Scotland United Kingdom 68 G6 54 38N 4 50W
Mull of Kintyre c. Scotland United Kingdom 68 F7 55 17N 5 55W
Multan Pakistan 53 C6 30 10N 71 36E
Mumeng Papua New Guinea 45 M3 6 57S 146 34E
Mumuni Papua New Guinea 45 K2 8 00S 142 38E
München (Munich) Germany 71 B1 48 08N 11 35E
Muncie Indiana U.S.A. 92 C2 40 11N 85 22W
Munda Solomon Islands 82 C5 8 18S 157 15E
Münden Germany 71 A2 51 25N 9 39E
Mundo r. Spain 72 B2 38 30N 2 00W
Mungbere Zaïre 110 E8 2 40N 28 25E
Munger India 53 F5 25 24N 86 29E
Munia i. Fiji 83 F9 17 23S 178 51W
Munich see München
Municipal Colony India 52 L4 28 42N 77 12E
Munsan South Korea 50 C3 37 56N 126 42E
Münster Germany 71 A2 51 58N 7 37E
Muntinlupa The Philippines 40 B3 14 25N 121 02E
Muntok Indonesia 42 C3 2 04S 105 12E
Muojärvi l. Finland 69 F4 65 52N 29 30E
Muong Man Vietnam 37 C2 10 59N 108 02E
Muong Te Vietnam 37 B4 22 28N 102 38E
Muonio älv r. Finland/Sweden 69 E4 68 20N 22 00E
Muqdisho (Mogadishu) Somalia 110 I8 2 02N 45 21E
Murai Reservoir Singapore 41 B4 1 24N 103 41E
Muraroa Atoll Pacific Ocean 81 F2 23 00S 140 00W
Murat r. Turkey 54 F6 38 50N 40 20E
Murchison r. Australia 78 B4 26 00S 117 00E
Murcia Spain 72 B2 37 59N 1 08W
Mureș r. Romania 75 D2 46 00N 22 00E
Murfreesboro Tennessee U.S.A. 91 I4 35 50N 86 25W
Murgab r. Asia 59 J2 37 00N 62 30E
Murilo i. Micronesia 80 B4 9 00N 154 00E
Müritz l. Germany 71 B2 53 00N 12 00E
Murmansk Russia 56 F9 68 59N 33 08E
Murom Russia 56 G7 55 34N 42 04E
Muroran Japan 46 D3 42 21N 140 59E
Muroto Japan 46 B1 33 13N 134 11E
Muroto-zaki c. Japan 46 B1 33 13N 134 11E
Murray r. Australia 78 G3 34 00S 142 00E
Murray Bridge Australia 78 F2 35 10S 139 17E
Murray Hill Christmas Island 81 P2 10 28S 105 35E
Murray, Lake Papua New Guinea 45 J3 7 25S 141 15E
Murray Seascarp Pacific Ocean 23 M11 32 00N 138 00W
Murrumbidgee r. Australia 78 H3 34 30S 146 30E
Murwara India 53 E4 23 49N 80 28E
Murzuq Libya 110 B13 25 55N 13 55E
Muş Turkey 54 F6 38 45N 41 30E
Musa r. Papua New Guinea 45 N2 9 30S 148 30E
Musala i. Indonesia 42 A4 1 30N 98 30E
Musan North Korea 50 D6 42 12N 129 15E
Musashino Japan 47 B3 35 43N 139 35E
Musgrave Ranges Australia 78 E4 26 00S 132 00E
Mushin Nigeria 109 V3 6 33N 3 25E
Musin Nigeria 112 F4 6 30N 3 15E
Muskegon Michigan U.S.A. 92 C2 43 13N 86 15W
Muskegon r. Michigan U.S.A. 92 C2 43 00N 86 00W
Muskogee Oklahoma U.S.A. 91 G4 35 35N 95 21W
Musquiz Mexico 90 F2 27 50N 101 00W
Mussau Island Papua New Guinea 45 N6 1 30S 149 30E
Musselshell r. Montana U.S.A. 90 E6 47 00N 108 00W
Mustafa Kemalpaşa Turkey 74 E2 40 03N 28 52E
Mutarara Mozambique 111 G4 17 30S 35 06E
Mutare Zimbabwe 111 F4 18 58N 32 40E
Mutkyi Myanmar 38 B3 16 35N 97 30E
Mutsu Japan 46 D3 41 18N 141 15E
Mutsu-wan b. Japan 46 D3 41 05N 140 40E
Muyun Kum d. Kazakhstan 59 L3 44 00N 70 00E
Muzaffarnagar India 53 D5 29 28N 77 42E
Muzaffarpur India 53 F5 26 07N 85 23E
Mwanza Tanzania 110 F7 2 31S 32 56E
Mweru, Lake (Lac Moero) Zaïre/Zambia 111 E6 8 30S 28 30E
Myabandar Andaman Islands 38 A2 12 52N 92 49E
Myanaung Myanmar 38 B3 18 17N 95 19E
MYANMAR (BURMA) 38
Myaungmya Myanmar 38 A3 16 33N 94 55E
Myawadi Myanmar 38 B3 16 42N 98 30E
Myingyan Myanmar 38 B4 21 25N 95 20E
Myitkyina Myanmar 38 B5 25 24N 97 25E
Myitmaka r. Myanmar 38 B3 16 00N 95 10E
Myittha Myanmar 38 B4 21 21N 96 06E
Myittha r. Myanmar 38 A4 22 00N 94 05E
Mymensingh Bangladesh 53 G4 24 45N 90 23E
Myohaung Myanmar 38 A4 20 35N 93 12E
Myotha Myanmar 38 B4 21 43N 95 44E
Mýrdalsjökull ice cap Iceland 69 I6 63 40N 19 00W
Mys Chelyuskin c. Russia 57 M11 77 44N 103 55E
Mys Kanin Nos c. Russia 56 G9 68 38N 43 20E
Mys Navarin c. Russia 57 T8 62 17N 179 13E
Mys Olyutorskiy c. Russia 57 T7 59 58N 170 25E
Mysore India 53 D2 12 18N 76 37E
Mys Tolstoy c. Russia 57 R7 59 00N 155 00E
My Tho Vietnam 37 C2 10 21N 106 21E
Mytinge r. Myanmar 38 B4 22 15N 97 00E
Mytishchi Russia 58 D6 55 54N 37 47E
Mže r. Czech Republic 71 B1 49 00N 13 00E
Mzuzu Malawi 111 F5 11 31S 34 00E

N

9 de Julio (Nueve de Julio) tn. Argentina 103 E5 35 28S 60 58W
Naaldwijk Netherlands 70 D3 52 00N 4 10E
Naas Irish Republic 68 E5 53 13N 6 39W
Nabari Japan 46 H1 34 37N 136 05E
Nabavatu Fiji 83 C10 16 35S 178 56E
Naberezhnyye Chelny (Brezhnev) Russia 56 H7 55 42N 52 19E
Nabeul Tunisia 74 B2 36 30N 10 44E
Nabire Irian Jaya Indonesia 44 F5 3 23S 135 31E
Nablus Jordan 54 O11 32 13N 35 16E
Naboutini Fiji 83 B8 18 16S 177 50E
Nabouwalu Fiji 83 C10 17 00S 178 43E
Nabq Egypt 54 O9 28 04N 34 26E
Nacogdoches Texas U.S.A. 91 H3 31 36N 94 40W
Nacula i. Fiji 83 B10 16 55S 177 25E
Nadarivatu Fiji 83 B9 17 32S 177 58E
Nadi Fiji 83 B9 17 47S 177 29E
Nadiad India 53 C4 22 42N 72 55E
Nadi Bay Fiji 83 B9 17 45S 177 23E
Nador Morocco 112 E10 35 10N 3 00W
Naduri Fiji 83 D10 16 26S 179 08E
Nadym Russia 57 J9 65 25N 72 40E
Naestved Denmark 69 C2 55 14N 11 47E
Naga The Philippines 40 B3 13 36N 123 12E
Nagahama Japan 46 H2 35 25N 136 16E
Naga Hills India 53 G5/H5 26 00N 95 00E
Nagai Japan 47 B1 35 11N 139 37E
Nagaland admin. India 53 G5 26 00N 94 30E
Nagano Japan 46 C2 36 39N 138 10E
Nagaoka Japan 46 C2 37 27N 138 50E
Nagasaki Japan 46 A1 32 45N 129 52E
Nagato Japan 46 B1 34 22N 131 11E
Nagatsuda Japan 47 B3 35 31N 139 30E
Nagercoil India 53 D1 8 11N 77 30E
Nagornyy Russia 57 O7 55 57N 124 54E
Nagoya Japan 46 H2 35 08N 136 53E
Nagpur India 53 D4 21 10N 79 12E
Nagqu China 53 G6 31 30N 91 57E
Nagykanizsa Hungary 75 C2 46 27N 17 00E
Nahanni Butte Northwest Territories Canada 88 K5 61 30N 123 20W
Nahanni National Park Northwest Territories Canada 88 K5 61 30N 123 00W
Nahariya Israel 54 O11 33 01N 35 05E
Nahe r. Germany 71 A1 49 00N 7 00E
Naidi Fiji 83 D10 16 49S 179 21E
Naigani i. Fiji 83 C9 17 36S 178 40E
Naihāti India 52 K3 22 53N 88 27E
Nailaga Fiji 83 B9 17 30S 177 40E
Nain Newfoundland Canada 89 W4 56 30N 61 45W
Nairai i. Fiji 83 D9 17 50S 179 26E
Nairobi Kenya 110 G7 1 17S 36 50E
Naitaba i. Fiji 83 E9 17 00S 179 18W
Najd geog. reg. Saudi Arabia 54 F4 25 40N 42 30E
Najin North Korea 50 E6 42 10N 130 20E
Najrān Saudi Arabia 54 F2 17 37N 44 40E
Naju South Korea 50 C2 35 03N 126 39E
Naka Japan 47 B2 35 25N 139 38E
Nakahara Japan 47 B3 35 34N 139 39E
Nakamura Japan 46 B1 33 02N 132 58E
Nakanai Mountains Papua New Guinea 45 O4 5 35S 151 15E
Nakano Japan 47 B3 35 42N 139 40E
Nakatsu Japan 46 B1 33 37N 131 11E
Nakawakawa Fiji 83 C10 16 51S 178 51E
Nakéty New Caledonia 82 V2 21 34S 166 03E
Nakhichevan' Azerbaijan 58 F2 39 12N 45 24E
Nakhodka Russia 57 P4 42 53N 132 54E
Nakhon Nayok Thailand 39 B2 14 15N 101 12E
Nakhon Pathom Thailand 39 B2 13 50N 100 01E
Nakhon Phanom Thailand 39 B3 17 22N 104 50E
Nakhon Ratchasima (Khorat) Thailand 39 B2 14 59N 102 06E
Nakhon Sawan Thailand 39 B3 15 42N 100 10E
Nakhon Si Thammarat Thailand 39 A1 8 24N 99 58E
Nakhon Thai Thailand 39 B3 17 04N 100 51E
Nakoroutari Fiji 83 D10 16 31S 179 23E
Nakskov Denmark 71 B2 54 50N 11 10E
Naktong r. South Korea 50 D2 35 20N 128 20E
Nakuru Kenya 110 G7 0 16S 36 05E
Nal r. Pakistan 52 B5 26 10N 65 30E
Nal'chik Russia 56 G4 43 31N 43 38E
Nam r. North Korea 50 C4 39 00N 126 30E
Namacu Fiji 83 D9 17 21S 179 24E
Namangan Uzbekistan 59 L3 40 59N 71 41E
Namatanai Papua New Guinea 45 P5 3 40S 152 26E
Nam Beng r. Laos 37 B4 20 15N 101 30E
Namber Irian Jaya Indonesia 44 F6 1 06S 134 49E
Nam Can Vietnam 37 B1 8 46N 104 59E
Namch'ŏnjom North Korea 50 C4 38 15N 126 26E
Nam Chon Reservoir Thailand 39 A3 15 30N 98 45E
Nam Chung Hong Kong U.K. 51 C3 22 31N 114 12E
Nam Co l. China 53 G6 30 50N 90 30E
Namdalen geog. reg. Norway 69 C3 64 40N 12 00E
Nam Dinh Vietnam 37 C4 20 25N 106 12E
Namena Barrier Reef Fiji 83 D9 17 06S 179 07E
Namenalala i. Fiji 83 D9 17 05S 179 06E
Namhae South Korea 50 C2 34 49N 127 54E
Nam Het r. Laos 37 B4 20 30N 103 45E
Namib Desert Namibia 111 B3/C2 22 00S 14 00E
Namibe Angola 111 B4 15 10S 12 09E
NAMIBIA 111 C3
Nam Khan r. Laos 37 B3 19 45N 102 30E
Nam Lang r. Myanmar 38 B4 21 00N 97 00E
Namlea Indonesia 43 G3 3 15S 127 07E
Nam Loi r. Myanmar 38 C4 21 30N 100 20E
Nam Mit r. Myanmar 38 B4 23 10N 96 50E
Nam Neun r. Laos 37 B3 19 45N 104 00E
Nam Ngum r. Laos 37 B3 18 15N 103 00E
Nam Ngum Reservoir Laos 37 B3 18 35N 102 40E
Nam On r. Laos 37 C3 17 45N 105 30E
Namosi Peaks mt. Fiji 83 C9 17 59S 178 08E
Nam Ou r. Laos 37 B4 20 15N 102 25E
Nampa Idaho U.S.A. 90 C5 43 35N 116 34W
Nam Pai r. Myanmar 38 B4 22 50N 96 30E
Nam Pang r. Myanmar 38 B4 21 20N 98 30E
Nam Pawn r. Myanmar 38 B4 20 00N 97 00E
Nam Phong Thailand 39 B3 16 44N 102 51E
Nam Pilu r. Myanmar 38 B3 19 40N 97 10E
Namp'o North Korea 50 B4 38 51N 125 10E
Nampula Mozambique 111 G4 15 09S 39 14E
Nam Pung Reservoir Thailand 39 B3 16 55N 103 55E
Namrole Indonesia 44 B5 3 50S 126 43E
Namsang Myanmar 38 B4 20 53N 97 45E
Nam Sha Po Hong Kong U.K. 51 A2 22 29N 113 59E
Namsos Norway 69 C3 64 28N 11 30E
Nam Taung r. Myanmar 38 B4 20 30N 98 00E
Nam Tha r. Laos 37 B4 20 20N 101 15E
Nam Theun Laos 37 C3 17 57N 105 04E
Nam Tok Thailand 39 A2 14 18N 99 01E
Namtu Myanmar 38 B4 23 04N 97 26E
Nam Tu r. Myanmar 38 B4 22 55N 97 20E
Namuamua Fiji 83 C8 18 05S 178 05E
Namuka Fiji 83 F8 18 51S 178 49W
Namuka-i-lau i. Fiji 83 F8 18 50S 178 41W
Nam Un Reservoir Thailand 39 B3 17 10N 103 45E
Namur Belgium 70 D2 50 28N 4 52E
Namur admin. Belgium 70 D2 50 10N 4 45E
Namwŏn South Korea 50 C2 35 23N 127 23E
Namyia Chaung r. Myanmar 38 B5 25 00N 96 40E
Nan Thailand 39 B3 18 47N 100 50E
Nanaimo British Columbia Canada 88 K2 49 08N 123 58W
Nanam North Korea 50 D5 41 44N 129 40E
Nanau-i-ra i. Fiji 83 C9 17 17S 178 18E
Nanao Japan 46 C2 37 03N 136 58E
Nanase Papua New Guinea 45 K3 7 32S 143 22E
Nanchang China 49 N4 28 33N 115 58E
Nanchong China 49 L5 30 54N 106 06E
Nancowry i. Nicobar Islands 36 A3 7 50N 93 00E
Nancy France 73 C2 48 42N 6 12E
Nanda Devi mt. India 53 D6 30 21N 79 58E
Nandai New Caledonia 82 U2 21 30S 165 25E
Nānded India 53 D3 19 11N 77 21E
Nanding He r. China 38 B4 23 40N 99 10E
Nandu Jiang r. China 37 C3 19 25N 110 00E
Nanga Eboko Cameroon 112 H3 4 38N 12 21E
Nangapinoh Indonesia 42 D3 0 21S 111 44E
Nangatayap Indonesia 42 D3 1 30S 110 33E
Nanggu Solomon Islands 83 M3 10 50S 166 00E
Nangi India 52 J1 22 30N 88 13E
Nangnim North Korea 50 C5 40 58N 127 12E
Nangnim-Sanmaek mts. North Korea 50 C4/5 40 00N 127 00E
Nang Rong Thailand 39 B2 14 39N 102 50E
Nanhai l. China 47 G1 39 55N 116 22E
Nanhua China 38 C5 25 12N 101 20E
Nanjian China 38 C5 25 02N 100 33E
Nanjing China 49 N5 32 03N 118 47E
Nanka Jiang r. Myanmar 38 B4 22 30N 99 00E
Nan Ling mts. China 49 M2/M3 25 00N 112 00E
Nanning China 49 L3 22 50N 108 19E
Nanortalik Greenland 89 Z5 60 10N 45 05W
Nanoumea Atoll Pacific Ocean 80 C3 5 40S 176 10E
Nanpan Jiang r. China 49 L3 25 00N 106 00E
Nanping China 49 N4 26 40N 118 07E
Nanri Dao i. China 51 F8 25 13N 119 29E
Nansei-shoto see Ryukyu Islands
Nanterre France 67 A2 48 53N 2 12E
Nantes France 73 A2 47 14N 1 35W
Nanto Japan 46 H1 34 17N 136 30E
Nantong China 49 O5 32 06N 121 04E
Nan-t'ou Taiwan 51 G6 23 54N 120 42E
Nantucket Island Massachusetts U.S.A. 93 F2/G2 41 15N 70 05W
Nantucket Sound Massachusetts U.S.A. 93 F2 41 00N 70 00W
Nanuca Fiji 83 D10 16 45S 179 41E
Nanukuloa Fiji 83 C9 17 29S 178 14E
Nanuku Reef Fiji 83 E10 16 40S 179 25W
Nanuku Passage Fiji 83 E10 16 50S 179 20W
Nanxiong China 36 E7 25 14N 114 20E

North European Plain Europe **60** 54 00N 20 00E
North Fiji Basin Pacific Ocean **22** H6 18 00S 173 00E
North Frisian Islands *see* Nordfriesische Inseln
North Gauhati India **38** A5 26 15N 91 38E
North Head Australia **79** H2 33 49S 151 18E
North Hollywood California U.S.A. **95** A3 34 10N 118 22W
North Island New Zealand **79** B3/C3
NORTH KOREA 50 B4/D5
North Lakhimpur India **36** A7 27 12N 94 07E
North Little Rock Arkansas U.S.A. **91** H3 34 46N 92 16W
North Loup *r.* Nebraska U.S.A. **90** F5 42 00N 0 0 00W
North Platte Nebraska U.S.A. **90** F5 41 09N 100 45W
North Platte *r.* U.S.A. **90** F5 42 00N 103 00W
North Point Barbados **96** V13 13 20N 59 37W
North Point Hong Kong U.K. **51** C1 22 18N 114 12E
North Pole Arctic Ocean **20** 90 00N
North River *tn.* Manitoba Canada **89** Q4 58 55N 94 30W
North Sea Europe **64** C6
North Tuas Basin Singapore **41** A3 1 19N 103 39E
North Uist *i.* Scotland United Kingdom **68** D9 57 04N 7 15W
North West Cape Australia **78** A5 21 48S 114 10E
North West Christmas Island Ridge Pacific Ocean **23** J8 9 30N 170 00W
Northwestern Atlantic Basin Atlantic Ocean **25** B10 33 00N 70 00W
Northwest Highlands Scotland United Kingdom **68** F8/G10
Northwest Pacific Basin Pacific Ocean **22** F11 35 00N 150 00E
North West Point Christmas Island **81** P2 10 26S 105 33E
Northwest Territories *territory* Canada **88/89** M6 65 15N 115 00W
Northwood England United Kingdom **66** B3 51 36N 0 25W
North York Moors England United Kingdom **68** K6 55 22N 0 45W
Norton Kansas U.S.A. **90** G4 39 51N 99 53W
Norton Sound Alaska U.S.A. **88** C5 64 00N 162 30W
Norvegia, Cape Antarctica **21** 71 28S 122 25W
Norwalk California U.S.A. **95** B2 33 56N 118 04W
Norwalk Connecticut U.S.A. **93** F2 41 07N 73 25W
NORWAY 69 B3/F5
Norway House *tn.* Manitoba Canada **89** P3 53 59N 97 50W
Norwegian Basin Arctic Ocean **25** H13 67 00N 0 00
Norwegian Sea Arctic Ocean **20** 70 00N 5 00E
Norwich England United Kingdom **68** M4 52 38N 1 18E
Norwich Connecticut U.S.A. **93** F2 41 32N 72 05W
Noshiro Japan **46** D3 40 13N 140 00E
Nosop *r.* Southern Africa **111** D2 25 00S 20 30E
Nosy Bé *i.* Madagascar **111** I5 13 00S 47 00E
Notéc *r.* Poland **75** C3 53 00N 17 00E
Notre Dame Bay Newfoundland Canada **89** X2 49 40N 55 00W
Notre-Dame du Lac *tn.* Québec Canada **93** G3 47 38N 68 49W
Nottaway River Québec Canada **93** E4 51 00N 78 00W
Nottingham England United Kingdom **68** J4 52 58N 1 10W
Nottingham Island Northwest Territories Canada **89** T5 62 15N 77 30W
Nouadhibou Mauritania **112** B7 20 54N 17 01W
Nouakchott Mauritania **112** B6 18 09N 15 58W
Nouméa *i.* New Caledonia **82** V1 22 16S 166 26E
Nouvelle Caledonia *(New Caledonia) i.* Pacific Ocean **82** R6/X2 22 00S 165 00E
Nouzonville France **70** D1 49 49N 4 45E
Nova Friburgo Brazil **103** I8 22 16S 42 34W
Nova Iguaçu Brazil **103** I8 22 46S 43 23W
Novolazarevskaya *r.s.* Antarctica **21** 70 46S 11 50E
Novara Italy **74** A4 45 27N 8 37E
Nova Scotia *province* Canada **89** W1 44 30N 65 00W
Nova Scotia Basin Atlantic Ocean **25** C10 39 00N 55 00W
Novaya Zemlya *is.* Russia **57** H10 74 00N 55 00E
Novgorod Russia **56** F7 58 30N 31 20E
Novi Pazar Serbia Yugoslavia **74** D3 43 09N 20 29E
Novi Sad Serbia Yugoslavia **74** D4 45 15N 19 51E
Novocheboksarsk Russia **58** F6 56 05N 47 27E
Novocherkassk Russia **58** E4 47 25N 40 05E
Novo Hamburgo Brazil **103** G7 29 37S 51 07W
Novokazalinsk Kazakhstan **59** J4 45 48N 62 06E
Novokuybyshevsk Russia **58** G5 53 05N 49 59E
Novokuznetsk Russia **57** K6 53 45N 87 12E
Novomoskovsk Russia **58** D5 54 06N 38 15E
Novorossiysk Russia **56** F4 44 44N 37 46E
Novoshakhtinsk Russia **58** D4 47 46N 39 55E
Novosibirsk Russia **57** K7 55 04N 83 05E
Novosibirskiye Ostrova *(New Siberian Islands) is.* Russia **20** 75 00N 145 00E
Novotroitsk Russia **59** H5 51 11N 58 16E
Novvy Port Russia **57** J9 67 38N 72 33E
Novvy Urengoy Russia **57** J9 66 00N 77 20E
Nowai *r.* India **52** K2 22 39N 88 28E
Nowa Sól Poland **75** C3 51 49N 15 41E
Nowgong India **53** G5 26 20N 92 41E
Nowy Dwor Poland **75** D3 52 27N 20 41E
Nowy Sącz Poland **75** D2 49 39N 20 40E
Nuapapu *i.* Tonga **83** B4 18 42S 174 05W
Nubian Desert Sudan **110** F12 21 00N 33 00E
Nueces *r.* Texas U.S.A. **90** G2 28 00N 99 00W
Nueltin Lake Northwest Territories Canada **89** P5 60 30N 99 00W
Nueva Rosita Mexico **96** D5 27 58N 101 11W
Nueva San Salvador El Salvador **96** G2 13 40N 89 18W
Nuevitas Cuba **97** I4 21 34N 77 18W
Nuevo Casas Grandes Mexico **96** C6 30 22N 107 53W
Nuevo Laredo Mexico **96** E5 27 39N 99 30W
Nuku'alofa Tonga **83** D1 21 09S 175 14W
Nukubasaga *i.* Fiji **83** E10 16 20S 179 15W
Nukufetau *i.* Pacific Ocean **80** C3 7 00S 178 00E
Nuku Hiva *i.* Pacific Ocean **81** E3 8 56S 140 00W
Nukuilau Fiji **83** B9 17 53S 177 51E
Nukunono Atoll Pacific Ocean **80** D3 9 10S 171 55W
Nukunuku Tonga **83** D1 21 80S 175 10W
Nukuoro *i.* Micronesia **80** B4 4 00S 155 00E
Nukus Uzbekistan **59** H3 42 28N 59 07E
Nullarbor Plain Australia **78** D3 32 00S 128 00E
Num *i.* Irian Jaya Indonesia **44** F6 1 30S 135 15E
Numazu Japan **46** K2 35 08N 138 50E
Numedal *geog. reg.* Norway **69** B3 60 40N 9 00E
Nunivak Island Alaska U.S.A. **88** B5 60 00N 166 00W
Nunspeet Netherlands **70** E4 52 22N 5 47E
Nupani *i.* Solomon Islands **82** L3 10 11S 165 32E
Nura *r.* Kazakhstan **59** L5 51 00N 71 00E
Nurakita *i.* Pacific Ocean **80** C3 9 00S 179 00E
Nuremberg *see* Nürnberg
Nürnberg *(Nuremberg)* Germany **71** B2 49 27N 11 05E
Nürtingen Germany **71** A1 48 37N 9 20E
Nusa Tenggara Barat *admin.* Indonesia **42** E2 8 00S 117 00E
Nusa Tenggara Timur *admin.* Indonesia **43** F2 10 00S 122 00E
Nuseybin Turkey **54** F6 37 05N 41 11E
Nu Shan *mts.* China **38** B5 26 30N 99 00E
Nushki Pakistan **52** B5 29 33N 66 01E
Nutak Newfoundland Canada **89** W4 57 30N 61 59W
Nuthe *r.* Germany **67** E1 52 21N 13 07E
Nuuk *see* Godthåb
Nuussuaq *p.* Greenland **89** Y7 70 50N 53 00W
Nu'utele *i.* Western Samoa **82** B10 14 03S 171 22W
Nuuuli American Samoa **82** E12 14 19S 170 42W
Nyainqântênglha Shan *mts.* China **48** G4/H5 30 00N 90 00E
Nyala Sudan **110** D10 12 01N 24 50E
Nyasa, Lake *(Lake Malawi)* Southern Africa **111** F5 12 00S 35 00E
Nyaungbitho Myanmar **38** B4 22 02N 96 11E
Nyaunglebin Myanmar **38** B3 17 59N 94 44E
Nyaung U Myanmar **38** A4 21 12N 94 55E
Nyíregyháza Hungary **75** D2 47 57N 21 43E
Nykøbing Denmark **69** C1 54 47N 11 53E
Nyköping Sweden **69** D2 58 45N 17 03E
Nyngan Australia **78** H3 31 34S 147 14E
Nyons France **73** C1 44 22N 5 08E
Nysa Poland **75** C3 50 30N 17 20E
Nysa *(Niesse) r.* Poland **75** B3 52 00N 14 00E
Nyūdō-zaki *c.* Japan **46** C2 40 00N 139 42E

O

Oahe, Lake U.S.A. **90** F6 45 00N 100 00W
Oahu *i.* Hawaiian Islands **23** X18-Y18 21 30N 158 10W
Oakes North Dakota U.S.A. **92** A3 46 08N 98 07W
Oak Hill *tn.* West Virginia U.S.A. **93** D1 37 58N 81 11W
Oakland California U.S.A. **90** B4 37 50N 122 15W
Oakland City Indiana U.S.A. **92** C1 38 21N 87 19W
Oak Ridge *tn.* Tennessee U.S.A. **91** J4 36 02N 84 12W
Oakville Ontario Canada **93** E2 43 27N 79 41W
Oamaru South Island New Zealand **79** B1 45 06S 170 58E
Oano Islands Pitcairn Islands **23** N5 23 32S 125 00W
Ōarai Japan **46** M3 36 18N 140 35E
Oates Land *geog. reg.* Antarctica **21** 70 00S 150 00E
Oaxaca Mexico **96** E3 17 05N 96 41W
Ob' *r.* Russia **57** I9 65 30N 66 00E
Oba Ontario Canada **89** S2 48 38N 84 17W
Obama Japan **46** G2 35 25N 135 45E
Oban Scotland United Kingdom **68** F8 56 25N 5 29W
Oberhausen Germany **71** A2 51 27N 6 50E
Oberösterreich *admin.* Austria **71** B1 48 00N 14 00E
Oberpfälzer Wald *see* Bohmer Wald
Oberursel Germany **71** A2 50 12N 8 35E
Ob', Gulf of Russia **57** J9 68 00N 74 00E
Obidos Brazil **102** F12 1 52S 55 30W
Obihiro Japan **46** D3 42 56N 143 10E
Obitsu *r.* Japan **47** C2 35 25N 139 53E
Ocala Florida U.S.A. **91** J2 29 11N 82 09W
Ocaña Colombia **102** C14 8 16N 73 21W
Ocatlán Mexico **96** D4 20 21N 102 42W
Ocean City Maryland U.S.A. **93** E1 38 21N 75 06W
Ochokovo Russia **56** L1 55 39N 37 30E
Ocho Rios Jamaica **97** Q8 18 24N 77 06W
Oconto Wisconsin U.S.A. **92** C2 44 55N 87 52W
Ōda Japan **46** B2 35 10N 132 29E
Odaejin North Korea **50** D5 41 23N 129 51E
Odate Japan **46** D3 40 18N 140 32E
Odawara Japan **46** L2 35 15N 139 08E
Odda Norway **69** B3 60 03N 6 34E
Ödemiş Turkey **74** E2 38 11N 27 58E
Odense Denmark **69** C2 55 24N 10 25E
Odenwald *mts.* Germany **71** A1 49 00N 9 00E
Oder *(Odra) r.* Europe **71** B2 52 00N 15 30E
Oder-Spree Kanal *can.* Germany **67** G1 52 21N 13 43E
Odessa Ukraine **58** C4 46 30N 30 46E
Odessa Delaware U.S.A. **93** E1 39 27N 75 40W
Odessa Texas U.S.A. **90** F3 31 50N 102 23W
Odiel *r.* Spain **72** A2 37 32N 7 00W
Odioñgan The Philippines **40** B3 12 24N 121 59E
Oekusi *see* Dili
Oema *i.* Solomon Islands **82** B7 6 40S 156 10E
Ofanto *r.* Italy **74** C3 41 00N 15 00E
Offenbach am Main Germany **71** A2 50 06N 8 46E
Offenburg Germany **71** A1 48 29N 7 57E
Ofolanga *i.* Tonga **83** B3 19 43S 174 29W
Ofu *i.* American Samoa **82** F12 14 11S 169 40W
Ofuna Japan **47** B2 53 21N 139 32E
Ofunato Japan **46** D2 39 04N 141 43E
Ogaden *geog. reg.* Africa **110** I9 7 00N 51 00E
Ōgaki Japan **46** H2 35 22N 136 36E
Ogano Japan **46** L2 35 55N 139 11E
Ogasawara Guntō *i.* Pacific Ocean **22** E10 27 30N 43 00E
Ogawa Japan **47** A3 35 43N 135 29E
Ogbomosho Nigeria **112** F4 8 05N 4 11E
Ogden Utah U.S.A. **90** D5 41 14N 111 59W
Ogdensburg New York U.S.A. **93** E2 44 42N 75 31W
Ogea Driki *i.* Fiji **83** F7 19 12S 178 25W
Ogea Levu *i.* Fiji **83** F7 19 09S 178 25W
Ogho Solomon Islands **82** B7 6 50S 156 50E
Ogilvie Mountains Yukon Territory Canada **88** H6 65 05N 139 00W
Ogoki *r.* Ontario Canada **89** R3 51 00N 87 00W
Ogonue *r.* Gabon **110** A7 0 30S 10 00E
Ogooué *r.* Gabon **112** G2 0 50S 9 50E
Ōhara Japan **46** M2 35 16N 140 22E
Ōhata Japan **46** D3 41 22N 141 11E
Ohio *r.* U.S.A. **92** C1 38 00N 88 00W
Ohio *state* U.S.A. **93** D2 40 00N 83 00W
'Ohonua Tonga **83** E1 21 22S 174 58W
Ohře *r.* Czech Republic **71** B2 50 00N 14 00E
Ohre *r.* Germany **71** B2 52 00N 11 00E
Ohridsko ozero *l.* Europe **74** D3 41 00N 21 00E
Oil City Pennsylvania U.S.A. **93** E2 41 26N 79 44W
Oise *r.* France **73** B2 49 10N 2 10E
Oistins Barbados **96** V12 13 04N 59 35W
Oistins Bay Barbados **96** V12 13 03N 59 34W
Ōita Japan **50** E1 33 15N 131 36E
Ojinaga Mexico **96** D5 29 35N 104 26W
Oka *r.* Russia **58** D5 55 00N 42 00E
Okaba Irian Jaya Indonesia **44** H2 8 06S 139 46E
Okanagan *r.* North America **90** C6 49 00N 119 00W
Okara Pakistan **53** C6 30 49N 73 31E
Okavango *r.* Southern Africa **111** C4 17 50S 20 00E
Okavango Basin Botswana **111** D4 19 00S 23 00E
Okaya Japan **46** C2 36 03N 138 00E
Okayama Japan **46** B1 34 40N 133 54E
Okazaki Japan **46** J1 34 58N 137 10E
Okeechobee, Lake Florida U.S.A. **91** J2 27 00N 81 00W
Okehampton England United Kingdom **73** A3 50 44N 4 00W
Okene Nigeria **112** G4 7 31N 6 14E
Okha Russia **57** Q6 53 35N 143 01E
Okhla India **52** M4 28 33N 77 16E
Okhotsk Russia **57** Q7 59 20N 143 15E
Okhotsk, Sea of Russia **57** Q7 55 00N 148 00E
Oki *is.* Japan **46** B2 36 05N 133 00E
Okinawa *i.* Japan **49** P4 26 30N 128 00E
Oklahoma *state* U.S.A. **91** G4 36 00N 98 00W
Oklahoma City Oklahoma U.S.A. **91** G4 35 28N 97 33W
Okpo Myanmar **38** B3 18 03N 95 43E
Oksapmin Papua New Guinea **45** K4 5 20S 142 12E
Oktyabr'skiy Russia **57** R6 52 43N 156 14E
Okushiri-tō *i.* Japan **46** C3 42 15N 139 30E
Olal Vanuatu **83** H5 16 05S 168 10E
Öland *i.* Sweden **69** D2 56 45N 51 50E
Olbia Italy **74** A3 40 56N 9 30E
Old Crow Yukon Territory Canada **88** H6 67 34N 139 43W
Oldenburg Germany **71** A2 53 08N 8 13E
Oldenzaal Netherlands **70** F4 52 19N 6 55E
Oldham England United Kingdom **68** I5 53 33N 2 07W
Old Harbour *tn.* Jamaica **97** Q7 17 56N 77 07W
Old Harbour Bay *tn.* Jamaica **97** Q7 17 54N 77 06W
Old Head of Kinsale *c.* Irish Republic **68** C3 51 40N 8 30W
Olds Alberta Canada **88** M3 51 50N 114 06W
Old Town Maine U.S.A. **93** G2 44 55N 68 41W
Olean New York U.S.A. **93** E2 42 05N 78 26W
Olekma *r.* Russia **57** O7 59 00N 121 00E
Olekminsk Russia **57** O8 60 25N 120 25E
Olenëk Russia **57** N9 68 28N 112 18E
Olenëk *r.* Russia **57** O10 72 00N 122 00E
Olhão Portugal **72** A2 37 01N 7 50W
Ólimbos *(Olympus) mt.* Greece **74** D3 40 05N 22 21E
Olinda Brazil **102** J11 8 00S 34 51W
Olivia Minnesota U.S.A. **92** B2 44 47N 94 58W
Olomouc Czech Republic **75** C2 49 38N 17 15E
Olongapo The Philippines **40** B3 14 49N 120 17E
Olorua *i.* Fiji **83** F8 18 24S 178 45W
Olosega American Samoa **82** F12 14 12S 169 38W
Olpoy Vanuatu **83** F7 14 50S 166 35E
Olsztyn Poland **75** D3 53 48N 20 29E
Olt *r.* Romania **75** D1 44 00N 24 00E
Olten Switzerland **73** C2 47 22N 7 55E
O'luan-pi *c.* Taiwan **51** G4 21 54N 120 53E
Olutanga *i.* The Philippines **40** B2 7 23N 122 50E
Olympia Washington U.S.A. **90** B6 47 03N 122 53W
Olympus *mt.* Cyprus **54** D5 34 55N 32 52E
Olympus *see* Ólimbos
Olympus, Mount Washington U.S.A. **90** B6 47 49N 123 42W
Om' *r.* Russia **57** J7 55 00N 79 00E
Omagh Northern Ireland United Kingdom **68** D6 54 36N 7 18W
Omaha Nebraska U.S.A. **92** A2 41 15N 96 00W
OMAN 55 I2
Oman, Gulf of Iran/Oman **55** I3 24 30N 58 30E
Omba *see* Aoba
Omboué Gabon **112** G2 1 38S 9 20E
Omdurman Sudan **110** F11 15 37N 32 29E
Ome Japan **46** L2 35 48N 139 17E
Omihachiman Japan **46** H2 35 08N 136 04E
Ōmiya Japan **46** L2 35 54N 139 39E
Omo *r.* Ethiopia **110** G9 7 00N 37 00E
Omolon *r.* Russia **57** R9 65 00N 160 00E
Omoloy *r.* Russia **57** P9 69 00N 132 00E
Omona *i.* Solomon Islands **82** D6 7 30S 158 40E
Omsk Russia **57** J7 55 00N 73 22E
Ōmuta Japan **46** B1 33 02N 130 26E
Omutinskiy Russia **59** K6 56 30N 67 40E
Ondo Nigeria **112** F4 7 05N 4 55E
Oneata *i.* Fiji **83** F8 18 27S 178 30W
Onega, Lake *see* Ozero Onezhskoy
Oneonta New York U.S.A. **93** E2 42 28N 75 04W
Onetar Vanuatu **83** G7 14 16S 167 26E
Ongjin North Korea **50** B3 37 56N 125 21E
Onitsha Nigeria **112** G4 6 10N 6 47E
Ono Japan **46** F1 34 52N 134 55E
Ono *i.* Fiji **83** C8 18 53S 178 30E
Onoda Japan **50** E1 34 00N 131 11E
Ono-i-lau *i.* Fiji **83** F6 20 48S 178 45W
Onomichi Japan **46** B1 34 25N 33 11E
Onon *r.* Russia/Mongolia **49** M9 51 00N 114 00E
Onslow Australia **78** B5 21 41S 115 12E
Onsong North Korea **50** D6 42 55N 129 59E
Ontario California U.S.A. **90** C3 34 04N 117 38W
Ontario *province* Canada **89** Q3 51 00N 91 00W
Ontario, Lake Canada/U.S.A. **93** E2 43 45N 78 00W
Ontonagon Michigan U.S.A. **92** C3 46 52N 89 18W
Ontong Java Atoll Solomon Islands **82** E8 5 20S 159 30E
Oologah Lake Oklahoma U.S.A. **92** A1 36 00N 95 00W
Oostelijk Flevoland *geog. reg.* Netherlands **70** E4 52 30N 5 40E
Oostende Belgium **70** B3 51 13N 2 55E
Oosterhout Netherlands **70** D3 51 39N 4 52E
Oosterschelde *sd.* Netherlands **70** C3 51 30N 3 58E
Oost-Vlaanderen *admin.* Belgium **70** C3 51 10N 3 45E
Opala Zaïre **110** D7 0 40S 24 20E
Opava Czech Republic **75** C2 49 58N 17 55E
Open Bay Papua New Guinea **45** O4 4 45S 151 30E
Opochka Russia **69** F2 56 41N 28 42E
Opole Poland **75** C3 50 40N 17 56E
Oporto *see* Porto
Opotiki North Island New Zealand **79** C3 38 01S 177 17E
Optic Lake *tn.* Manitoba Canada **89** O3 54 47N 101 15W
Oradea Romania **75** D2 47 03N 21 55E
Oradell Reservoir New Jersey U.S.A. **94** B2 40 58N 74 00W
Orai India **53** D5 26 00N 79 26E
Oran Algeria **112** E10 35 45N 0 38W
Orán Argentina **103** E8 23 07S 64 16W
Orange Australia **78** H3 33 19S 149 10E
Orange France **73** B1 44 08N 4 48E
Orange California U.S.A. **95** C2 33 43N 117 54W
Orange New Jersey U.S.A. **94** B2 40 45N 74 14W
Orange Texas U.S.A. **91** H3 30 05N 93 43W
Orange *r.* Southern Africa **111** C2 28 30S 17 30E
Orangeburg South Carolina U.S.A. **91** J3 33 28N 80 53W
Orange Free State *admin.* Republic of South Africa **111** E2 27 30S 27 30E
Oranienburg Germany **71** B2 52 46N 13 15E
Oransbari Irian Jaya Indonesia **44** F6 1 16S 134 18E
Oras The Philippines **40** C3 12 10N 125 28E
Oravița Romania **75** D2 45 02N 21 43E
Orbigo *r.* Spain **72** A3 42 15N 5 45W
Orcadas *r.s.* Antarctica **21** 60 44S 44 44W
Orchies France **70** C2 50 28N 3 15E
Orcia *r.* Italy **74** B3 42 00N 11 00E
Ordu Turkey **58** D3 41 00N 37 52E
Ordzhonikidze *see* Vladikavkaz
Örebro Sweden **69** D2 59 17N 15 13E
Oregon *state* U.S.A. **90** B5 44 00N 120 00W
Oregon City Oregon U.S.A. **90** B6 45 21N 122 36W
Orekhovo-Zuyevo Russia **58** D6 55 47N 39 00E
Orël Russia **56** F6 52 58N 36 04E
Orem Utah U.S.A. **90** D5 40 20N 111 45W
Orenburg Russia **56** H6 51 50N 55 00E
Orense Spain **72** A3 42 20N 7 52W
Orient Bay *tn.* Ontario Canada **92** C3 49 23N 88 08W
Orihuela Spain **72** B2 38 05N 0 56W
Orillia Ontario Canada **93** E2 44 36N 79 26W
Orissa *admin.* India **53** E4 20 20N 83 00E
Oristano Italy **74** A2 39 54N 8 36E
Orizaba Mexico **96** E3 18 51N 97 08W
Orkney Islands Scotland United Kingdom **68** H11 59 00N 3 00W
Orlando Florida U.S.A. **91** J2 28 33N 81 21W
Orléans France **73** B2 47 54N 1 54E
Orly France **67** B1 48 44N 2 24E
Ormoc The Philippines **40** B3 11 01N 124 36E
Orne *r.* France **73** A2 48 50N 0 16W
Örnsköldsvik Sweden **69** D3 63 19N 18 45E
Orohena, Mount Tahiti **82** T9 17 37S 149 27W
Orona *(Hull Island) i.* Pacific Ocean **80** D3 4 35S 172 20W
Oropucha *r.* Trinidad and Tobago **96** T10 10 36N 61 05W
Oroquieta The Philippines **40** B2 8 31N 123 46E
Orpington England United Kingdom **66** D2 51 23N 0 05E
Orsay France **67** A1 48 42N 2 11E
Orsk Russia **56** H6 51 13N 58 35E
Orthez France **73** A1 43 29N 0 46W
Ortigueira Spain **72** A3 43 43N 8 13W
Ortoire *r.* Trinidad and Tobago **96** T9 10 16N 61 15W
Ortonville Minnesota U.S.A. **92** A3 45 18N 96 28W
Ortze *r.* Germany **71** B2 53 00N 10 00E
Orūmīyeh Iran **54** F6 37 40N 45 00E
Oruro Bolivia **102** D9 17 59S 67 08W
Osage *r.* U.S.A. **92** B1 38 00N 93 00W
Ōsaka Japan **46** G1 34 40N 135 30E
Ōsaka *pref.* Japan **46** G1 34 30N 135 10E
Ōsaka-wan *b.* Japan **46** G1 34 30N 135 18E
Osceola Iowa U.S.A. **92** B2 41 02N 93 46W
Osh Kirgyzstan **59** L3 40 37N 72 49E
Oshawa Ontario Canada **93** E2 43 53N 78 51W
Ō-shima *i.* Japan **46** C1 34 45N 139 25E
Oshkosh Wisconsin U.S.A. **92** C2 44 01N 88 32W
Oshogbo Nigeria **112** F4 7 50N 4 35E
Osijek Croatia **74** C4 45 33N 18 41E
Oskaloosa Iowa U.S.A. **92** B2 41 16N 92 40W
Oslo Norway **69** C2 59 56N 10 45E
Oslofjorden *fj.* Norway **69** C2 59 20N 10 37E
Osmaniye Turkey **54** E6 37 04N 36 15E
Osnabrück Germany **71** A2 52 17N 8 03E
Osorno Chile **103** C4 40 35S 73 14W
Oss Netherlands **70** E3 51 46N 5 31E
Ossa, Mount Australia **78** H1 41 52S 146 04E
Ostankino Russia **56** M2 55 50N 37 37E
Österdalälven *r.* Sweden **69** C3 61 40N 13 30E
Østerdalen *geog. reg.* Norway **69** C3 62 00N 10 30E
Osterode Germany **71** B2 51 44N 10 15E
Östersund Sweden **69** C3 63 10N 14 40E
Östervall Sweden **69** D3 62 20N 15 20E
Ostfriesische Inseln *(East Frisian Islands) is.* Germany **71** A2 53 00N 7 00E
Ostrava Czech Republic **75** C2 49 50N 18 15E
Ostróda Poland **75** C3 53 42N 19 59E
Ostrołęka Poland **75** D3 53 05N 21 32E
Ostrov Russia **69** F2 57 52N 28 20E
Ostrowiec Swietokrzyski Poland **75** D3 50 58N 21 22E
Ostrów Mazowiecki Poland **75** D3 52 50N 21 51E
Ostrów Wielkopolski Poland **75** C3 51 39N 17 50E
Oswego New York U.S.A. **93** E2 43 27N 76 31W
Ōta Japan **47** B3 33 15N 131 36E
Otaheite Bay Trinidad and Tobago **96** S9 10 15N 61 30W
Otaki North Island New Zealand **79** C2 40 46S 175 09E
Otakwa Irian Jaya Indonesia **44** G4 4 45S 137 10E
Otaru Japan **46** D3 43 14N 140 59E
Otava *r.* Czech Republic **71** B1 49 00N 13 00E
Otavalo Ecuador **102** B13 0 13N 78 15W
O' The Cherokees, Lake Oklahoma U.S.A. **92** B1 37 00N 95 00W
Otra *r.* Norway **69** B2 56 17N 7 30E
Otranto Italy **74** C3 40 08N 18 30E
Otranto, Strait of Adriatic Sea **74** C2/3 40 00N 19 00E
Otsego Michigan U.S.A. **92** C2 42 46N 85 42W
Ōtsu Japan **46** G2 35 00N 135 50E
Otsuki Japan **46** K2 35 38N 138 53E
Ottawa Illinois U.S.A. **92** C2 41 21N 88 51W
Ottawa Kansas U.S.A. **92** A1 38 35N 95 16W
Ottawa Ontario Canada **93** E3 45 24N 75 38W
Ottawa *r.* Ontario/Québec Canada **93** E3 46 00N 77 00W
Ottawa Islands Northwest Territories Canada **89** S4 59 10N 80 25W
Otter Rapids *tn.* Ontario Canada **93** D4 50 12N 81 40W
Ottumwa Iowa U.S.A. **92** B2 41 02N 92 26W
Otu Tolu Group Tonga **83** B2 20 20S 174 25W
Oua *i.* Tonga **83** B2 20 01S 174 44W
Ouaco New Caledonia **82** T3 20 50S 164 30E
Ouadda Central African Republic **110** D9 8 09N 22 20E
Ouagadougou Burkina **112** E5 12 20N 1 40W
Ouahigouya Burkina **112** E5 13 31N 2 20W
Ouargla Algeria **112** G9 32 00N 5 16E
Ouassel *r.* Algeria **72** C2 35 30N 2 00E
Oubangui *r.* Africa **112** I3 0 00 17 30E
Oudenaarde Belgium **70** C2 50 50N 3 37E
Oude Rijn *r.* Netherlands **70** D4 52 06N 4 46E

Oudong Cambodia **37** B2 11 48N 104 47E
Oudtshoorn Republic of South Africa **111** D1 33 35S 22 12E
Oued Dra *r.* Morocco **112** C8 28 10N 11 00W
Oued Zem Morocco **112** D9 32 55N 6 33W
Ouégoa New Caledonia **82** T3 20 20S 164 35E
Ouerrha *r.* Morocco **72** A1 34 00N 6 00W
Ouesso Congo **112** I3 1 38N 16 03E
Ouezzane Morocco **72** A1 34 25N 5 35W
Ouham *r.* Central African Republic **110** C9 7 00N 17 30E
Ouichita *r.* U.S.A. **91** H3 34 00N 93 00W
Ouichita Mountains U.S.A. **91** G3/H3 34 00N 95 00W
Ouinné New Caledonia **82** V2 21 59S 166 40E
Oujda Morocco **112** E9 34 41N 1 45W
Oulu Finland **69** F4 65 02N 25 27E
Oulu järvi *l.* Finland **69** F3 64 20N 27 00E
Oulujöki *r.* Finland **69** F3 64 50N 26 00E
Ounasjoki *r.* Finland **69** F4 67 00N 25 00E
Our *r.* Luxembourg/Germany **70** F1 50 00N 6 00E
Ouro Vanuatu **83** G5 16 15S 167 56E
Ourthe *r.* Belgium **70** E2 50 20N 5 50E
Ōu-sanmyaku *mts.* Japan **46** D2 39 20N 141 00E
Ouse *r.* England United Kingdom **68** J5 53 40N 1 00W
Oust *r.* France **73** A2 47 50N 2 30W
Outer Hebrides *is.* Scotland United Kingdom **68** D9 58 00N 7 00W
Outreau France **70** A2 50 42N 1 36E
Ouvéa *i.* New Caledonia **82** V3 20 25S 166 39E
Ovalau *i.* Fiji **83** C9 17 40S 178 47E
Ovalle Chile **103** C6 30 33S 71 16W
Overflakkee *i.* Netherlands **70** D3 51 45N 4 10E
Overijssel *admin.* Netherlands **70** F4 52 23N 6 28E
Övertorneå Sweden **69** E4 66 22N 23 40E
Oviedo Spain **72** A3 43 21N 7 18E
Owando Congo **112** I2 0 27S 15 44E
Owatonna Minnesota U.S.A. **92** B2 44 06N 93 10W
Owen Falls Dam Uganda **110** F8 0 29N 33 11E
Owen Fracture Zone Indian Ocean **24** E7/8 10 00N 55 00E
Owen, Mount South Island New Zealand **79** B2 41 33S 172 33E
Owensboro Kentucky U.S.A. **92** C1 37 45N 87 05W
Owens Lake California U.S.A. **90** C4 36 25N 117 56W
Owen Sound *tn.* Ontario Canada **93** D2 44 3N 80 56W
Owen Stanley Range Papua New Guinea **45** M2/N2 9 15S 148 30E
Owo Nigeria **112** G4 7 10N 5 39E
Owosso Michigan U.S.A. **93** D2 43 00N 84 11W
Owyhee *r.* U.S.A. **90** C5 43 00N 117 00W
Oxford England United Kingdom **68** J3 51 46N 1 15W
Oxnard California U.S.A. **90** C3 34 11N 119 10W
Oxted England United Kingdom **66** C1 51 15N 0 01W
Oyama Japan **46** C2 36 18N 139 48E
Oyapock *r.* Brazil **102** G13 3 00N 52 30W
Oyem Gabon **112** H3 1 34N 11 31E
Oyo Nigeria **112** F4 7 50N 3 55E
Ozamiz The Philippines **40** B2 8 09N 123 51E
Ozark Plateau Missouri U.S.A. **91** H4 37 00N 93 00W
Ozarks, Lake of the Missouri U.S.A. **92** B1 38 00N 93 00W
Ozero Sevan *l.* Armenia **58** F3 40 00N 45 00E
Ozero Alakol' *salt l.* Kazakhstan **59** N4 46 00N 82 00E
Ozero Aydarkul' *l.* Kazakhstan **59** K3 41 00N 68 00E
Ozero Balkhash *(Lake Balkhash) l.* Kazakhstan **59** L4/M4 46 00N 75 00E
Ozero Baykal *(Lake Baykal) l.* Russia **57** M6 54 00N 109 00E
Ozero Chany *salt l.* Russia **57** J6 55 00N 77 30E
Ozero Chudskoye *(Lake Peipus) l.* Estonia/Russia **69** F2 58 40N 27 30E
Ozero Imandra *l.* Russia **69** G4 67 45N 33 00E
Ozero Issyk-Kul' *salt l.* Kirgyzstan **59** M3 42 30N 77 30E
Ozero Kulundinskoye *l.* Russia **59** M5 53 00N 80 00E
Ozero Leksozero *l.* Russia **69** G3 64 00N 31 20E
Ozero Manych Gudilo *l.* Russia **58** E4 46 30N 43 00E
Ozero Nyuk *l.* Russia **69** G3 64 30N 31 50E
Ozero Onezhskoye *(Lake Onega) l.* Russia **56** F8 62 00N 40 00E
Ozero Pskovskoye *l.* Estonia/Russia **69** F2 58 00N 28 00E
Ozero Pyazero *l.* Russia **69** G4 66 00N 31 15E
Ozero Seletyteniz *l.* Kazakhstan **59** L5 53 30N 73 00E
Ozero Sredneye Kuyto *l.* Russia **69** G4 65 00N 31 15E
Ozero Taymyr *l.* Russia **57** M10 74 00N 102 30E
Ozero Teletskoye *l.* Russia **59** O5 52 00N 88 00E
Ozero Tengiz *salt l.* Kazakhstan **59** K5 51 00N 69 00E
Ozero Topozero *l.* Russia **69** G4 65 45N 32 10E
Ozero Zaysan *l.* Kazakhstan **59** N4 48 00N 84 00E
Ozieri Italy **73** C1 40 35N 9 01E

P
Paagoumène New Caledonia **82** T3 20 30S 164 10E
Paama *i.* Vanuatu **83** H5 16 29S 168 15E
Pa-an Myanmar **38** B3 16 51N 97 37E
Pabjanice Poland **75** C3 51 40N 19 20E
Pabna Bangladesh **53** F4 24 00N 89 15E
Pacasmayo Peru **102** B11 7 27S 79 33W
Pachuca Mexico **96** E4 20 10N 98 44W
Pacific-Antarctic Ridge Pacific Ocean **23** L2/O2 55 00S 135 00W
Pacific Grove California U.S.A. **90** B4 36 36N 121 56W
Pacific Ocean 22/23
Pacitan Indonesia **42** P6 8 12S 111 05E
Padang Indonesia **42** B3 1 00S 100 21E
Padangpanjang Indonesia **42** B3 0 30S 100 26E
Padangsidempuan Indonesia **42** A4 1 23N 99 15E
Paderborn Germany **71** A2 51 43N 8 44E
Padilla Bolivia **102** E9 19 18S 64 20W
Padova Italy **74** B4 45 24N 11 53E
Padstow England United Kingdom **73** A3 50 33N 4 56W
Paducah Kentucky U.S.A. **92** C1 37 03N 88 36W
Paéa Tahiti **82** S9 17 41S 149 35W
Paeroa North Island New Zealand **79** C3 37 23S 175 40E
Paeu Bay *tn.* Solomon Islands **83** M2 11 40S 166 50E
Pag *i.* Croatia **74** B3/C3 44 00N 15 00E
Pagadian The Philippines **40** B2 7 50N 123 30E
Pagai Selatan *i.* Indonesia **42** B3 3 00S 100 20E
Pagai Utara *i.* Indonesia **42** B3 2 40S 100 00E
Pagan Myanmar **38** A4 21 07N 94 53E
Pagatan Indonesia **42** E3 3 36S 115 58E
Pago Pago American Samoa **82** E12 14 16S 170 43W
Pahala Hawaiian Islands **23** Z17 19 12N 155 28W
Paharganj India **52** L4 28 38N 77 12E
Päijänne *l.* Finland **69** F3 61 30N 25 25E
Pailin Cambodia **37** B2 12 51N 102 34E
Painan Indonesia **42** B3 1 21S 100 34E
Painesville Ohio U.S.A. **93** D2 41 43N 81 15W
Pai-sha Tao *i.* Taiwan **51** F6 23 40N 119 33E
Paisley Scotland United Kingdom **68** G7 55 50N 4 26W
Paita New Caledonia **82** V1 22 08S 166 28E
Paita Peru **102** A11 5 11S 81 09W
Pakanbaru Indonesia **42** B4 0 33N 101 30E
Pakbeng Laos **37** B3 19 57N 101 08E
Pak Chong Thailand **39** B2 14 43N 101 28E
PAKISTAN 52 A5/C5
Pakitsoq *(Jakobskavn)* Greenland **20** 69 10N 51 05W
Pakokku Myanmar **38** B4 21 20N 95 05E
Pak Phanang Thailand **39** B1 8 20N 100 10E
Pak Sha Tsuen Hong Kong U.K. **51** B2 22 25N 114 01E
Pak Tam Chung Hong Kong U.K. **51** C2 22 24N 114 19E
Pak Tho Thailand **39** A2 13 22N 99 50E
Pakxan Laos **37** B3 18 29N 103 46E
Pakxé Laos **37** C3 15 05N 105 55E
Pakxèng Laos **37** B4 20 09N 102 46E
Pakxong Laos **37** C3 15 06N 106 05E
Palaiseau France **67** A1 48 43N 2 15E
Palana Russia **57** R7 59 05N 159 59E
Palanan Point The Philippines **40** B4 17 08N 122 30E
Palangkaraya Indonesia **42** D3 2 16S 113 55E
PALAU *(BELAU)* **80** A4
Palau *(Belau) i.* Pacific Ocean **43** H5 7 30N 134 30E
Palaw Myanmar **38** B2 12 57N 98 39E
Palawan *i.* The Philippines **40** A2/A3 10 00N 119 00E
Palawan Passage The Philippines **40** A2/A3 10 00N 118 00E
Palayankottai India **53** D1 8 42N 77 46E
Paleleh Indonesia **43** F4 1 05N 121 59E
Palembang Indonesia **42** B3 2 59S 104 45E
Palencia Spain **72** B3 41 01N 4 32W
Palermo Italy **74** B2 38 08N 13 23E
Palestine Texas U.S.A. **91** G3 31 45N 95 39W
Paletwa Myanmar **38** A4 21 25N 92 49E
Palghat India **53** D2 10 46N 76 42E
Palian Thailand **39** A1 7 10N 99 38E
Paliat *i.* Indonesia **42** R7 6 55S 115 35E
Palk Strait India **53** D2 10 00N 80 00E
Palliser, Cape North Island New Zealand **79** C2 41 37S 175 15E
Palma de Mallorca Balearic Islands **72** E4 39 35N 2 39E
Palmar Sur Costa Rica **97** H1 8 57N 83 28W
Palmas Bellas Panama **97** X2 9 16N 80 05W
Palmas, Cape Liberia **112** D3 4 25N 7 50W
Palm Beach Australia **79** H3 33 36S 151 19E
Palmer Alaska U.S.A. **88** F5 61 35N 149 10W
Palmer *r.s.* Antarctica **21** 64 46S 64 03W
Palmer Land *geog. reg.* Antarctica **21** 72 00S 62 00W
Palmerston Atoll *i.* Pacific Ocean **81** D3 18 04S 163 10W
Palmerston North North Island New Zealand **79** C2 40 22S 175 37E
Palmira Colombia **102** B13 3 33N 76 17W
Palmyra Atoll Pacific Ocean **81** D3 5 52N 162 05W
Paloh Indonesia **42** C4 1 43N 109 18E
Palomares Mexico **96** E3 17 10N 95 04W
Palopo Indonesia **43** F3 3 01S 120 12E
Palo Seco Trinidad and Tobago **96** S9 10 06N 61 36W
Palos Verdes Hills California U.S.A. **95** A1/2 33 46N 118 23W
Palu Indonesia **43** E3 0 54S 119 52E
Pamekasan Indonesia **42** Q7 7 11S 113 30E
Pameunpeuk Indonesia **42** C2 7 39S 107 40E
Pamiers France **73** B1 43 07N 1 36E
Pamirs *mts.* Asia **59** L2/M2 38 00N 74 00E
Pamlico Sound North Carolina U.S.A. **91** K4 35 00N 76 00W
Pa Mok Thailand **39** B2 14 29N 100 26E
Pampas *geog. reg.* Argentina **103** E5 36 00S 63 00W
Pamplona Colombia **102** C14 7 24N 72 38W
Pamplona Spain **72** B3 42 49N 1 39W
Pamua Solomon Islands **82** G3 10 25S 161 45E
Panaitan *i.* Indonesia **42** M7 6 40S 105 15E
Panajam Indonesia **42** E3 1 18S 116 40E
PANAMA 97 H1
Panamá Panama **97** I1 8 57N 19 30W
Panama City Florida U.S.A. **91** I3 30 10N 85 41W
Panama Isthmus Central America **84** 9 00N 80 00W
Panaon *i.* The Philippines **40** C3 10 00N 125 00E
Panay *i.* The Philippines **40** B3 11 00N 122 00E
Panay *r.* The Philippines **40** B3 11 00N 122 00E
Panay Gulf The Philippines **40** B3 10 00N 122 00E
Pančevo Serbia Yugoslavia **74** D3 44 52N 20 40E
Panch'iao Taiwan **51** H8 25 01N 121 27E
Panchla India **52** J2 22 32N 88 08E
Panchur India **52** K2 22 31N 88 15E
Pandan Singapore **41** B3 1 19N 103 45E
Pandan Reservoir Singapore **41** B3 1 19N 103 45E
Pandan Strait Singapore **41** B2/C3 1 15N 103 44E
Pandu India **38** A5 26 10N 91 40E
Panevežys Lithuania **69** E2 55 44N 24 24E
Pangai Tonga **83** B3 19 50S 174 23W
Pangaimotu Tonga **83** C4 18 40S 174 00W
Panggoe Solomon Islands **82** C7 7 01S 157 05E
Pangkalanbuun Indonesia **42** D3 2 43S 111 38E
Pangkalansusu Indonesia **42** A4 4 05N 98 13E
Pangkal Kalong Malaysia **39** B1 5 56N 102 14E
Pangkalpinang Indonesia **42** C3 2 05S 106 09E
Pangnirtung Northwest Territories Canada **89** V6 66 05N 65 45W
Panguna Papua New Guinea **45** Q3 6 22S 155 20E
Pangutaran The Philippines **40** B2 6 19N 120 33E
Panié, Mount New Caledonia **82** T3 20 36S 164 47E
Pānihāti India **52** K2 22 41N 88 23E
Panipat India **53** D5 29 24N 76 58E
Paniqui The Philippines **40** B4 15 40N 120 35E
Panke *r.* Germany **67** F2 52 38N 13 27E
Pankow Germany **67** F2 52 35N 13 25E
Pantelleria *i.* Italy **74** B2 36 00N 12 00E
Pantin France **67** B2 48 54N 2 25E
Pan Xian China **38** C5 25 45N 104 41E
Pão de Açúcar *(Sugar Loaf) mt.* Brazil **103** Q2 22 57S 43 09W
Paoni Indonesia **44** C5 2 50S 129 05E
Paopao Tahiti **82** R9 17 28S 149 48W
Papa Hawaiian Islands **23** Z17 19 12N 155 53W
Pápa Hungary **75** C2 47 20N 17 29E
Papantla Mexico **96** E4 20 30N 97 21W
Papara Tahiti **82** S9 17 45S 149 33W
Papatura Faa *i.* Solomon Islands **82** D6 7 35S 158 45E
Papatura Ite *i.* Solomon Islands **82** D6 7 35S 158 50E
Papeete Tahiti **82** S9 17 32S 149 34W
Papenburg Germany **71** A2 53 05N 7 25E
Papendrecht Netherlands **70** D3 51 50N 4 42E
Papenoo Tahiti **82** T9 17 29S 149 25W
Papetoai Tahiti **82** R9 17 29S 149 52W
Papua, Gulf of Papua New Guinea **45** L2 8 15S 144 45E
PAPUA NEW GUINEA 45
Papun Myanmar **38** B3 18 05N 97 26E
Pará *admin.* Brazil **102** G12 4 30S 52 30W
Paraburdoo Australia **78** B5 23 15S 117 45E
Paracel Islands South China Sea **36** E5 16 00N 113 30E
PARAGUAY 102/103 F8
Paraiba *admin.* Brazil **102** J11 7 20S 37 10W
Parakou Benin **112** F4 9 23N 2 40E
Paramaribo Surinam **102** F14 5 52N 55 14W
Paramonga Peru **102** B10 10 42S 77 50W
Paramus New Jersey U.S.A. **94** B2 40 55N 74 03W
Paraná Argentina **103** E6 31 45S 60 30W
Parana *admin.* Brazil **103** G8 24 30S 53 00W
Paraná Plateau Brazil **98** 25 00S 50 00W
Paranguá Brazil **103** H7 25 32S 48 36W
Parbhani India **53** D3 19 16N 76 51E
Parchim Germany **71** B2 53 26N 11 51E
Pardubice Czech Republic **75** C3 50 03N 15 45E
Pare Indonesia **42** Q7 7 43S 112 13E
Parepare Indonesia **43** E3 4 00S 119 40E
Paria, Gulf of Trinidad and Tobago **96** S9 10 30N 61 45W
Pariaman Indonesia **42** B3 0 36S 100 09E
Parintins Brazil **102** F12 2 38S 56 45W
Paris France **73** B2 48 52N 2 20E
Paris Missouri U.S.A. **92** B1 39 27N 91 59W
Paris Texas U.S.A. **91** G3 33 41N 95 33W
Paris Basin France **60** 48 00N 2 30E
Parish New York U.S.A. **93** E2 43 24N 76 07W
Parkano Finland **69** E3 62 03N 23 00E
Parker, Mount Hong Kong U.K. **51** C1 22 16N 114 13E
Parkersburg West Virginia U.S.A. **93** D1 39 17N 81 33W
Park Royal England United Kingdom **66** B3 51 32N 0 17W
Parma Italy **74** B3 44 48N 10 19E
Parma Ohio U.S.A. **93** D2 41 24N 81 44W
Parnaíba Brazil **102** I12 2 58S 41 46W
Parnassós *mt.* Greece **74** D2 38 30N 22 37E
Pärnu Estonia **69** E2 58 28N 24 30E
Paroo *r.* Australia **78** G4 27 00S 144 00E
Páros *i.* Greece **74** E2 37 00N 25 00E
Parramatta Australia **79** G2 33 50S 151 00E
Parramatta River Australia **79** G2 33 49S 151 05E
Parras Mexico **96** D5 25 30N 102 11W
Parry, Cape Northwest Territories Canada **88** K7 70 08N 124 34W
Parry Island Northwest Territories Canada **89** N8 75 15N 109 00W
Parry Sound *tn.* Ontario Canada **93** E3 45 21N 80 03W
Parthenay France **73** A2 46 39N 0 14W
Pasadena California U.S.A. **95** B3 34 10N 118 09W
Pasadena Texas U.S.A. **91** G2 29 42N 95 14W
Pascagoula Mississippi U.S.A. **91** I3 30 21N 88 32W
Pas-de-Calais *admin.* France **70** A2 50 45N 2 00E
Pas de Calais *(Strait of Dover) sd.* English Channel **73** B3 51 00N 1 20W
Pasir Mas Malaysia **42** B5 6 03N 102 08E
Pasir Panjang Singapore **41** C3 1 18N 103 47E
Pasir Ris Singapore **41** E4 1 23N 103 57E
Passage Lolvavana Vanuatu **83** H6 15 25S 168 10E
Passaic New Jersey U.S.A. **94** B2 40 50N 74 08W
Passaic River New Jersey U.S.A. **94** B2 40 46N 74 09W
Passau Germany **71** B1 48 35N 13 28E
Passe d'Anemata *sd.* New Caledonia **82** V3 20 32S 166 10E
Passe de la Sarcelle *sd.* New Caledonia **82** W1 22 30S 167 10E
Passi The Philippines **40** B3 11 06N 122 40E
Passo Fundo Brazil **103** G7 28 16S 52 20W
Pasto Colombia **102** B13 1 12N 77 17W
Pasuruan Indonesia **42** Q7 7 38S 112 44E
Pata *i.* The Philippines **40** B2 5 49N 121 13E
Patagonia *geog. reg.* Argentina **103** C2/D4 48 00S 70 00W
Patan India **53** C4 23 51N 72 11E
Patan Nepal **53** F5 27 40N 85 20E
Patchogue New York U.S.A. **93** F2 40 46N 73 01W
Patea North Island New Zealand **79** B3 39 45S 174 28E
Pate Island Kenya **110** H7 2 05S 41 05E
Paterson New Jersey U.S.A. **94** B2 40 55N 74 08W
Pathankot India **53** D6 32 16N 75 43E
Pathiu Thailand **39** A2 10 41N 99 18E
Pathum Thani Thailand **39** B2 14 00N 100 29E
Pati Indonesia **42** P7 6 45S 111 00E
Patiala India **53** D6 30 21N 76 27E
Pātipukur India **52** K2 22 36N 88 24E
Patkai Range India/Myanmar **38** B5 27 00N 95 30E
Patna India **53** F5 25 37N 85 12E
Patnanongan *i.* The Philippines **40** B3 14 50N 122 13E
Patos Brazil **102** J11 6 55S 37 15W
Pátrai Greece **74** D2 38 14N 21 44E
Pattani Thailand **39** B1 6 50N 101 20E
Pattani *r.* Thailand **39** B1 6 30N 101 10E
Pattaya Thailand **39** B2 12 57N 100 53E
Pauk Myanmar **38** A4 21 25N 94 30E
Pauksa Taung *mt.* Myanmar **38** A3 19 58N 94 15E
Paungde Myanmar **38** B3 18 30N 95 30E
Pausin Germany **67** E2 52 39N 13 04E
Pavia Italy **74** A4 45 12N 9 09E
Pavlodar Kazakhstan **59** M5 52 21N 76 59E
Pavlograd Ukraine **58** D4 48 34N 35 50E
Pavuvu *i.* Solomon Islands **82** E4 9 05S 159 05E
Pawan *r.* Indonesia **42** D3 1 00S 110 30E
Pawtucket Massachusetts U.S.A. **93** F2 41 53N 71 23W
Paxton Illinois U.S.A. **92** C2 40 28N 88 07W
Payakumbuh Indonesia **42** B3 0 10S 100 30E
Paya Lebar Singapore **41** D4 1 21N 103 53E
Payamala *r.* Myanmar **38** A3 15 45N 94 40E
Paysandú Uruguay **103** F6 32 21S 58 05W
Pazardzhik Bulgaria **74** D3 42 10N 24 20E
Peace River British Columbia/Alberta Canada **88** L4 57 30N 117 00W
Peace River *tn.* Alberta Canada **88** L4 56 15N 117 18W
Peake Deep Atlantic Ocean **25** F11 43 00N 20 05W
Pearl Ontario Canada **92** C3 48 41N 88 39W
Pearl *r.* Mississippi U.S.A. **91** H3 32 00N 90 00W
Pearl Harbor Hawaiian Islands **23** Y18 21 22N 158 00W
Pebble Island Falkland Islands **25** M16 51 20S 59 40W
Peć Serbia Yugoslavia **74** D3 42 40N 20 19E
Pechenga Russia **69** G4 69 28N 31 04E
Pechora Russia **56** H9 65 14N 57 18E
Pechora *r.* Russia **56** G9 66 00N 52 00E
Pecos Texas U.S.A. **90** F3 30 00N 102 00W
Pecos *r.* U.S.A. **90** F3 30 0N 102 00W
Pécs Hungary **75** C2 46 04N 18 15E
Pedreiras Brazil **102** I12 4 32S 44 40W
Pedro Juan Caballero Paraguay **103** F8 22 30S 55 44W
Pedro Miguel Locks Panama **97** Y2 9 01N 79 36W
Peekskill New York U.S.A. **93** F2 41 18N 73 56W
Peel *r.* Yukon Territory Canada **88** H6 66 00N 135 00W
Peel Sound Northwest Territories Canada **89** P7 73 50N 95 55W
Peene *r.* Germany **71** B2 53 00N 14 00E
Pegalan *s.* Malaysia **40** A2 5 00N 116 00E
Pegasus Bay South Island New Zealand **79** B2 43 22S 172 55E
Pegu Myanmar **38** B3 17 18N 96 31E
Pegu *admin.* Myanmar **38** B3 18 00N 96 00E
Pegunungan Barisan *mts.* Indonesia **42** B3 2 30S 102 30E
Pegunungan Iran *mts.* Indonesia/Malaysia **42** D4/E4 2 00N 115 00E
Pegunungan Jayawijaya *mts.* Irian Jaya Indonesia **44** H4 4 45S 138 30E
Pegunungan Kapuas Hulu *mts.* Indonesia/Malaysia **42** D4 1 00N 113 00E
Pegunungan Maoke *mts.* Irian Jaya Indonesia **44** F5-H4 4 00S 137 00E
Pegunungan Muller *mts.* Indonesia **42** D4 0 00 113 00E
Pegunungan Sudirman *mts.* Irian Jaya Indonesia **44** G4 4 30S 136 30E
Pegunungan Tamrau *mts.* Irian Jaya Indonesia **44** E6 0 30S 132 30E
Pegunungan Van Rees *mts.* Irian Jaya Indonesia **44** G5-H5 2 45S 138 30E
Pegu Yoma *mts.* Myanmar **38** B3 19 00N 96 00E
Pei-kang Taiwan **51** G6 23 38N 120 18E
Peipus, Lake *see* Ozero Chudskoy
Pekalongan Indonesia **42** O7 6 54S 109 37E
Peking *see* Beijing
Pelabuhanratu Indonesia **42** N7 7 05S 106 30E
Pelaihari Indonesia **42** D3 4 00S 114 40E
Pelee Point Ontario Canada **93** D2 41 45N 82 39W
Pelican Point Namibia **111** B3 22 54S 14 25E
Pelješac *i.* Croatia **74** C3 43 00N 17 00E
Pellworm *i.* Germany **71** A2 54 00N 8 00E
Pelly Lake Northwest Territories Canada **89** O6 65 10N 102 30W
Peloponnese *see* Pelopónnisos
Pelopónnisos *(Peloponnese) geog. reg.* Greece **74** D2 37 00N 22 00E
Pelotas Brazil **103** G6 31 45S 52 20W
Pemalang Indonesia **42** O7 6 53S 109 21E
Pematangsiantar Indonesia **42** A4 2 59N 99 01E
Pemba Mozambique **111** H5 13 00S 40 30E
Pemba National Park Zaïre **111** E6 9 00S 26 30E
Pembroke Ontario Canada **93** E3 45 49N 77 08W
Penal Trinidad and Tobago **96** T9 10 10N 61 28W
Peñarroya-Pueblonuevo Spain **72** A2 38 19N 5 16W
Pendleton Oregon U.S.A. **90** C6 45 40N 118 46W
Penedo Brazil **102** J10 10 16S 36 33W
Peng Chau Hong Kong U.K. **51** B1 22 17N 114 02E
Peng Chau *i.* Hong Kong U.K. **51** B1 22 17N 114 02E
P'eng-chia Hsü *i.* Taiwan **51** I8 24 38N 122 02E
Penghu *see* Makung
P'eng-hu Lieh-tao *(Pescadores Islands) i.* Taiwan **51** F6 23 30N 119 30E
Peng-hu Shuitao *sd.* Taiwan **51** F6 23 30N 119 30E
P'eng-hu Tao *i.* Taiwan **51** F6 23 34N 119 35E
Penha Brazil **103** P2 22 49S 43 17W
Penida *i.* Indonesia **42** R6 8 45S 115 30E
Peninsula de Paria *p.* Venezuela **96** S10 10 44N 61 52W
Peninsula de Taitao *p.* Chile **103** C3 46 30S 75 00W
Peninsular Malaysia *(Malaya) admin.* Malaysia **42** B4 5 00N 102 00E
Péninsule d'Ungava *p.* Québec Canada **89** U5 60 00N 74 00W
Pennant Hills Australia **79** G3 33 44S 151 04E
Penner *r.* India **53** D2 14 30N 77 30E
Pennines *hills* England United Kingdom **68** I6
Pennsylvania *state* U.S.A. **93** E2 41 00N 78 00W
Penonomé Panama **97** H1 8 30N 80 20W
Penrith England United Kingdom **68** I6 54 40N 2 44W
Pensacola Florida U.S.A. **91** I3 30 26N 87 12W
Pensacola Mountains Antarctica **21** 84 00S 60 00W
Pentecost Island *(Île Pentecôte)* Vanuatu **83** H6 15 45S 168 11E
Pentenwell Lake Wisconsin U.S.A. **92** C2 44 00N 90 00W
Penticton British Columbia Canada **88** L2 49 29N 119 38W
Pentland Firth *sd.* Scotland United Kingdom **68** H10 58 45N 3 10W
Penwegon Myanmar **38** B3 18 14N 96 34E
Penza Russia **56** G6 53 11N 45 00E
Penzance England United Kingdom **68** F2 50 07N 5 33W
Peoria Illinois U.S.A. **92** C2 40 43N 89 38W
Pereira Colombia **102** B13 4 47N 75 46W
Perhojöki *r.* Finland **69** E3 63 30N 24 00E
Peribonca River Québec Canada **93** F3 49 00N 71 00W
Périgeuex France **73** B2 45 12N 0 44E
Perm' Russia **56** H7 58 01N 56 10E
Pernambuco *admin.* Brazil **102** J11 8 00S 37 30W
Pernik Bulgaria **74** D3 42 36N 23 03E
Péronne France **73** B2 49 56N 2 57E
Perovo Russia **56** M1 55 44N 37 46E
Perpignan France **73** B1 42 42N 2 54E
Perros-Guirec France **73** A2 48 49N 3 27W
Perryville Missouri U.S.A. **92** C1 37 43N 87 52W
Perth Australia **78** B3 31 58S 115 49E
Perth Scotland United Kingdom **68** H8 56 42N 3 28W
Perth Amboy New York U.S.A. **94** B1 40 31N 74 17W
PERU 102 B10
Peru Basin Pacific Ocean **23** Q6 18 00S 95 00W
Peru-Chile Trench Pacific Ocean **23** S6 13 00S 87 00W
Perugia Italy **74** B3 43 07N 12 23E
Peruweiz Belgium **70** C2 50 30N 3 35E
Pervoural'sk Russia **59** H6 56 59N 59 58E
Pesaro Italy **74** B3 43 54N 12 54E
Pescadores Islands *see* P'eng-hu Lieh-tao
Pescara Italy **74** B3 42 27N 14 13E
Peshawar Pakistan **53** C6 34 01N 71 40E
Pessac France **73** A1 44 49N 0 37W
Petah Tiqwa Israel **54** O11 32 05N 34 53E
Petaluma California U.S.A. **90** B4 38 13N 12 39W
Pétange Luxembourg **70** E1 49 33N 5 53E
Petare Venezuela **102** D15 10 31N 66 50W
Petauke Zambia **111** F5 14 15S 31 20E
Peterborough Australia **78** F3 33 00S 138 51E
Peterborough Ontario Canada **93** E2 44 19N 78 20W

San Lucas Mexico **96** C4 22 50N 109 52W
San Luis Argentina **103** D6 33 20S 66 23W
San Luis Obispo California U.S.A. **90** B4 35 16N 120 40W
San Luis Potosí Mexico **96** D4 22 10N 101 00W
San Marcos Texas U.S.A. **91** G2 29 54N 97 57W
Sanmenxia China **49** M5 34 46N 111 17E
San Miguel El Salvador **96** G2 13 28N 88 10W
San Miguel de Tucumán Argentina **103** D7 26 47S 65 15W
Sanming China **49** N4 26 16N 117 35E
Sannan Japan **46** G2 35 05N 135 03E
San Pablo The Philippines **40** B3 14 03N 121 19E
San Pedro Argentina **103** E8 24 12S 64 55W
San Pedro Côte d'Ivoire **112** D3 4 45N 6 37W
San Pedro Dominican Republic **97** K3 18 30N 69 18W
San Pedro California U.S.A. **95** A1 33 45N 118 19W
San Pedro Bay California U.S.A. **95** B1 33 43N 118 12W
San Pedro Channel California U.S.A. **95** A1 33 43N 118 22W
San Pedro de las Colonias Mexico **96** D5 25 50N 102 59W
San Pedro Sula Honduras **96** G3 15 26N 88 01W
San Rafael Argentina **103** D6 34 35S 68 24W
San Rafael California U.S.A. **90** B4 37 58N 122 30W
San Remo Italy **74** A3 43 48N 7 46E
San Salvador El Salvador **96** G2 13 40N 89 10W
San Salvador *i.* The Bahamas **97** J4 24 00N 74 32W
San Salvador de Jujuy Argentina **103** D8 24 10S 65 48W
San Sebastián Spain **72** B3 43 19N 1 59W
San Severo Italy **74** C3 41 41N 15 23E
Santa Ana Bolivia **102** D10 13 46S 65 37W
Santa Ana El Salvador **96** G2 14 00N 89 31W
Santa Ana Mexico **90** D3 30 31N 111 08W
Santa Ana California U.S.A. **95** C2 33 44N 117 54W
Santa Ana *i.* Solomon Islands **82** H3 10 53S 162 28E
Santa Ana River California U.S.A. **95** C2 33 46N 117 54W
Santa Barbara Mexico **96** C5 26 48N 105 50W
Santa Barbara California U.S.A. **90** C3 33 29N 119 01W
Santa Catalina *i.* Solomon Islands **82** H3 10 55S 16 30E
Santa Catalina Island California U.S.A. **90** C3 33 25N 118 25W
Santa Catarina *admin.* Brazil **103** G7 27 00S 51 00W
Santa Clara Cuba **97** I4 22 25N 79 58W
Santa Cruz Bolivia **102** E9 17 50S 63 10W
Santa Cruz Canary Islands **112** B8 28 28N 16 15W
Santa Cruz Jamaica **97** Q8 18 03N 77 43W
Santa Cruz Luzon The Philippines **40** B3 14 16N 121 24E
Santa Cruz Marinduque The Philippines **40** B3 13 28N 122 03E
Santa Cruz California U.S.A. **90** B4 36 58N 122 03W
Santa Cruz Island California U.S.A. **90** C3 34 00N 119 40W
Santa Cruz Islands Solomon Islands **83** M3/N3 11 00S 166 30E
Santa Cruz *r.* Argentina **103** D2 50 00S 70 00W
Santa Eulalia del Rio Balearic Islands **72** D4 38 59N 1 33E
Santa Fé Argentina **103** E6 31 35S 60 50W
Santa Fe New Mexico U.S.A. **90** E4 35 41N 105 57W
Santa Isabel Solomon Islands **82** D6/E5 8 00S 159 00E
Santa Maria Brazil **103** G7 29 45S 53 40W
Santa Maria California U.S.A. **90** B3 34 56N 120 25W
Santa Maria *see* Gaua
Santa Marta Colombia **102** C15 11 18N 74 10W
Santa Monica California U.S.A. **95** A3 34 00N 118 25W
Santa Monica Moutains California U.S.A. **95** A3 33 07N 118 27W
Santana do Livramento Brazil **103** F6 30 52S 55 30W
Santander Colombia **102** B13 3 00N 76 25W
Santander Spain **72** B3 43 28N 3 48W
Sant' Antioco Italy **74** A2 39 04N 8 27E
Santañy Balearic Islands **72** E4 39 22N 3 07E
Santarém Brazil **102** G12 2 26S 54 41W
Santarém Portugal **72** A2 39 14N 8 40W
Santa Rosa Argentina **103** E5 36 37S 64 17W
Santa Rosa Honduras **96** G2 14 48N 88 43W
Santa Rosa California U.S.A. **90** B4 38 26N 122 43W
Santa Rosa New Mexico U.S.A. **90** F3 34 56N 104 42W
Santa Rosa Island California U.S.A. **90** B3 34 00N 120 05W
Santa Rosalia Mexico **96** B5 27 20N 112 20W
Santa Teresa Brazil **103** Q2 22 57S 43 12W
Santa Teresa Gallura Italy **73** C1 41 14N 9 12E
Santiago Chile **103** C6 33 30S 70 40W
Santiago Panama **97** H2 8 08N 80 59W
Santiago The Philippines **40** B4 16 45N 121 34E
Santiago de Compostela Spain **72** A3 42 52N 8 33W
Santiago de Cuba Cuba **97** I4 20 00N 75 49W
Santiago del Estero Argentina **103** E7 27 47S 64 15W
Santiago Ixcuintla Mexico **96** C4 21 50N 105 11W
San Tin Hong Kong U.K. **51** B3 22 30N 114 04E
Santi Nagar India **52** L4 28 40N 77 10E
Santo *(Luganville)* Vanuatu **83** G6 15 32S 167 32E
Santo Andre Brazil **103** H8 23 39S 46 29W
Santo Domingo Dominican Republic **97** K3 18 30N 69 57W
Santong He *r.* China **50** C6 42 00N 125 45E
Santos Brazil **103** H8 23 56S 46 22W
San Uk Ha Hong Kong U.K. **51** C3 22 30N 114 14E
San Vicente El Salvador **96** G2 13 38N 88 42W
San Vicente The Philippines **40** B4 18 30N 122 09E
São Bernardo do Campo Brazil **103** H8 23 45S 46 34W
São Borja Brazil **103** F7 28 35S 56 01W
São Cristovão Brazil **103** Q2 22 52S 43 15S
São Gonçalo Brazil **103** Q2 22 48S 43 08W
São João de Meriti Brazil **103** P2 22 47S 43 22W
São José Brazil **103** H7 27 35S 48 40W
São José do Rio Prêto Brazil **102** H8 20 50S 49 20W
São José dos Campos Brazil **103** H8 23 07S 45 52W
São Luís Brazil **102** I12 2 34S 44 16W
Saône *r.* France **73** B2 46 28N 4 55E
São Paulo Brazil **103** H8 23 33S 46 39W
São Paulo de Olivença Brazil **102** D12 3 34S 68 55W
São Paulo *admin.* Brazil **102** G8/H8 21 30S 50 00W
São Tomé *i.* Gulf of Guinea **112** G3 0 25N 6 35E
SÃO TOMÉ AND PRINCIPE 112 G3
São Vicente Brazil **103** H8 23 57S 46 23W
Saparua Indonesia **44** C5 3 35S 128 37E
Sape Indonesia **42** E2 8 35S 118 59E
Sappemeer Netherlands **70** F5 53 10N 6 47E
Sapporo Japan **46** D3 43 05N 141 21E
Sapudi *r.* Indonesia **42** R7 7 00S 114 15E
Sapulot Malaysia **42** E4 4 50N 117 00E
Saqqez Iran **55** G6 36 14N 46 15E
Saraburi Thailand **39** B2 14 32N 100 53E
Sarajevo Bosnia-Herzegovina **74** C3 43 52N 18 26E
Sarakhs Iran **55** J6 36 32N 61 07E
Saramati *mt.* India/Myanmar **38** B5 25 45N 95 02E
Saranac Lake *tn.* New York U.S.A. **93** F2 44 19N 74 10W
Sarang Papua New Guinea **45** L4 4 48S 145 40E
Sarangani *i.* The Philippines **40** C2 5 28N 125 28E
Saransk Russia **56** G6 54 12N 45 10E
Sarapui *r.* Brazil **103** P3 22 44S 43 17W
Sarapul Russia **59** G6 56 30N 53 49E
Sarasota Florida U.S.A. **91** J2 27 20N 82 32W
Sarata Ukraine **75** E2 46 00N 29 40E
Saratov Russia **56** G6 51 30N 45 55E
Saravan Iran **55** J4 27 25N 62 17E
Saravan Laos **37** C3 15 43N 106 24E
Sarawak *admin.* Malaysia **42** D4 1 00N 111 00E
Sarcelles France **67** B2 48 59N 2 22E
Sardegna *(Sardinia)* *i.* Italy **74** A2/A3 40 00N 9 00E
Sardindida Plain Kenya **110** G8/H8 2 00N 40 00E
Sardinia *see* Sardegna
Sar-e Pol Afghanistan **55** K6 36 13N 65 55E
Sargasso Sea Atlantic Ocean **25** B9 27 00N 66 00W
Sargeant Barbados **96** V12 13 05N 59 35W
Sargodha Pakistan **53** C6 32 01N 72 40E
Sarh Chad **110** C9 9 08N 18 22E
Sarikei Malaysia **42** D4 2 09N 111 31E
Sarimbun Reservoir Singapore **41** B5 1 26N 103 41E
Sarīr Calanscio *d.* Libya **110** D13 26 00N 22 00E
Sariwon North Korea **50** B4 38 30N 125 45E
Sark *i.* Channel Islands British Isles **68** I1 49 26N 2 22W
Sarmet Vanuatu **83** G5 16 11S 167 32E
Sarmi Irian Jaya Indonesia **44** H6 1 51S 138 45E
Sarmiento Argentina **103** D3 45 38S 69 08W
Sarnia Ontario Canada **93** D2 42 58N 82 23W
Sarolangun Indonesia **42** B3 2 14S 102 44E
Saronikós Kólpos *g.* Greece **74** D2 38 00N 23 00E
Sarpsborg Norway **69** C2 59 17N 11 06E
Sarraméa New Caledonia **82** U2 21 38S 165 50E
Sarrebourg France **73** C2 48 43N 7 03E
Sarreguemines France **73** C2 49 06N 6 55E
Sartène Corsica **73** C1 41 37N 8 58E
Sarthe *r.* France **73** A2 47 45N 0 30W
Sartrou-ville France **67** A2 48 56N 2 11E
Sary Ishikotrau *d.* Kazakhstan **59** M3/4 45 00N 77 00E
Sarysu *r.* Kazakhstan **59** K4 47 00N 67 30E
Sasamungga Solomon Islands **82** B6 7 05S 156 45E
Sasayama Japan **46** G2 35 03N 135 12E
Sasebo Japan **46** A1 33 10N 129 42E
Saskatchewan *province* Canada **88** N3 53 50N 109 00W
Saskatoon Saskatchewan Canada **88** N3 52 10N 106 40W
Sassandra Côte d'Ivoire **112** D3 4 58N 6 08W
Sassandra *r.* Côte d'Ivoire **112** D4 5 50N 6 55W
Sassari Italy **74** A3 40 43N 8 34E
Sassnitz Germany **71** B2 54 32N 13 40E
Sataua Western Samoa **82** A11 13 26S 172 40W
Satlayev *(Nikol'skiy)* Kazakhstan **59** K4 47 54N 67 25E
Satna India **53** E4 24 33N 80 50E
Satpura Range *mts.* India **53** C4/D4 21 40N 75 00E
Sattahip Thailand **39** B2 12 36N 100 56E
Satuk Thailand **39** B3 15 17N 103 20E
Satu Mare Romania **75** D2 47 48N 22 52E
Satun Thailand **39** B1 6 40N 100 01E
SAUDI ARABIA 94/95
Sauer *(Sûre)* *r.* Europe **70** F1 49 45N 6 30E
Sault Ste. Marie Ontario Canada **93** D3 46 31N 84 20W
Sault Ste. Marie Michigan U.S.A. **93** D3 46 29N 84 22W
Saumlaki Indonesia **43** H2 7 59S 131 22E
Saumur France **73** A2 47 16N 0 05W
Saurimo Angola **111** D6 9 39S 20 24E
Savai'i *i.* Western Samoa **82** A11 13 44S 172 18W
Savanna Illinois U.S.A. **92** B2 42 06N 90 07W
Savannah Georgia U.S.A. **91** J3 32 04N 81 07W
Savannah *r.* U.S.A. **91** J3 33 00N 82 00W
Savannakhet Laos **37** B3 16 34N 104 45E
Savanna la Mar Jamaica **97** P8 18 13N 78 08W
Saverne France **71** A1 48 45N 7 22E
Savo *i.* Solomon Islands **82** E4 9 10S 159 50E
Savona Italy **74** A3 44 18N 8 28E
Savusavu Vanua Levu Fiji **83** D10 16 48S 179 20E
Savusavu Viti Levu Fiji **83** C9 17 34S 178 16E
Savusavu Bay Fiji **83** D10 16 48S 179 15E
Saw Myanmar **38** A4 21 12N 94 08E
Sawahlunto Indonesia **42** B3 0 41S 100 52E
Sawaleke Fiji **83** D9 17 59S 179 15E
Sawankhalok Thailand **39** A3 17 19N 99 50E
Sawara Japan **46** M2 35 52N 140 31E
Sawi Thailand **39** A2 10 15N 99 06E
Shawinigan Québec Canada **89** U2 46 33N 72 45W
Sawpit Canyon Reservoir California U.S.A. **95** C3 34 10N 117 59W
Sawu Sea Indonesia **43** F2 9 00S 122 00E
Sayabec Québec Canada **93** G3 48 35N 67 41W
Sayabouri *see* Xaignabouri
Sayanogorsk Russia **57** L6 53 00N 91 26E
Sayano-Shushenskoya Vodokhranilishche *res.* Russia **59** P5 52 00N 92 00E
Saylac Somalia **110** H10 11 21N 43 30E
Saynshand Mongolia **49** M7 44 58N 111 10E
Sayram Hu *l.* China **59** N3 44 45N 80 30E
Say'ūn Yemen Republic **55** G2 15 59N 48 44E
Scafell Pike *mt.* England United Kingdom **68** H6 54 27N 3 14W
Scandinavia *geog. reg.* Europe **60**
Scarborough England United Kingdom **68** K6 54 17N 0 24W
Scarsdale New York U.S.A. **94** B2 40 59N 73 49W
Sceaux France **67** B2 48 46N 218E
Schaerbeek Belgium **70** D2 50 52N 4 22E
Schaffhausen Switzerland **73** C2 47 42N 8 38E
Schagen Netherlands **70** D4 52 47N 4 47E
Schefferville *(Kawawachikamach)* Québec Canada **89** V3 54 50N 67 00W
Schelde *(Scheldt)* *r.* Netherlands **70** D3 51 15N 4 16E
Scheldt Estuary Europe **60** 51 30N 3 30E
Schenectady New York U.S.A. **93** F2 42 48N 73 57W
Schiedam Netherlands **70** D3 51 55N 4 25E
Schiermonnikoog *i.* Netherlands **70** F5 53 28N 6 10E
Schildow Germany **67** F2 52 40N 13 21E
Schleswig Germany **71** A2 54 32N 9 34E
Schleswig-Holstein *admin.* Germany **71** A2/B2 54 00N 10 00E
Schönebeck Germany **71** B2 52 01N 11 45E
Schöneberg Germany **67** F1 52 24N 13 22E
Schöneiche Germany **67** G1 52 28N 13 43E
Schönwalde Frankfurt Germany **67** F2 52 43N 13 26E
Schönwalde Potsdam Germany **67** E2 52 41N 13 27E
Schorndorf Germany **71** A1 48 48N 9 33E
Schoten Belgium **70** D3 51 15N 4 30E
Schouten Islands Papua New Guinea **45** L5 3 15S 144 30E
Schouwen *i.* Netherlands **70** C3 51 40N 3 50E
Schreiber Ontario Canada **92** C3 48 48N 87 17W
Schulzendorf Germany **67** G1 52 20N 13 34E
Schwäbisch Alb *mts.* Germany **71** A1/B1 48 00N 9 00E
Schwäbisch Gmünd Germany **71** A1 48 49N 9 48E
Schwabisch Hall Germany **71** A1 49 07N 9 45E
Schwandorf Germany **71** B1 49 20N 12 07E
Schwanebeck Germany **67** F2 52 40N 13 27E
Schwarze Elster *r.* Germany **71** B2 52 00N 13 00E
Schwarzwald *(Black Forest)* *mts.* Germany **71** A1 47 00N 8 00E
Schwarzwälder Hochwald *mts.* Germany **70** F1 49 00N 7 00E
Schwedt Germany **71** B2 53 04N 14 17E
Schweinfurt Germany **71** B2 50 03N 10 16E
Schwerin Germany **71** B2 53 38N 11 25E
Schwielowsee *l.* Germany **67** D1 52 19N 13 57E
Schwyz Switzerland **73** C2 47 02N 8 34E
Scilly, Isles of England United Kingdom **68** E1 49 56N 6 20W
Scioto *r.* Ohio U.S.A. **93** D1 40 00N 83 00W
Scoresbysund *(Ittoqqortoormiit)* *sd.* Greenland **89** EE7 70 30N 22 45W
Scotia Ridge Atlantic Ocean **25** C1 53 00S 50 00W
Scotia Sea Atlantic Ocean **25** C1 56 30N 50 00W
Scotland United Kingdom **68** F8
Scott Base *r.s.* Antarctica **21** 77 51S 166 45E
Scott Island Southern Ocean **22** H1 66 35S 180 00
Scottsbluff Nebraska U.S.A. **90** F5 41 52N 103 40W
Scranton Pennsylvania U.S.A. **93** E2 41 25N 75 40W
Scunthorpe England United Kingdom **68** K5 53 35N 0 39W
Sealdah India **52** K2 22 32N 88 22E
Seal River Manitoba Canada **89** P4 59 10N 97 00W
Seattle Washington U.S.A. **90** B6 47 35N 122 20W
Sebakung Indonesia **42** E3 1 36S 116 30E
Sebisseb *r.* Algeria **72** C2 35 30N 4 00E
Sebkra Sidi El Hani *salt l.* Tunisia **74** B2 35 30N 10 00E
Sedalia Missouri U.S.A. **92** B1 38 42N 93 15W
Sedan France **73** B2 49 42N 4 57E
Seddinsee *l.* Germany **67** G1 52 23N 13 42E
Segama *r.* Malaysia **40** A2 5 10N 118 30E
Segamat Malaysia **42** B4 2 30N 102 49E
Seghe Solomon Islands **82** C5 8 25S 157 50E
Ségou Mali **112** D5 13 28N 6 18W
Segovia Spain **72** B3 40 57N 4 07W
Segre *r.* Spain **72** C3 42 00N 1 10E
Segura *r.* Spain **72** B2 38 00N 1 00W
Sehulea Papua New Guinea **45** O2 9 59S 151 15E
Seine *r.* France **73** B2 49 15N 1 15E
Seki Japan **46** H2 35 30N 136 54E
Sekondi Takoradi Ghana **112** E3 4 59N 1 43W
Se Kong *r.* Cambodia **37** C2 13 45N 106 10E
Selaphum Thailand **39** B3 16 03N 103 59E
Selat Bali *sd.* Indonesia **42** R6 8 30S 114 30E
Selat Dampier *sd.* Irian Jaya Indonesia **44** D6 0 30S 131 15E
Selat Gaspar *sd.* Indonesia **42** C3 3 00S 107 00E
Selat Johor *sd.* Singapore/Malaysia **41** C5 1 27N 103 45E
Selat Jurong *sd.* Singapore **41** B3 1 18N 103 42E
Selat Lombok *sd.* Indonesia **42** E2 8 20S 116 00E
Selat Madura *sd.* Indonesia **42** Q7 7 30S 113 30E
Selat Melaka *see* Strait of Malacca
Selatpanjang Indonesia **42** B4 0 58N 102 40E
Selat Serasan *sd.* Indonesia **42** C4 2 00N 109 00E
Selat Sumba *sd.* Indonesia **43** F2 9 00S 120 00E
Selat Sunda *sd.* Indonesia **42** C2 5 50S 105 30E
Selat Wetar *sd.* Indonesia **44** B2 8 00S 126 15E
Selat Yapen *sd.* Irian Jaya Indonesia **44** G6 1 30S 136 15E
Seldovia Alaska U.S.A. **88** E4 59 29N 151 45W
Sele Irian Jaya Indonesia **44** D6 1 22S 131 06E
Selemdzha *r.* Russia **57** P6 52 30N 132 00E
Selenge *r.* Mongolia **49** K8 49 00N 102 00E
Seletar Singapore **41** D4 1 23N 103 52E
Seletar Reservoir Singapore **41** C4 1 24N 103 48E
Selety *r.* Kazakhstan **59** L5 52 50N 73 00E
Selima Oasis Sudan **110** E12 21 22N 29 19E
Selkirk Manitoba Canada **92** A4 50 10N 96 52W
Selma Alabama U.S.A. **91** I3 32 24N 87 01W
Selpele Irian Jaya Indonesia **44** D6 0 15S 130 15E
Sélune *r.* France **73** A2 48 40N 1 15W
Selvas *geog. reg.* South America **98** 7 00S 65 00W
Selwyn Mountains British Columbia Canada **88** I5 63 00N 131 00W
Selwyn Recreational Reserve Norfolk Island **81** K5 29 00S 167 55E
Semarang Indonesia **42** P7 6 58S 110 29E
Sematan Malaysia **42** C4 1 50N 109 48E
Sembakung *r.* Indonesia **42** E4 4 00N 117 00E
Sembawang Singapore **41** C5 1 27N 103 49E
Semenovskoye Russia **56** M1 55 39N 37 32E
Seminoe Reservoir Wyoming U.S.A. **90** E5 42 00N 106 00W
Seminole Oklahoma U.S.A. **91** G4 35 15N 96 40W
Semiozernoye Kazakhstan **59** J5 52 22N 64 06E
Semipalatinsk Kazakhstan **59** N5 50 26N 80 16E
Semirara Islands The Philippines **40** B3 12 00N 121 00E
Semitau Indonesia **42** D4 0 30N 111 59E
Semnān Iran **55** H6 35 30N 53 25E
Semo Fiji **83** B8 18 05S 177 24E
Semois *r.* Belgium **70** E1 49 40N 5 30E
Semuda Indonesia **42** D3 2 51S 112 58E
Sendai Honshu Japan **46** D2 38 16N 140 52E
Sendai Kyūshū Japan **46** B1 31 50N 130 17E
Seneca Lake New York U.S.A. **93** E2 43 00N 77 00W
SENEGAL 112 B5/C6
Sénégal *r.* Senegal/Mauritania **112** C6 16 45N 14 45W
Senftenberg Germany **71** B2 51 31N 14 01E
Senhor do Bonfim Brazil **102** I10 10 28S 40 11W
Senja *i.* Norway **69** D4 69 15N 17 20E
Senlis France **73** B2 49 12N 2 35E
Senmonorom Cambodia **37** C2 12 31N 107 41E
Sennar Sudan **110** F10 13 31N 33 38E
Sennar Dam Sudan **54** D1 13 20N 33 45E
Sennett Singapore **41** D3 1 20N 103 53E
Senobe Japan **46** G2 35 09N 135 25E
Sens France **73** B2 48 12N 3 18E
Senyavin Islands Pacific Ocean **22** G8 7 00N 161 30E
Seo de Urgel Spain **73** B1 42 22N 1 27E
Seoul *see* Sŏul
Sepanda Papua New Guinea **45** M3 7 20S 146 31E
Sepasu Indonesia **42** E4 0 42N 117 40E
Sepik *r.* Papua New Guinea **45** L4 4 15S 144 00E
Sept-Îles *tn.* Québec Canada **89** V3 50 10N 66 00W
Seraing Belgium **70** E2 50 37N 5 31E
Seram *(Ceram)* *i.* Indonesia **43** G3 3 30S 129 30E
Seram Sea Indonesia **43** G3/H3 2 30S 130 00E
Serang Indonesia **42** N7 6 07S 106 09E
Serangoon Singapore **41** D4 1 22N 103 52E
Serangoon Harbour Singapore **41** E4 1 23N 103 57E
Serbia *admin.* Yugoslavia **74** D3
Serdan Mexico **96** C5 28 40N 105 57W
Seremban Malaysia **42** B4 2 43N 102 57E
Serengeti National Park Tanzania **110** F7 2 30S 35 00E
Serenje Zambia **111** F5 13 12S 30 15E
Sergiev Posad *(Zagorsk)* Russia **56** F7 56 20N 38 10E
Sergino Russia **57** I8 62 30N 65 40E
Sergipe *admin.* Brazil **102** J10 11 00S 38 00W
Seria Brunei Darussalam **32** E4 4 39N 114 23E
Serikkembelo Indonesia **44** B5 3 20S 127 55E
Serov Russia **56** I7 59 42N 60 32E
Serowe Botswana **111** E3 22 25S 26 44E
Serpukhov Russia **58** D5 54 53N 37 25E
Serra Brazil **102** I9 20 06S 40 16W
Serra do Mar *mts.* Brazil **103** H7 27 30S 49 00W
Serra do Navio Brazil **102** G13 1 00N 52 05W
Sérrai Greece **74** D3 41 03N 23 33E
Serrania de Cuenca *mts.* Spain **72** B3 40 30N 2 15W
Serra Tumucumaque *mts.* Brazil **102** F13/G13 2 00N 55 00W
Serre *r.* France **70** C1 49 40N 3 52E
Serua *i.* Indonesia **44** D3 6 20S 130 02E
Serui Irian Jaya Indonesia **44** G6 1 53S 136 15E
Seruwai Indonesia **42** A4 4 10N 98 00E
Seruyan *r.* Indonesia **42** D3 2 20S 112 30E
Se San *r.* Cambodia **37** C2 13 40N 106 30E
Sesayap Indonesia **42** E4 3 34N 117 01E
Setagaya Japan **47** B3 35 37N 139 38E
Sète France **73** B1 43 25N 3 43E
Sete Lagoas Brazil **102** I9 19 29S 44 15W
Sete Pontes Brazil **103** Q2 22 51S 43 04W
Setesdal *geog. reg.* Norway **69** B2 59 30N 7 10E
Setit *r.* Sudan **110** G10 14 20N 36 15E
Seto Japan **46** J2 35 14N 137 06E
Seto-Naikai *sd.* Japan **46** B1 34 00N 132 30E
Settat Morocco **112** D9 33 04N 7 37W
Settlement *tn.* Christmas Island **81** R2 10 25S 105 41E
Setúbal Portugal **72** A2 38 31N 8 54W
Sevastopol' Ukraine **58** C3 44 36N 33 31E
Sevenoaks England United Kingdom **66** D2 51 16N 0 12E
Severn *r.* Ontario Canada **89** R4 55 10N 89 00W
Severn *r.* England United Kingdom **68** I4 52 30N 2 30W
Severnaya Sos'va *r.* Russia **56** I8 62 30N 62 00E
Severnaya Zemlya *(North Land)* *is.* Russia **57** L12 80 00N 95 00E
Severočsky *admin.* Czech Republic **71** B2 50 00N 14 00E
Severodonetsk Ukraine **58** D4 48 58N 38 29E
Severodvinsk Russia **56** F8 64 35N 39 50E
Severoural'sk Russia **59** J7 60 10N 59 56E
Sevier *r.* Utah U.S.A. **90** D4 39 00N 113 00W
Sevilla *(Seville)* Spain **72** A2 37 24N 5 59W
Seville *see* Sevilla
Sèvre *r.* France **73** A2 47 00N 1 10W
Sèvres France **67** A2 48 49N 2 13E
Seward Alaska U.S.A. **88** F5 60 05N 149 34W
Seward Peninsula Alaska U.S.A. **88** B5/C5 65 20N 165 00W
SEYCHELLES 24 E6
Seychelles Ridge Indian Ocean **24** E6/F5
Seym *r.* Russia/Ukraine **58** C5 51 00N 34 00E
Seymchan Russia **57** R8 62 54N 152 26E
Seymour Indiana U.S.A. **92** C1 38 57N 85 55W
Sézannes France **73** B2 48 44N 3 44E
Sfax Tunisia **112** H9 34 45N 10 43E
Sfîntu Gheorghe Romania **75** E2 45 51N 25 48E
's-Gravenhage *(Den Haag, The Hague)* Netherlands **70** D4 52 05N 4 16E
Shabaqua Ontario Canada **92** C3 48 35N 89 54W
Sha Chau *i.* Hong Kong U.K. **51** A2 22 21N 113 53E
Shache China **48** E6 38 27N 77 16E
Shackleton Ice Shelf Antarctica **21** 66 00S 100 00E
Shackleton Range Antarctica **21** 81 00S 20 00W
Shah Alam Malaysia **32** C4 3 02N 101 31E
Shahdara India **52** M4 28 40N 77 17E
Shahdol India **53** E4 23 19N 81 26E
Shahjahanpur India **53** D5 27 53N 79 55E
Shakhty Russia **58** E4 47 43N 40 16E
Shaki Nigeria **112** F4 8 39N 3 25E
Sha Lo Wan Hong Kong U.K. **51** A1 22 17N 113 54E
Sham Chung Hong Kong U.K. **51** C2 22 26N 114 17E
Sham Chun River Hong Kong U.K. **51** B3 22 30N 114 00E
Shamokin Pennsylvania U.S.A. **93** E2 40 45N 76 34W
Sham Shek Tsuen Hong Kong U.K. **51** A1 22 17N 113 53E
Sham Shui Po Hong Kong U.K. **51** B1 22 20N 114 09E
Sham Tseng Hong Kong U.K. **51** B2 22 22N 114 03E
Shangani *r.* Zimbabwe **111** E4 19 00S 29 00E
Shanghai China **49** O5 31 06N 121 22E
Shangqui China **49** N5 34 27N 115 07E
Shangrao China **49** N4 28 28N 117 54E
Shangshui China **49** M5 33 36N 114 38E
Shan State *admin.* Myanmar **38** B4 22 00N 98 00E
Shanngaw Range Myanmar **38** B5 26 10N 98 05E
Shannon *r.* Irish Republic **68** C4 53 30N 9 00W
Shantou China **49** N3 23 23N 116 39E
Shanyao China **51** E8 25 07N 118 44E
Shaoguan China **49** M3 24 54N 113 33E
Shaoxing China **49** O5 30 02N 120 35E
Shaoyang China **49** M4 27 10N 111 25E
Shaqrā' Saudia Arabia **55** G4 25 18N 45 15E
Sharon Pennsylvania U.S.A. **93** D2 41 46N 80 30W
Sharp Island Hong Kong U.K. **51** C2 22 22N 114 17E
Sharp Peak Hong Kong U.K. **51** D2 22 26N 114 22E
Shashi China **49** M5 30 16N 112 20E
Shasta Lake California U.S.A. **90** B5 40 45N 122 20W
Shasta, Mount California U.S.A. **90** B5 41 25N 122 12W
Sha Tau Kok Hong Kong U.K. **51** C3 22 33N 114 13E
Sha Tin Hong Kong U.K. **51** C2 22 22N 114 10E
Shatsky Rise Pacific Ocean **22** G11 34 00N 160 00E
Shau Kei Wan Hong Kong U.K. **51** C1 22 16N 114 13E
Shebelë *r.* Ethiopia/Somalia **110** H9 6 00N 44 00E
Sheberghān Afghanistan **55** K6 36 41N 65 45E
Sheboygan Wisconsin U.S.A. **92** C2 43 46N 87 44W

Sheffield England United Kingdom **68** J5 53 23N 1 30W
Shek Kip Mei Hong Kong U.K. **51** C2 22 20N 114 10E
Shek Kong Hong Kong U.K. **51** B2 22 26N 114 06E
Shek Kwu Chau *i.* Hong Kong U.K. **51** A1 22 12N 113 59E
Shek O Hong Kong U.K. **51** C1 22 14N 114 15E
Shek Pik Hong Kong U.K. **51** A1 22 13N 113 53E
Shek Pik Reservoir Hong Kong U.K. **51** A1 22 14N 113 54E
Shek Uk Shan *mt.* Hong Kong U.K. **51** C2 22 26N 114 18E
Shek Wu Hui Hong Kong U.K. **51** B3 22 30N 114 07E
Shelburne Nova Scotia Canada **89** V1 43 37N 65 20W
Shelburne Ontario Canada **93** D2 44 05N 80 13W
Shelby Montana U.S.A. **90** D6 48 30N 111 52W
Shelbyville Indiana U.S.A. **92** C1 39 31N 85 46W
Shelekhov Bay Russia **57** R8 60 00N 157 00E
Shelikof Strait Alaska U.S.A. **88** D4/E4 57 30N 155 00W
Shelter Island Hong Kong U.K. **51** C1 22 19N 114 19E
Shenandoah Iowa U.S.A. **92** A2 40 48N 95 22W
Shenandoah *r.* Virginia U.S.A. **93** E1 39 00N 78 00W
Shenandoah Mountains U.S.A. **93** E1 39 00N 79 00W
Shenyang China **49** O7 41 50N 123 26E
Shenzhen China **49** M3 22 31N 114 08E
Sheoraphuli India **52** K3 22 46N 88 20E
Shepherd Group Vanuatu **83** H5 17 00S 168 30E
Sher *r.* India **38** A4 24 30N 92 50E
Sherbrooke Québec Canada **93** F3 45 24N 71 54W
Sheridan Wyoming U.S.A. **90** E5 44 48N 106 57W
's-Hertogenbosch Netherlands **70** E3 51 41N 5 19E
Shetland Islands Scotland United Kingdom **68** J12 60 00N 1 15W
Sheung Shui Hong Kong U.K. **51** B3 22 31N 114 07E
Sheyenne *r.* North Dakota U.S.A. **92** A3 47 00N 98 00W
Shibuya Japan **47** B3 35 39N 139 42E
Shiderty *r.* Kazakhstan **59** L5 51 30N 75 00E
Shiga *pref.* Japan **46** H2 35 10N 136 07E
Shihezi China **48** G7 44 19N 86 10E
Shijiazhuang China **49** M6 38 04N 114 28E
Shikarpor Pakistan **52** B5 27 58N 68 42E
Shikoku *i.* Japan **46** B1 33 40N 134 00E
Shikotan *i.* Japan **46** E3 43 47N 148 45E
Shiliguri India **53** F5 26 42N 88 30E
Shilka *r.* Russia **57** N6 52 30N 117 30E
Shillong India **53** G5 25 34N 91 53E
Shima-hantō *p.* Japan **46** H1 34 25N 136 30E
Shimizu Japan **46** C2 35 01N 138 29E
Shimoga India **53** D2 13 56N 75 31E
Shimonita Japan **46** K3 36 12N 138 47E
Shimonoseki Japan **46** B1 33 59N 130 58E
Shimono-shima *i.* Japan **50** D2 34 12N 129 15E
Shimotsuma Japan **46** L3 36 10N 139 58E
Shinagawa Japan **47** B3 35 37N 139 44E
Shinagawa Bay Japan **47** C3 35 56N 139 50E
Shinano *r.* Japan **46** C2 37 40N 139 00E
Shindand Afghanistan **55** J5 33 16N 62 05E
Shingbwiyang Myanmar **38** B5 26 41N 96 10E
Shingū Japan **46** C1 33 42N 136 00E
Shinjō Japan **46** D2 38 45N 140 18E
Shinjuku Japan **47** B3 35 41N 139 42E
Shinyanga Tanzania **111** F7 3 40S 33 25E
Shiono-misaki *c.* Japan **46** C1 33 28N 135 47E
Shiping China **38** C4 23 41N 102 31E
Shipki Pass India **53** D6 31 50N 78 50E
Shirakawa Japan **46** D2 37 07N 140 11E
Shiraoi Japan **46** D3 42 34N 141 19E
Shirāz Iran **55** H4 29 38N 52 34E
Shiretoko-misaki *c.* Japan **46** E3 44 24N 145 20E
Shirinthorn Reservoir Thailand **39** C3 15 00N 105 25E
Shishmaref Alaska U.S.A. **88** B6 66 15N 166 11W
Shivaji Park *tn.* India **52** L4 28 40N 77 07E
Shiwan Dashan *mts.* China **37** C4 21 45N 108 00E
Shizong China **38** C4 24 45N 104 01E
Shizuishan China **49** L6 39 04N 106 22E
Shizuoka Japan **46** C1 34 59N 138 24E
Shizuoka *pref.* Japan **46** K2 35 10N 138 50E
Shkodër Albania **74** C3 42 03N 19 01E
Shomolu Nigeria **109** V3 6 34N 3 26E
Shortland Islands Solomon Islands **82** A6/B6 7 00S 156 00E
Shreveport Louisiana U.S.A. **91** H3 32 30N 93 46W
Shrewsbury England United Kingdom **68** I4 52 43N 2 45W
Shrirampur India **52** K3 22 45N 88 21E
Shuangbai China **38** C4 24 40N 101 40E
Shuangjiang China **38** B4 23 29N 99 54E
Shuangliao China **49** O7 43 30N 123 29E
Shuangyashan China **49** Q8 46 42N 131 20E
Shuen Wan Hong Kong U.K. **51** C2 22 28N 114 12E
Shuicheng China **38** C5 26 36N 104 57E
Shui-feng Reservoir China **50** B5 40 40N 125 30E
Shuiluo He *r.* China **38** C5 28 00N 100 30E
Shui Tau Hong Kong U.K. **51** B2 22 27N 114 04E
Shumagin Islands Alaska U.S.A. **88** D4 55 00N 159 00W
Shumen Bulgaria **74** E3 43 17N 26 55E
Shunde China **49** M3 22 50N 113 16E
Shuqrā Yemen Republic **55** G1 13 23N 45 44E
Shwebo Myanmar **38** B4 22 35N 95 42E
Shwedaung Myanmar **38** B3 18 44N 95 12E
Shweli *r.* Myanmar **38** B4 23 25N 96 55E
Shwenyaung Myanmar **38** B4 20 48N 96 58E
Shyamnagar India **52** K3 22 50N 88 24E
Siabu Indonesia **42** A4 1 00N 99 28E
Sialkot Pakistan **53** C6 32 29N 74 35E
Siargao *i.* The Philippines **40** C2 10 00N 126 00E
Siasi The Philippines **40** B2 5 33N 120 50E
Siasi *i.* The Philippines **40** B2 5 33N 120 52E
Šiauliai Lithuania **69** E2 55 51N 23 20E
Šibenik Croatia **74** C3 43 45N 15 55E
Sibi Pakistan **52** B5 29 31N 67 54E
Sibidiri Papua New Guinea **45** K2 8 58S 142 16E
Sibiti Congo **112** H2 3 40S 13 24E
Sibiu Romania **75** D2 45 46N 24 09E
Sibolga Indonesia **42** A4 1 42N 98 48E
Sibpur India **52** K2 22 34N 88 19E
Sibsagar India **36** A7 26 58N 94 39E
Sibu Malaysia **42** D4 2 19N 111 50E
Sibuguey *r.* The Philippines **40** B2 8 00N 123 00E
Sibuguey Bay The Philippines **40** B2 7 00N 122 00E
Sibut Central African Republic **110** C9 5 46N 19 06E
Sibuyan *i.* The Philippines **40** B3 12 00N 122 00E
Sibuyan Sea The Philippines **40** B3 12 00N 122 00E
Sicapoo *mt.* The Philippines **40** B4 18 01N 120 58E
Sichon Thailand **39** A1 8 59N 99 56E
Sichuan Basin *see* Sichuan Pendi
Sichuan Pendi *(Sichuan Basin)* China **49** K5/L5 32 00N 107 00E
Sicilian Channel Mediterranean Sea **74** B2 37 00N 12 00E
Sicily *i.* Italy **74** B2/C2 37 00N 14 00E
Sicuani Peru **102** C10 14 21S 71 13W
Sidcup England United Kingdom **66** D2 51 26N 0 07E
Sidi Barrani Egypt **110** E14 31 38N 25 58E
Sidi Bel Abbès Algeria **112** E10 35 15N 0 39W
Sidi Ifni Morocco **112** C8 29 24N 10 12W
Sidlaw Hills Scotland United Kingdom **68** H8 56 30N 3 10W
Sidney Lanier, Lake Georgia U.S.A. **91** J3 34 00N 84 00W
Sidoarjo Indonesia **42** Q7 7 27S 112 42E
Sidon *see* Saïda
Siedlce Poland **75** D3 52 10N 22 18E
Sieg *r.* Germany **71** A2 50 00N 8 00E
Siegburg Germany **71** A2 50 48N 7 13E
Siegen Germany **71** A2 50 52N 8 02E
Siemensstadt Germany **67** F2 52 33N 13 14E
Siem Pang Cambodia **37** C2 14 09N 106 23E
Siem Reap Cambodia **37** B2 13 21N 103 50E
Siena Italy **74** B3 43 19N 11 19E
Sierra Blanca *tn.* Texas U.S.A. **90** E3 31 10N 105 22W
Sierra da Estrêla *mts.* Portugal **72** A3 40 17N 8 00W
Sierra de Alcaraz *mts.* Spain **72** B2 38 30N 2 30W
Sierra de Alfabia *mts.* Balearic Islands **72** E4 39 30N 2 45E
Sierra de Gata *mts.* Spain **72** A3 40 15N 6 40W
Sierra de Gredos *mts.* Spain **72** A3 40 18N 5 20W
Sierra de Guadarrema *mts.* Spain **72** B3 40 45N 4 00W
Sierra del Cadi *mts.* Spain **72** C3 42 20N 1 30E
Sierra de Maracaju *mts.* Brazil **102** F8/G9 20 00S 55 00W
Sierra de Perija *mts.* Colombia/Venezuela **97** J1 10 00N 73 00W
Sierra de Segura *mts.* Spain **72** B2 38 00N 2 45W
Sierra dos Parecis *hills.* Brazil **98** 7 00S 60 00W
SIERRA LEONE **112** C4
Sierra Madre *mts.* The Philippines **40** B4 17 00N 122 00E
Sierra Madre del Sur *mts.* Mexico **96** D3/E3 17 30N 100 00W
Sierra Madre Occidental *mts.* Mexico **96** C5/D4 26 00N 107 00W
Sierra Madre Oriental *mts.* Mexico **96** D5/E4 23 30N 100 00W
Sierra Morena *mts.* Spain **72** A2/B2 38 05N 5 50W
Sierra Nevada *mts.* Spain **72** B2 37 00N 3 20W
Sierra Nevada *mts.* U.S.A. **90** C4 37 00N 119 00W
Sierras de Córdoba *mts.* Argentina **103** D6/E6 32 30S 65 00W
Sigatoka Fiji **83** B8 18 10S 177 30E
Sighetu Marmaţiei Romania **75** D2 47 56N 23 53E
Sighişoara Romania **75** D2 46 12N 24 48E
Sigli Indonesia **42** A5 5 21N 95 56E
Siglufjördur Iceland **69** I7 66 09N 18 55W
Signy *r.s.* South Orkney Islands **21** 60 43S 45 36W
Sigüenza Spain **72** B3 41 04N 2 38W
Siguiri Guinea **112** D5 11 28N 9 07W
Sikar India **53** D5 27 33N 75 12E
Sikasso Mali **112** D5 11 18N 5 38W
Si Khiu Thailand **39** B2 14 55N 101 45E
Sikhote-Alin' *mts.* Russia **57** P5 45 00N 137 00E
Sikkim *admin.* India **53** F5 27 30N 88 30E
Sil *r.* Spain **72** A3 42 25N 7 05W
Silay The Philippines **40** B3 10 45N 122 59E
Silchar India **53** G4 24 49N 92 47E
Silifke Turkey **54** D6 36 22N 33 57E
Siling Co *l.* China **53** F6 31 45N 88 50E
Silisili, Mount Western Samoa **82** A11 13 34S 172 27W
Silistra Bulgaria **74** E3 44 06N 27 17E
Siljan *l.* Sweden **69** D3 60 55N 14 50E
Silver Bay *tn.* Minnesota U.S.A. **92** B3 47 15N 91 17W
Silver City Christmas Island **81** R2 10 25S 105 42E
Silver City New Mexico U.S.A. **90** E3 32 47N 108 16W
Silver Lake Reservoir California U.S.A. **95** A3 34 05N 118 16W
Silves Portugal **72** A2 37 11N 8 26W
Simanggang Malaysia **32** E4 1 10N 111 32E
Simbo *i.* Solomon Islands **82** B5 8 15S 156 30E
Simcoe Ontario Canada **93** D2 42 50N 80 19W
Simcoe, Lake Ontario Canada **93** E2 44 23N 79 18W
Simei Singapore **41** E4 1 20N 103 57E
Simferopol Ukraine **58** C3 44 57N 34 05E
Simla India **53** D6 31 07N 77 09E
Simpson Desert Australia **78** F4/5 24 30S 137 30E
Sinabang Indonesia **42** A4 2 27N 96 24E
Sinai *p.* Egypt **54** N9/O9 29 15N 34 00E
Sinai, Mount *see* Gebel Mûsa
Sincelejo Colombia **102** B14 9 17N 75 23W
Sinchaingbyin Myanmar **38** A4 20 53N 92 27E
Sinch'ang North Korea **50** D5 40 07N 128 28E
Sinch'ŏn North Korea **50** B4 38 28N 125 27E
Sind *geog. reg.* Pakistan **52** B5 26 20N 68 40E
Sindañgan The Philippines **40** B2 8 13N 123 01E
Sindangbarang Indonesia **42** N7 7 26S 107 01E
Sindelfingen Germany **71** A1 48 43N 9 01E
Sines Portugal **72** A2 37 58N 8 52W
Sineu Balearic Islands **72** E4 39 39N 3 00E
SINGAPORE **42** B4
Singapore River Singapore **41** D3 1 17N 103 51E
Singapore, Straits of Singapore **41** A3/B2 1 15N 103 40E
Singaraja Indonesia **42** R6 8 06S 115 04E
Sing Buri Thailand **39** B2 14 56N 100 21E
Singen Germany **71** A1 47 45N 8 50E
Singkaling Hkamti Myanmar **38** B5 26 01N 95 39E
Singkang Indonesia **43** F3 4 09S 120 02E
Singkawang Indonesia **42** C4 0 57N 108 57E
Singkil Indonesia **42** A4 2 16N 97 47E
Sinhyo-ri South Korea **50** C1 33 16N 126 35E
Sinjai Indonesia **43** F2 5 07S 120 15E
Sinkiang Uighur Autonomous Region *see* Xinjiang Uygur Zizhiqu
Sinmak North Korea **50** C4 38 25N 126 17E
Sinmi-do *i.* North Korea **50** B4 39 30N 124 50E
Sinop Turkey **54** E7 42 02N 35 09E
Sinp'o North Korea **50** D5 40 00N 128 13E
Sintang Indonesia **42** D4 0 03N 111 31E
Sintra Portugal **72** A2 38 48N 9 22W
Sinŭiju North Korea **50** B5 40 04N 124 25E
Sion Switzerland **73** C2 46 14N 7 22E
Sioux City Iowa U.S.A. **92** A2 42 30N 96 28W
Sioux Falls *tn.* South Dakota U.S.A. **92** A2 43 34N 96 42W
Sioux Lookout Ontario Canada **92** B4 50 07N 91 54W
Sioux Narrows *tn.* Ontario Canada **92** B3 49 27N 94 06W
Sipalay The Philippines **40** B2 9 45N 122 25E
Siparia Trinidad and Tobago **96** S9 10 08N 61 31W
Siping China **49** O7 43 15N 124 25E
Sipiwesk Manitoba Canada **89** P4 55 27N 97 24W
Siple, Mount Antarctica **21** 73 25S 122 50W
Siquijor *i.* The Philippines **40** B2 9 13N 123 35E
Sira *r.* Norway **69** B2 58 50N 6 40E
Si Racha Thailand **39** B2 13 09N 100 48E
Siracusa Italy **74** C2 37 04N 15 19E
Sire *r.* Romania **75** D2 47 00N 26 00E
Sirikit Reservoir Thailand **39** B3 17 50N 100 30E
Sirte *see* Surt
Sirte Desert Libya **110** C14 30 00N 16 00E
Sirte, Gulf of Libya **110** C14 31 00N 17 00E
Sisak Croatia **74** C4 45 30N 16 22E
Si Sa Ket Thailand **39** B3 15 08N 104 18E
Si Satchanalai Thailand **39** A3 17 30N 99 50E
Sisophon Cambodia **37** B2 13 37N 102 58E
Sisseton South Dakota U.S.A. **92** A3 45 39N 97 03W
Sisteron France **73** C1 44 16N 5 56E
Sitka Alaska U.S.A. **88** I4 57 05N 135 20W
Sittang *r.* Myanmar **38** B3 18 00N 96 30E
Sittard Netherland **70** F3 51 00N 5 52E
Sittwe *(Akyab)* Myanmar **38** A4 20 09N 92 55E
Situbondo Indonesia **42** R7 7 40S 114 01E
Sivas Turkey **54** E6 39 44N 37 01E
Siwa Egypt **110** E13 29 11N 25 31E
Sjaelland *i.* Denmark **69** C2 55 15N 11 30E
Skadarsko ezero *l.* Europe **74** C3 42 00N 19 00E
Skagerrak *sd.* Denmark/Norway **69** B2 57 30N 8 00E
Skagway Alaska U.S.A. **88** H4 59 23N 135 20W
Skåne *geog. reg.* Sweden **60** 56 00N 14 00E
Skeena *r.* British Columbia Canada **88** J3 54 20N 128 30W
Skeena Mountains British Columbia Canada **88** J4 57 30N 129 00W
Skegness England United Kingdom **68** L5 53 10N 0 21E
Skellefteå Sweden **69** E3 64 45N 21 00E
Skellefte älv *r.* Sweden **69** D4 65 30N 19 00E
Skien Norway **69** B2 59 14N 9 37E
Skierniewice Poland **75** D3 51 58N 20 10E
Skikda Algeria **112** G10 36 53N 6 54E
Skiros *i.* Greece **74** D2 39 00N 24 00E
Skopje Macedonia (Former Yugoslav Republic) **74** D3 42 00N 21 28E
Skövde Sweden **69** C2 58 24N 13 52E
Skovorodino Russia **57** O6 54 00N 123 53E
Skowhegan Maine U.S.A. **93** G2 44 46N 69 44W
Skye *i.* Scotland United Kingdom **68** E9 57 20N 6 15W
Slaney *r.* Irish Republic **68** E4 52 30N 6 35W
Slatina Romania **75** D1 44 26N 24 22E
Slave Lake *tn.* Alberta Canada **88** M4 55 17N 114 43W
Slave River Alberta/Northwest Territories Canada **88** M4 59 20N 111 10W
Slavonski Brod Croatia **74** C4 45 09N 18 02E
Slavyansk Ukraine **58** D4 48 51N 37 36E
Slawi Indonesia **42** O7 6 57S 109 05E
Slessor Glacier Antarctica **21** 79 00S 22 00W
Sliedrecht Netherlands **70** D3 51 50N 4 46E
Slieve Donard *mt.* Northern Ireland United Kingdom **68** E6 54 11N 5 55W
Sligo Irish Republic **68** C6 54 17N 8 28W
Sliven Bulgaria **74** E3 42 40N 26 19E
Slonim Belarus **75** E3 53 05N 25 21E
Slough England United Kingdom **66** A3 51 31N 0 36W
SLOVAKIA **75** C2/D2
SLOVENIA **74** B4
Słubice Poland **71** B2 52 20N 14 35E
Sluch' *r.* Ukraine **58** B5 50 00N 27 00E
Słupsk Poland **75** C3 54 28N 17 00E
Slutsk Belarus **75** E3 53 02N 27 31E
Slyne Head *c.* Irish Republic **68** A5 53 25N 10 10W
Smallwood Reservoir Newfoundland Canada **89** W3 54 00N 63 00W
Smederevo Serbia Yugoslavia **74** D3 44 40N 20 56E
Smith Alberta Canada **88** M4 55 10N 114 02W
Smithers British Columbia Canada **88** J3 54 45N 127 10W
Smith Mountain Lake Virginia U.S.A. **93** E1 37 00N 79 00W
Smith Point Christmas Island **81** Q2 10 26S 105 39E
Smiths Falls *tn.* Ontario Canada **93** E2 44 45N 76 01W
Smithson Bight Christmas Island **81** Q1 10 32S 105 37E
Smoky Hills Kansas U.S.A. **90** G4 39 00N 100 00W
Smøla *i.* Norway **69** B3 63 25N 8 00E
Smolensk Russia **56** F6 54 49N 32 04E
Smolyan Bulgaria **74** D3 41 34N 24 42E
Smyrna Mills Maine U.S.A. **93** G3 46 07N 68 09W
Snaefell *mt.* Isle of Man British Isles **68** G6 54 16N 4 28W
Snake *r.* U.S.A. **90** C6 47 00N 118 00W
Snake River Plain U.S.A. **90** D5 43 00N 114 00W
Sneek Netherlands **70** E5 53 02N 5 40E
Snoul Cambodia **37** C2 12 05N 106 25E
Snowdon *mt.* Wales United Kingdom **68** G5 53 04N 4 05W
Snow Lake *tn.* Manitoba Canada **89** P3 54 56N 100 00W
Snowy Mountains Australia **78** H2 36 50S 147 00E
Snyder Texas U.S.A. **90** F3 32 43N 100 54W
Soar *r.* England United Kingdom **68** J4 52 40N 1 20W
Soa-Siu Indonesia **32** H4 0 40N 127 30E
Sobat *r.* Sudan **110** F9 8 00N 33 00E
Sobral Brazil **102** I12 3 45S 40 20W
Sochi Russia **56** F4 43 35N 39 46E
Socotra *i.* Yemen Republic **55** H1 12 05N 54 10E
Soc Trang *(Khanh Hung)* Vietnam **37** C1 9 36N 105 59E
Sodankylä Finland **69** F4 67 26N 26 35E
Söderhamn Sweden **69** D3 61 19N 17 10E
Södertälje Sweden **69** D2 59 11N 17 39E
Sodo Ethiopia **110** G9 6 49N 37 41E
Soë Indonesia **44** A2 9 51S 124 16E
Soest Germany **71** A2 51 34N 8 06E
Soest Netherlands **70** E4 52 10N 5 20E
Sofiya Bulgaria **74** D3 42 40N 23 18E
Sogamoso Colombia **102** C14 5 43N 72 56W
Sognefjorden *fj.* Norway **69** B3 61 05N 5 30E
Sogod The Philippines **40** B3 10 22N 124 59E
Sohâg Egypt **110** F13 26 33N 31 42E
Sohano Papua New Guinea **45** Q4 5 26S 154 39E
Soignies Belgium **70** D2 50 35N 4 04E
Soissons France **73** B2 49 23N 3 20E
Söjosŏn-man *b.* North Korea **50** B4 39 20N 125 00E
Sok Kwu Wan Hong Kong U.K. **51** B1 22 13N 114 08E
Sokodé Togo **112** F4 8 59N 1 11E
Soko Islands Hong Kong U.K. **51** A1 22 10N 113 54E
Sokoto Nigeria **112** G5 13 02N 5 15E
Sokoto *r.* Nigeria **112** F5 13 02N 4 55E
So Kwun Wat Tsuen Hong Kong U.K. **51** B2 22 23N 114 00E
Solana The Philippines **40** B4 17 40N 121 41E
Solander, Cape Australia **79** G1 34 01S 151 14E
Solāpur India **53** D3 17 43N 75 56E
Soligorsk Belarus **75** E3 52 50N 27 32E
Solihull England United Kingdom **68** J4 52 25N 1 45W
Solikamsk Russia **56** H7 59 40N 56 45E
Sol'-Iletsk Russia **59** G5 51 09N 55 00E
Solingen Germany **71** A2 51 10N 7 05E
Sollefteå Sweden **69** D3 63 09N 17 15E
Sóller Balearic Islands **72** E4 39 46N 2 42E
Solntsevo Russia **56** L1 55 36N 37 25E
Solo *r.* Indonesia **42** P7 7 05S 111 35E
Sologne *geog. reg.* France **73** B2 47 35N 1 47E
Solok Indonesia **42** B3 0 45S 100 42E
SOLOMON ISLANDS **80** C3
Solomon Sea Papua New Guinea **45** O3 7 00S 150 00E
Solothurn Switzerland **73** C2 47 13N 7 32E
Soltau Germany **71** A2 52 59N 9 50E
Solway Firth *est.* Scotland United Kingdom **68** H6 54 40N 3 40W
SOMALIA **110** H8/I9
Somali Basin Indian Ocean **24** E7 5 00N 55 00E
Sombor Serbia Yugoslavia **74** C4 45 46N 19 09E
Sombrerete Mexico **96** D4 23 38N 103 40W
Somerset Island Northwest Territories Canada **89** Q7 73 00N 92 30W
Somme *r.* France **73** B3 50 00N 1 45E
Sommen *l.* Sweden **69** D2 58 05N 15 15E
Som Mong Vietnam **37** B4 21 12N 104 20E
Somosomo Fiji **83** E10 16 48S 179 59W
Somosomo Strait Fiji **83** D10 16 55S 179 50E
Somoto Nicaragua **97** G2 13 29N 86 36W
Son *r.* India **53** E4 24 00N 81 00E
Sonārpur India **52** K1 22 26N 88 26E
So'nch'on North Korea **50** B4 39 43N 124 57E
Sønderborg Denmark **69** B1 54 55N 9 48E
Søndre Strømfjord *see* Kangerlussuaq
Sondrio Italy **73** C2 46 11N 9 52E
Song Malaysia **42** D4 2 00N 112 34E
Song Ba *r.* Vietnam **37** C2 13 15N 108 45E
Song Be *r.* Vietnam **37** C2 11 15N 106 45E
Song Ca *r.* Vietnam **37** B3/C3 19 00N 105 00E
Song Cau Vietnam **37** C2 13 26N 109 12E
Song Chay *r.* Vietnam **37** B4 22 20N 104 30E
Song Da *(Black)* *r.* China/Vietnam **37** B4 21 00N 104 45E
Song Dong Nai *r.* Vietnam **37** C2 11 30N 107 20E
Songea Tanzania **111** G5 10 42S 35 39E
Song Gam *r.* Vietnam **37** C4 22 15N 105 20E
Song Ha Giao *r.* Vietnam **37** C2 14 00N 108 55E
Song Hua Giang *r.* Vietnam **37** C1/2 9 45N 106 00E
Songhua Jiang *r.* China **49** P8 46 30N 128 00E
Sŏngjin *(Kimch'aek)* North Korea **50** D5 40 41N 129 12E
Songjŏng South Korea **50** C2 35 08N 126 48E
Songkhla Thailand **39** B1 7 12N 100 35E
Song-koi *(Hong, Merah, Yuan Jiang)* *r.* China/Vietnam **37** B4 22 00N 104 00E
Song-koi, Mouths of the *est.* Vietnam **37** C4 20 15N 106 45E
Song Lo *r.* Vietnam **37** C4 22 10N 105 00E
Song Ma *r.* Laos/Vietnam **37** B4 20 30N 104 45E
Song Mi *r.* Vietnam **37** C3 15 30N 107 58E
Sŏngnam South Korea **50** C3 37 29N 127 12E
Song Phi Nong Thailand **39** B2 14 14N 100 02E
Song Saigon *r.* Vietnam **37** C2 11 00N 106 00E
Song Tien Giang Vietnam **37** C2 10 20N 105 10E
Song Tra Khuc *r.* Vietnam **37** C2 15 00N 108 40E
Songŭm-ni South Korea **50** C1 38 25N 127 00E
Song Vom Co Dong *r.* Vietnam **37** C2 11 00N 106 15E
Song Vom Co Tay *r.* Vietnam **37** C2 10 35N 106 00E
Son Ha Vietnam **37** C3 15 03N 108 33E
Son La Vietnam **37** B4 21 20N 103 55E
Sonneberg Germany **71** B2 50 22N 11 10E
Sonoita Mexico **96** B6 31 53N 112 52W
Sonsonate El Salvador **96** G2 13 43N 89 44W
Sonsoral *i.* Palau **80** A4 5 20N 132 13E
Sonsorol Islands Caroline Islands **43** H5 5 20N 132 13E
Son Tay Vietnam **37** C4 21 06N 105 32E
Sopa Sopa Head Papua New Guinea **45** M6 1 55S 146 15E
Sopkhao Laos **37** B3 19 55N 103 16E
Sopot Poland **75** C3 54 27N 18 31E
Sopron Hungary **75** C2 47 40N 16 35E
Sorel Québec Canada **93** F3 46 03N 73 06W
Soria Spain **72** B3 41 46N 2 28W
Sorocaba Brazil **103** H8 23 30S 47 32W
Soroki Moldova **75** E2 48 08N 28 12E
Sorong Irian Jaya Indonesia **44** D6 0 50S 131 17E
Soroti Uganda **110** F8 1 42N 33 37E
Sørøya *i.* Norway **69** E5 70 35N 22 30E
Sorraia *r.* Portugal **72** A2 38 55N 9 30W
Sorsogon The Philippines **40** B3 12 59N 124 01E
Sŏsan South Korea **50** C3 36 49N 126 26E
Sosnowiec Poland **75** C3 50 16N 19 07E
Sŏsura North Korea **50** E6 42 15N 130 38E
Souillac France **73** B1 44 53N 1 29E
Souk Ahras Algeria **74** A2 36 14N 8 00E
Sŏul *(Seoul)* South Korea **50** C3 37 32N 127 00E
Soûr *(Tyre)* Lebanon **54** O11 33 16N 35 12E
Sousse Tunisia **112** H10 35 50N 10 38E
South African National Antarctic Expedition *see* SANAE
Southall England United Kingdom **66** B3 51 31N 0 23W
Southampton Ontario Canada **93** D2 44 29N 81 22W
Southampton England United Kingdom **68** J2 50 55N 1 25W
Southampton Island Northwest Territories Canada **89** R5 64 50N 85 00W
South Andaman *i.* Andaman Islands **38** A2 12 00N 92 40E
South Atlantic Ocean Atlantic Ocean **25** G5
South Australia *state* Australia **78** E3/F4
South Australian Basin Indian Ocean **24** L3 38 00S 125 00E
South Bend Indiana U.S.A. **92** C2 41 40N 86 15W
South Cape Fiji **83** D9 17 00S 179 57E
South Cape *see* Kalae
South Carolina *state* U.S.A. **91** J3 34 00N 81 00W
South China Sea Pacific Ocean **42** C5-D5 15 00N 110 00E
South Dakota *state* U.S.A. **90** F5 45 00N 102 00W

W

Glossary

Ákra	cape (Greek)
Älv	river (Swedish)
Bahia	bay (Spanish)
Bahr	stream (arabic)
Baie	bay (French)
Bugt	bay (Danish)
Cabo	cape (Portuguese; Spanish)
Cap	cape (French)
Capo	cape (Italian)
Cerro	hill (Spanish)
Chaîne	mountain range (French)
Chapada	hills (Portuguese)
Chott	salt lake (Arabic)
Co	lake (Chinese)
Collines	hills (French)
Cordillera	mountain range (Spanish)
Costa	coast (Spanish)
Côte	coast (French)
-dake	peak (Japanese)
Danau	lake (Indonesian)
Dao	island (Chinese)
Dasht	desert (Persian; Urdu)
Djebel	mountain (Arabic)
Do	island (Korean; Vietnamese)
Embalse	reservoir (Spanish)
Erg	dunes (Arabic)
Estrecho	strait (Spanish)
Estreito	strait (Portuguese)
Gebel	mountain (Arabic)
Golfe	gulf; bay (French)
Golfo	gulf; bay (Italian; Spanish)
Göiü	lake (Turkish)
Gora	mountain (Russian)
Gunto	islands (Japanese)
Gunung	mountain (Indonesian; Malay)
Hafen	harbour (German)
Hai	sea (Chinese)
Ho	river (Chinese)
Hu	lake (Chinese)
Île; Isle	island (French)
Ilha	island (Portuguese)
Inseln	islands (German)
Isla	island (Spanish)
Istmo	isthmus (Spanish)
Jabal;Jebel	mountain (Arabic)
Jezero	lake (Serbo-Croat)
Jezioro	lake (Polish)
Jiang	river (Chinese)
-jima	island (Japanese)
-kaikyō	strait (Japanese)
Kamen'	rock (Russian)
Kap	cape (Danish)
Kepulauan	islands (Indonesian)
-ko	lake (Japanese)
Lac	lake (French)
Lago	lake (Italian; Portuguese; Spanish)
Laguna	lagoon (Spanish)
Ling	mountain range (Chinese)
Llyn	lake (Welsh)
-misaki	cape (Japanese)
Mont	mountain (French)
Montagne	mountain (French)
Monts	mountains (French)
Monti	mountains (Italian)
More	sea (Russian)
Muang	city (Thai)
Mys	cape (Russian)
-nada	gulf; sea (Japanese)
-nama	cape (Japanese)
Ostrova	islands (Russian)
Ozero	lake (Russian)
Pegunungan	mountain range (Malay)
Pergunungan	mountain range (Indonesia)
Pendi	basin (Chinese)
Pic	summit (French; Spanish)
Pico	summit (Spanish)
Pik	summit (Russian)
Planalto	plateau (Portuguese)
Planina	mountain range (Bulgarian; Serbo-Croat)
Poluostrov	peninsula (Russian)
Puerto	port (Spanish)
Pulau-pulau	islands (Indonesian)
Puncak	mountain (Indonesian)
Punta	cape (Italian; Spanish)
Ras; Râs	cape (Arabic)
Ra's	cape (Persian)
Rio	river (Portuguese; Spanish)
Rivière	river (French)
Rubha	cape (Gaelic)
-saki	cape (Japanese)
Salina	salt pan (Spanish)
-san	mountain (Japanese)
-sanchi	mountains (Japanese)
-sanmyaku	mountain range (Japanese)
Sebkra	salt pan (Arabic)
See	lake (German)
Selat	strait (Indonesian)
Seto	strait (Japanese)
Shan	mountains (Chinese)
-shima	island (Japanese)
-shotō	islands (Japanese)
Sierra	mountain range (Spanish)
Song	river (Vietnamese)
-suidō	strait (Japanese)
Tassili	plateau (Berber)
Tau	island (Chinese)
Teluk	bay (Indonesian)
-tō	island (Japanese)
Tonle	lake (Cambodian)
Vodokhran-ilishche	reservoir (Russian)
-wan	bay (Japanese)
-zaki	cape (Japanese)
Zaliv	bay (Russian)

Abbreviations used on the maps

A.C.T.	Australian Capital Territory
Ákr.	Ákra
App.	Appennino
Arch.	Archipelago
Austl.	Australia
C.	Cape; Cabo; Cap
Ck.	Creek
Col.	Colombia
D.C.	District of Columbia
Den.	Denmark
E.	East
Ec.	Ecuador
Eq.	Equatorial
Fj.	Fjord
Fr.	France
Fwy.	Freeway
G.	Gunung; Gebel
Hwy.	Highway
I.	Island; Île; Ilha; Isla
Is.	Islands; Îles; Ilhas; Islas
J.	Jezioro
Jez.	Jezero
Kep.	Kepulauan
M.	Muang
Mt.	Mount; Mountain; Mont
Mte.	Monte
Mts.	Mountains; Monts
N.	North
Nat. Pk.	National Park
NCD	National Capital District
Neths.	Netherlands
N.P.	National Park
Pa.	Passage
Peg.	Pegunungan
Pen.; Penin.	Peninsula
Pl.	Planina
Port.	Portugal
proj.	projected
Pt.	Point
Pta.	Punta
Pte.	Pointe
Pto.	Porto; Puerto
R.	River; Rio
Ra.	Range
Res.	Reservoir
Résr.	Réservoir
S.	San; South
S.A.	South Africa
Sa.	Sierra
Sd.	Sound
Sev.	Severnaya
Sp.	Spain
S.R.A.	State Recreation Area
St.	Saint
Ste.	Sainte
Str.	Strait
Terr.	Territory
U.A.E.	United Arab Emirates
u/c	under construction
U.K.	United Kingdom
U.N.	United Nations
U.S.A.	United States of America
U.S.S.R.	Union of Soviet Socialist Republics
W.	West

Abbreviations used in the gazetteer

admin.	administrative area
ACT	Australian Capital Territory
b.	bay or harbour
c.	cape, point or headland
can.	canal
co.	county
d.	desert
dep.	depression
est.	estuary
fj.	fjord
g.	gulf
geog. reg.	geographical region
h.	homestead
hist. site	historical site
i.	island
is.	islands
ist.	isthmus
l.	lake, lakes, lagoon
m.s.	mission
mt.	mountain, peak or spot height
mts.	mountains
NSW	New South Wales
NT	Northern Territory
NWT	Northwest Territories
p.	peninsula
plat.	plateau
pn.	plain
Qld	Queensland
r.	river
r.s.	research station
reg.	region
rep.	republic
res.	reservoir
SA	South Australia
salt l.	salt lake
sd.	sound, strait or channel
sum.	summit
Tas.	Tasmania
tn.	town or other populated place
trig. point	trigonometrical point
U.A.E.	United Arab Emirates
U.K.	United Kingdom
U.S.A.	United States of America
v.	valley
Vic.	Victoria
vol.	volcano
WA	Western Australia